VISIONS ACROSS THE AMERICAS

Short Essays for Composition

Fifth Edition

J. Sterling Warner
Evergreen Valley College

Judith Hilliard
San Jose State University

THOMSON
—*—
HEINLE

Australia   Canada   Mexico   Singapore   Spain   United Kingdom   United States

Visions Across the Americas, Fifth Edition
Short Essays for Composition
Warner · Hilliard

Publisher: *Michael Rosenberg*
Acquisitions Editor: *Stephen Dalphin*
Development Editor: *Cathlynn Richard*
Associate Production Editor: *Matt Drapeau*
Director of Marketing: *Lisa Kimball*
Executive Marketing Manager: *Carrie Brandon*

Senior Print Buyer: *Mary Beth Hennebury*
Compositor: *WestWords, Inc.*
Project Manager: *Pat McCutcheon*
Cover Designer: *Dutton and Sherman Design*
Printer: *Transcontinental Printing*

Cover Art: *Lamberto Alvarez*

For permission to use material from this text or product contact us:
Tel   1-800-730-2214
Fax   1-800-730-2215
Web   www.thomsonrights.com

**Library of Congress
Cataloging-in-Publication Data**

Visions across the Americas[compiled by] J. Sterling Warner, Judith Hilliard.—5th ed.
   p. cm.
   Includes index.
   ISBN 0-8384-0678-5
   1. College Readers. 2. English language—Rhetoric—Problems, exercises, etc. 3. America—Civilization—Problems, exercises, etc. 4. Report writing—Problems, exercises, etc. 5. Readers—America. I. Warner, J. Sterling. II. Hilliard, Judith.

PE1417.V56 2003
808'.0427—dc21

2003047390

Preface to the Fifth Edition

*A **Cross-Cultural Emphasis:** Visions Across the Americas* takes an intensive look at cross-cultural issues and themes affecting the lives of Americans today as well as those in the past. Overall, these essays offer a broad perspective of selected topics, providing students with a chance to evaluate and re-evaluate their biases, prejudices, or "programmed notions" about subjects. Most importantly, our selections present good writings that are valuable tools for generating material, for writing logs and journals, for collaborative work activities, and for individual writing assignments, all of which encourage creativity and help the student to think and write clearly and critically.

New Essays: Seven new essays appear in the fifth edition of this text, offering a range of topics and issues for reading, discussion, critical thinking, and writing. In *Chapter 1: Communicating is Language at Work,* Toni Morrison's "Writers Together," continues to illustrate the practice of active reading, and Peter Elbow's "Freewriting," presents a method for generating ideas *freely,* avoiding writer's block. Meanwhile, the student essay by Joanne Jaime, "Marriage: The Changing Institution," demonstrates how writers develop a controlling idea or thesis in stages.

Current Issues: From essays related to popular culture in American society such as Grace Sumabat Mateo's "The Anima of Anime," Bill Swanson's "How Films Feed the Mind *or* When I'm Hungry, I Don't Want to Eat Candy," and Rose Anna Higashi's "Eating With Immigrants," to articles on social, political, and ecological issues like Gard E. Norberg's "Jingo Bells, Jingo Bells," Cobie Kwasi Harris' "River of Memory: The Ebb and Flow of Black Consciousness Across the Americas," Michael Segell's "The Politics of Greeting," and Ann Scheid's *"Where Have All the Flowers Gone?:* Is Humanity its Own Worst Enemy?" the newest essays in *Visions Across the Americas* create additional opportunities for progressive language study.

A Progressive Level of Difficulty: Generally, the reading selections in *Visions Across the Americas* are arranged from easiest to most difficult, and, with the exception of the narration, description, comparison/contrast, combined strategies, argumentation, and persuasion chapters that contain six reading selections, each chapter contains five reading selections. As in the fourth edition of *Visions Across the Americas,* whenever possible we have also complemented our brief biographies with photographs of the selection authors.

Pedagogy: To re-enforce an understanding of rhetorical modes and their purposes in context, there is a short discussion of them at the beginning of each chapter. Following chapter introductions are brief lists of tips on how to effectively compose a particular type of essay (i.e., comparison/contrast or cause/effect). For greater accessibility, we include additional writing topics at the end of each rhetorical chapter, and to increase *Visions'* usefulness as a reference, we feature a glossary of common literary and rhetorical terms at the back of the text. This reader primarily is designed to consider short essay development through rhetorical mode but does more than merely acquaint students with cause/effect, argumentation, narration, and so on. The selections also enrich student's vocabulary because clear, written expression often is a matter of good reasoning coupled with a broad command of words in the English language. Thus, many of the reading selections challenge and test the readers' growing abilities.

An Emphasis on the Reading and Writing Connection: To emphasize the connection between reading and writing, we have designed specific questions and activities to engage students in reading. While your instructor may modify our basic guidelines a bit, generally we suggest that you *first,* thoroughly consider pre-reading questions and do what they suggest prior to reading the selection. *Second,* scan the composition, underline, list, and then write the definition of each unfamiliar word. *Third,* carefully read the composition and jot down any notes or questions that come to mind in the margins of the text. *Fourth,* reread the selection after looking over the post-reading questions and then write the answers to the questions found in the following sections: *Content, Strategies and Structures,* and *Language and Vocabulary.*

An Overview of the Writing Process: We are aware that many students may be unfamiliar with the reading-writing process.

Therefore, apart from a discussion of reading strategies, we have included an overview of the writing process in Chapter 1 which (1) serves as a resource for students, and (2) allows instructors flexibility in teaching what we offer, disregarding it, and/or combining our information with information from a standard rhetoric. We have narrowed our discussion of the writing process to:

- generating writing topics,
- organizing material for paragraphs and essays,
- strengthening and developing one's thesis or controlling ideas, and
- revising and editing compositions.

Once students have made the connection between reading and writing, how the two go hand-in-hand, they will not only read more clearly with greater retention but also be able to respond to material critically and confidently, which will be important growth as writers.

Instructor's Manual: The *Instructor's Manual* for the fifth edition of *Visions Across the Americas: Short Essays for Composition* continues to include suggested approaches to rhetorical sections, suggested responses to content and strategies and structures questions; a section about poetry and word use; and an expanded bibliography of great literature from the Americas and beyond. Additionally, the fifth edition *Instructor's Manual* continues to offer brief professional essays describing writing techniques and tools, as well as approaches to writing assignments. Just as we offered "Distance Learning and American Society" as a counterpoint to Mark Charles Fissel's "Online Learning and Student Success" in the fourth edition, the fifth edition *Instructor's Manual* for *Visions Across the Americas* offers other essays that may serve as counterpoints to articles read in the main text such as Barbara Mikulski's "A Young Polish American Speaks Up: The Myth of the Melting Pot" and Jane and Michael Stern's "Valley Girl." While both feature a complete pre- and post-reading apparatus, "Valley Girl" also outlines an extensive slang project. Rounding off the *Instructor's Manual* are reading comprehension quizzes/study guides initially featured in part—and now for each essay—in the *Instructor's Manual* to the fifth edition of *Visions*.

Acknowledgments: Getting from one edition of a text to the next is a long process, and so we want to acknowledge our appreciation to all the instructors whose careful, critical comments helped us to shape the five editions of *Vision Across the Americas*: Shirley Brozzo, Northern Michigan University; Lawrence Carlson, Orange Coast College; Lynn M. Lowery Darby, Kentucky State University; Sarah Dye, Elgin Community College; Jeannie Edwards, Memphis State University; Lloyd A. Flanigan, Piedmont Virginia Community College; Mary J. Flores, Lewis-Clark State College; Gail J. Gerlach, Indiana University of Pennsylvania; Margie Glazier, Merced College; Carolyn Hartnett, College of the Mainland; Shirley Kahlert, Evergreen Valley College; William L. Knox, Northern Michigan University; Regina Lebowitz, New York City Technical College; Reginald F. Lockett, San Jose City College; Robert Mehaffy, American River College; Margaret Murray, Temple University; Tamara O'Hearn, Ball State University; Joanne Pinkston, Daytona Beach Community College; Harry Rubinstein, Hudson Community College; Nancy Sessano, American River College; John Sklute, San Jose City College; Barbara Smith-Cunningham, Olivet College; Sherry Sullivan, South Puget Sound Community College; Sandra Trammell, Kentucky State University; George T. Vaughn, Maysville Community College; Regina Van Epps, Atlantic Cape Community College; Jessica Stephens, Eastern Kentucky University; Linda Sloan, King's College; Brenda Dillard, Brazosport Community College; and Jane Davis, Heald Business College.

Finally, our indebtedness to Stephanie Surface deserves special mention; her enthusiasm, support and critical advice never wavered as she followed the first edition of our text from its inception to its completion.

We also want to thank the authors who have contributed to the present edition of *Visions Across the Americas,* Kevin Warner for his technical support, and our family, friends, and colleagues for their encouragement and patience. We also want to thank those at Heinle Publishers, particularly: Steve Dalphin, Senior Acquisitions Editor; Cathy Richard Dodson, Developmental Editor; Matt Drapeau, Production Editor, for their time, enthusiasm, and support in preparing the fifth edition of our text.

Sterling Warner
Judith Hilliard

Rhetorical Contents

Rose Anna Higashi and her husband share a hobby: eating in immigrant restaurants. Yet she finds much more to be gained than just a good meal because a person who eats in an immigrant restaurant can receive a refresher course in the positive effects that traditional cultures can have on life in America.

Thematic Contents

Lifestyles

Old Age

Racism, Sexism, and Ageism _____

American Society _____

Prejudices and Stereotypes _____

Working in America

Tradition and Ritual

Popular Culture

Technology, Cyberspace, and the Cosmos _____

Politics and Ecology _____

Visual, Written, and Verbal Arts _____

1

Communicating Is Language at Work

Listening, speaking, reading, and writing all deal with communication. If you write a word, you create meaning by simply arranging letters in some sort of recognizable pattern. Words, whether spoken or written, assist people in expressing themselves, for instance, in relating a story, presenting an argument, or explaining a misunderstanding. The ability to communicate in one way or another enables you to explore ideas and issues outside of your realm of personal experience.

In the following essays, the authors explore many different issues about language use. Amy Tan looks at her mother's English and how it influences the way others perceive her. Peter Elbow is interested in the writing process, particularly in how you can generate topics and ideas by "freewriting." Examining her own motivations for writing, Pat Mora says she writes because she likes to express herself and, more importantly, because she is Hispanic and feels a need to correct images of self-worth that have been hurt by the society around her. She believes *that Hispanics need to take their rightful place in American literature.* In each instance, the author illustrates the power of language.

Before you begin reading, it would be helpful to review the *process* of reading—how to read carefully and correctly and how to become actively involved in the reading process. The following tips will help you to become an active reader.

Tips on Becoming an Active Reader

1. **Preview Your Reading.** Before you begin to read, preview the selection and get an idea of what to expect from the piece. Previewing means that you:

   - Read the title. Does it suggest what the article or story will be about?
   - Scan the subheadings. What do they suggest about the order of this piece?
   - Read the opening and concluding paragraphs because main ideas are often presented and summarized in these sections. Is there a thesis or controlling idea presented in the first paragraph? Is there a concluding statement in the final paragraph?
   - Read any bibliographical or biographical prefaces. Who wrote the piece? When and where was the piece written? How might this information suggest something about the essay or story?

2. **Ask Questions.** Remain active while reading by asking questions about the piece. You can start with the title; turn it into a question by using one of the journalist's six queries (who, what, where, when, why, and how). As you read, question a character's motives, the validity of an argument, or the "meaning" of the piece. Ask yourself what the author is trying to accomplish, what the main point of his or her argument is, and what makes this an effective or ineffective composition. (You should jot these questions down in the margins.)

3. **Make Connections.** To make connections between what you have read and your own life, constantly ask yourself what in your life is similar to this author's experiences or ideas. Begin by looking into (1) your past to find connections between the reading and yourself, (2) the world around you to see what relates to your reading, (3) history to see what in the past connects to what you are reading now, and (4) your past readings to see what you already have experienced that affirms or repudiates the ideas of this author.

4. **Learn to Recognize Patterns That Lead to Coherence.** Try to discover a pattern of development: Is the author comparing and contrasting, moving from general to specific, showing cause and effect, or exploring a problem and solution? How do patterns of development help to establish re-

lationships between words, clauses, and phrases leading to an understanding of the writer's ultimate purpose?

5. **Underline and Jot Down Notes.** If you are an active reader, you will write a great deal, underlining points you feel are essential to an understanding of the piece: the thesis, the main ideas, important examples and images, key words, and new vocabulary. Terms that cause confusion— unknown words, confusing passages that need rereading, and unfamiliar names—are also underlined or noted in some way.

   You also will write in the margins quite a bit. Sometimes, it's as simple as noting "thesis!" or "key term." Other times, it's to help with rereading: "What does all this mean?" "Confusing." At times, notes in the margins make judgments, such as "good point—we do all need love" or "this example does not prove the point."

6. **Reread and Reevaluate.** Since reading is a process similar to writing, there is a rereading stage. It is necessary to go back over particularly illustrative examples or what you feel are the main points of the essay; reread confusing sections, and search the passage for a key phrase that will clarify an idea. It is particularly helpful to read a confusing passage aloud, paying careful attention to the punctuation.

7. **Write.** After reading and rereading, you may begin to write by summarizing the ideas found in the essay, writing an evaluation of the piece, or establishing connections between different readings.

8. **Share with Others.** Sharing your thoughts with others can often produce a new line of thinking and better ideas for writing. How? You can discuss what you enjoyed or disliked about a piece, what you felt the author hoped to accomplish, what connections you made between the reading and your own experiences and observations, what passages you found confusing, what ideas you have on the subject matter, and how they either validate or reject the author's ideas. The following excerpt from Toni Morrison's article "Writers Together" has been annotated in the same fashion that you will use to mark your own reading assignments. It further illustrates steps a writer might take to become actively involved in an article or story he or she is reading.

Toni Morrison

Writers Together

A celebrated poet, essayist, playwright, novelist and editor, Toni Morrison was born Chloe Anthony Wofford in Lorain, Ohio, and she received her college education at Cornell and Howard University. Following her divorce of Jamaican husband, Harold Morrison, she worked for Random House Publishers, often editing books by other African Americans such as Muhammad Ali, Toni Cade Bambara, Angela Davis, Gayle Jones, and Andrew Young. Morrison fully embraces her role as one of the most influential African-American women writers of the twentieth century, and her works are filled with memorable female characters whose stories frequently deal with growing up in a predominantly white, racist—and sexist—society. Some notable characteristics of her fiction include a sparse use of poetic language, emotional intensity, human sensitivity, and historical contexts for her plots. Morrison's works include The Bluest Eye *(1970),* Sula *(1974),* Song of Solomon *(1977, winner of the National Book Award and the National Book Critics' Circle Award),* Tar Baby *(1981),* Beloved *(1987, winner of the Pulitzer Prize and the Robert F. Kennedy Book Award),* Jazz *(1992), and* Paradise *(1998). In 1992, Morrison also published a collection of essays:* Race-ing Justice, Re-Gendering Power.

Something is wrong. The puddle of public funds   *good imagery*
allocated to writers (always the least amount of all

the arts) has been reduced to drops. Government support has been so (blasted) that it is at the moment a gesture of nickels and dimes so humiliating, so contemptuous of writers, that one is staggered by the sheer gall.

strange term— why did author choose this?

Editors are judged by the profitability of what they acquire, not by the way they edit or the talent they nourish. Major publishers—for whom mere solvency is death—are required to burst with growth or attach themselves to a parent bursting with growth. Otherwise they (wither.) Small presses that do not starve hang on—hungry, feisty and always in danger of eclipse.

good analogy— flower— like

dry up

That this notion of the writer as toy—manipulable toy, profitable toy—jeopardizes the literature of the future is abundantly clear. But not only is the literature of the near future endangered; so is the literature of the recent past. This country has had an unsurpassed literary presence in the world for several decades now. But it will be lucky, in the coming decade, if it can hold its

//

own. What emerges as the best literature of the 1980s or even the 1990s may be written elsewhere by other people. Not because of an absence of native genius but because something is very wrong in the writers' community. Writers are less *[What's wrong with the writers' community?]* and less central to the idea and subject of literature. Whole schools of criticism have dispossessed the writer of any place whatever in the critical value of his work: Ideas, craft, vision, meaning—all of them are just so much baggage in these critical systems. The text itself is a mere point of departure for philology, philosophy, psychiatry, *[study of mind disorder]* *[love of learning]* theology, and other disciplines. *[love of wisdom]*

[study of religious doctrine] The political consequences for minority workers, dissident writers and writers committed to social change are devastating. For it means that there is no way to talk about what we mean, because to mean anything is not in vogue. Just as to feel anything about what one reads is "sentimental" and also not in vogue. If our works are prohibited *[not hidden]* *[secret]* from having overt or covert meaning—if our

meaning has no meaning—then we have no

meaning either. *interesting*

The literature of the past is endangered not

only by brilliant intellectualism but also by glar-

ing anti-intellectualism. Apparently there are still

such things as books (already written, already

loved) that are so evil they must be burnt like

witches at the stake for fear of contaminating

other books and other minds. Censorship in new

unchecked, unrestrained

and old disguises is rampant. And contempt gives

way to fear. There has been a ritual spasm of

book-snatching—rivaling that in South Africa

deadly for pernicious oppressiveness. *tyranny cruelty*

I think it is our sense of that danger to both

the future and the past that has brought us here.

What is it? Does the danger really come from

large organization, corporation

the monolithic publishers or are they symptoms

disease

of some larger malady? Is the disease really local

censorship and outraged illiterates, or are those

also symptomatic of a larger malady? It is perhaps

characteristic of an event

the mood of a terrified, defensive, bullying nation

no longer sure of what the point is? A nation em-

barrassed by its own Bill of Rights? Burdened by

its own constitutional guarantees and promises of

liberty and equal protection under the law? A

country so hungry for a purely imagined past of

being clear, lucid

innocence and (clarity) that it is willing to (subvert) *to destroy*

the future and, in fact, to declare that there is none,

luxuriate, revel

in order to (wallow) in illusion? If that were the

case, if the country as a whole decided to have no

to hold back,

future — then one of its jobs would be to (stifle,) *suppress*

to chain, (fetter,) and dismiss the artists it could not whip
restrict

into market shape. Because a writer let loose on

the world, uncompromised and untamed, would

notice what had become of the country, and

might say so.

You can't have unmarketable writers roaming

around if you have opted for an improved past in

exchange for no future. After all, the future is

hard, even dangerous, because it may involve

change and it may involve loss. And writers

would say that, too.

We are, some of us, significant individual writers in the cultural life of a group or of an institution, but as writers we are no longer central to the cultural life of this country.   *Why?*

Is that the reason? The mood of the country?

Writer asks questions to get reader to think and analyze the problem

The times we live in? Have we given over our power and our (primacy) to others? Or is there

state of being first

something frail in the nature of our work? Much of what we as writers do and how we do it is shaped by our belief in the (sacredness) of the indi-

holiness, venerableness

vidual artist and his freedom. Individualism in its particularly interesting American form may be at the heart of our dilemma. The idea of the individual in the artistic arena has its own

mutually conflicting feelings, i.e. love and hate

(ambivalence) and contradiction, just as it does in the political arena: governance by many committed to preserving the rights of a few. Ralph Ellison said: "In the beginning was the Word — and its contradiction."

Constructing Responses to Readings: Paragraphs and Essays

All compositions have at least one principle in common: a need to develop a unified thought. A unified composition makes a point and does not wander as the writer develops the paragraph. The facts, examples, reasoning, and evidence used to support a topic sentence—the idea controlling the focus of a paragraph—specifically back up what you initially say. For instance, to ensure unity in a paragraph with a topic sentence such as *"The physicians at Elizabeth Scott Memorial Hospital give the medical profession a bad name,"* a writer must show how and why *the physicians* give the medical profession a bad name. Discussing the nursing staff or hospital rooms is wandering from the controlling idea—the focus—of the paragraph, confusing the reader in the process.

Another topic sentence might be *"In the late twentieth century, graffiti became the artistic expression of street youth."* Here again, evidence will be required to prove the point or to justify an opinion. Your essay must include examples and reasons to illustrate how and why graffiti is more than just defacing and vandalizing public property. In other words, you will be *showing* your reader how graffiti is an art form.

Whether writing a paragraph or an essay, on paper or on a word processor, authors must first generate ideas to determine which direction they wish to take in the development of their topic. Thus, generating ideas is the first step in achieving an overall focus.

Generating Ideas and Establishing a Focus

One of the more difficult tasks a writer faces is coming up with original ideas about a topic. Original ideas don't just pop out of our heads every time we would like them to, so we must learn how to generate fresh perspectives about a topic by brainstorming in a variety of written ways such as clustering, freewriting, and listing. After generating several ideas on a topic, the author will want to focus on a specific controlling idea, either a topic sentence or a thesis statement.

Clustering words creates a visual picture of the relationships between ideas associated with a topic. To cluster thoughts, begin with a topic or stimulus word, freely associating words and ideas around the topic and drawing connections

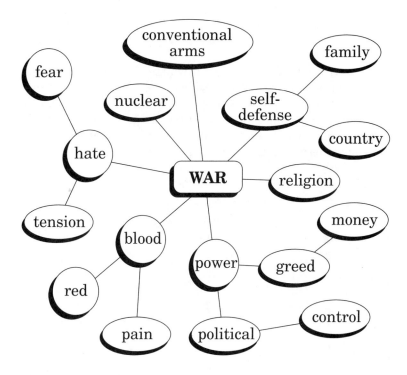

between your responses. For example, the cluster above helped a student generate ideas and arrive at a focus on the general topic of war.

After analyzing her cluster, this student decided that, out of all the associations she had made with the word "war," there were four ideas that dominated her cluster—the major causes of war: hatred, power, self-defense, and religion. While her other information dealt with warfare, she decided to write on only the causes of war to give her paper focus. By eliminating information that did not fall into one of these four categories, the author narrowed her focus and prevented herself from wandering off the topic. Initially, the free association of thoughts allowed her to reach her controlling idea and major discussion points.

Listing is yet another way to examine your thoughts on a subject. Though there is no specific format for listing, most writers who make use of this technique simply write down one word or phrase and then another. Like other prewriting strategies—especially clustering—used to generate ideas, listing is based on the concept that *one thought generates another,* and for this reason, all items on a list may be important. When freely associating words, it's hard to determine which word will lead the writer to a specific focus—the ultimate objective of the activity.

Freewriting is another popular way to brainstorm a general topic in order to arrive at a specific focus. When you freewrite, you should compose as quickly as you can, never stopping to edit. Since your goal is to associate ideas freely, you need not worry about formal essay structure, mechanics, or grammatical correctness. You are exploring your ideas by getting them into writing.

Peter Elbow

Freewriting

A graduate of Williams College, Peter Elbow has published numerous articles and books about the writing process, including Writing with Power, Writing Without Teachers, Embracing Contraries: Explorations in Learning and Teaching, *and* Sharing and Responding. *In the following essay, Elbow offers some suggestions on how to begin the writing process: freewrite!*

Pre-reading Questions

1. Have you ever used a pre-writing exercise to generate ideas for essay topics? Do you ever freewrite?

2. Write nonstop for five minutes expressing everything that comes to mind when you hear the word *freewriting*. Don't be concerned about grammatical or mechanical correctness at this time.

1   The most effective way I know to improve your writing is to do freewriting exercises regularly. At least three times a week. They are sometimes called "automatic writing," "babbling," or "jabbering" exercises. The idea is simply to write for ten minutes (later on, perhaps fifteen or twenty). Don't stop for anything. Go quickly without rushing. Never stop to look back, to cross something out, to wonder how to spell something, to wonder what word or thought to use, or to think about what you are doing. If you can't think of a word or a spelling, just use a squiggle or else write, "I can't think of it." Just put down something. The easiest thing is just to put down whatever is in your mind. If you get stuck it's fine to write "I can't think what to say, I can't think what to say" as many times as you want; or

repeat the last word you wrote over and over again; or any-thing else. The only requirement is that you *never* stop.

2   What happens to a freewriting exercise is important. It must be a piece of writing which, even if someone reads it, doesn't send any ripples back to you. It is like writing some-thing and putting it in a bottle in the sea. The teacherless class helps your writing by providing maximum feedback. Free-writings help you by providing no feedback at all. When I as-sign one, I invite the writer to let me read it. But also tell him to keep it if he prefers. I read it quickly and make no comments at all and I do not speak with him about it. The main thing is that a freewriting must never be evaluated in any way; in fact there must be no discussion or comment at all.

3   Here is an example of a fairly coherent exercise (sometimes they are very incoherent, which is fine):

> I think I'll write what's on my mind, but the only thing on my mind right now is what to write for ten minutes. I've never done this before and I'm not prepared in any way—the sky is cloudy today, how's that? Now I'm afraid I won't be able to think of what to write when I get to the end of the sentence—well, here I am at the end of the sentence—here I am again, again, again, again, at least I'm still writing—Now I ask is there some reason to be happy that I'm still writing—ah yes! Here comes the question again—What am I getting out of this? What point is there in it? It's almost obscene to always ask it but I seem to question everything that way and I was gonna say something else pertaining to that but I got so busy writing down the first part that I forgot what I was leading into. This is kind of fun oh don't stop writing—cars and trucks speeding by somewhere out the window, pens clitter-ing across peoples' papers. The sky is still cloudy—is it sym-bolic that I should be mentioning it? Huh? I dunno. Maybe I should try colors, blue, red, dirty words—wait a minute—no can't do that, orange, yellow, arm tired, green pink violet ma-genta lavender red brown black green—now that I can't think of any more colors—just about done—relief? Maybe.

Freewriting may seem crazy but actually it makes simple sense. Think of the difference between speaking and writing. Writing has the advantage of permitting more editing. But that's its downfall too. Almost everybody interposes a massive and complicated series of editings between the time words start to be born into consciousness and when they finally come off the end of the pencil or typewriter onto the page. This is partly because schooling makes us obsessed with the "mis-takes" we make in writing. Many people are constantly think-ing about spelling and grammar as they try to write. I am always thinking about the awkwardness, wordiness, and general mushiness of my natural verbal product as I try to write down words.

4   But it's not just "mistakes" or "bad writing" we edit as we write. We also edit unacceptable thoughts and feelings, as we do in speaking. In writing there is more time to do it so the editing is heavier: when speaking, there's someone right there waiting for a reply and he'll get bored or think we're crazy if we don't come out with *something*. Most of the time in speaking, we settle for the catch-as-catch-can way in which the words tumble out. In writing, however, there's a chance to try to get them right. But the opportunity to get them right is a terrible burden: you can work for two hours trying to get a paragraph "right" and discover it's not right at all. And then give up.

5   Editing, *in itself,* is not the problem. Editing is usually necessary if we want to end up with something satisfactory. The problem is that editing goes on *at the same time* as producing. The editor is, as it were, constantly looking over the shoulder of the producer and constantly fiddling with what he's doing while he's in the middle of trying to do it. No wonder the producer gets nervous, jumpy, inhibited, and finally can't be coherent. It's an unnecessary burden to try to think of words and also worry at the same time whether they're the right words.

6   The main thing about freewriting is that it is *nonediting*. It is an exercise in bringing together the process of producing words and putting them down on the page. Practiced regularly, it undoes the ingrained habit of editing at the same time you are trying to produce. It will make writing less blocked because words will come more easily. You will use up more paper, but chew up fewer pencils.

7   Next time you write, notice how often you stop yourself from writing down something you were going to write down. Or else cross it out after it's written. "Naturally," you say, "it wasn't any good." But think for a moment about the occasions when you spoke well. Seldom was it because you first got the beginning just right. Usually it was a matter of a halting or even garbled beginning, but you kept going and your speech finally became coherent and even powerful. There is a lesson here for writing: trying to get the beginning just right is a formula for failure—and probably a secret tactic to make yourself give up writing. Make some words, whatever they are, and then grab hold of that line and reel in as hard as you can. Afterwards you

can throw away lousy beginnings and make new ones. This is the quickest way to get into good writing.

8   The habit of compulsive, premature editing doesn't just make writing hard. It also makes writing dead. Your voice is damped out by all the interruptions, changes, and hesitations between the consciousness and the page. In your natural way of producing words there is a sound, a texture, a rhythm—a voice—which is the main source of power in your writing. I don't know how it works, but this voice is the force that will make a reader listen to you, the energy that drives the meanings through his thick skull. Maybe you don't *like* your voice; maybe people have made fun of it. But it's the only voice you've got. It's your only source of power. You better get back into it, no matter what you think of it. If you keep writing in it, it may change into something you like better. But if you abandon it, you'll likely never have a voice and never be heard.

9   Freewritings are vacuums. Gradually you will begin to carry over into your regular writing some of the voice, force, and connectedness that creep into those vacuums.

Post-reading Questions

Content
1. What is freewriting? How do you begin to do it?
2. What does Elbow suggest is one of the biggest obstacles in the writing process? To what extent do you agree with him? Why?
3. How can freewriting overcome "writer's block"?
4. According to Elbow, what is the result of "compulsive, premature editing"?

Strategies and Structures
1. Why does Elbow offer such an extensive example of freewriting? What questions does it tend to answer?
2. How does the author address his reader in this essay? Does he seem to be lecturing and/or "talking down" to his audience? Explain your answer.
3. Why does Elbow devote so much time to the issue of editing? What point is he trying to make? How does he succeed or fail in his effort?

Language and Vocabulary
1. In writing this essay, Elbow was careful to avoid words that would have distracted the reader—

words the reader would need to look up in the dictionary. How does his simple word choice help to establish a reader/writer relationship? How is Elbow's own use of language and vocabulary "free" from the narrow confines of academic writing?

2. Elbow uses a simile to explain that freewriting "is like writing something and putting it in a bottle in the sea." After reading his entire essay, what do you think he meant by that comparison?

Group Activities

1. To explore the possibilities freewriting can offer you in the way of generating ideas or focusing in on essay topics/issues, get together with two other students in class, pick an initial topic (it will serve as a starting point), and all three of you write without stopping for five minutes. Then pick a second topic and write for another five minutes, this time editing your work as you write (precisely what Elbow warns against doing). At the end of ten minutes, have other group members evaluate both pieces of writing. Which was more natural?

2. Share other methods of freewriting you have found useful with the rest of your group. Show group members how you use a particular strategy to overcome writing blocks and to generate specific, meaningful paragraph/essay topics.

Writing Activities

1. Write for ten minutes without stopping, putting down every word or thought that creeps into your mind. Do not worry about grammar, mechanics, or even making sense. Next, write down a specific topic of your choice at the top of a clean page, underline it, and then freewrite for ten more minutes. What sorts of things did you end up saying about the topic or issue you wrote on? Pick one of them to function as the controlling idea in your thesis statement. How would you develop it?

2. Beginning today, freewrite for five minutes daily. Keep your freewritings in a bound notebook or

portfolio of your choice. Like any prewriting technique, freewriting is bound to be a bit disorganized and at times confusing, but don't worry about it. The objective of freewriting is not to produce a finished copy of an essay. As Elbow himself said, freewriting "is an exercise in bringing together the process of producing words and putting them down on the page."

Structuring Essays

Your essay is structured to support a thesis or controlling idea. Once you have arrived at a specific focus, the next step in the writing process is to organize your supporting points (topic sentences). Based on the purpose of your essay, you may want to arrange material in chronological or emphatic order. Leaving out steps in a process paper, for instance, will only confuse the reader. However you choose to organize your material, it should always develop your thesis logically and coherently.

Traditionally, essays have three different types of paragraphs. *Introductory paragraphs* expose the reader to an idea, concept, or argument and lead to a specific thesis. *Body paragraphs* contain specific topic sentences or discussion points that support a writer's thesis. *Concluding paragraphs* draw the discussion to a close, either summarizing major points and relating them to the thesis or providing a definite sense of closure. In essence, you have a beginning, middle, and end.

Introductory paragraphs acquaint your reader with a specific topic and ultimately focus on the controlling idea or thesis you plan to develop. Though a one-sentence introduction might inform your reader of your thesis, it seldom captures the reader's imagination or engages his or her intellect. Some of the more effective ways of leading a reader to a thesis or controlling idea include telling an illustrative story, providing startling or revealing facts or statistics, asking some provocative questions (often rhetorical questions—questions you plan to answer), or using a relevant quote. All of these introductory strategies lead quite naturally to a thesis statement.

A thesis statement introduces your subject, what you have to say about a subject, and how you plan to defend your point of view. Your plan of development breaks a broad topic into manageable units—paragraphs—and suggests the structure of your composition. How many paragraphs should you include in an es-

Introductory paragraph
leading to a thesis
statement or a
controlling idea

Topic sentence #1
Supporting examples
and details

Topic sentence #2
Supporting examples
and details

Body Paragraphs
Note: The complexity
of your thesis, not an
arbitrary formula (e.g.,
an essay equals five
paragraphs), will
determine the number
of paragraphs needed
to develop your essay.

Topic sentence #3
Supporting examples
and details

Concluding paragraph
relating discussion
points back to
the thesis

say? While most people are familiar with a five-paragraph
format—one introductory paragraph, three supporting paragraphs, and one concluding paragraph—in reality, an essay
should contain as many paragraphs as necessary to justify or develop your thesis or controlling idea.

For instance, in "Creatures That Haunt the Americas," in
order to develop fully her controlling idea that *"When
Africans reached the New World, the creatures [of African
folktales] stepped ashore with them,"* Constance García-Barrio

presents the reader with several illustrative paragraphs containing examples that support her thesis. Because her controlling idea is broad, García-Barrio must explore, explain, and support her thesis in several paragraphs in order to develop it adequately.

Body paragraphs support or develop your thesis through argument and examples. Like miniature essays, paragraphs tend to have a beginning, a middle, and an end. For example, a topic sentence is usually the starting point of a paragraph. Here the author alerts the reader to the controlling idea. Supporting examples and details, often referred to as primary and secondary support, comprise the bulk of the paragraph. Such information illustrates what an author has claimed. At the end of a paragraph, an author may offer a closing or transitional statement, which either summarizes the paragraph or leads to the next discussion point.

In "Distance Learning and American Society," Mark Fissel *focuses* paragraph 2 with the topic sentence: *"Distance learning via interactive video instruction makes teaching student-oriented and decentralized as opposed to instructor-oriented, centralized instruction in the traditional classroom."* The rest of Fissel's paragraph supports this claim by supplying examples and interviews. His paragraph is unified because he sticks to supporting his main point (topic sentence).

Concluding paragraphs draw the discussion to a close. In concluding paragraphs, the author strives to come up with a solution to a problem, refers to the information presented in the introductory paragraph, and makes predictions based upon the evidence presented. Just as he or she does not want to begin to develop an essay in an introductory paragraph, a writer will not want to develop new ideas in a conclusion. Keep in mind that the final sentence ideally should leave a lasting impression upon your reader. Once again, you may draw upon an anecdote or refer to information presented in your introduction to frame your essay as a whole.

Point of View: Position of Authority

Point of view in its simplest sense can be considered a position of authority. A personal experience, for instance, can best be expressed in first person (I, me, my; we, us, our). The particular point of view one selects to use in a composition indicates who is controlling the essay.

Point of View	Subject	Object	Possessive
First Person Singular	I	me	my, mine
Second Person Singular	you	you	your, yours
Third Person Singular	he, she, it	him, her, it	his, his, her, hers, its, its
First Person Plural	we	us	our, ours
Second Person Plural	you	you	your, yours
Third Person Plural	they	them	their, theirs

First person point of view: The author speaks through his or her personal experience (I, me, my; we, us, our). *I* and *we* are subject pronouns, *me* and *us* are object pronouns, and *my* and *our* indicate possession.

Second person point of view: The author speaks to another person (you, your). In the case of *you,* it is both subject and object, and *your* is possessive.

Third person point of view: The authors speaks about other people, places and things (he, him, his; she, her, hers; it, its; they, them, their), where *he, she, it,* and *they* are subject pronouns, *him, her, it,* and *them* are object pronouns, and *his, her, its,* and *their* denote possession.

Appropriate Use of Point of View

First Person: When writing an expository essay where you provide details and examples based on your own experience, use the first person point of view. Why? You, the author, are the authority of the situation. When writing in first person, be careful not to mention what people are thinking. The way to reveal this is by using dialogue and quotation marks, since you are not able to read a person's mind, which is known as the omniscient (all-knowing) point of view. (See third person.)

> *Example:* When the car hit me, I knew that my arm and leg were broken and my recovery would take months.

Second Person: The second person point of view has an author or speaker addressing at least one other person. Second person point of view is effective in process essays (those that tell the reader how to construct an object or complete a task).

> *Example*: Once you have combined all the ingredients, pour the batter into the baking pan, place in the oven, and bake for 35 minutes at 375 degrees.

Unless you are writing a process-oriented paper (how to do something or how something was done), avoid the use of second person, for it too often can sound preachy and alienate readers by seemingly talking down to them.

Third Person: The third person point of view features an anonymous narrator who has virtually free license to talk or write about people, objects, and locations. The narrator, above all, is allowed to go into people's minds and reveal what they are thinking. This is known as the omniscient or all-knowing point of view, and only the third person point of view lends itself to this.

> *Example:* When Mary encountered the rapist, fear ran rampant through her body,and she could not imagine how she would survive.

Above all, writers must be careful to avoid shifting their points of view. Begin with one (i.e., first, second or third person), and stay with that point of view. Below is an example of shifting points of view, which must be avoided:

> *Example: One* must always change *their* clothes when *you* are going to a formal dinner, or *we* could be refused entry.

Rewritten correctly in *third person plural*, the sentence would read:

> *People* must always change *their* clothes when *they* are going to a formal dinner, or *they* could be refused entry.

Lead-Ins and Concluding Sentences

Both *lead-in* and *concluding* sentences can play a crucial role in an effective essay. Lead-in sentences are those that expose readers to a topic or an issue, grabbing their interest and actively engaging them with the text. The following lead-in sentences taken from various essays presented in *Visions Across the Americas* all invite or intrigue people to read on:

- "The last inch of space was filled, yet people continue to wedge themselves along the walls of the Store."—*Maya Angelou*
- "What is intelligence, anyway?"—*Isaac Asimov*
- "From the neck up, I am a nudist."—*Karen Ray*
- "I mean, it's like, today's teens, they just don't get it! Sure, for them, life is totally phine—er, phat."—*Mark Katz*

- "It is possible to stop most drug addiction in the United States within a very short time."—*Gore Vidal*
- "You ask me what is poverty? Listen to me. Here I am, dirty, smelly, and with no 'proper' underwear on and with the stench of my rotting teeth near you."—*Jo Goodwin Parker*
- "Do you know the difference between shame and guilt." —*Philip Persky*
- "The beguiling presence of anime in North American culture cannot be ignored."—*Grace Sumabat Mateo*

Drawing essays to effective, satisfying conclusions can also be a difficult task. It is no secret that even professional writers often wait until they revise an essay before they construct a clincher sentence. Regardless of when the concluding sentence or sentences are written—in your first draft or revised draft— they should complement your work by drawing your discussion to a definite close. Concluding sentences are usually one of the following: (1) a call to action, (2) a prediction, (3) a quotation, (4) a final anecdote, or (5) a statement about the broader implications of your topic or issue. Note how the following conclusions exemplify these methods of bringing closure to an essay.

- ". . . Between Mr. Muhammad's teachings, my correspondence, my visitors—usually Ella and Reginald—and my reading of books, months passed without my even thinking about being imprisoned. In fact, up to then, I had never been so truly free in my life."—*Malcolm X*
- ". . . A country song I once heard said it all for me: 'You've got to stand for something or you'll fall for anything.'" —*Stephanie Ericsson*
- ". . . Apart from what any critic had to say about my writing, I knew I had succeeded where it counted when my mother finished reading my first book and gave me her verdict. 'So easy to read.'"—*Amy Tan*
- ". . . Certainly to ponder, to imagine, to contemplate, or to change their [students'] minds gets them nowhere in their goals to move from point A to point B. And the various cultural elements that should nourish us—from our college classrooms and textbooks to the articles that fill our homes—reinforce an American sense of self based on the objects of life—the commodities—and less on living, by doing, with manners."—*Martha L. Henning*
- ". . . Nonviolent resistance is not aimed against oppressors but against oppression. Under its banner consciences, not racial groups, are enlisted."—*Dr. Martin Luther King, Jr.*

- "... But fetal alcohol syndrome is preventable—it need not ever happen again. The future of society, in this instance more than most, is in our hands. We can't claim ignorance any longer."—*Michael Dorris*

Revising and Editing

One draft of a paper, of course, will not usually result in a polished essay. Polished writing requires a great deal of work and is more than just a neatly rewritten or a grammatically or mechanically correct paper (a paper without a comma splice or subject–verb agreement error can still be thoroughly disunified and disorganized). Therefore, you will probably write several drafts before arriving at a finished product. After you get your basic material down on paper, you will be ready for the next step in the writing process: revision. A good rule of thumb is to remember that "good writing is a matter of *rewriting.*"

When you revise, you'll want to consider your work from the viewpoint of the receptor (reader), rather than the creator (writer). In doing so, you will critique *what has been written* as opposed to *what you intended.* One way to approach the second draft—and all subsequent drafts—of an essay is to ask yourself questions like "How could I have said this better?" or "What seems to be missing here?" Jot down your answers to such questions in your margins because they will come in handy later on. Following are some other questions you may wish to bear in mind:

- Are there awkward, imprecise sentences? Where? Which sentences could be condensed and combined with other sentences?
- Do transitions and linking words establish clear relationships and promote coherence between words, clauses, sentences, and paragraphs?
- Is there a clearly defined thesis? Do all paragraphs support the thesis? How?
- Where might sentence variety improve the flow of information?
- Have major points been thoroughly justified or illustrated? How?
- Where might concrete nouns and active verbs replace vague nouns and passive verbs?

- Are the supporting paragraphs logically organized and thoroughly developed?
- Does the essay contain a satisfying and appropriate concluding paragraph?
- Are paragraphs unified?
- Is reasoning sound? Are conclusions logically drawn? How?

As you move from one draft to the next, organizing material, developing weak points, eliminating awkward constructions, and rewriting confusing sentences, you'll want to remember the distinction between revision and editing skills. They are two different steps in the composition process—not one and the same. You revise your material in order to present it in a logical, coherent, effective manner; you edit your writing so that it adheres to recognizable conventions of style, grammar, and usage. Each time you *finish revising a paper,* edit and correct grammatical and mechanical errors which interfere with clear written communication. The following student, Joanne Jaime, wrote three drafts of her essay, *discussing* the full range of her observations and feelings toward marriage and divorce in the first draft; revising awkward constructions and *addressing* unity, organization, coherence, and paragraph structure in the second draft; and *refining* syntax, *varying* sentence patterns, and *editing* careless grammatical or mechanical errors which could interfere with or impair a clear understanding of her subject in the third and final draft.

Marriage: The Changing Institution

Over the past thirty years, the institution of marriage has fallen victim to the changes in our social and moral values. Infidelity, physical abuse, substance abuse, financial instability, job-related stress, conflicting goals and lack of communication are problems often associated with the breakup of marriages. The current high divorce rate in the United States is directly

Lead-in to thesis

Thesis statement

related to our views about marriage, our motives for marriage, and our expectations of marriage.

Discussion point #1 (views on marriage) with examples & reasoning

The vows ". . . in sickness and in health, 'til death do us part" were once taken literally. Marriage was viewed as a lifelong commitment. People married their first loves, settled down, and started a family. They didn't question whether their lives were fulfilling; they simply accepted the wisdom of tradition and their parents. In the end, the security of it all was comforting and they thanked God for their children and grandchildren. Divorce, on the other hand, was practically unheard of. It carried a social stigma and was synonymous with failure; something must have been wrong with people if they couldn't hold their marriages together. Divorced women, especially, were considered no good and sinful.

Paragraph #3 takes discussion point #1 a step further by contrasting the social values of the past with those held today.

Today, all this does not necessarily hold true. Because of numerous social revolutions and movements in the 1960s—the sexual revolution, the civil rights movement, and the women's movement, among others—divorce is no longer considered an unacceptable practice. In fact, marriage conforms almost to the same rules as a business deal. If we are not getting our money's worth, or if promises are broken, we have every right to dissolve our agreement. We are considered smart for cutting our losses and moving on with our lives. Besides, the beauty of marriage is what it symbolizes, not its true rewards and sacrifices. Although some of us like the idea of growing old with that one special person, the pursuit of individual happiness is what we truly cherish.

Why bother getting married? Why don't people just live together and see what happens? Nowadays, many people do choose to live together indefinitely. However, before the sexual revolution, marriage was the only acceptable predecessor to having sex and children. Afterwards, the number of unmarried women who became pregnant increased. Pregnancy is still a strong reason that many people get married. The pressure to get married under this circumstance could easily account for many unhappy marriages. Going from a one-night stand to a marriage, baby included, is a long distance to travel in a short period of time. The absence of quality time can weaken the foundation of a marriage. Divorce is the most likely outcome.

Discussion point #2 (motives for marrying). Note the effective use of rhetorical questions to establish the controlling idea about "motives."

Paragraph #5 is an extension of discussion point #2 with some examples drawn from personal experiences.

People everywhere tend to get married for the wrong reasons, reasons other than love. Some people marry for financial gain, others for status or citizenship, and still others marry just because they are afraid of being alone. An acquaintance of mine, for instance, accepted $10,000 to marry her husband, François, and stay with him until he gained American citizenship. Another person I know married her husband so they could file a joint income tax return; they neither lived nor spent time with each other. If a person's motive for getting married is primarily self-serving, then the decision needs to be reconsidered. We should not get married to get divorced.

Discussion point #3 (the change in expectations of a marriage)

A final reason for the increase in divorce rates is that marriage expectations have changed considerably over the years. Due to the increase of women in the work force, they are no longer dependent on men to be sole supporters. There is no longer any financial incentive for women to remain in bad marriages. On the contrary, divorce settlements sometimes offer considerable financial gain! Also, education has not only improved, it has become more accessible. There is a wealth of knowledge spewing forth from books, magazines, and TV talk shows: information about laws, domestic violence, support groups, and other social and moral issues. Education enables us to make better decisions in our lives, but we also learn to expect more from ourselves and others.

People constantly get married hoping to change their partners so they fit their ideals of the perfect husband or wife. Even worse, some people like my former math instructor marry a dysfunctional person with any number of problems and decide their mission in life is to become a "miracle worker," reforming or saving that individual from himself or herself. Such relationships inevitably end in violence, despair, or disillusionment—such relationships should be avoided. Nowadays we do not have to stay in a rotten marriage or accept abuse from anyone. At the same time, in order to avoid these situations to begin with, we should take a good look at whom we are marrying before saying, "I do." Today we are ready to file for divorce at the least provocation. If we are not happy, we must ask ourselves whose responsibility it is to make us happy. Marriage is give-and-take. Divorce is giving up.

Paragraph #7 expands upon discussion point #3.

Conclusion reiterates main discussion points.

There are several forces inside of marriage that can lead to discord and divorce. Some, such as the changing views about, the motivation for, and the expectations of a marriage, are more obvious than others. Still, the relationship between the husband and wife figures prominently in the success or failure of a marriage. More than ever before, love and respect are essential ingredients in a good marriage, for the future of marriage commitments is no longer tied to the dictates of the past. As the institution of marriage continues to evolve in the twenty-first century, we may go through even more changes and eventually come full circle. This ultimate

Concludes essay with a prediction

decision, however, will be made by individuals—couples—not morality imposed by society at large.

Special Writing Activities: The Individual and Group Response

There are many ways an individual becomes an active writer and a creative thinker. Individually, a person might write notes and impressions in a journal, record responses to a reading in a reading/writing log, or create, analyze, and solve a problem in a thesis notebook. Other times, writers work together as a group, examine issues, exchange ideas, and ultimately write a composition. Whether you write alone or with others, the ultimate goals are usually the same: to generate ideas, to analyze a problem, and to structure a meaningful response to the issue or reading. The following section offers a few writing strategies to use individually or as a group that will assist you in completing some of the pre-reading and post-reading activities in this text.

Journals, Reading/Writing Logs, and Thesis Notebooks

A journal is one of the most popular resources used by writers. In a journal, the writer freely records observations (sometimes in a diary format), notes events and daily activities, and jots down plans and goals. Journal entries are usually informal, and the writer's concern is to record ideas and observations with little regard for grammatical or mechanical perfection. A journal should be a place to examine new ideas and reevaluate old ones; it's a place to explore feelings and attitudes without the fear of censorship or any type of judgment or evaluation. Many techniques such as freewriting and brainstorming offer ideal strategies for writing journal entries.

Both readers and writers alike record their responses to an analysis of a book, story, poem, essay, or play in reading/writing logs. What do they write about? After reading, they jot down their emotional responses to the issues or topics discussed. They may also create a dialogue with the text, asking questions and stating opinions such as "This is seldom true!" or "Why doesn't the author support her claim?" Under "Tips on Becoming an Active Reader" earlier in Chapter 1, you will find useful hints for keeping a reading/writing log.

Much like a journal or a reading/writing log, a thesis notebook records information. However, whereas the reading/writing log focuses on your reactions and perceptions about readings, a thesis notebook deals mostly with expository writings. In particular, the writer probes ideas to determine whether they can function as a controlling idea and be developed into an essay. During this process, the writer attempts to narrow a topic, construct a thesis, and support it. As a result, a thesis notebook often contains several drafts of writing assignments. In addition to its usefulness when structuring essays, a thesis notebook provides a place to rough out creative writings such as poems, short stories, and even plays. Since many of the pre- and post-reading questions in this text invite both informal and formal reader response, they are ideally suited for journal and reading/writing log assignments.

In many instances, authors will combine characteristics of journals, logs, and notebooks under one cover because they all deal with the same thing: exploring and recording ideas and perceptions. A journal or notebook is seldom an end in itself but a means of working out ideas that will lead to a formal written response.

Response and Summary

A summary takes a longer work and briefly condenses it for a reader. Oftentimes, practice in writing summaries can be a valuable exercise for a reader/writer. A summary, which is about one-fourth as long as the original material in length, requires the reader to reflect upon what he or she has read. Then, the *reader* will have to consider the main points (though often details are omitted) and as a *writer* will place them in some orderly sequence. As an ongoing journal activity, frequently summarize the essays you read in *Visions Across the Americas* to get a clear sense of other writers' ideas, and to practice critical thinking and writing. You might follow each summary you write with a personal response about the topic, issue, or essay in question. For instance, J. J., a student, wrote the following journal entry:

Summary   "Euphemisms" by Neil Postman explores the practice of calling things by a different name in order to attract more positive reactions and sentiment towards those things. He often uses the examples of changing "garbage man" to "sanitation engineer." In his essay, Postman doesn't outrightly criticize the practice of using euphemisms; he does, however, stress that it is mostly an art of disguising the true meaning of something. (Then again, even Postman states that there is no *true meaning of something.*)

Personal   What Postman says is interesting. All of his exam-
response
ples are not completely fitting for the points he tries to make, but the general idea seems on target to me. We often have to fool ourselves in order to feel good—

or to fool others to wake them up and get them fo-

cused. Of course, it is only our acceptance of a name

or word that makes its definition concrete. If we

squabble over what to call things, we'd be nowhere

fast. On the other hand, I suppose people will always

think what they want, and they'll be sure to make up

new names to fit their way of thinking. Priorities and

values don't necessarily change because of a name.

Writing a summary requires you to read material carefully in order to extract the part that represents the whole (the major discussion points that support a thesis). If a work is inaccurately represented, then the summary is of no use to anyone. You might also follow your close analytical reading, summary, and personal response with a comparative evaluation of viewpoints: an author's and your own.

A summary is not a paraphrase. When you paraphrase a written work, you place someone else's words into your own. Whereas a summary provides your reader with a brief gist of a longer work, a paraphrase offers a more detailed rewording of a piece of writing— usually to clarify meaning—and is approximately as long as the original work. (There is nothing brief about a paraphrase!)

Group Activities and Collaborative Writing

Although writers often work out concepts individually, they also collaborate (work together) to generate and evaluate ideas. In the Group Activities sections of this textbook, for instance, you will often be asked to brainstorm a topic or issue as a group, meaning you will initially share information or opinions without evaluating or judging them. Ideally, your group will have a wide range of responses to any given subject; that way, you will be able to consider a topic from as many points of view as possible before analyzing or writing about it. Group activities generate dialogue; each group member both listens and contributes to group discussion without the anxiety of being judged.

One outcome of group activities might be a collaborative composition. Here, authors work together to generate and compose an essay. To begin with, writers examine an issue in order to arrive at a specific focus and formulate a thesis. Next, after thorough discussion, they break the thesis down into sections which will serve as major points or topic sentences to structure their composition. Collaborative writers then use an essay map or outline in order to guide them as they write. Then, with one person acting as recorder/secretary, group members develop each major point (topic sentence); every individual offers his or her experiences or examples to support the group's thesis, thereby developing the rough draft. Once a draft is complete, all group members go over their collaborative effort, correcting careless errors and noting parts of the composition in need of revision or more development.

There are many variations to a collaborative writing project. Sometimes, for instance, every group member may write a rough draft of an agreed-upon thesis and then the group may combine them into one essay. Other times, group members may be responsible for individual sections of the collaborative essay. Regardless of how you approach a collaborative writing assignment, its strength rests on cooperation with, and participation by, each group member.

Summation

From reading and marking textbooks to generating ideas, structuring compositions, and engaging in group (collaborative) activities, the connection between reading and writing is ever-present. As you read through the remaining essays on language in this chapter—and the essays in this book as a whole—we suggest that you review this brief section on reading and writing frequently. Doing so will enable you to keep a clear perspective on how to read and write "actively."

Pat Mora

Why I Am a Writer

Pat Mora was born and educated in Texas, first at Texas Western College, where she earned her bachelor's degree in 1963, and later at the University of El Paso, where she received her master's degree in 1967. Since then, she has been actively involved in cross-cultural studies, both as an instructor and an administrator. In her own work, Mora frequently draws from her Hispanic heritage. Her poetry and prose frequently appear in literary journals, popular magazines, and anthologies. She has published three award-winning poetry collections, Chants *(1984),* Borders *(1986), and* Communion *(1991). She also wrote* Agua Santa: Holy Water *(1997), and* A Library for Juana: The World of Sor Juana Ines *(2002). The following essay explaining why Mora is a writer first appeared in the July/August 1990 issue of* The Horn Book Magazine.

Pre-reading Questions

1. The title of Mora's essay, "Why I Am a Writer," seems to promise some sort of explanation or answer. Why do you imagine Mora or any other person would want to be a writer?

2. Do a freewriting in which you explain why and when you write.

1   I like people. I like long, slow lunches with my friends. I like to dance. I'm no hermit, and I'm not shy. So why do I sit with my tablet and pen and mutter to myself?

2   There are many answers. I write because I am a reader. I want to give to others what writers have given me, a chance to hear the voices of people I will never meet. Even if I met these

authors, I wouldn't hear what I hear alone with the page—words carefully chosen, woven into a piece unlike any other, enjoyed by me in a way no other person will enjoy them. I love the privateness of writing and reading.

3   I write because I am curious. I am curious about me. Writing is a way of finding out how I feel about anything and everything. Now that I've left the desert where I grew up, for example, I'm discovering how it feels to walk on spongy autumn leaves and to watch snow drifting up on a strong wind. I notice what's around me in a special way because I am a writer. I notice my world more, and then I talk to myself about it on paper. Writing is my way of saving my feelings.

4   I write because I believe that Hispanics need to take their rightful place in American literature. We need to be published and to be studied in schools and colleges so that the stories and ideas of our people won't quietly disappear. Although I am happy when I finish the draft of a poem or story, I always wish that I wrote better, that I could bring more honor and attention to the *abuelitas*—grandmothers—I write about. That mix of sadness and pleasure frequently occurs in a writer's life.

5   Although we don't discuss it often because it is depressing, my people have been and sometimes still are viewed as inferior. We have all been hurt by someone who said, "You're not like us; you are not one of us. Speaking Spanish is odd; your family looks funny." Some of us decide we don't want to be different; we don't want to be part of a group that is often described as poor and uneducated. I spoke Spanish at home to my grandmother and aunt, but I didn't always want my friends at school to know that I spoke Spanish. And I didn't like myself for feeling that way. I sensed it was wrong, but I didn't know why. Now I know.

6   I know that the society we live in affects us. It is not easy to learn to disregard the unimportant things about people—the car they drive, the house they live in, the color of their skin, the language they speak at home. It takes courage to face the fact that we all have ten toes, get sleepy at night, get scared in the dark. Some families, some cities, some states, and even some countries foolishly convince themselves that they are better than others. Then they teach their children this ugly lie. It's like a weed with burrs and stickers that prick people.

7   How are young people who are Hispanic or members of any ethnic group supposed to feel about themselves? Some are proud of their cultural roots. But television commercials are busy trying to convince us that our cars, clothes, and even our families

aren't good enough. It is so hard to be yourself, your many interesting selves, because billboards and magazine ads tell you that being beautiful is being thin, blond, and rich, rich, rich. No wonder we don't always like ourselves when we look in the mirror.

8   So I write to try to correct these images of worth. I take pride in being a Hispanic writer. I will continue to write and to struggle to say what no other writer can say in quite the same way.

Post-reading Questions

Content

1. What are some of the reasons Mora gives for writing?
2. Why does she say that "a mix of sadness and pleasure frequently occurs in a writer's life"?
3. Why didn't Mora speak Spanish in school? How did she feel about this decision?
4. In what ways does Mora attempt to "correct images of worth" through her writings?

Strategies and Structures

1. What personal example does Mora give to show that some people don't want to be different? How does Mora illustrate the unimportant "things about people"?
2. In what way do specific topic sentences help to lead the reader through each paragraph and organize the essay?
3. What is the effect of the repetition of lead-in phrases like "I write because"? What do you imagine the author is attempting to achieve?
4. In what way do the first and last paragraphs function as a framing device for the whole essay?

Language and Vocabulary

1. A simile is a comparison with the use of *like* or *as*. At the end of paragraph 6, Mora uses a simile to illustrate the effects of the ugly lies we tell about others. What is this simile? Is it an accurate image of cultural lies? Why? Why not?
2. Mora uses one Spanish word in her essay, *abuelitas*. How does she define this word for the non-Spanish speakers? When do you feel this would be an effective strategy in your own writing?

Group Activities

1. Mora claims that Hispanic authors need "to be studied in schools and colleges." Divide into small groups, go to the library, and find stories, essays, poems, and/or articles written by Hispanic authors. Choose one you like best and write a summary of it to present to the class. Why do you imagine your particular author likes to write?

2. The author tells us that "billboards and magazine ads tell you that being beautiful is being thin, blond, and rich, rich, rich." In small groups, look through several magazines and discuss whether Mora's claim is true or not and compare your findings with the other groups.

Writing Activities

1. In a short composition, briefly explain why you are not "a writer." You might begin your paper much like Mora, using topic sentences with lead-ins such as *I write because . . .* or *I don't write because . . .*

2. Using ideas generated from Group Activity 2, write a brief essay in which you support or disprove Mora's claim that "magazine ads tell you that being beautiful is being thin, blond, and rich, rich, rich" with specific examples from your observations.

Ray Bradbury

The Joy of Writing

An esteemed author of many science fiction classics, Ray Bradbury is
also well-known for his non-fiction works, his screenplays, his
television scripts, and futuristic novels. Among his many works are:
The Martian Chronicles *(1950),* Fahrenheit 451 *(1953),* Something
Wicked This Way Comes *(1962),* Death Is a Lonely Business *(1985),*
Yestermorrow: Obvious Answers to an Impossible Future *(1991),*
Green Shadow, White Whale *(1992),* Quicker Than the Eye *(1996),*
Driving Blind *(1997),* From The Dust Returned *(2001), and* One
More For the Road: A New Short Story Colection *(2002). In addition*
to all of these, Bradbury frequently authors articles like "The Joy of
Writing," offering insights into the composition process. In the preface
to Zen and the Art of Writing *(1996), for instance, Bradbury invites*
his readers to approach writing the same way he does: "Every
morning I jump out of bed and step on a landmine. The landmine is
me. After the explosion, I spend the rest of the day putting the pieces
together. Now, it's your turn. Jump!"

Pre-reading Questions

1. Who are some of your favorite authors, poets, musicians,
   artists, actors/actresses? Make a brief list of them.
2. How would you define "zest" and "gusto"? In what sort of
   situation might you use these words?

---

1   Zest. Gusto. How rarely one hears these words used. How
rarely do we see people living, or for that matter, creating by
them. Yet if I were asked to name the most important items in
a writer's make-up, the things that shape his material and

rush him along the road to where he wants to go, I could only warn him to look to his zest, see to his gusto.

2   You have your list of favorite writers; I have mine. Dickens, Twain, Wolfe, Peacock, Shaw, Molière, Jonson, Wycherly, Sam Johnson. Poets: Gerard Manley Hopkins, Dylan Thomas, Pope. Painters: El Greco, Tintoretto. Musicians: Mozart, Haydn, Ravel, Johann Strauss (!). Think of all these names and you think of big or little, but nonetheless important, zests, appetites, hungers. Think of Shakespeare and Melville and you think of thunder, lightning, wind. They all knew the joy of creating in large or small forms, on unlimited or restricted canvasses. These are the children of the gods. They knew fun in their work. No matter if creation came hard here and there along the way, or what illnesses and tragedies touched their most private lives. The important things are those passed down to us from their hands and minds and these are full to bursting with animal vigor and intellectual vitality. Their hatreds and despairs were reported with a kind of love.

3   Look at El Greco's elongation and tell me, if you can, that he had no joy in his work? Can you really pretend that Tintoretto's *God Creating the Animals of the Universe* is a work founded on anything less than "fun" in its widest and most completely involved sense? The best jazz says, "Gonna live forever; don't believe in death." The best sculpture, like the head of Nefertiti, says again and again, "The Beautiful One was here, is here, and will be here, forever." Each of the men I have listed seized a bit of the quicksilver of life, froze it for all time and turned, in the blaze of their creativity, to point at it and cry, "Isn't this good!" And it was good.

4   What has all this to do with writing the short story in our times?

5   Only this: if you are writing without zest, without gusto, without love, without fun, you are only half a writer. It means you are so busy keeping one eye on the commercial market, or one ear peeled for the avant-garde coterie, that you are not being yourself. You don't even know yourself. For the first thing a writer should be is—excited. He should be a thing of fevers and enthusiasms. Without such vigor, he might as well be out picking peaches or digging ditches; God knows it'd be better for his health.

6   How long has it been since you wrote a story where your real love or your real hatred somehow got onto the paper? When was the last time you dared release a cherished prejudice so it slammed the page like a lightning bolt? What are the

best things and the worst things in your life, and when are you going to get around to whispering or shouting them?

7   Wouldn't it be wonderful, for instance, to throw down a copy of *Harper's Bazaar* you happened to be leafing through at the dentist's, and leap to your typewriter and ride off with hilarious anger, attacking their silly and sometimes shocking snobbishness? Years ago I did just that. I came across an issue where the *Bazaar* photographers, with their perverted sense of equality, once again utilized natives in a Puerto Rican backstreet as props in front of which their starved-looking mannikins postured for the benefit of yet more emaciated half-women in the best salons in the country. The photographs so enraged me I ran, did not walk, to my machine and wrote "Sun and Shadow," the story of an old Puerto Rican who ruins the *Bazaar* photographer's afternoon by sneaking into each picture and dropping his pants.

8   I dare say there are a few of you who would like to have done this job. I had the fun of doing it; the cleansing after effects of the hoot, the holler, and the great horselaugh. Probably the editors at the *Bazaar* never heard. But a lot of readers did and cried, "Go it, *Bazaar,* go it, Bradbury!" I claim no victory. But there was blood on my gloves when I hung them up.

9   When was the last time you did a story like that, out of pure indignation?

10   When was the last time you were stopped by the police in your neighborhood because you like to walk, and perhaps think, at night? It happened to me just often enough that, irritated, I wrote "The Pedestrian," a story of a time, fifty years from now, when a man is arrested and taken off for clinical study because he insists on looking at un-televised reality, and breathing un-air-conditioned air.

11   Irritations and angers aside, what about loves? What do you love most in the world? The big and little things, I mean. A trolley car, a pair of tennis shoes? These, at one time when we were children, were invested with magic for us. During the past year I've published one story about a boy's last ride in a trolley that smells of all the thunderstorms in time, full of cool–green moss-velvet seats and blue electricity, but doomed to be replaced by the more prosaic, more practical-smelling bus. Another story concerned a boy who wanted to own a pair of new tennis shoes for the power they gave him to leap rivers and houses and streets, and even bushes, sidewalks, and dogs. The shoes were to him, the surge of antelope and gazelle on African summer veldt. The energy of unleashed rivers and

summer storms lay in the shoes; he had to have them more than anything else in the world.

12   So, simply then, here is my formula.

13   What do you want more than anything else in the world? What do you love, or what do you hate?

14   Find a character, like yourself, who will want something or not want something, with all his heart. Give him running orders. Shoot him off. Then follow as fast as you can go. The character, in his great love, or hate, will rush you through to the end of the story. The zest and gusto of his need, and there *is* zest in hate as well as in love, will fire the landscape and raise the temperature of your typewriter thirty degrees.

15   All of this is primarily directed to the writer who has already learned his trade; that is, has put into himself enough grammatical tools and literary knowledge so he won't trip himself up when he wants to run. The advice holds good for the beginner, too, however, even though his steps may falter for purely technical reasons. Even here, passion often saves the day.

16   The history of each story, then, should read almost like a weather report: Hot today, cool tomorrow. This afternoon, burn down the house. Tomorrow, pour cold critical water upon the simmering coals. Time enough to think and cut and rewrite tomorrow. But today—explode—fly apart—disintegrate! The other six or seven drafts are going to be pure torture. So why not enjoy the first draft, in the hope that your joy will seek and find others in the world who, reading your story, will catch fire, too?

17   It doesn't have to be a big fire. A small blaze, candlelight perhaps; a longing for a mechanical wonder like a trolley or an animal wonder like a pair of sneakers rabbiting the lawns of early morning. Look for the little loves, find and shape the little bitternesses. Savor them in your mouth, try them on your typewriter. When did you last read a book of poetry or take time, of an afternoon, for an essay or two? Have you ever read a single issue of *Geriatrics,* the Official Journal of the American Geriatrics Society, a magazine devoted to "research and clinical study of the diseases and processes of the aged and aging"? Or read, or even seen, a copy of *What's New,* a magazine published by the Abbott Laboratories in North Chicago, containing articles such as "Tubocurarene for Cesarean Section" or "Phenurone in Epilepsy," but also utilizing poems by William Carlos Williams, Archibald Macleish, stories by Clifton Fadiman and Leo Rosten; covers and interior illustrations by John Groth, Aaron Bohrod, William Sharp, Russell Cowles? Absurd? Perhaps. But ideas lie everywhere, like apples fallen and melt-

ing in the grass for lack of wayfaring strangers with an eye and a tongue for beauty, whether absurd, horrific, or genteel.

18   Gerard Manley Hopkins put it this way:

> *Glory be to God for dappled things—*
> *For skies of couple-color as a brinded cow;*
> *For rose-moles all in stipple upon trout that swim;*
> *Fresh-firecoal chestnut-falls; finches' wings;*
> *Landscape plotted and pieced—fold, fallow, and plow;*
> *And all trades, their gear and tackle and trim.*
> *All things counter, original, spare, strange;*
> *Whatever is fickle, freckled (who knows how?)*
> *With swift, slow; sweet, sour; adazzle, dim;*
> *He fathers-forth whose beauty is past change:*
> *Praise Him.*

19   Thomas Wolfe ate the world and vomited lava. Dickens dined at a different table every hour of his life. Molière, tasting society, turned to pick up his scalpel, as did Pope and Shaw. Everywhere you look in the literary cosmos, the great ones are busy loving and hating. Have you given up this primary business as obsolete in your own writing? What fun you are missing, then. The fun of anger and disillusion, the fun of loving and being loved, of moving and being moved by this masked ball which dances us from cradle to churchyard. Life is short, misery sure, mortality certain. But on the way, in your work, why not carry those two inflated pig-bladders labeled Zest and Gusto. With them, traveling to the grave, I intend to slap some dummox's behind, pat a pretty girl's coiffure, wave to a tad up a persimmon tree.

20   Anyone wants to join me, there's plenty of room in Coxie's Army.

Post-reading Questions

Content

1. What is the basic message in Bradbury's essay? Explain.

2. How does Bradbury's list of favorite authors, poets, musicians, artists, actors/actresses, and so on, compare with your own list of favorite people?

3. What does Bradbury imply about the power of the written word?

4. Explain what you imagine Bradbury means when he says, "Look for the little loves, find and shape the

little bitternesses. Savor them in your mouth, [and] try them on your typewriter."

Strategies and Structures

1. What basic human instincts does Bradbury appeal to in order to engage his readers and connect with their lives and experiences?

2. How is Bradbury's insight that writing is ". . . almost like a weather report: Hot today, cool tomorrow," useful information for any writer? Why?

3. What does Bradbury imply about his own mind and his approach to writing? How might his approach to diverse topics and issues be beneficial to you as a writer?

4. In what way does beginning and concluding his essay with the words "zest" and "gusto" provide a framing device for the entire composition? Explain how this strategy unifies the essay and brings it full circle.

Language and Vocabulary

1. Vocabulary: *zest, gusto, mannikins, emaciated, prosaic, Cesarean Section, epilepsy, wayfaring, cosmos, dummox, persimmon.* After looking up the definitions for the above words and phrases, write each in an original sentence using a variety of sentence patterns.

2. To what extent might some of Bradbury's references seem dated in "The Joy of Writing" (written in 1973)? Write a journal entry citing specific words, phrases, or references which might distinguish his prose from contemporary authors writing at the beginning of the twenty-first century.

Group Activities

1. After gathering in groups of four to five people, compare your responses to Language and Vocabulary question #2. What was the most common criticism among members of your group? To what extent was your criticism a heartfelt response to the question? If your group had an opportunity to discuss Bradbury's essay with him, what would you suggest that he revise or change and why?

2. Divide the list of authors, painters, and musicians in paragraphs 2 and 17 among members in your group. Then, go to your campus library (or online) and investigate the lives of these people. Do you find any evidence of their approaching their respective craft with "zest" and "gusto"? Share your findings and conclusions with the rest of the class. (Each group should research all the individuals Bradbury mentions in order to prepare for the class forum.)

Writing Activities

1. Write to a magazine, business, social agency, or restaurant and either attack or praise its policies, its snobbish, elitist attitudes, preferential treatment of topics, issues, or employees, and so on. A letter of praise, of course, would highlight positive rather than negative attributes of the magazine, business, social agency or restaurant.

2. Following Bradbury's instructions, select a topic you either love or hate. Then write an essay, using "zest" and "gusto" to explain and defend your position on the topic. You might want to begin by making two lists—one for topics you love and one for topics you hate. Narrow each list by asking yourself, "what do I feel most passionate about?" Then, as Bradbury suggests, "Jump [right into the essay]!"

Amy Tan

My Mother's English

A freelance writer and author of the prize-winning book The Joy Luck
Club *(1989), Amy Tan currently lives in San Francisco with her
family and is a popular lecturer. Her second novel,* The Kitchen God's
Wife, *was released in 1991. In 1992, she published* The Moon Lady, *a
children's book based on one of the chapters in* The Joy Luck Club.
Her other children's books include The Siamese Cat *(1994). Tan's
other novels include:* The Hundred Secret Senses *(1995) and* The
Bonesetter's Daughter *(2001). In addition to writing, Tan sings for*
The Rock Bottom Remainders, *a rock group that includes such
popular writers as Dave Barry and Stephen King (their motto is "We
play music as well as Metallica writes novels"). The following excerpt
about her "mother's English" is from a speech Tan delivered at the
CATE (California Association of Teachers of English) '90 Conference
in San Francisco.*

Pre-reading Questions

1. Who influenced the way you speak the most—your parents, your peers, or your teachers?

2. How do you use language when speaking with relatives,
friends, teachers, and strangers? How does your language change depending on to whom you are speaking?
When do you feel your verbal English accurately represents the "real you"? (Do you ever feel as if another person is doing the talking when you are speaking to others?
When?)

3. When have you felt limited or particularly effective due to
your inability or ability to read and write? (For example,
have you ever had writer's block on an essay test?)

1   As you know, I am a writer and by that definition I am someone who has always loved language. I think that is first and
foremost with almost every writer I know. I'm fascinated by
language in daily life. I spend a great deal of time thinking
about the power of language—the way it can evoke an emotion, a visual image, a complex idea or a simple truth. As a
writer, language is the tool of my trade and I use them all, all
the Englishes I grew up with.

2   A few months back, I was made keenly aware of the Englishes I do use. I was giving a talk to a large group of people,
the same talk I had given many times before and also with
notes. And the nature of the talk was about my writing, my life,
and my book, *The Joy Luck Club*. The talk was going along well
enough until I remembered one major difference that made the
whole thing seem wrong. My mother was in the room, and it
was perhaps the first time she had heard me give a lengthy
speech, using a kind of English I had never used with her. I was
saying things like "the intersection of memory and imagination," and "there is an aspect of my fiction that relates to this
and thus." A speech filled with carefully wrought grammatical
sentences, burdened to me it seemed with nominalized forms,
past perfect tenses, conditional phrases, all the forms of standard English that I had learned in school and through books, a
form of English I did not use at home or with my mother.

3   Shortly after that I was walking down the street with my
mother and my husband and I became self-conscious of the
English I was using, the English that I do use with her. We
were talking about the price of new and used furniture and I
heard myself saying to her, "Not waste money that way." My
husband was with me as well, and he didn't notice any switch
in my English. And then I realized why: because over the
twenty years that we've been together he's often used that
English with me and I've used that with him. It is sort of the
English that is our language of intimacy, the English that relates to family talk, the English that I grew up with.

4   I'd like to give you some idea what my family talk sounds
like and I'll do that by quoting what my mother said during a
recent conversation which I videotaped and then transcribed.
During this conversation, my mother was talking about a political gangster who had the same last name as her family, Du,
and how the gangster in his early years wanted to be adopted
by her family which was by comparison very rich. Later the
gangster became more rich, more powerful than my mother's
family and one day showed up at my mother's wedding to pay

his respects. And here's what she said about that, in part, "Du You Sung having business like food stand, like off the street kind; he's Du like Du Zong but not Tsung-ming Island people. The local people call him Du, from the river east side. He belong that side, local people. That man want to ask Du Zong father take him in become like own family. Du Zong father look down on him but don't take seriously until that man becoming big like, become a Mafia. Now important person, very hard inviting him. Chinese way: come only to show respect, don't stay for dinner. Respect for making big celebration; he shows up. Means gives lots of respect, Chinese custom. Chinese social life that way—if too important, won't have to stay too long. He come to my wedding; I didn't see it I heard it. I gone to boy's side. They have YMCA dinner; Chinese age I was nineteen."

5   You should know that my mother's expressive command of English belies how much she actually understands. She reads the *Forbes Report,* listens to *Wall Street Week,* converses daily with her stockbroker, reads all of Shirley MacLaine's books with ease, all kinds of things I can't begin to understand. Yet some of my friends tell me that they understand 50 percent of what my mother says. Some say maybe they understand maybe 80 percent. Some say they understand almost nothing at all. As a case in point, a television station recently interviewed my mother and I didn't see this program when it was first aired, but my mother did. She was telling me what happened. She said that everything she said, which was in English, was subtitled in English, as if she had been speaking in pure Chinese. She was understandably puzzled and upset. Recently a friend gave me that tape and I saw that same interview and I watched. And sure enough—subtitles—and I was puzzled because listening to that tape it seemed to me that my mother's English sounded perfectly clear and perfectly natural. Of course, I realize that my mother's English is what I grew up with. It is literally my mother tongue, not Chinese, not standard English, but my mother's English which I later found out is almost a direct translation of Chinese.

6   Her language as I hear it is vivid and direct, full of observation and imagery. That was the language that helped shape the way that I saw things, expressed things, made sense of the world. Lately I've been giving more thought to the kind of English that my mother speaks. Like others I have described it to people as broken or fractured English, but I wince when I say that. It has always bothered me that I can think of no other

way to describe it than broken, as if it were damaged or needed to be fixed, that it lacked a certain wholeness or soundness to it. I've heard other terms used, "Limited English" for example. But they seem just as bad, as if everything is limited, including people's perceptions of the Limited English speaker.

7   I know this for a fact, because when I was growing up my mother's limited English limited my perception of her. I was ashamed of her English. I believed that her English reflected the quality of what she had to say. That is, because she expressed it imperfectly, her thoughts were imperfect as well. And I had plenty of empirical evidence to support me: The fact that people in department stores, at banks, at supermarkets, at restaurants did not take her as seriously, did not give her good service, pretended not to understand her, or even acted as if they did not hear her.

8   My mother has long realized the limitations of her English as well. When I was fifteen she used to have me call people on the phone to pretend I was she. In this guise, I was forced to ask for information or oftentimes to complain and yell at people that had been rude to her. One time it was a call to her stockbroker in New York. She had cashed out her small portfolio and it just so happened that we were going to New York the next week, our very first trip outside of California. I had to get on the phone and say in my adolescent voice, which was not very convincing, "This is Mrs. Tan." And my mother was in the back whispering loudly, "Why don't he send me check already? Two weeks late. So mad he lie to me, losing me money." Then I said in perfect English, "Yes, I'm getting rather concerned. You had agreed to send the check two weeks ago, but it hasn't arrived." And she began to talk more loudly, "What you want—I come to New York, tell him front of his boss you cheating me?" And I was trying to calm her down, making her be quiet, while telling this stockbroker, "I can't tolerate any more excuses. If I don't receive the check immediately I'm going to have to speak to your manager when I arrive in New York." And sure enough the following week, there we were in front of this astonished stockbroker. And there I was, red-faced and quiet, and my mother the real Mrs. Tan was shouting at his boss in her impeccable broken English.

9   We used a similar routine a few months ago for a situation that was actually far less humorous. My mother had gone to the hospital for an appointment to find out about a benign brain tumor a CAT scan had revealed a month ago. And she had spoken very good English she said—her best English, no

mistakes. Still she said the hospital had not apologized when
they said they had lost the CAT scan and she had come for nothing. She said that they did not seem to have any sympathy
when she told them she was anxious to know the exact diagno-
sis since her husband and son had both died of brain tumors.
She said they would not give her any more information until
the next time; she would have to make another appointment for
that, so she said she would not leave until the doctor called her
daughter. She wouldn't budge, and when the doctor finally
called her daughter, me, who spoke in perfect English, lo-and-
behold, we had assurances the CAT scan would be found, they
promised a conference call on Monday, and apologies were given
for any suffering my mother had gone through for a most re-
grettable mistake. By the way, apart from the distress of that
episode, my mother is fine.

10   But it has continued to disturb me how much my mother's
English still limits people's perceptions of her. I think my
mother's English almost had an effect on limiting my possibilities as well. Sociologists and linguists will probably tell you
that a person's developing language skills are more influenced
by peers. But I do think the language spoken by the family, especially immigrant families, which are more insular, plays a
large role in shaping the language of the child. . . . [While this
may be true, I always wanted, however,] to capture what language ability tests can never reveal—her intent, her passion,
her imagery, the rhythms of her speech, and the nature of her
thoughts. Apart from what any critic had to say about my writing, I knew I had succeeded where it counted when my mother
finished reading my first book and gave me her verdict. "So
easy to read."

Post-reading Questions

Content

1. What is the focus of Tan's essay? Who and what
   does she talk about?
2. Tan speaks of many different "Englishes." What are
   they?
3. How do others characterize her mother's English?
   How does Tan feel about her mother's English?
4. What steps does Tan's mother take to hide her "broken English"? Why does she feel it is necessary to
   conceal the "limitations of her English"?

Strategies and Structures

1. What is the purpose of Tan's opening paragraph? What does it establish? How does it prepare you for her discussion of her mother's English?
2. Tan says her mother's language is "full of observation and imagery." How does she support such claims throughout her essay?
3. How does the author demonstrate the difficulties others have with her mother's English?
4. How does Tan illustrate the effectiveness of her mother's direct, "broken English" in comparison to the author's use of the English language?

Language and Vocabulary

1. Vocabulary: *intersection, wrought, nominalized, transcribed, belies, empirical, portfolio, CAT scan, linguists.* To increase your vocabulary, look up the definitions of the above words in a dictionary. Even if you think you know the meanings, look them up to confirm what you know and expand your vocabulary with additional meanings. Then write synonyms (words or word groups with similar meanings) in your writing log or journal for each word.
2. This essay is an excerpt from a speech. For the most part, Tan keeps her language straightforward and simple. Why is her style particularly appropriate to listeners as opposed to readers? What limitations does a speaker face that a writer does not?

Group Activities

1. Many minorities face language discrimination. There have been several attempts by states to recognize English as the official language of American citizens. As a group, research articles debating both sides of such initiatives and then discuss the following questions: Why are some people in favor of a national language and others against it? Do you feel Tan would feel such initiatives are necessary or fair?
2. Go back through the text and note all passages where Tan's mother expresses herself. In the incident with the stockbroker, Tan claims her mother's English was more effective than Tan's own "proper"

English. Compare the two Englishes and discuss
why Tan would make such a claim (e.g., what was
ineffective about Tan's use of the English language).

Writing Activities

1. Write a paragraph or so in which you discuss the
   differences in the language you use with your family and friends. Which is more formal? Which includes more slang? If you feel you speak to family
   and friends exactly alike, write a topic sentence expressing as much and then support your controlling
   idea with some specific, representative examples.
2. Briefly describe a situation where you felt your use
   of the English language—whether it was "standard"
   or "broken"—played an important part in the way
   others perceived you.

2

Narration

People told stories long before written languages appeared. The only way many cultures preserved their history was through stories passed down from generation to generation. In many cultures, the storyteller's position in society was second only to royalty. Chants, a form of storytelling, were so important to the Hawaiians that a chanter was put to death for missing even one word of a story. Today, we still enjoy hearing and telling stories but need not fear the fate of Hawaiian chanters. Whether we're sitting around a roaring fire telling jokes or ghost stories, recalling memorable moments (good or bad), or narrating a humorous happening, we are engaged in the process of narration. We tell stories for many reasons: to inform, to entertain, or to persuade. Regardless of purpose, narration has many common elements.

Common Elements of Narration

Creating Chronological Order

Most narratives have a chronological order; that is, the events are told in the sequence in which they occurred. To unify their essays and to help readers through them, authors frequently use *time transitions,* words such as *initially, next, in addition, once, finally,* and so on. These transitional devices, often called linking words, appear in strategic places in the essay, indicating the relationship between phrases, clauses, and entire paragraphs. In

"Saigon, April 1975," Nguyen Ngoc Ngan uses transitional expressions like "later," "after waiting," "the very next day," "first," and "then" in order to lead his reader through the things he did to survive when the Viet Cong took over South Vietnam.

Alma Luz Villanueva uses similar transitional expressions in her narrative, "Leaps of Faith," with phrases such as "during the time," "when I began," "about two weeks later," and "as I sit," in order to clearly indicate time order crucial to understanding and appreciating how fictional characters evolved out of her personal experiences.

Developing Character

In order to develop a character, you will want to use concrete nouns and active verbs whenever possible. Doing so will *show* your reader what the person is like through his or her actions. For example, in "The Origins of the Pipe," rather than telling readers the Buffalo Woman is supernatural, Black Elk shows us by writing, *"And as she sang, there came from her mouth a white cloud that was good to smell."* Similarly, Maxine Hong Kingston uses vividly descriptive words and phrases like *"Wei saw his arrow sticking in a ball of flesh entirely covered with eyes, some rolled back to show the dulling whites"* to describe a ghost. Such passages may horrify, amuse, or inform the reader, but one thing is certain: They rarely will put the reader to sleep!

Establishing Mood and Tone

Often authors use concrete details to engage the reader's imagination, establishing mood and tone; they often draw on sensory imagery. In "Journey to Nine Miles," when Alice Walker writes, *"By five o'clock, we were awake, listening to the soothing slapping of the surf and watching the sky redden over the ocean,"* she appeals to the reader's senses of sight and sound to establish a colorful, sensual tone that pervades the essay. In "American Horse," Louise Erdrich creates a textured, visual panorama when she writes, *"The way he said it, grace meant everything the butterfly was. The sharp delicate wings. The way it floated over grass. The way its wings seem to breathe fanning in the sun. The wisdom of the way it blended into flowers or changed into a leaf."*

Whether narratives are meant to inform, entertain, or persuade, they have been used by storytellers and writers for ages—and continue to be used—to engage their readers' imaginations. In the process, writers have manipulated the elements of character, imagery, and plot to achieve their goals.

Tips on Writing Narrative Essays

1. Determine the purpose of your narrative. Do you plan to inform, argue an issue, define something, or simply write an amusing account for your reader?

2. Ask yourself for whom you are writing this narrative. (Your audience will determine how you will approach your topic and what sort of language you will use.)

3. Freewrite, brainstorm, or cluster your topic using the five Ws (who, what, where, when, and why) and *H* (how). Once you have decided upon a particular focus or controlling idea for your composition, write the idea in the form of a thesis statement and construct your introductory paragraph.

4. Using time transitions (first, second, third, then, also) to highlight chronological order, write out your entire narrative, referring to your thesis statement to ensure continuity.

5. Create mood and tone in your narrative by using concrete nouns and active verbs. During the revision stage of writing, add small descriptive details to appeal to your reader's five senses. Attempt to enable your reader to visualize everything you are recounting.

6. Before writing your final copy, have someone read your paper and tell you whether he or she felt like a participant— or an observer—at the event you described. An impartial reader can often point out areas in your paper where you've assumed too much reader knowledge or sections that require additional attention.

Maxine Hong Kingston

Ghosts

The daughter of Chinese immigrants, Maxine Hong Kingston was born in Stockton, California. Her articles and stories have appeared in such publications as Ms., The New York Times, *and* New West. *Kingston's books include* The Woman Warrior: Memoirs of a Girlhood among Ghosts, *which won the National Book Critics Circle award in 1976,* China Men, *winner of the American Book Award in 1981;* Tripmaster Monkey *(1990),* Hawaii One Summer *(1998), and* To Be a Poet *(2002). The following narrative was taken from* The Woman Warrior.

Pre-reading Questions

1. What does the title "Ghosts" lead you to expect in Kingston's story?

2. Brainstorm the word *ghosts* in small groups or as a class. Use the *W* and *H* questions (who, what, when, where, why, and how) to generate ideas.

---

1   When the thermometer in our laundry reached one hundred and eleven degrees on summer afternoons, either my mother or my father would say that it was time to tell another ghost story so that we could get some good chills up our backs. My parents, my brothers, sisters, great-uncle, and "Third Aunt," who wasn't really our aunt but a fellow villager, someone else's third aunt, kept the presses crashing and hissing and shouted out the stories. Those were our successful days, when so much laundry came in, my mother did not have to pick tomatoes. For breaks we changed from pressing to sorting.

2   "One twilight," my mother began, and already the chills travelled my back and crossed my shoulders; the hair rose at

the nape and the back of the legs. "I was walking home after doctoring a sick family. To get home I had to cross a footbridge. In China the bridges are nothing like the ones in Brooklyn and San Francisco. This one was made from rope, laced and knotted as if by magpies. Actually it had been built by men who had returned after harvesting sea swallow nests in Malaya. They had had to swing over the faces of the Malayan cliffs in baskets they had woven themselves. Though this bridge pitched and swayed in the updraft, no one had ever fallen into the river, which looked like a bright scratch at the bottom of the canyon, as if the Queen of Heaven had swept her great silver hairpin across the earth as well as the sky."

3   Only twilight, just as my mother stepped on the bridge, two smoky columns spiraled up taller than she. Their swaying tops hovered over her head like white cobras, one at either handrail. From stillness came a wind rushing between the smoke spindles. A high sound entered her temple bones. Through the twin whirlwinds she could see the sun and the river, the river twisting in circles, the trees upside down. The bridge moved like a ship, sickening. The earth dipped. She collapsed to the wooden slats, a ladder up the sky, her fingers so weak she could not grip the rungs. The wind dragged her hair behind her, then whipped it forward across her face. Suddenly the smoke spindles disappeared. The world righted itself, and she crossed to the other side. She looked back, but there was nothing there. She used the bridge often, but she did not encounter those ghosts again.

4   "They were Sit Dom Kuei," said Great-Uncle. "Sit Dom Kuei."

5   "Yes, of course," said my mother. "Sit Dom Kuei."

6   I keep looking in dictionaries under those syllables. "Kuei" means "ghost," but I don't find any other words that make sense. I only hear my great-uncle's river-pirate voice, the voice of a big man who had killed someone in New York or Cuba, make the sounds—"Sit Dom Kuei." How do they translate?

7   When the Communists issued their papers on techniques for combating ghosts, I looked for "Sit Dom Kuei." I have not found them described anywhere, although now I see that my mother won in ghost battle because she can eat anything—quick, pluck out the carp's eyes, one for Mother and one for Father. All heroes are bold toward food. In the research against ghost fear published by the Chinese Academy of Science is the story of a magistrate's servant, Kao Chung, a capable eater who in 1683 ate five cooked chickens and drank ten bottles of wine that belonged to the sea monster with branching teeth. The monster had arranged its food around a fire on the beach

and started to feed when Kao Chung attacked. The swan-feather sword he wrested from this monster can be seen in the Wentung County Armory in Shantung today.

8   Another big eater was Chou Yi-han of Changchow, who fried a ghost. It was a meaty stick when he cut it up and cooked it. But before that it had been a woman out at night.

9   Chen Luan-feng, during the Yuan Ho era of the T'ang dynasty (A.D. 806–820), ate yellow croaker and pork together, which the thunder god had forbidden. But Chen wanted to incur thunderbolts during drought. The first time he ate, the thunder god jumped out of the sky, its legs like old trees. Chen chopped off the left one. The thunder god fell to the earth, and the villagers could see that it was a blue pig or bear with horns and fleshy wings. Chen leapt on it, prepared to chop its neck and bite its throat, but the villagers stopped him. After that, Chen lived apart as a rainmaker, neither relatives nor the monks willing to bring lightning upon themselves. He lived in a cave, and for years whenever there was drought the villagers asked him to eat yellow croaker and pork together, and he did.

10   The most fantastic eater of them all was Wei Pang, a scholar-hunter of the Ta Li era of the T'ang dynasty (A.D. 766–779). He shot and cooked rabbits and birds, but he could also eat scorpions, snakes, cockroaches, worms, slugs, beetles, and crickets. Once he spent the night in a house that had been abandoned because its inhabitants feared contamination from the dead man next door. A shining, twinkling sphere came flying through the darkness at Wei. He felled it with three true arrows—the first making the thing crackle and flame; the second dimming it; and the third putting out its lights, sputter. When his servant came running in with a lamp, Wei saw his arrows sticking in a ball of flesh entirely covered with eyes, some rolled back to show the dulling whites. He and the servant pulled out the arrows and cut up the ball into little pieces. The servant cooked the morsels in sesame oil, and the wonderful aroma made Wei laugh. They ate half, saving half to show the household, which would return now.

11   Big eaters win. When the other passers-by stepped around the bundle wrapped in white silk, the anonymous scholar of Hanchow took it home. Inside were three silver ingots and a froglike evil, which sat on the ingots. The scholar laughed at it and chased it off. That night two frogs the size of year-old babies appeared in his room. He clubbed them to death, cooked them, and ate them with white wine. The next night a

dozen frogs, together the size of a pair of year-old babies, jumped from the ceiling. He ate all twelve for dinner. The third night thirty small frogs were sitting on his mat and staring at him with their frog eyes. He ate them too. Every night for a month smaller but more numerous frogs came so that he always had the same amount to eat. Soon his floor was like the healthy banks of a pond in spring when the tadpoles, having just turned, sprang in the wet grass. "Get a hedgehog to help eat," cried his family. "I'm as good as a hedgehog," the scholar said, laughing. And at the end of the month the frogs stopped coming, leaving the scholar with the white silk and silver ingots.

Post-reading Questions

Content
1. What image(s) do you find powerful or interesting? Why?
2. What does it mean to be heroic from Kingston's cultural perspective? How does this compare or contrast with America's perspective on heroism?
3. How and why did her mother defeat the ghost? How and why did the others defeat the ghosts?
4. Why does the author bring Chinese words into the story?

Strategies and Structures
1. Where do you imagine Kingston could have obtained the information on the different ghost warriors?
2. How does Kingston illustrate what it takes to defeat a ghost?
3. How does Kingston arrange the examples of the ghost warriors?
4. What linking words does Kingston use to unify and lead the reader through the essay?
5. How does she illustrate what it takes to be a ghost warrior?

Language and Vocabulary
1. Vocabulary: *spindle, whirlwind, croaker, pluck, sputter, anonymous, ingots.* Look up these words in your dictionary and write a ten-sentence paragraph about one of the words.

2. Kingston's language is descriptive. What "mental pictures" did or can you draw from this story? What words make her descriptions vivid?

Group Activities

1. Write a collaborative ghost story. As a group, decide what the plot of your story will be. Next, have each member of the group write consecutive paragraphs. Then link your paragraphs together carefully, using transitions. Finally, proofread your essays, eliminating mechanical and grammatical errors, and as a group, read the essay, making final corrections.
2. As a group, discuss the peculiar habits of ghosts or heroes in your culture just as Kingston narrates the peculiar eating habits of ghosts in her culture.

Writing Activities

1. Using specific examples, write a narrative essay wherein you illustrate your definition of a fiercely independent person at odds with the world around him or her.
2. Narrate a ghost story you remember hearing as a child.

Black Elk

The Offering of the Pipe

Born in 1863, Black Elk was a holy man (wichash wakon) of the Oglala Sioux. As a boy, he witnessed the Battle of the Little Big Horn in 1876 and the near demise of his people. In Black Elk Speaks *(1931), the source of the following narrative, he tells his life story— which he was instructed to do in a vision—to John G. Niehardt. Niehardt himself is the author of several books on the American West and Native Americans.*

Pre-reading Questions

1. Black Elk, a holy man, makes offerings to nature. In your cultural tradition, who are the holy men or women who make similar offerings to *unseen* powers?

2. Freewrite in your journal about ceremonies and sacred offerings. Then read Black Elk's narrative.

---

1   *Black Elk Speaks:*
My friend, I am going to tell you the story of my life, as you wish; and if it were only the story of my life I think I would not tell it; for what is one man that he should make much of his winters, even when they bend him like a heavy snow? So many other men have lived and shall live that story, to be grass upon the hills.

2   It is the story of all life that is holy and is good to tell, and of us two-leggeds sharing in it with the four-leggeds and the wings of the air and all green things; for these are children of one mother and their father is one Spirit.

3   This, then, is not the tale of a great hunter or of a great warrior, or of a great traveler, although I have made much meat in my time and fought for my people both as boy and man, and have gone far and seen strange lands and men. So also have

many others done, and better than I. These things I shall remember by the way, and often they may seem to be the very tale itself, as when I was living them in happiness and sorrow. But now that I can see it all as from a lonely hilltop, I know it was the story of a mighty vision given to a man too weak to use it; of a holy tree that should have flourished in a people's heart with flowers and singing birds, and now is withered; and of a people's dream that died in bloody snow.

4   But if the vision was true and mighty, as I know, it is true and mighty yet; for such things are of the spirit, and it is in the darkness of their eyes that men get lost.

5   So I know that it is a good thing I am going to do; and because no good thing can be done by any man alone, I will first make an offering and send a voice to the Spirit of the World, that it may help me to be true. See, I fill this sacred pipe with the bark of the red willow; but before we smoke it, you must see how it is made and what it means. These four ribbons hanging here on the stem are the four quarters of the universe. The black one is for the west where the thunder beings live to send us rain; the white one for the north, whence comes the great white cleansing wind; the red one for the east, whence springs the light and where the morning star lives to give men wisdom; the yellow for the south, whence come the summer and the power to grow.

6   But these four spirits are only one Spirit after all, and this eagle feather here is for that One, which is like a father, and also it is for the thoughts of men that should rise high as eagles do. Is not the sky a father and earth a mother, and are not all living things with feet or wings or roots their children? And this hide upon the mouthpiece here, which should be bison hide, is for the earth, from whence we came and at whose breast we suck as babies all our lives, along with all the animals and birds and trees and grasses. And because it means all this, and more than any man can understand, the pipe is holy.

7   There is a story about the way the pipe first came to us. A very long time ago, they say, two scouts were out looking for bison; and when they came to the top of a high hill and looked north, they saw something coming a long way off, and when it came closer they cried out, "It is a woman!," and it was. Then one of the scouts, being foolish, had bad thoughts and spoke them; but the other said: "That is a sacred woman; throw all bad thoughts away." When she came still closer, they saw that she wore a fine white buckskin dress, that her hair was very long and that she was young and very beautiful. And she knew their thoughts and said in a voice that was like singing: "You

do not know me, but if you want to do as you think, you may come." And the foolish one went; but just as he stood before her, there was a white cloud that came and covered them. And the beautiful young woman came out of the cloud, and when it blew away the foolish man was a skeleton covered with worms.

8   Then the woman spoke to the one who was not foolish: "You shall go home and tell your people that I am coming and that a big tepee shall be built for me in the center of the nation." And the man, who was very much afraid, went quickly and told the people, who did at once as they were told; and there around the big tepee they waited for the sacred woman. And after a while she came, very beautiful and singing, and as she went into the tepee this is what she sang:

> *With visible breath I am walking*
> *A voice I am sending as I walk.*
> *In a sacred manner I am walking.*
> *With visible tracks I am walking.*
> *In a sacred manner I walk.*

And as she sang, there came from her mouth a white cloud that was good to smell. Then she gave something to the chief, and it was a pipe with a bison calf carved on one side to mean the earth that bears and feeds us, and with twelve eagle feathers hanging from the stem to mean the sky and the twelve moons, and these were tied with a grass that never breaks. "Behold!" she said. "With this you shall multiply and be a good nation. Nothing but good shall come from it. Only the hands of the good shall take care of it and the bad shall not even see it." Then she sang again and went out of the tepee; and as the people watched her going, suddenly it was a white bison galloping away and snorting, and soon it was gone.

9   This they tell, and whether it happened so or not I do not know; but if you think about it, you can see that it is true.

10   Now I light the pipe, and after I have offered it to the powers that are one Power, and sent forth a voice to them, we shall smoke together. Offering the mouthpiece first of all to the One above—so—I send a voice:

11   Hey hey! hey hey! hey hey! hey hey!

12   Grandfather, Great Spirit, you have been always, and before you no one has been. There is no other one to pray to but you. You yourself, everything that you see, everything has been made by you. The star nations all over the universe you have finished. The four quarters of the earth you have finished. The day, and in that day, everything you have finished. Grandfather, Great

Spirit, lean close to the earth that you may hear the voice I send. You towards where the sun goes down, behold me; Thunder Beings, behold me! You where the White Giant lives in power, behold me! You where the sun shines continually, whence come the day-break star and the day, behold me! You where the summer lives, behold me! You in the depth of the heavens, an eagle of power, behold! And you, Mother Earth, the only Mother, you who have shown mercy to your children!

13   Hear me, four quarters of the world—a relative I am! Give me the strength to walk the soft earth, a relative to all that is! Give me the eyes to see and the strength to understand, that I may be like you. With your power only can I face the winds.

14   Great Spirit, Great Spirit, my Grandfather, all over the earth the faces of living things are all alike. With tenderness have these come up out of the ground. Look upon these faces of children without number and with children in their arms, that they may face the winds and walk the good road to the day of quiet.

15   This is my prayer; hear me! The voice I have sent is weak, yet with earnestness I have sent it. Hear me!

16   It is finished. *Hetchetu aloh!*

17   Now, my friend, let us smoke together so that there may be only good between us.

Post-reading Questions

Content

1. In this essay, what is the purpose of smoking the sacred pipe?
2. What is the significance of the four ribbons on Black Elk's pipe?
3. Who is the young woman in the white buckskin dress? Why does she come to Black Elk's people?
4. To whom does Black Elk pray and why? What other spirits does he mention and why?

Strategies and Structures

1. In paragraph 7, why does Black Elk digress from his main narrative? What purpose does the story of the Buffalo Woman serve?
2. How does Black Elk explain the origins of the sacred pipe?
3. Why does Black Elk begin and conclude this narrative with the same ceremony? What effect does this have on the reader?

Language and Vocabulary

1. Vocabulary: *withered, cleansing, bison, skeleton, tepee, earnestness.* Check your dictionary for the meanings of these words and write two or three paragraphs in which you first make up and then narrate an event in the life of a Native American using each of the following words from the list above—*withered, bison,* and *tepee*—at least twice.
2. What context clues suggest the meaning of *hetchetu aloh?*

Group Activities

1. In groups of four, pair off and take turns interviewing each other. Then write a brief profile of each member in your group.
2. Compare your freewritings on ceremonies and sacred offerings with others in your group. What did your freewritings have in common? How did they differ? Overall, how does your group assess the importance of ritual in modern life in America?

Writing Activities

1. Write a story explaining your origins. Who were your ancestors? What significant events can you recall during different stages of growing up?
2. Write a narrative essay wherein you start with some sort of ceremony, digress, and then conclude with the initial ceremony.

Alice Walker

Journey to Nine Miles

In 1944, Alice Walker was born in Eatonton, Georgia—the eighth child of African-American sharecroppers. Her works include The Third Life of Grange Copeland *(1970),* Revolutionary Petunias *(1973),* Meridian *(1976),* You Can't Keep a Good Woman Down *(1981),* The Color Purple, *for which she won the Pulitzer Prize for fiction (1983),* Temple of My Familiar *(1989),* Her Blue Body Everything We Know: Earthling Poems, 1965–1990 *(1991),* Possessing the Secret of Joy *(1992),* The Same River Twice: Honoring the Difficult *(1996),* Anything We Love Can Be Saved *(1997),* Sent by Earth *(2001), and* The Way Forward is With a Broken Heart *(2001). In addition to her own work, Walker writes and lectures on African-American authors like Zora Neal Hurston, Jean Toomer, and Langston Hughes—individuals who provided some of the models and inspiration for her own writing. Walker, who has always considered herself a "womanist," became a spokesperson for problems in African-American families (especially those dealing with gender inequities), began one of the first women's studies courses in the United States, and served as an editor for* Ms. *magazine. In the following essay, excerpted from her second collection of essays,* Living by the Word *(1989), Walker relates a journey to the gravesite of reggae legend Bob Marley, a journey of cultural and spiritual significance.*

Pre-reading Questions

1. In your culture, is there a tradition of visiting the gravesites of ancestors or respected persons? Why do you go? What purpose(s) does it serve?
2. What sorts of preparations do you make for such visitations?

---

1   By five o'clock we were awake, listening to the soothing slapping of the surf and watching the sky redden over the ocean. By six we were dressed and knocking on my daughter's door. She and her friend Kevin were going with us (Robert and me) to visit Nine Miles, the birthplace of someone we all loved, Bob Marley. It was Christmas Day, bright, sunny, and very warm, and the traditional day of thanksgiving for the birth of someone sacred.

2   I missed Bob Marley when his body was alive, and I have often wondered how that could possibly be. It happened, though, because when he was singing all over the world, I was living in Mississippi being political, digging into my own his/her story, writing books, having a baby—and listening to local music, B. B. King, and the Beatles. I liked dreadlocks, but only because I am an Aquarian; I was unwilling to look beyond the sexism of Rastafarianism. The music stayed outside my consciousness. It didn't help either that the most political and spiritual of reggae music was suppressed in the United States, so that "Stir It Up" and not "Natty Dread" or "Lively Up Yourself" or "Exodus" was what one heard. And then, of course, there *was* disco, a music so blatantly soulless as to be frightening, and impossible to do anything to but exercise.

3   I first really *heard* Bob Marley when I was writing a draft of the screenplay for *The Color Purple*. Each Monday I drove up to my studio in the country, a taxing three-hour drive, worked steadily until Friday, drove back to the city, and tried to be two parents to my daughter on weekends. We kept in touch by phone during the week, and I had the impression that she was late for school every day and living on chocolates.

4   My friends Jan and Chris, a white couple nearby, seeing my stress, offered their help, which I accepted in the form of dinner at their house every night after a day's work on the script. One night, after yet another sumptuous meal, we pushed back the table and, in our frustration at the pain that rides on the seat next to joy in life (cancer, pollution, invasions, the bomb, etc.), began dancing to reggae records: UB-40, Black Uhuru . . . Bob Marley. I was transfixed. It was hard to believe the beauty of the soul I heard in "No Woman No Cry," "Coming In from the Cold," "Could You Be Loved," "Three Little Birds," and "Redemption Song." Here was a man who loved his roots (even after he'd been nearly assassinated in his own country) and knew they extended to the ends of the earth. Here was a soul who loved Jamaica and loved Jamaicans and loved *being* a Jamaican (nobody got more pleasure out of the history, myths, traditions, and language of Jamaica than Bob Marley), but who knew it was not meant to limit itself (or even could) to an island of any sort. Here

was the radical peasant-class, working-class consciousness that fearlessly denounced the *wasichu* (the greedy and destructive) and did it with such grace you could dance to it. Here was a man of extraordinary sensitivity, political acumen, spiritual power, and sexual wildness; a free spirit if ever there was one. Here, I felt, was my brother. It was as if there had been a great and gorgeous light on all over the world, and somehow I'd missed it. Every night for the next two months I listened to Bob Marley. I danced with his spirit—so much more alive still than many people walking around. I felt my own dreadlocks begin to grow.

5   Over time, the draft of the script I was writing was finished. My evenings with my friends came to an end. My love of Marley spread easily over my family, and it was as neophyte Rastas (having decided that *Rasta* for us meant a commitment to a religion of attentiveness and joy) that we appeared when we visited Jamaica in 1984.

6   What we saw was a ravaged land, a place where people, often Rastas, eat out of garbage cans and where, one afternoon in a beach cafe during a rainstorm, I overheard a 13-year-old boy offer his 11-year-old sister (whose grown-up earrings looked larger, almost, than her face) to a large hirsute American white man (who blushingly declined) along with some Jamaican pot.

7   The car we rented (from a harried, hostile dealer who didn't even seem to want to tell us where to buy gas) had already had two flats. On the way to Nine Miles it had three more. Eventually, however, after an agonizing seven hours from Negril, where we were staying, blessing the car at every bump in the road to encourage it to live through the trip, we arrived.

8   Nine Miles (because it is nine miles from the nearest village of any size) is one of the most still and isolated spots on the face of the earth. It is only several houses, spread out around the top of a hill. There are small, poor farms, with bananas appearing to be the predominant crop.

9   Several men and many children come down the hill to meet our car. They know we've come to visit Bob. They walk with us up the hill where Bob Marley's body is entombed in a small mausoleum with stained-glass windows: the nicest building in Nine Miles. Next to it is a small one-room house where Bob and his wife, Rita, lived briefly during their marriage. I think of how much energy Bob Marley had to generate to project himself into the world beyond this materially impoverished place; and of how exhausted, in so many of his later photographs, he looked. On the other hand, it is easy to understand—listening to the deep stillness that makes a jet soaring overhead sound like the

buzzing of a fly—why he wanted to be brought back to his home village, back to Nine Miles, to rest. We see the tomb from a distance of about 50 feet, because we cannot pass through (or climb over) an immense chain link fence that has recently been erected to keep the too eager (and apparently destructive and kleptomaniacal) tourists at bay. One thing that I like very much: built into the hill facing Bob's tomb is a permanent stage. On his birthday, February 6, someone tells us, people from all over the world come to Nine Miles to sing to him.

10 The villagers around us are obviously sorry about the fence. (Perhaps we were not the ones intended to be kept out?) Their faces seem to say as much. They are all men and boys. No women or girls among them. On a front porch below the hill I see some women and girls, studiously avoiding us.

11 One young man, the caretaker, tells us that though we can't come in, there is a way we can get closer to Bob. (I almost tell him I could hardly be any closer to Bob and still be alive, but I don't want to try to explain.) He points out a path that climbs the side of the hill and we—assisted by half a dozen of the more agile villagers—take it. It passes through bananas and weeds, flowers, past goats tethered out of the sun, past chickens. Past the home, one says, of Bob Marley's cousin, a broken but gallant-looking man in his 50s, nearly toothless, with a gentle and generous smile. He sits in his tiny, nearly bare house and watches us, his face radiant with the pride of relationship.

12 From within the compound now we hear singing. Bob's songs come from the lips of the caretaker, who says he and Bob were friends. That he loved Bob. Loved his music. He sings terribly. But perhaps this is only because he is, though about the age Bob would have been now, early 40s, lacking his front teeth. He is very dark and quite handsome, teeth or no. And it is his humble, terrible singing—as he moves proprietarily about the yard where his friend is enshrined—that makes him so. It is as if he sings Bob's songs *for* Bob, in an attempt to animate the tomb. The little children are all about us, nearly underfoot. Beautiful children. One little boy is right beside me. He is about six, of browner skin than the rest—who are nearer to black—with curlier hair. He looks like Bob.

13 I ask his name. He tells me. I have since forgotten it. As we linger by the fence, our fingers touch. For a while we hold hands. I notice that over the door to the tomb someone has plastered a bumper sticker with the name of Rita Marley's latest album. It reads: "Good Girl's Culture." I am offended by it; there are so many possible meanings. For a moment I try to imagine the sticker plastered across Bob's forehead. It drops off immediately,

washed away by his sweat (as he sings and dances in the shamanistic trance I so love) and his spirit's inability to be possessed by anyone other than itself (and Jah). The caretaker says Rita erected the fence. I understand the necessity.

14   Soon it is time to go. We clamber back down the hill to the car. On the way down the little boy who looks like Bob asks for money. Thinking of our hands together and how he is so like Bob must have been at his age, I don't want to give him money. But what else can I give him, I wonder.

15   I consult "the elders," the little band of adults who've gathered about us.

16   "The children are asking for money," I say. "What should we do?"

17   "You should give it," is the prompt reply. So swift and unstudied is the answer, in fact, that suddenly the question seems absurd.

18   "They ask because they have none. There is nothing here."

19   "Would Bob approve?" I ask. Then I think, "Probably. The man has had himself planted here to feed the village."

20   "Yes," is the reply. "Because he would understand."

21   Starting with the children, but by no means stopping there (because the grown-ups look as expectant as they), we part with some of our "tourist" dollars, realizing that tourism is a dead thing, a thing of the past; that no one can be a tourist anymore, and that, like Bob, all of us can find our deepest rest and most meaningful service at home.

22   It is a long hot anxious drive that we have ahead of us. We make our usual supplications to our little tin car and its four shiny tires. But even when we have another flat, bringing us to our fourth for the trip, it hardly touches us. Jamaica is a poor country reduced to selling its living and its dead while much of the world thinks of it as "real estate" and a great place to lie in the sun; but Jamaicans as a people have been seen in all their imperfections and beauty by one of their own, and fiercely sung, even from the grave, and loved. There is no poverty, only richness in this. We sing "Redemption Song" as we change the tire; feeling very Jamaica, very Bob, very Rasta, very *no woman no cry.*

Post-reading Questions

Content

1. Why did Walker "miss" Marley's music at first? What event put her in touch with it?

2. Where does her appreciation of Marley lead her and her family? What does she find at the end of her journey?

3. What does Walker learn about the Jamaican people and "Rasta" culture?

4. Walker claims that "Jamaica is a poor country reduced to selling its living and its dead. . . ." Is this much different than America or any other country? How? Why? Explain.

Strategies and Structures

1. Walker uses a "journey motif" to structure her essay. Why does she choose to use this motif? What does this symbolize?

2. What sorts of linking devices does Walker use? How do they allow the reader to follow her on the journey to Marley's grave?

3. What images or descriptions create a definite mood in this essay?

4. How does the tone at the end of Walker's essay (when she is changing her tire for the *fourth* time) compare with the beginning? What might her return from her journey suggest?

Language and Vocabulary

1. Vocabulary: *Aquarian, acumen, sumptuous, neophyte, hirsute, kleptomaniacal, shamanistic, expectant.* Find the definitions of these words and be prepared to discuss how Walker uses them as she moves through her essay. Since you may not have encountered many of these words before reading this selection, choose three or four of them and write at least three sentences for each.

2. How is the title of this essay, "Journey to Nine Miles," significant?

Group Activities

1. Go to the library and find the lyrics to a Bob Marley song. How does he use words? (Pay particular attention to syntax.) Then, as a group, rewrite (paraphrase) his song lyrics using a complete paragraph

for each word group. What do his lyrics lose in translation?

2. As a group, visit a rest home for elderly people, and after your visit, write a collaborative narrative detailing your group's reaction to what you see. Did the visit depress you, or did you leave with a renewed outlook on life?

Writing Activities

1. Narrate a journey you took to fulfill some significant purpose. How did it begin? What obstacle(s) did you have to overcome before reaching your ultimate destination?

2. Write about a nonphysical journey—mental or spiritual—which has greatly changed your way of thinking. Consider what you were like prior to your journey as well as after it.

Louise Erdrich

American Horse

*Of Chippewa and German-American descent, Louise Erdrich is both
a poet and a novelist and frequently writes about the Native-
American experience. Erdrich's published works include collections of
poetry* Jacklight *(1984) and* Baptism of Desire *(1989), and several
novels:* Love Medicine *(1984),* The Beet Queen *(1986),* Tracks *(1988),*
The Bingo Palace *(1994),* The Blue Jay's Dance: A Birth Year *(1995),
a nonfiction work regarding small and large events all parents will
relate to, and* Tales of Burning Love *(1996). In 1992, Erdrich
published* The Crown of Columbus, *a novel she coauthored with her
husband, the late Michael Dorris. Her most recent works are:* The
Antelope Wife *(1998),* The Birchbark House *(1999), and* The Last
Report on the Miracles at Little No Horse *(2001). The following
narrative from* The Bingo Palace *presents a parent / child
relationship at odds with a social service agency.*

Pre-reading Questions

1. How many times have you—or someone you know—done
   something because another person said, "It's for your own
   good"? Describe one of these situations in your journal.
2. What welfare or social agency are you aware of through
   personal experience, observations, or readings?

---

1   The woman sleeping on the cot in the woodshed was Albertine
American Horse. The name was left over from her mother's
short marriage. The boy was the son of the man she had loved
and let go. Buddy was on the cot too, sitting on the edge because he'd been awake three hours watching out for his mother

and besides, she took up the whole cot. Her feet hung over the edge, limp and brown as two trout. Her long arms reached out and slapped at things she saw in her dreams.

2   Buddy had been knocked awake out of hiding in a washing machine while herds of policemen with dogs searched through a large building with many tiny rooms. When the arm came down, Buddy screamed because it had a blue cuff and sharp silver buttons. "Tss," his mother mumbled, half awake, "wasn't nothing." But Buddy sat up after her breathing went deep again, and he watched.

3   There was something coming and he knew it.

4   It was coming from very far off but he had a picture of it in his mind. It was a large thing made of metal with many barbed hooks, points, and drag chains on it, something like a giant potato peeler that rolled out of the sky, scraping clouds down with it and jabbing or crushing everything that lay in its path on the ground.

5   Buddy watched his mother. If he woke her up, she would know what to do about the thing, but he thought he'd wait until he saw it for sure before he shook her. She was pretty, sleeping, and he liked knowing he could look at her as long and close up as he wanted. He took a strand of her hair and held it in his hands as if it was the rein to a delicate beast. She was strong enough and could pull him along like the horse their name was.

6   Buddy had his mother's and his grandmother's name because his father had been a big mistake.

7   "They're all mistakes, even your father. But *you* are the best thing that ever happened to me."

8   That was what she said when he asked.

9   Even Kadie, the boyfriend crippled from being in a car wreck, was not as good a thing that had happened to his mother as Buddy was. "He was a medium-sized mistake," she said. "He's hurt and I shouldn't even say that, but it's the truth." At the moment, Buddy knew that being the best thing in his mother's life, he was also the reason they were hiding from the cops.

10   He wanted to touch the satin roses sewed on her pink tee shirt, but he knew he shouldn't do that even in her sleep. If she woke up and found him touching the roses, she would say, "Quit that, Buddy." Sometimes she told him to stop hugging her like a gorilla. She never said that in the mean voice she used when he oppressed her, but when she said that he loosened up anyway.

11   There were times he felt like hugging her so hard and in such a special way that she would say to him, "Let's get married." There were also times he closed his eyes and wished that

she would die, only a few times, but still it haunted him that his wish might come true. He and Uncle Lawrence would be left alone. Buddy wasn't worried, though, about his mother getting married to somebody else. She had said to her friend, Madonna, "All men suck," when she thought Buddy wasn't listening. He had made an uncertain sound, and when they heard him they took him in their arms.

12 "Except for you, Buddy," his mother said. "All except for you and maybe Uncle Lawrence, although he's pushing it."

13 "The cops suck the worst, though," Buddy whispered to his mother's sleeping face, "because they're after us." He felt tired again, slumped down, and put his legs beneath the blanket. He closed his eyes and got the feeling that the cot was lifting up beneath him, that it was arching its canvas back and then traveling, traveling very fast and in the wrong direction for when he looked up he saw the three of them were advancing to meet the great metal thing with hooks and barbs and all sorts of sharp equipment to catch their bodies and draw their blood. He heard its insides as it rushed toward them, purring softly like a powerful motor and then they were right in its shadow. He pulled the reins as hard as he could and the beast reared, lifting him. His mother clapped her hand across his mouth.

14 "Okay," she said. "Lay low. They're outside and they're gonna hunt."

15 She touched his shoulder and Buddy leaned over with her to look through a crack in the boards.

16 They were out there all right, Albertine saw them. Two officers and that social worker woman. Vicki Koob. There had been no whistle, no dream, no voice to warn her that they were coming. There was only the crunching sound of cinders in the yard, the engine purring, the dust sifting off their car in a fine light brownish cloud and settling around them.

17 The three people came to a halt in their husk of metal—the car emblazoned with the North Dakota State Highway Patrol emblem which is the glowing profile of the Sioux policeman, Red Tomahawk, the one who killed Sitting Bill. Albertine gave Buddy the blanket and told him that he might have to wrap it around him and hide underneath the cot.

18 "We're gonna wait and see what they do." She took him in her lap and hunched her arms around him. "Don't you worry," she whispered against his ear. "Lawrence knows how to fool them."

19 Buddy didn't want to look at the car and the people. He felt his mother's heart beating beneath his ear so fast it seemed to push the satin roses in and out. He put his face to them carefully and

breathed the deep, soft powdery woman smell of her. That smell was also in her little face cream bottles, in her brushes, and around the washbowl after she used it. The satin felt so unbearably smooth against his cheek that he had to press closer. She didn't push him away, like he expected, but hugged him still tighter until he felt as close as he had ever been to back inside her again where she said he came from. Within the smells of her things, her soft skin, and the satin of her roses, he closed his eyes then, and took his breaths softly and quickly with her heart.

20   They were out there, but they didn't dare get out of the car yet because of Lawrence's big, ragged dogs. Three of these dogs had loped up the dirt driveway with the car. They were rangy, alert, and bounced up and down on their cushioned paws like wolves. They didn't waste their energy barking, but positioned themselves quietly, one at either car door and the third in front of the bellied-out screen door to Uncle Lawrence's house. It was six in the morning but the wind was up already, blowing dust, ruffling their short moth-eaten coats. The big brown one on Vicki Koob's side had unusual black and white markings, stripes almost, like a hyena and he grinned at her, tongue out and teeth showing.

21   "Shoo!" Miss Koob opened her door with a quick jerk.

22   The brown dog sidestepped the door and jumped before her, tiptoeing. Its dirty white muzzle curled and its eyes crossed suddenly as if it was zeroing its cross-hair sights in on the exact place it would bite her. She ducked back and slammed the door.

23   "It's mean," she told Officer Brackett. He was printing out some type of form. The other officer, Harmony, a slow man, had not yet reacted to the car's halt. He had been sitting quietly in the back seat, but now he rolled down his window and with no change in expression unsnapped his holster and drew his pistol out and pointed it at the dog on his side. The dog smacked down on its belly, wiggled under the car and was out and around the back of the house before Harmony drew his gun back. The other dogs vanished with him. From wherever they had disappeared to they began to yap and howl, and the door to the low shoebox-style house fell open.

24   "Heya, what's going on?"

25   Uncle Lawrence put his head out the door and opened wide the one eye he had in working order. The eye bulged impossibly wider in outrage when he saw the police car. But the eyes of the two officers and Miss Vicki Koob were wide open too because they had never seen Uncle Lawrence in his sleeping getup or, indeed, witnessed anything like it. For his ribs, which were cracked from a bad fall and still mending, Uncle Lawrence wore

a thick white corset laced up the front with a striped sneakers' lace. His glass eye and his set of dentures were still out for the night so his face puckered here and there, around its absences and scars, like a damaged but fierce little cake. Although he had a few gray streaks now, Uncle Lawrence's hair was still thick, and because he wore a special contraption of elastic straps around his head every night, two oiled waves always crested on either side of his middle part. All of this would have been sufficient to astonish, even without the most striking part of his outfit—the smoking jacket. It was made of black satin and hung open around his corset, dragging a tasseled belt. Gold thread dragons struggled up the lapels and blasted their furry red breath around his neck. As Lawrence walked down the steps, he put his arms up in surrender and the gold tassels in the inner seams of his sleeves dropped into view.

26   "My heavens, what a sight." Vicki Koob was impressed.

27   "A character," apologized Officer Harmony.

28   As a tribal police officer who could be counted on to help out the State Patrol, Harmony thought he always had to explain about Indians or get twice as tough to show he did not favor them. He was slow-moving and shy but two jumps ahead of other people all the same, and now, as he watched Uncle Lawrence's splendid approach, he gazed speculatively at the torn and bulging pocket of the smoking jacket. Harmony had been inside Uncle Lawrence's house before and knew that above his draped orange-crate shelf of war medals a blue-black German luger was hung carefully in a net of flat-headed nails and fishing line. Thinking of this deadly exhibition, he got out of the car and shambled toward Lawrence with a dreamy little smile of welcome on his face. But when he searched Lawrence, he found that the bulging pocket held only the lonesome-looking dentures from Lawrence's empty jaw. They were still dripping denture polish.

29   "I had been cleaning them when you arrived," Uncle Lawrence explained with acid dignity.

30   He took the toothbrush from his other pocket and aimed it like a rifle.

31   "Quit that, you old idiot." Harmony tossed the toothbrush away. "For once you ain't done nothing. We came for your nephew."

32   Lawrence looked at Harmony with a faint air of puzzlement.

33   "Ma Frere, listen," threatened Harmony amiably, "those two white people in the car came to get him for the welfare. They got papers on your nephew that give them the right to take him."

34   "Papers?" Uncle Lawrence puffed out his deeply pitted cheeks. "Let me see them papers."

35   The two of them walked over to Vicki's side of the car and she pulled a copy of the court order from her purse. Lawrence put his teeth back in and adjusted them with busy workings of his jaw.

36   "Just a minute," he reached into his breast pocket as he bent close to Miss Vicki Koob. "I can't read these without I have in my eye."

37   He took the eye from his breast pocket delicately, and as he popped it into his face the social worker's mouth fell open in a consternated O.

38   "What is this?" she cried in a little voice.

39   Uncle Lawrence looked at her mildly. The white glass of the eye was cold as lard. The black iris was strangely charged and menacing.

40   "He's nuts," Bracket huffed along the side of Vicki's neck. "Never mind him."

41   Vicki's hair had sweated down her nape in tiny corkscrews and some of the hairs were so long and dangly now that they disappeared into the zippered back of her dress. Brackett noticed this as he spoke into her ear. His face grew red and the backs of his hands prickled. He slid under the steering wheel and got out of the car. He walked around the hood to stand with Leo Harmony.

42   "We could take you in too," said Brackett roughly. Lawrence eyed the officers in what was taken as defiance. "If you don't cooperate, we'll get out the handcuffs," they warned.

43   One of Lawrence's arms was stiff and would not move until he'd rubbed it with witch hazel in the morning. His other arm worked fine though, and he stuck it out in front of Brackett.

44   "Get them handcuffs," he urged them. "Put me in a welfare home."

45   Brackett snapped one side of the handcuffs on Lawrence's good arm and the other to the handle of the police car.

46   "That's to hold you," he said. "We're wasting our time. Harmony, you search that little shed over by the tall grass and Miss Koob and myself will search the house."

47   "My rights is violated!" Lawrence shrieked suddenly. They ignored him. He tugged at the handcuff and thought of the good heavy file he kept in his tool box and the German luger oiled and ready but never loaded, because of Buddy, over his shelf. He should have used it on these bad ones, even Harmony in his big-time white man job. He wouldn't last long in that job anyway before somebody gave him what for.

48   "It's a damn scheme," said Uncle Lawrence, rattling his chains against the car. He looked over at the shed and thought maybe Albertine and Buddy had sneaked away before the car pulled into the yard. But he sagged, seeing Albertine move like a shadow within the boards. "Oh, it's all a damn scheme," he muttered again.

49   "I want to find that boy and salvage him," Vicki Koob explained to Officer Brackett as they walked into the house. "Look at his family life—the old man crazy as a bedbug, the mother intoxicated somewhere."

50   Brackett nodded, energetic, eager. He was a short hopeful redhead who failed consistently to win the hearts of women. Vicki Koob intrigued him. Now, as he watched, she pulled a tiny pen out of an ornamental clip on her blouse. It was attached to a retractable line that would suck the pen back, like a child eating one strand of spaghetti. Something about the pen on its line excited Brackett to the point of discomfort. His hand shook as he opened the screen door and stepped in, beckoning Miss Koob to follow.

51   They could see the house was empty at first glance. It was only one rectangular room with whitewashed walls and a little gas stove in the middle. They had already come through the cooking lean-to with the other stove and washstand and rusty old refrigerator. That refrigerator had nothing in it but some wrinkled potatoes and a package of turkey necks, Vicki Koob noted in her perfect-bound notebook. The beds along the walls of the big room were covered with quilts that Albertine's mother, Sophie, had made from bits of old wool coats and pants that the Sisters sold in bundles at the mission. There was no one hiding beneath the beds. No one was under the little aluminum dinette table covered with a green oil-cloth, or the soft brown wood chairs tucked up to it. One wall of the big room was filled with neatly stacked crates of things—old tools and springs and small half-dismantled appliances. Five or six television sets were stacked against the wall. Their control panels spewed colored wires and at least one was cracked all the way across. Only the topmost set, with coathanger antenna angled sensitively to catch the bounding signals around Little Shell, looked like it could possibly work.

52   Not one thing escaped Vicki Koob's trained and cataloguing gaze. She made note of the cupboard that held only commodity flour and coffee. The unsanitary tin oil drum beneath the kitchen window, full of empty surplus pork cans and beer bottles, caught her eye as did Uncle Lawrence's physical and

mental deteriorations. She quickly described these "benchmarks of alcoholic dependency within the extended family of Woodrow (Buddy) American Horse" as she walked around the room with the little notebook open, pushed against her belly to steady it. Although Vicki had been there before, Albertine's presence had always made it difficult for her to take notes.

53   "Twice the maximum allowable space between door and threshold," she wrote now. "Probably no insulation. Two three-inch cracks in walls inadequately sealed with white-washed mud." She made a mental note but could see no point in describing Lawrence's stuffed reclining chair that only reclined, the shadeless lamp with its plastic orchid in the bubble glass base, or the three-dimensional picture of Jesus that Lawrence had once demonstrated to her. When plugged in, lights rolled behind the water the Lord stood on so that he seemed to be strolling although he never actually went forward, of course, but only pushed the glowing waves behind him forever like a poor tame rat in a treadmill.

54   Brackett cleared his throat with a nervous rasp and touched Vicki's shoulder.

55   "What are you writing?"

56   She moved away and continued to scribble as if thoroughly absorbed in her work. "Officer Brackett displays an undue amount of interest in my person," she wrote. "Perhaps?"

57   He snatched playfully at the book, but she hugged it to her chest and moved off smiling. More curls had fallen, wetted to the base of her neck. Looking out the window, she sighed long and loud.

58   "All night on brush rollers for this. What a joke."

59   Brackett shoved his hands in his pockets. His mouth opened slightly, then shut with a small throttled cluck.

60   When Albertine saw Harmony ambling across the yard with his big brown thumbs in his belt, his placid smile, and his tiny black eyes moving back and forth, she put Buddy under the cot. Harmony stopped at the shed and stood quietly. He spread his arms to show her he hadn't drawn his big police gun.

61   "Ma Cousin," he said in the Michif dialect that people used if they were relatives or sometimes if they needed gas or a couple of dollars, "why don't you come out here and stop this foolishness?"

62   "I ain't your cousin," Albertine said. Anger boiled up in her suddenly. "I ain't related to no pigs."

63   She bit her lip and watched him through the cracks, circling, a big tan punching dummy with his boots full of sand so he never stayed down once he fell. He was empty inside, all stale

air. But he knew how to get to her so much better than a white cop could. And now he was circling because he wasn't sure she didn't have a weapon, maybe a knife or the German luger that was the only thing that her father, Albert American Horse, had left his wife and daughter besides his name. Harmony knew that Albertine was a tall strong woman who took two big men to subdue when she didn't want to go in the drunk tank. She had hard hips, broad shoulders, and stood tall like her Sioux father, the American Horse who was killed threshing in Belle Prairie.

64　"I feel bad to have to do this," Harmony said to Albertine. "But for godsakes, let's nobody get hurt. Come on out with the boy, why don't you? I know you got him in there."

65　Albertine did not give herself away this time. She let him wonder. Slowly and quietly she pulled her belt through its loops and wrapped it around and around her hand until only the big oval buckle with turquoise chunks shaped into a butterfly stuck out over her knuckles. Harmony was talking but she wasn't listening to what he said. She was listening to the pitch of his voice, the tone of it that would tighten or tremble at a certain moment when he decided to rush the shed. He kept talking slowly and reasonably, flexing the dialect from time to time, even mentioning her father.

66　"He was a damn good man. I don't care what they say, Albertine, I knew him."

67　Albertine looked at the stone butterfly that spread its wings across her fist. The wings looked light and cool, not heavy. It almost looked like it was ready to fly. Harmony wanted to get to Albertine through her father but she would not think about American Horse. She concentrated on the sky blue stone.

68　Yet the shape of the stone, the color, betrayed her.

69　She saw her father suddenly, bending at the grille of their old gray car. She was small then. The memory came from so long ago it seemed like a dream—narrowly focused, snapshot-clear. He was bending by the grille in the sun. It was hot summer. Wings of sweat, dark blue, spread across the back of his work shirt. He always wore soft blue shirts, the color of shade cloudier than this stone. His stiff hair had grown out of its short haircut and flopped over his forehead. When he stood up and turned away from the car, Albertine saw that he had a butterfly.

70　"It's dead," he told her. "Broke its wings and died on the grille."

71　She must have been five, maybe six, wearing one of the boy's tee shirts Mama bleached in Hilex-water. American Horse took the butterfly, a black and yellow one, and rubbed it on Albertine's collarbone and chest and arms until the color and the powder of it were blended into her skin.

72   "For grace," he said.

73   And Albertine had felt a strange lightening in her arms, in her chest, when he did this and said, "For grace." The way he said it, grace meant everything the butterfly was. The sharp delicate wings. The way it floated over grass. The way its wings seemed to breathe fanning in the sun. The wisdom of the way it blended into flowers or changed into a leaf. In herself she felt the same kind of possibilities and closed her eyes almost in shock or pain, she felt so light and powerful at that moment.

74   Then her father had caught her and thrown her high into the air. She could not remember landing in his arms or landing at all. She only remembered the sun filling her eyes and the world tipping crazily behind her, out of sight.

75   "He was a damn good man," Harmony said again.

76   Albertine heard his starched uniform gathering before his boots hit the ground. Once, twice, three times. It took him four solid jumps to get right where she wanted him. She kicked the plank door open when he reached for the handle and the corner caught him on the jaw. He faltered, and Albertine hit him flat on the chin with the butterfly. She hit him so hard the shock of it went up her arm like a string pulled taut. Her fist opened, numb, and she let the belt unloop before she closed her hand on the tip end of it and sent the stone butterfly swooping out in a wide circle around her as if it was on the end of a leash. Harmony reeled backward as she walked toward him swinging the belt. She expected him to fall but he just stumbled. And then he took the gun from his hip.

77   Albertine let the belt go limp. She and Harmony stood within feet of each other, breathing. Each heard the human sound of air going in and out of the other person's lungs. Each read the face of the other as if deciphering letters carved into softly eroding veins of stone. Albertine saw the pattern of tiny arteries that age, drink, and hard living had blown to the surface of the man's face. She saw the spoked wheels of his iris and the arteries like tangled threads that sewed him up. She saw the living net of springs and tissue that held him together, and trapped him. She saw the random, intimate plan of his person.

78   She took a quick shallow breath and her face went strange and tight. She saw the black veins in the wings of the butterfly, roads burnt into a map, and then she was located somewhere in the net of veins and sinew that was the tragic complexity of the world so she did not see Officer Brackett and Vicki Koob

rushing toward her, but felt them instead like flies caught in the same web, rocking it.

79   "Albertine!" Vicki Koob had stopped in the grass. Her voice was shrill and tight. "It's better this way, Albertine. We're going to help you."

80   Albertine straightened, threw her shoulders back. Her father's hand was on her chest and shoulders lightening her wonderfully. Then on wings of her father's hands, on dead butterfly wings, Albertine lifted into the air and flew toward the others. The light powerful feeling swept her up the way she had floated higher, seeing the grass below. It was her father throwing her up into the air and out of danger. Her arms opened for bullets but no bullets came. Harmony did not shoot. Instead, he raised his fist and brought it down hard on her head.

81   Albertine did not fall immediately, but stood in his arms a moment. Perhaps she gazed still farther back behind the covering of his face. Perhaps she was completely stunned and did not think as she sagged and fell. Her face rolled forward and hair covered her features, so it was impossible for Harmony to see with just what particular expression she gazed into the head-splitting wheel of light, or blackness, that overcame her.

82   Harmony turned the vehicle onto the gravel road that led back to town. He had convinced the other two that Albertine was more trouble than she was worth, and so they left her behind, and Lawrence too. He stood swearing in his cinder driveway as the car rolled out of sight. Buddy sat between the social worker and Officer Brackett. Vicki tried to hold Buddy fast and keep her arm down at the same time, for the words she'd screamed at Albertine had broken the seal of antiperspirant beneath her arms. She was sweating now as though she'd stored an ocean up inside of her. Sweat rolled down her back in a shallow river and pooled at her waist and between her breasts. A thin sheen of water came out on her forearms, her face. Vicki gave an irritated moan but Brackett seemed not to take notice, or take offense at least. Air-conditioned breezes were sweeping over the seat anyway, and very soon they would be comfortable. She smiled at Brackett over Buddy's head. The man grinned back. Buddy stirred. Vicki remembered the emergency chocolate bar she kept in her purse, fished it out, and offered it to Buddy. He did not react, so she closed his fingers over the package and peeled the paper off one end.

83   The car accelerated. Buddy felt the road and wheels pummeling each other and the rush of the heavy motor purring in

high gear. Buddy knew that what he'd seen in his mind that morning, the thing coming out of the sky with barbs and chains, had hooked him. Somehow he was caught and held in the sour tin smell of the pale woman's armpit. Somehow he was pinned between their pounds of breathless flesh. He looked at the chocolate in his hand. He was squeezing the bar so hard that a thin brown trickle had melted down his arm. Automatically he put the bar in his mouth.

84   As he bit down he saw his mother very clearly, just as she had been when she carried him from the shed. She was stretched flat on the ground, on her stomach, and her arms were curled around her head as if in sleep. One leg was drawn up and it looked for all the world like she was running full tilt into the ground, as though she had been trying to pass into the earth, to bury herself, but at the last moment something had stopped her.

85   There was no blood on Albertine, but Buddy tasted blood now at the sight of her, for he bit down hard and cut his own lip. He ate the chocolate, every bit of it, tasting his mother's blood. And when he had the chocolate down inside him and all licked off his hands, he opened his mouth to say thank you to the woman, as his mother had taught him. But instead of a thank you coming out he was astonished to hear a great rattling scream, and then another, rip out of him like pieces of his own body and whirl onto the sharp things all around him.

Post-reading Questions

Content

1. What is the subject or theme of Erdrich's narrative? What is the plot? (See Glossary.)

2. Why did Harmony believe he had "to explain about Indians to others" or treat them tougher than anyone else?

3. Who was American Horse? Explain the significance of his role and the incident with the dead butterfly in the story. Why do you think that Erdrich titles her story "American Horse"?

4. What happened when *"American Horse took the butterfly, a black and yellow one, and rubbed it on Albertine's collarbone and chest and arms until the color and the powder of it were blended into her skin"?*

5. Why does Buddy start screaming at the end of the story? What does he realize?

Strategies and Structures

1. How might you divide Erdrich's narrative into four distinct parts? How does each division blend into the next?
2. Explain the function of transitions and linking words throughout this narrative story.
3. What strategy does Erdrich use to frame her narrative? Where does her tale begin, how does it conclude, and what—if anything—is resolved?
4. How does Erdrich use her characters' observations of each other as a means of developing individual personalities while advancing the plot?

Language and Vocabulary

1. Vocabulary: *loped, luger, dentures, deterioration, antiperspirant, grille, pummeling, emblazoned, retractable.* Locate the definition for each of the vocabulary words in your dictionary. Then write a descriptive narrative in the manner of Louise Erdrich using at least five of the words.
2. *The American Heritage Dictionary*'s definition of the verb *salvage* is "to save (discarded or damaged material) for further use." With this definition in mind, when Vicki Koob says, *"I want to find that boy and salvage him,"* who and what do you think she is really interested in *saving* or *salvaging?* What is her opinion of herself? Choose some lines from the story to support your position.

Group Activities

1. As a class, weigh the pros and cons of Buddy's staying with Albertine, his mother. Then, divide the class in half and debate the rights of a social agency versus the rights of a blood relative regarding the custody of a child.
2. After selecting groups, make plans to visit the child care center at your campus. Plan to take copious notes on what you observe at the center—notes worthy of Vicki Koob's *"trained and cataloguing gaze."* Finally, share your notes with each other at your next class session. What sort of observation was the most common among your peers? What

kind of details were most frequently cited? How did they differ?

Writing Activities

1. Write a narrative wherein you show how a significant incident in your past enables you to act well under pressure in the present.
2. Construct a narrative about a time in your life when you or someone you know hid from an authority figure.

Nguyen Ngoc Ngan

Saigon, April 1975

Now living in Toronto, Canada, Nguyen Ngoc Ngan, a refugee from South Vietnam, wrote The Will of Heaven, *which details his experiences from the fall of South Vietnam to his escape to the free world. The following piece was excerpted from the prologue to the book.*

Pre-reading Questions

1. What unavoidable conflict have you ever faced? Have you ever been powerless to do what you wanted or thought was best for others? How did you react?

2. What do you know about Saigon or Vietnam? Read the first two paragraphs and then, based upon your own knowledge of Vietnam and what you read, make a list in which you guess (speculate) what will happen next.

---

1   Early in the morning of April 29, 1975, I sat bolt upright in bed, awakened by the sudden explosions shaking predawn Saigon. I glanced with concern at my wife, Tuyet Lan, asleep beside me, and my one-year-old son, Tran, lying peacefully in his crib by the window. Then I raced to the roof.

2   Reddish glows pulsated in the darkness to the west, accompanied by the deep rumbling of artillery. The glows seemed to be coming from the general direction of Tan Son Nhut airport. I shuddered, for there I knew that thousands of Vietnamese had assembled for the American airlift. That throbbing brilliance seemed the final incinerating flash of an almost endless war. From it could come only the blackened cinder of my country's defeat.

3   I stared at the scene with an aching heart. Who would have thought that all our agonizing years of death and sacrifice

would finally be reduced to simply a reddish glow in the darkened western sky? I turned, and with leaden steps descended the stairs.

4   When I returned to the bedroom, my wife was sitting on the edge of our bed.

5   "Where have you been? When I woke up from the noise and found you gone, I was frightened." She stared up at me, her dark eyes large and fearful.

6   "I've just been up on the roof, checking. Those shells are falling miles away," I tried to reassure her. "You might as well try to get some more rest. It's only twenty past four."

7   "No, Ngan," she said, shaking her head. "Let's talk, be honest with me now, don't treat me like a child. I have to know! It's almost over, isn't it? They're not going to negotiate, are they? The Viet Cong are going to come right in with their tanks and soldiers. There'll be fighting in the streets." Then there was stark fear in her voice. "They'll do the same thing here that they did at Hue."

8   Tuyet Lan was referring to the Hue horror of Tet, 1968. She had had relatives among the more than two thousand civilians in the Northern city of Hue who were forced to dig shallow trenches, then were lined up in front of them and shot in cold blood. That grisly recollection now filled her with terror. She clung to me, her body trembling with sobs.

9   I brushed the tears from Tuyet Lan's eyes and tried to comfort her. She stared up at me, her gentle eyes full of fear.

10   "Isn't it possible," she finally asked tremulously, "that we could get on one of the flights out of Tan Son Nhut? I know there are many leaving who don't have proper credentials."

11   "There are no more flights out of Tan Son Nhut, Tuyet Lan," I said gently. "That's where they're shelling now."

12   Tuyet Lan paled. "But there must be boats," she persisted. "Yes, we must try to get on a boat down at the harbor. There'll be some American ships out there somewhere. They'll pick us up."

13   I was surprised to hear these words. Only two days before when I had asked her whether we should leave the country she had had entirely different views. But at that time there had been much talk about a negotiated peace and that General Duong Van ("Big") Minh, appointed president only the day before, was the one person who could achieve it. Then Tuyet Lan had said, "The war has kept you away from me so much, Ngan! Now that peace is coming, why not stay here and enjoy our life together for a change? Certainly, there's no better place to be than in our own homeland."

14   I recalled those words now as my wife stood before me, pale and tense.

15   "There'll be plenty of American ships out there, Ngan," she repeated, looking up at me imploringly.

16   I gathered her again in a gentle embrace. "We can try, Tuyet Lan," I said softly. "We can try."

17   So later that morning Tuyet Lan and I said good-bye to our parents and soon, with Tran, became part of the seething mass of humanity we found milling around the waterfront. It seemed hopeless. Thousands and thousands of people were there ahead of us, trying to get aboard the few boats. After waiting for two hours and still finding ourselves on only the periphery of the crowd, we edged our way out of the growing throng and set out again on the motor scooter for the American Embassy. We had heard that helicopter flights were beginning to leave from there.

18   As we approached the embassy, we saw its fortress-like walls surrounded by a boundless sea of people. Coming closer, we could see no evidence of any helicopters, and, upon inquiring, learned that the flights had not yet begun. Reluctantly I admitted to myself that it would require a miracle for the three of us ever to get past the huge, grim-faced Marines at the gates, and finally we headed back home.

19   As we passed now-deserted American installations, we saw Vietnamese leaving the buildings, bending under the heavy burdens of boxes of food and cases of beer and soft drinks. At long last, it seemed, American aid was finally reaching the people.

20   That night I lay sleepless, twisting the radio dial, trying to pick up the BBC or the Voice of America broadcasts. Lately I had begun to lose faith in the BBC because of their consistently premature announcements of the fall of cities to the north, which added to the general panic prevailing there. Now they were saying that the Viet Cong would occupy Saigon tomorrow. With the night alive with the stammering clatter of machine-gun fire and the crash of distant shells, the BBC pronouncement was very believable indeed.

21   The very next day, April 30, 1975, the North Vietnamese Army, with disarming cries of *hoa binh* ("peace"), swept triumphantly into Saigon. The world as I had known it for twenty-eight years ended abruptly.

22   I rose apprehensively at six-fifteen and opened the side window of the living room. It was still a bit dark, but I was able to discern some figures lying in our small yard near the cassia shrub. I called out, "Who's there?"

23   "Please excuse us for trespassing," came a woman's polite voice out of the semidarkness, "but the grass looked so inviting. We're from Hoc Mon. The Viet Cong are already there. In fact, they are here in Saigon. We have been running from the fighting but there's no place now to run."

24   A few minutes later I heard a heavy rumble that seemed to be getting closer to the house. I ran out into the street and looked up and down in the hazy morning light. In the distance I could see a tank approaching, loaded with ARVN (our Army of the Republic of Vietnam) soldiers.

25   From the other direction I could hear the ominous roar of several approaching tanks and blasts from other guns. Russian T-54's! There was going to be a battle right on our street, I thought, running back inside. The refugees were right. The Viet Cong were here and in strength. I roused Tuyet Lan and Tran and a few minutes later we were on my motor scooter, fleeing the scene of probable confrontation.

26   Frantically hopeful, we once again approached the Saigon harbor, which had become a scene of chaos. Cars, motorcycles, and people were hopelessly snarled as thousands fought to get aboard the few boats. Ahead of us at the waterfront we could see a boat pulling out, loaded almost to sinking. The crowd surged forward, fighting to be first on the next boat, and there was a wild melee to get aboard. This scene repeated itself several times until there were no more boats.

27   A few people had begun to drift sadly away when the shelling began. There was screaming. Everyone panicked and ran wildly for cover, blindly trampling the fallen. I clutched Tuyet Lan tightly by the hand and fled with Tran in my arms, looking helplessly for a building that would afford some protection. We passed the Saigon market and the sprawled bodies of some shelling victims. Finally I came upon a school building, and, thrusting Tuyet Lan ahead of me, went inside. It was packed. We all huddled fearfully there, waiting for the roof to crash down on us. At least it would take a direct hit to kill us; we were safe from random shell fragments.

28   It was in that building, over a tiny radio, that we heard our president of three days, General Duong Van Minh, offer his unconditional surrender and order a cease-fire. Some people heaved sighs of relief; others wept. A few sat staring silently into space. Someone near me commented that, earlier that morning, Minh had appealed to his army to put an end to all hostilities, and had implored "our brothers of the provisional government" to do likewise.

29   "They're our 'brothers' now," said my neighbor, smiling bitterly. "They're no longer the 'murdering Viet Cong.'"

30   Tuyet Lan and I sat in stunned silence as the building began to empty. It had all happened so quickly, but still, I was filled with self-recrimination for having been so indecisive during the last few days. I should have been firmer with Tuyet Lan, I thought. We could probably have gotten on one of those flights out of Tan Son Nhut. And instead of giving up so easily yesterday and going home, we should have tried the port at Nha Be. Boats most surely were leaving from there. I had just not planned properly; I had waited too long. Even though I had anticipated this inevitable moment for the past few days, some small part of me had hoped right up to the end that somehow the United States would ultimately come to our rescue. How could they do otherwise? Who would have thought that after all these years they would let this happen?

31   With a start I suddenly realized that everyone had left the building. Tuyet Lan and I were sitting there alone. We got up and headed for home through streets now filled with a palpable sorrow. We passed gruesomely mutilated shell victims sprawled on the streets. People hurried by them with averted eyes.

32   "How terrible it is to die like that at the last moment of the war," I said. "Just as peace comes."

33   Tuyet Lan made no answer. She held tightly to my hand as we hurried along the saddened street. A soft, warm rain was falling. Once Tuyet Lan stumbled slightly, and as I reached out to steady her, I saw that her eyes were blinded by tears.

34   Discarded weapons—M-16 rifles, Colt .45 automatics, grenades, bayonets, cartridge clips—were scattered where our soldiers had dropped them in their rush to acquire the anonymity of civilian attire. More than the words I had just heard on the radio, they brought home to me the full realization that now the war was completely lost.

35   When we arrived at home about three-thirty that afternoon, my father anxiously met us at the door. "You didn't make it!" he exclaimed sadly. "You didn't get away."

36   There were tears in his eyes, and despite his words, I could tell that he was glad to see us back. Now he would not be lonely. His shoulders sagged and his deeply lined face was haggard. In just the past few days he'd grown much older than his sixty years. I asked him about the tank battle that had seemed imminent when we had fled early that morning. He said he thought that a small flurry of fighting had taken

place a considerable distance down the street, but it had not amounted to much.

37 *"Troi oi* [Good heavens], Ngan!" he then said impatiently. "Everybody's burning things—you'd better get busy! Burn everything that might be incriminating. They'll be here soon with their questions, making their eternal lists."

38 I spent that evening collecting and burning anything that would connect me or my family with active support of the fallen regime. This may perhaps seem to be a less than courageous thing to do by some who have never had their own instincts for survival put to a severe test. But the vivid recollections of Hue in 1968, and entire families of military officers and civil servants being put to death, gave impetus to all our actions now.

39 First I burned all my uniforms. Then I searched through Tuyet Lan's photograph albums for pictures of me in uniform. What a flood of memories that brought forth. I stared in amused disbelief at the very first photograph I found. It was of me standing alone in front of the barracks at the Infantry Officer Training Academy in Thu Duc in 1970. How raw and youthful I looked in my ill-fitting uniform and short military-style haircut! And how naive I actually was, then, of the war and the political situation. Except for the Tet Offensive I had been virtually untouched by the war. There was another photograph of me with Tuyet Lan, snapped by one of my fellow cadets. I had to smile, seeing how skinny and solemn I looked. But how lovely and innocent was Tuyet Lan. I came to another that had been enlarged and put on display on the table in the living room. It showed me, looking very fierce and proud, receiving my officer's commission from the academy deputy commandant, a colonel who was later murdered by the Viet Cong when he answered his doorbell one evening in Thu Duc. I stared at these photographs of only a few years ago as though they belonged to another age, and then slowly dropped them into the flames.

Post-reading Questions

Content

1. What does the author describe in his narrative account? What unavoidable conflict is he forced to face? Why?
2. Why was the author angry with the BBC network? Explain why his anger was or was not justified, logical, and fair.

3. Why did the author say, *"The world as I had known it for twenty-eight years ended abruptly"*? What did he mean?

Strategies and Structures

1. How does the author's firsthand experience of the U.S. pullout of Vietnam strengthen this narrative?
2. What is the tone or mood in Nguyen's passage? What events foreshadow his impending sense of doom?
3. Go through the text and underline specific words and phrases you believe the author uses to state a general point in a powerful, memorable manner. Include derogatory terms that force a reaction like shock or indignation in a reader. How are such words effective in context?
4. What makes Nguyen's descriptions vivid and clear? What sort of details can you recall after reading this essay?

Language and Vocabulary

1. Vocabulary: *imminent, haggard, melee, palpable, incriminating, impetus, ominous, self-recrimination, triumphantly, disarming, provisional.* Most of these vocabulary words suggest power or powerlessness in one way or another. Which words indicate futility and which words describe the impending military takeover, the source of panic among the South Vietnamese?
2. Go back through the essay and locate instances where the author uses images that suggest sadness. Using the author's images and your own, write a paragraph about a time in your life that was particularly sad.

Group Activities

1. War is usually not what one thinks it will be like. During a war, people are given license to kill other human beings, ideally clear of conscience because of their noble cause. However, once a war ends, the same people are expected to act humanely toward each other. As a group activity, discuss the problems

that you would expect people to have when they are
ordered to make friends with their enemies. What is
the difference between being told to become friends
and having the right to choose your own friends?

2. How does your image of Vietnam, possibly influenced
by the news media and movies like *Apocalypse Now,
Platoon,* and *Good Morning, Vietnam,* differ from the
picture Nguyen draws of Americans pulling out of
Saigon and the Viet Cong moving into what would
become Ho Chi Minh City? It may be a good idea to
select a group leader for this exercise so that everyone has an opportunity to talk, question, and respond
to each other in the time allotted for this activity.

Writing Activities

1. Write an essay wherein you rationalize or reason
how the instinct to survive would allow you to do
things you usually would consider cowardly, dishon-
est, degrading, or immoral.

2. Has there ever been a time in your life when you
figuratively or literally destroyed symbols of your
past hopes or beliefs in order to pursue a realistic
future? Limit your focus, and write a narrative
about the event.

Alma Luz Villanueva

Leaps of Faith

Alma Luz Villanueva, a multi-talented author, has earned popular acclaim and numerous awards for her poetry, short stories, essays, and novels. Her poetry blends the personal and political, anchoring the abstract in the sensual world, revealing a belief in the power of language to connect us to the world, to each other, and to ourselves. Collections of her verse include Bloodroot *(1977),* La Chingada *(1985),* Life Span *(1985),* Planet *(1994),* LUNA'S California Poppies *(2000), and* The VIDA *(2000). In 1994, the Latin American Writers Institute singled out* Planet, *a collection of her poetry, for its depth, sensitivity, and wit. Villanueva's most recent poetry collection,* Desire, *made its debut in July 1998, and was nominated for the Pulitzer Prize. Villanueva's fictional works include* Weeping Woman: La Llorona and Other Stories *(1994), a collection of short stories;* The Ultraviolet Sky *(1988), a novel, which won an American Book Award and is listed in* 500 Great Books By Women *(Penguin); and* Naked Ladies, *another novel, for which she received a PEN Oakland Award for Fiction. In addition to writing, Ms. Villanueva does guest teaching and gives readings and presentations at colleges and universities and literary events.*

Pre-reading Questions

1. Brainstorm the word "faith," and then jot down your personal definition of it. How might "faith" be a source of power and creativity?

2. What do you associate with the phrase, "waking dream"? Describe a "waking dream" of your own or that of a friend or a relative.

1   Today, March 25, 1996, I'm back at the beach (a beautiful, clear day after high winds yesterday). The comet Hyakutake is passing overhead, only ten million miles away. They say the last time it passed this way was 18,400 years ago, during the time humans were crossing the then-glaciated Bering Strait into North America. Last night Jules (who's fifteen now) and I went outside to see it through the binoculars. As I stared at the comet, its wide splash of light tail, it seemed I could see it move. I imagine my (our) ancestors crossing the Bering Strait, the immense, most incredible leap of faith to push forward. I imagine they dreamt their destination. They *knew* this continent was here. I imagined myself, 18,400 years ago, standing on ice; ice behind me, ice in front of me. I shuddered. How amazing we are, we humans.

2   I handed the binoculars to Jules. We were silent. Later, his father, Wilfredo, would come home late from teaching his class. Jules and I moved to Santa Cruz, California, in the fall of 1984 to be with his father (my partner and husband). This took a comparatively tiny leap of faith, but here we are. We rediscovered each other, with new boundaries, new territory, with some familiar expectations we had to resist (possessiveness, male/female roles, old, but ingrained, patriarchal roles), or we'd lose the together, again. We still have to resist, of course, and create (dream) our paths separately, and trust they will continue meet and converge.

3   Today I sit on the sand, facing a cliff with eucalyptus trees growing on the edge of it. The largest one has roots extending all the way down the steep cliff: gnarled, twining, *exposed*. Its other roots extend into the ground behind it, *hidden*. This, I think, is the ongoing task of the writer, and as I look at this tree, I see it's not an awkward sight. Not at all. It affords me a view of its life. There's beauty and grace in that.

4   During the time I've lived here in Santa Cruz, I've written three novels, a short story collection, and two books of poetry. When I began my first novel, *The Ultraviolet Sky*, it was with blind panic and seizures of terror; another leap of faith. I'd told family and friends I was going to write a novel (I told myself I was going to write a novel), and so not to was to admit defeat. Failure. So, I wrote the first fifty pages blind (yet dreaming), my heart in my throat.

5   My main character, Rosa, was a painter, and I had plans for her (until page one hundred or so). One morning when I sat down to write I just couldn't. Not a thing. I had no link. To the novel, to the plot, to any of the characters, and especially not to Rosa. It was as though everything and everyone, in the novel's

world, had died; they refused to speak to me, much less appear. Though Rosa's character had sprung from me, my life, I could already see what she looked like, and she didn't look like me or walk like me or talk like me. She looked, walked, talked like *herself*. That morning I couldn't even glimpse Rosa. She was dead, everything was dead. And I was absolutely devastated, to my surprise; this had never happened to me before. All I could do was mourn, though I told no one at this point. I assumed this was the end of novels for me.

6   About two weeks later I was in the shower listlessly washing my hair, feeling pretty damned depressed, as though my usual sense of purpose and will were absent. I was just washing my hair. Suddenly, large as life (more vividly than I'd ever seen her), Rosa strode, and I mean *strode*, right into me. It was electrifying, orgasmic.

7   Quickly, I towel-dried, found the notebook I'd hidden from view, a pen, and sat to write. Anything. I got a fix on Rosa; or rather she had a fix on me. There she was, looking right at me. Sternly. She had some things to say about *her life*, and she set me straight. About the number of children she had—one; I'd given her two. How she felt about her lover, her work, her friends, the painting *she* envisioned and had to create, the world as she perceived it. On and on. I sat there and listened. To my character, Rosa.

8   And that's how the novel was written; that's how I was allowed to write the novel, by allowing Rosa, and all the other characters, to reveal themselves to me, bit by bit, in their own time, in their own voice. Yet the vision, the central theme, was mine, and that's what I had to stay true to while struggling with the truth of the characters. As I look back on it now (and forward to future novels), I see a kind of passion play of self and ego(s). Self (eternal, wise, knowing) and ego (temporary, innocent/guilty, learning).

9   I learned a lot. There was magic in the writing process for me, the usual terror and wonder. Many times I would dream an especially difficult sequence—an outline, a piece of dialogue, a character's presence—making it possible to continue with fluidity.

10   The next novel, *Naked Ladies*, wasn't quite as terrifying. The process was similar, but certainly not the same. Each novel, each short story, each poem takes that leap of faith— that I ask (from my deepest longing) and that I'll be answered (from an endless, mysterious source: creation).

11   When I teach I try to convey this process to my students. I attempt to teach writing (creation) as the waking dream, dreaming awake, transformation of energy into matter. Imagine: it's the faith of a woman who's just learned she's pregnant. She imagines the darkness of her womb, the size of her womb, so small. She imagines the tiniest creature, a seahorse-child, a spiral-shaped creature, nestled in her womb. Invaded. Penetrated. Chosen. Blessed. Cursed. Captured. She imagines her life, whether it's possible. To create (this child, this novel, this poem, this painting, this equation). She imagines its birth (form, words, color, song, the unknown face). And she leaps. She allows. She struggles. She dreams. Until it is complete. Unto itself.

12   And then she lets go. She will create again. She will love again. If her faith is intact. If she is willing to leap, again and again, into the unknown. The undiscovered The uncreated source.

13   As I sit here in the sweet spring sun, I think of my daughter, Antoinette, now thirty-five and a critical care registered nurse, with two children of her own: Ashley, fourteen—born in the same year as Jules, and Cody, eleven. My grandchildren are intelligent, beautiful, and very humorous. My son Ed, now thirty-three, is a professional bike racer and also attends college. Marc, who's twenty-nine, teaches high school biology (and is track coach) in Boulder, Colorado, and is also a writer. And Jules (fifteen) is a handsome, sensitive, boy-man who also has a gift for writing, and he's a bodyboarder and a surfer. All of them continue to complete themselves, unto themselves. They are their own creations.

14   As I sit here, dolphins surface to breathe revealing their fins, their black, shiny bodies. I read that dolphins arrived in the Monterey Bay about ten years ago, about the time I did. Last summer when I was swimming I saw a flash of darkness in the water; I nearly screamed as I registered SHARK. Then, a silky, smooth body brushed alongside my own: a dolphin. It was like being brushed by a jolt of joy. At fifty-one, I can truly say that my joy outweighs my sorrow, and I'm *grateful* to know this.

15   As I sit here a group of teenagers with a small boy are building a fort with washed-up driftwood. I wonder if the boy is their son or brother (people often thought Antoinette was my sister). I can see the boy is loved; the way they play with him, touch him, include him. And I think: Wherever there's love, there's innocence. There's a beautiful innocence about this group. I feast my eyes.

16   There's a juggler a few feet away. He's very good, juggling three, then four frisbees.

17　And then there's the world, beyond what I can see, but I can *feel* it: Bosnia, China, Africa, Tibet, Mexico, Nicaragua, Russia, Turkey, Korea, Cambodia, India . . . The Earth as we're faced with a new, uncreated century.

18　As I sit here I pray that innocence survives, that the Earth survives (us), that we survive (as compassionate human beings), that the juggler be truly skilled. And I pray (to the Goddess and the God) that I may write for the rest of this lifetime, and dream always.

19　I wrote this poem yesterday ("Dear World" is a series of poems I started two years ago):

March 24, 1996

Dear World,

*18,400 years ago, this comet
we call (in 1996) Hyakutake,
came close to the Earth (10 million
miles away, 10 million), but we*

*can see it with the naked
eye, floating in the sky like
a tail of light. The last
time it came within 10 million*

*miles, humans were just crossing
the terrible, icy glaciers,
the Bering Strait, into this
land mass, North America, one*

*of the floating, enduring Turtles.
The Turtles whispered, "Leap of
faith, dream, leap of faith, dream,"
as the comet edged its way*

*10 million miles, so close. 18,400
years later, the Turtles whisper,
"Leap of faith, one planet, leap
of faith, one people." This planet*

*floating through the stars, comets
coming home to sing to the Turtles:
"Cross the terrible, icy glaciers,
the human heart, leap."*

20　It's mid-April. I've completed typing this essay, the poems, into my word processor. On my desk are two photographs, close together, that catch my eye. I realize I've never looked at them together. One is a photo of my grandmother, Jesus, at eighteen or nineteen, sitting with a friend. They're sitting in chairs next to each other; a large, white, fur rug extends from the floor to the back of their chairs. My grandmother's friend strikes an intellectual pose, placing her left hand to the side of her face as though considering something important; the other's in her lap. My grandmother has her left hand in her lap, while her right hand caresses the soft, sensual fur. Her face is sensual, intuitive, beautiful, a little sad. She is my ancestor.

21   The other photo is of me at nineteen with four-year-old Antoinette. I can't see my hands, but I remember. They washed diapers and sheets by hand when the children (Antoinette and Ed) had measles one after the other for a month, and I couldn't go to the laundry. I imagine my right hand is curled around my daughter's soft, slightly chubby baby's leg, exposed because of her dress. My face is sensual, intuitive, beautiful, a little sad. I imagine my left hand rests nervously in my lap (with nothing to do). My daughter's head eclipses the right side of my face; the left side is just me at nineteen.

22   I had no idea I would ever really write (and publish). In fact, I often thought I might not even survive. But I did. And I realize, now, that to survive I had to be transformed (reborn). I had to die. I have to do this dying cyclically in order to be reborn (a small, green snake slithered in front of me on a trail yesterday, reminding me of this truth, my new skin). But first, one must learn to die.

23   *I am my ancestor.* Thanks to the nineteen-year-old (twenty, thirty, forty-year-old) woman I was, I am the fifty-one-year-old woman I am now. Thanks to the dead and the living I have known (and not known), I am able to write these words. I write to remember the dead, all that is no more. I write to remember to love, all that yearns to be. Created.

Post-reading Questions

Content

1. Explain the significance of Villanueva's essay title, "Leaps of Faith."

2. Villanueva describes many leaps of faith in the course of her essay, beginning with her reference to the last time the Hyakutake comet passed earth 18,400 years ago when the first humans crossed the Bering Strait. What do her observations show readers about human nature?

3. What does Villanueva consider to be the "ongoing work of a writer"?

4. Why does Villanueva teach writing as a "waking dream"? What extended comparison does she use to illustrate the creative process in paragraphs 11 through 13?
5. Who was Rosa? How did Villanueva get a "fix" on her? Explain the significance of the "encounter" between the two women—one fictional, one flesh and blood.

Strategies and Structures

1. Describe the tone of this essay. How does it compliment Villanueva's subject matter?
2. How does the author's use of concrete nouns and active verbs make her narrative discussion vivid and clear? In what way does she enable readers to picture what she speaks about through her word choice?
3. Villanueva mentions her children at different stages in their lives throughout her essay. What might be her strategic purpose for so doing?
4. In what way does Villanueva's poem, dated March 24, 1996 and titled "Dear World," capture the essence— the entire mood, spirit, and point—of her essay?
5. How does the final paragraph in the essay, beginning with "I am my ancestor," relate back to her opening paragraph? How was Villanueva reborn?

Language and Vocabulary

1. *Glaciated, binoculars, ingrained, patriarchal, converge, seizures, devastated, orgasmic, envisioned, transformation, eclipses.* After checking definitions for the vocabulary in this essay, write a paragraph using at least five of them to describe the cause and/or effect of some sort of change.
2. What words used by Villanueva indicate the "leaps of faith" and the magical experiences she talks of throughout the essay?

Group Activities

1. In a small group, revisit how and why "there was magic in the writing process" for Villanueva. Consider, for instance, how the character of Rosa from *The Ultraviolet Sky* became dead to her, figuratively speaking, only to be reborn.

2. Individually, highlight all transitional words and linking devices that enable Villanueva to move from sentence to sentence, paragraph to paragraph with clarity and cohesiveness. Then, divide into groups and make an exhaustive collaborative list of connecting words in "Leaps of Faith." Next, read her essay out loud *omitting* all highlighted words. How did the relationship between words, clauses, sentences and paragraphs change? Briefly jot down your group's insight into the function of transitions and linking words based on your collaborative observations.

Writing Activities

1. Write an essay wherein you reflect upon, describe, and analyze special moments or experiences you would label as "leaps of faith" in your lifetime.
2. Compose an essay that uses a spin-off of the phrase "There was magic in the writing process" as your thesis statement. For instance, your thesis might be "There is magic in the process of making music," "There is magic in the process of earning money," "There is magic in the process of painting pictures," and so on.

Additional Topics and Issues for Narrative Essays

1. Write a short narrative essay about the culture shock you encountered after moving from one neighborhood or country to another.
2. Compose an essay about a time in your life when you gave in to peer pressure rather than sticking to your personal convictions.
3. As closely as you can remember, narrate a story one of your parents used to tell you about his or her life. To frame your composition, provide your reader with the reasons or occasions your mother or father would tell you the story. Then, relate the story and conclude with your present perceptions about such moments with your parent(s).
4. Write a narrative about a person you met on a bus, plane, train, elevator, or the like who began to talk to you like an

intimate friend. What was the person like? How did you react to him or her? Did you try to ignore the person? What was his or her response to what you did or said? What conclusions can you draw about such people?

5. Discuss a situation or event that taught you a valuable lesson about life or survival in America.

6. Write a personal narrative recounting a typical holiday meal with your family. What takes place before, during, and after the meal? It may be helpful to narrow your focus to a specific holiday like Thanksgiving, New Year's, Hanukkah, or Christmas.

7. Compose a narrative essay based on a social function or a sporting event you participated in during the past year. Make sure you mention what your expectations were prior to the event as well as your feelings following it.

8. Write a humorous account of a recent concert, play, night club act, or sporting event you attended. Your humor should reflect your attitude toward your subject matter (the event).

9. Write a narrative essay about a trip you made outside of or coming to the United States. Begin your narrative from your point of departure, highlighting significant points of your trip. Conclude your essay with some reflective thoughts about the trip. What did you like about it? Would you go again? Would you recommend that someone else make the trip?

10. Flip through the photographs of the authors in the Narration chapter, read their bylines, and select one author in particular to investigate in greater detail. Next, go to the internet and locate the author's website, read his or her biography and digest the material. Finally, compose a brief biography of your own about the author, narrating significant events and publications in his or her life.

3

Description

While many college readers include description in their narration chapter, we feel that the rhetorical strategy of description is worthy of consideration in its own right. To be sure, there is frequently a narrative element in descriptive compositions. You need only read Maya Angelou's "Champion of the World" to realize how narration and description tend to overlap, producing a visual picture of an event (Joe Louis defending his heavyweight title).

Details: Appealing to the Five Senses

What makes an essay memorable? How do specific details engage one's imagination and enable writers vividly to convey a setting, a person, an object, or a situation in general? One of the most effective strategies authors employ to accomplish such ends is to appeal to the five senses: sight, sound, taste, touch, and smell. Using such an appeal to sight, sound, and touch, N. Scott Momaday describes Rainy Mountain in the following way:

> Winter brings blizzards, hot tornadic winds arise in the spring, and in the summer the prairie is an anvil's edge. The grass turns brittle and brown and it cracks beneath your feet. There are green belts along the rivers and creeks, linear groves of hickory and pecan, willow and witch hazel. At a distance in July or August the steaming foliage seems almost to writhe in fire. Great green and yellow grasshoppers are everywhere in the tall grass, popping up with the corn to

> *sting the flesh, and tortoises crawl about on the red earth, go-*
> *ing nowhere in plenty of time.*

In "Notes from a Son to His Father," Russell C. Leong's vivid description of his father's culinary (cooking) skills appeals to our senses of taste and smell in addition to sight in phrases like *"the hardest, fibrous vegetables to be cooked first in a dash of oil, and then the more delicately flavored ones, with purple and orange-tipped spears of heat, sizzling them in the heart."*

Appealing to our sense of hearing, Toshio Mori writes, *"She says silence is the most beautiful symphony"* and *"the Southern Pacific trains rumble by and the vehicles whizz with speed."* In "Old Before Her Time," Katherine Barrett combines sight, sound, and touch when she writes, *"She saw only a blur of sneakers and blue jeans, heard the sounds of mocking laughter, felt the fists pummeling her—on her back, her legs, her breasts, her stomach."* Capitalizing on our natural ability to see, to smell, to hear, to feel, and to taste when we compose an essay allows us to write more creatively and make what we say easy to picture.

Figurative Language: Appealing to the Imagination

While literal language can convey specific information and facts, occasionally you'll find the figurative use of language quite effective because it stimulates the imagination. Since figurative language tends to use strong imagery, it can often make abstract concepts come to life. At the same time, it can make your material more accurate and precise. Of all the figurative devices, *similes* and *metaphors* are the most frequently used.

When you make a comparison between two unlike objects using the words *like* or *as,* you are using a simile. For example, Leong writes that his father arranges the bitter melons so that they *"come out in even green crescents, like perfect waves of a green sea."* When Momaday writes, *"Her long, black hair, always drawn and braided in the day, lay upon her shoulders and against her breasts like a shawl,"* we get a vivid description of what her hair resembled through association (it was *like* a shawl)—a *simile.* A metaphor compares one thing to another by stating that one thing is another. It is a device many authors in this chapter use at least once. Mori compares a room to a depot. When Joe Louis falls in the boxing ring. Angelou compares it to *"our people falling . . . another lynching, . . . One more woman ambushed and raped."*

Dialogue: Revealing Characters through Speech

In addition to using details to describe their characters, authors often employ dialogue that refines them, giving us a glimpse of their characters' actual personalities. In "Champion of the World," for example, Angelou uses colloquial language (slang/everyday speech) when one of her characters says, *"I ain't worried 'bout this fight. Joe's gonna whip that cracker like it's open season."* Also, an occasional use of dialogue adds variety and interest to a descriptive narrative. In the line, *"It's been a long time since anyone hugged me,"* for instance, Katherine Barrett reveals the loneliness of old age effectively *without* directly telling the reader that the woman is lonely.

Actions: Describing People by What They Do

Actions, just as dialogue, go a long way towards revealing the physical and mental make-up of a speaker or character in an essay. What motivates a person to do anything? In "Confessions of a Quit Addict," Barbara Graham explains the power of *quitting* school, severing relationships, and moving around in life: *"Suddenly it seemed possible to reinvent myself, to discard my old life like last year's outfit and step into a new one—free from the responsibilities and relationships that had dragged me down."* As Graham reflects on her subject, she also states, *"Still, I don't consider myself a 'recovering' quitter. That would put too negative a spin on an act that is sometimes the best, most honest, and most creative response to a life situation, as well as a tremendous source of energy and power."*

Tips on Writing Descriptive Essays

1. Ask yourself questions such as, "What is the purpose of my essay? How will description further advance my purpose?"

2. Write sentences that appeal to the five senses: sight, sound, touch, taste, and smell. Add dialogue to provide variety.

3. Use adjectives (descriptive words) to further modify an object. For instance, when the word *house* is mentioned, each of us, undoubtedly, has a different mental image. When we use adjectives, however, each of us will have similar mental images (e.g., the *little, red, ramshackle, two-story* house is surrounded by *knee-high, withered grass* and a *broken-down, unpainted wooden* fence).

4. Adverbs also are used to modify words—verbs, adjectives, and other adverbs. For example: The track star raced *half-heartedly* to the finish line. The word *half-heartedly* is an adverb modifying the verb *raced*. An example of an adverb modifying an adjective is thus: The *extremely* overdressed girl felt out of place at the barbecue. The adverb *extremely* modifies the adjective *overdressed*. In the sentence "The crippled train inched *very* slowly up the mountain," the adverb *very* is modifying the other adverb *slowly*. Try using more adverbs in your writing to aid in description.

5. Employ figurative language such as metaphors and similes in order to stimulate the imagination and leave a lasting impression on your reader.

Toshio Mori

The Woman Who Makes Swell Doughnuts

*A former professional baseball player, Mori started writing
extensively in his late teens. He wrote mostly about the Japanese-
American experience, trying to capture the way his people spoke in the
1930s and 1940s. When his family was interned at the Topaz
Relocation Camp during World War II, Mori co-founded a newspaper
there and acted as camp historian. His works have appeared in
several anthologies and magazines, including* New Directions, Best
American Short Stories of 1943, Common Ground, *and* Writer's
Forum. *His books include* Yokohama, California *(1949),* The
Chauvinist and Other Stories *(1979),* The Woman from Hiroshima
(1979), and Unfinished Message *(2002).*

Pre-reading Questions

1. What elderly person have you admired? Who? Why?

2. Using the 5 Ws and H (who, what, where, when, why, and
   how), make the title of this essay into questions. For example, "Who is the woman making swell doughnuts?"

---

1   There is nothing I like to do better than to go to her house
and knock on the door and when she opens the door, to go in. It
is one of the experiences I will long remember—perhaps the
only immortality that I will ever be lucky to meet in my short
life—and when I say experience I do not mean the actual movement, the motor of our lives. I mean by experience the dancing
of emotions before our eyes and inside of us, the dance that is
still but is the roar and the force capable of stirring the earth
and the people.

2   Of course, she, the woman I visit, is old and of her youthful beauty there is little left. Her face of today is coarse with hard water and there is no question that she has lived her life: given birth to six children, worked side by side with her man for forty years, working in the fields, working in the house, caring for the grandchildren, facing the summers and winters and also the springs and autumns, running the household that is completely her little world. And when I came on the scene, when I discovered her in her little house on Seventh Street, all of her life was behind, all of her task in this world was tabbed, looked into, thoroughly attended, and all that is before her in life and the world, all that could be before her now was to sit and be served; duty done, work done, time clock punched; old-age pension or old-age security; easy chair; soft serene hours till death take her. But this was not of her, not the least bit of her.

3   When I visit her she takes me to the coziest chair in the living room, where are her magazines and books in Japanese and English. "Sit down," she says, "Make yourself comfortable. I will come back with some hot doughnuts just out of oil."

4   And before I can turn a page of a magazine she is back with a plateful of hot doughnuts. There is nothing I can do to describe her doughnut; it is in a class by itself, without words, without demonstration. It is a doughnut, just a plain doughnut just out of oil but it is different, unique. Perhaps when I am eating her doughnuts I am really eating her; I have this foolish notion in my head many times and whenever I catch myself doing so I say, that is not so, that is not true. Her doughnuts really taste swell, she is the best cook I have ever known, Oriental dishes or American dishes.

5   I bow humbly that such a room, such a house exists in my neighborhood so I may dash in and out when my spirit wanes, when hell is loose. I sing gratefully that such a simple and common experience becomes an event, an event of necessity and growth. It is an event that is part of me, an addition to the elements of the earth, water, fire, and air, and I seek the day when it will become a part of everyone.

6   All her friends, old and young, call her Mama. Everybody calls her Mama. That is not new, it is logical. I suppose there is in every block of every city in America a woman who can be called Mama by her friends and the strangers meeting her. This is commonplace, it is not new and the old sentimentality may be the undoing of the moniker. But what of a woman who isn't a mama but is, and instead of priding in the expansion of her little world, takes her little circle, living out her days in the

little circle, perhaps never to be exploited in a biography or on everybody's tongue, but enclosed, shut, excluded from world news and newsreels; just sitting, just moving, just alive, planting the plants in the fields, caring for the children and the grandchildren and baking the tastiest doughnuts this side of the next world.

7   When I sit with her I do not need to ask deep questions, I do not need to know Plato or The Sacred Books of the East or dancing. I do not need to be on guard. But I am on guard and foot-loose because the room is alive.

8   "Where are the grandchildren?" I say. "Where are Mickey, Tadao, and Yaeko?"

9   "They are out in the yard," she says. "I say to them, play, play hard, go out there and play hard. You will be glad later for everything you have done with all your might."

10   Sometimes we sit many minutes in silence. Silence does not bother her. She says silence is the most beautiful symphony, she says the air breathed in silence is sweeter and sadder. That is about all we talk of. Sometimes I sit and gaze out the window and watch the Southern Pacific trains rumble by and the vehicles whizz with speed. And sometimes she catches me doing this and she nods her head and I know she understands that I think the silence in the room is great, and also the roar and the dust of the outside is great, and when she is nodding I understand that she is saying that this, her little room, her little circle, is a depot, a pause, for the weary traveler, but outside, outside of her little world there is dissonance, hugeness of another kind, and the travel to do. So she has her little house, she bakes the grandest doughnuts, and inside of her she houses a little depot.

11   Most stories would end with her death, would wait till she is peacefully dead and peacefully at rest but I cannot wait that long. I think she will grow, and her hot doughnuts just out of the oil will grow with softness and touch. And I think it would be a shame to talk of her doughnuts after she is dead, after she is formless.

12   Instead I take today to talk of her and her wonderful doughnuts when the earth is something to her, when the people from all parts of the earth may drop in and taste the flavor, her flavor, which is everyone's and all flavor; talk to her, sit with her, and also taste the silence of her room and the silence that is herself; and finally go away to hope and keep alive what is alive in her, on earth and in men, expressly myself.

Post-reading Questions

Content

1. What image(s) in Mori's essay do you find powerful or interesting? Why?
2. Why does Mori respect the woman who makes swell doughnuts?
3. Why does Mori write about "the woman" before she dies instead of after her death?
4. What do the doughnuts symbolize to Mori? If they are a symbol for the woman and her way of life, what do they symbolize about her and her lifestyle?

Strategies and Structures

1. For different paragraphs in the essay, Mori uses different controlling metaphors or images. What is the controlling image of paragraph 6? What is the controlling image of paragraph 10? What does each paragraph suggest about the old woman?
2. How does Mori illustrate different aspects of the old woman in paragraph 2? How does the description of events in her life show what kind of woman she is?
3. Mori uses dialogue only a few times. Why do you think he uses it when he does? Why do you imagine he doesn't use dialogue more often?
4. How does Mori suggest "the woman who makes swell doughnuts" is a person who has had varied experience in life?

Language and Vocabulary

1. Vocabulary: *immortality, tabbed, pension, serene, coziest, wanes, moniker, depot.* Reread Mori's essay noting where these vocabulary words appear. Which words do you feel need further definition, and which words are easy to understand because of their "context" (see Glossary)? What other words or descriptions make the vocabulary words easy to comprehend?
2. Mori's language is very descriptive. What mental pictures did or can you draw from this story? What words make his descriptions vivid?
3. Mori uses many active verbs in this story. List a few of them and explain how they make the story more descriptive.

Group Activities

1. In small groups, create a list of words that describes "the woman who makes swell doughnuts." Then, take quotes from the essay that illustrate each point. Be prepared to explain your choices to the rest of the class.

2. As a group, discuss some of the qualities you associate with old age. How do you imagine elderly people live? What concerns, hopes, and desires do they have? What activities, hobbies, or events might they participate in? Does your picture of an elderly person's life correspond with the picture of the life described by Mori?

Writing Activities

1. Write a portrait of someone you know. Include details from his or her life that best illustrate the type of person he or she is. Pick several key images and words to describe the person as you develop your paragraphs.

2. Interview an elderly person and then write a description of him or her based on your notes. First you'll want to make up a list of questions to take to the interview. Then you'll want to make an appointment with a person. (*Hint:* During the interview, you may want to use a tape recorder.) Also, see Kathleen Hudson's essay, "Interviews: Stories That Make a Difference," in Chapter 6, Process Analysis, for an insight into the interview process.

Maya Angelou
Champion of the World

*Born Marguerita Johnson in 1928, Maya Angelou spent her youth en-
countering one personal tragedy after another. Angelou's talents are
many; she has acted in the television miniseries* Roots, *produced a
series about Africa for* PBS-TV, *and written several volumes of poetry.
A recipient of several honorary doctorates, Angelou is best known for
her autobiography* I Know Why the Caged Bird Sings *(1970). Other
works include* Just Give Me a Cool Drink of Water 'for I Die *(1971),*
Gather Together in My Name *(1974),* Singin' and Swingin' & Gettin'
Merry Like Christmas *(1976),* And Still I Rise *(1978),* Shaker, Why
Don't You Sing? *(1983),* All God's Children Need Traveling Shoes
(1986), I Shall Not Be Moved *(1990),* Wouldn't Take Nothing for My
Journey Now *(1993),* Lessons in Living *(1993),* Kofi and His Magic
(1996), Even the Stars Look Lonesome *(1997), and* A Song Flung Up
To Heaven *(2002). Angelou's career as a dancer, singer, and writer con-
tinues to flourish. She is a popular speaker at literary gatherings and
conferences worldwide. Long esteemed by our nation's leaders, former
President Gerald Ford appointed Angelou to the American Revolution
Bicentennial Council in 1975, and she wrote and read the poem, "On
the Pulse of Morning" (1993), at the inauguration of William Jefferson
Clinton, the forty-second president of the United States.*

Pre-reading Questions

1. The following piece is an excerpt from Angelou's *I Know
   Why the Caged Bird Sings.* Without worrying about accu-
   racy, explain the meaning behind the title of her autobiography in your journal or writing log.
2. Think about the title of this descriptive narrative, *"Champion of the World,"* a title taken directly from a phrase in

the book. Then turn to the person sitting next to you and brainstorm the word *champion*. What qualities do you associate with a champion?

---

1   The last inch of space was filled, yet people continued to wedge themselves along the walls of the Store. Uncle Willie had turned the radio up to its last notch so that youngsters on the porch wouldn't miss a word. Women sat on kitchen chairs, dining-room chairs, stools and upturned wooden boxes. Small children and babies perched on every lap available and men leaned on the shelves or on each other.

2   The apprehensive mood was shot through with shafts of gaiety, as a black sky is streaked with lightning.

3   "I ain't worried 'bout this fight. Joe's gonna whip that cracker like it's open season."

4   "He gone whip him till that white boy call him Momma."

5   At last the talking finished and the string-along songs about razor blades were over and the fight began.

6   "A quick jab to the head." In the Store the crowd grunted. "A left to the head and a right and another left." One of the listeners cackled like a hen and was quieted.

7   "They're in a clinch, Louis is trying to fight his way out."

8   Some bitter comedian on the porch said, "That white man don't mind hugging that niggah now, I betcha."

9   "The referee is moving in to break them up, but Louis finally pushed the contender away and it's an uppercut to the chin. The contender is hanging on, now he's backing away. Louis catches him with a short left to the jaw."

10   A tide of murmuring assent poured out the door and into the yard.

11   "Another left and another left. Louis is saving that mighty right . . . " The mutter in the Store had grown into a baby roar and it was pierced by the clang of a bell and the announcer's "That's the bell for round three, ladies and gentlemen."

12   As I pushed my way into the Store I wondered if the announcer gave any thought to the fact that he was addressing as "ladies and gentlemen" all the Negroes around the world who sat sweating and praying, glued to their "master's voice."

13   There were only a few calls for R. C. Colas, Dr. Peppers, and Hires root beer. The real festivities would begin after the fight. Then even the old Christian ladies who taught their children and tried themselves to practice turning the other cheek would buy soft drinks, and if the Brown Bomber's victory was a particularly

bloody one they would order peanut patties and Baby Ruths also.

14 Bailey and I laid the coins on top of the cash register. Uncle Willie didn't allow us to ring up sales during a fight. It was too noisy and might shake up the atmosphere. When the gong rang for the next round we pushed through the near-sacred quiet to the herd of children outside.

15 "He's got Louis against the ropes and now it's a left to the body and a right to the ribs. Another right to the body, it looks like it was low . . . Yes, ladies and gentlemen, the referee is signaling but the contender keeps raining the blows on Louis. It's another to the body, and it looks like Louis is going down."

16 My race groaned. It was our people falling. It was another lynching, yet another Black man hanging on a tree. One more woman ambushed and raped. A Black boy whipped and maimed. It was hounds on the trail of a man running through slimy swamps. It was a white woman slapping her maid for being forgetful.

17 The men in the Store stood away from the walls and at attention. Women greedily clutched the babes on their laps while on the porch the shufflings and smiles, flirtings and pinching of a few minutes before were gone. This might be the end of the world. If Joe lost we were back in slavery and beyond help. It would all be true, the accusations that we were lower types of human beings. Only a little higher than apes. True that we were stupid and ugly and lazy and dirty and, unlucky and worst of all, that God Himself hated us and ordained us to be hewers of wood and drawers of water, forever and ever, world without end.

18 We didn't breathe. We didn't hope. We waited.

19 "He's off the ropes, ladies and gentlemen. He's moving towards the center of the ring." There was no time to be relieved. The worst might still happen.

20 "And now it looks like Joe is mad. He's caught Carnera with a left hook to the head and a right to the head. It's a left jab to the body and another left to the head. There's a left cross and a right to the head. The contender's right eye is bleeding and he can't seem to keep his block up. Louis is penetrating every block. The referee is moving in, but Louis sends a left to the body and it's an uppercut to the chin and the contender is dropping. He's on the canvas, ladies and gentlemen."

21 Babies slid to the floor as women stood up and men leaned toward the radio.

22 "Here's the referee. He's young. One, two, three, four, five, six, seven . . . Is the contender trying to get up again?"

23 All the men in the store shouted, "NO."

24 "—eight, nine, ten." There were a few sounds from the audience, but they seemed to be holding themselves in against tremendous pressure.

25 "The fight is all over, ladies and gentlemen. Let's get the microphone over to the referee . . . Here he is. He's got the Brown Bomber's hand, he's holding it up . . . Here he is . . . "

26 Then the voice, husky and familiar, came to wash over us— "The winnah, and still heavyweight champeen of the world . . . Joe Louis."

27 Champion of the world. A Black boy. Some Black mother's son. He was the strongest man in the world. People drank Coca-Colas like ambrosia and ate candy bars like Christmas. Some of the men went behind the Store and poured white lightning in their soft-drink bottles, and a few of the bigger boys followed them. Those who were not chased away came back blowing their breath in front of themselves like proud smokers.

28 It would take an hour or more before the people would leave the Store and head for home. Those who lived too far had made arrangements to stay in town. It wouldn't do for a Black man and his family to be caught on a lonely country road on a night when Joe Louis had proved that we were the strongest people in the world.

Post-reading Questions

Content

1. Why were so many people gathered at Uncle Willie's store at night? What did they all have in common, "even the old Christian ladies"?

2. Why did the people who lived far away from Uncle Willie's store make arrangements to stay "in town" for the night?

3. While we know he is literally defending his heavyweight boxing title, Joe Louis is figuratively defending something else. What is it? (See paragraphs 16 and 17.)

4. How did the radio announcer's description of the fight affect the people in Willie's store?

5. How did people at Uncle Willie's store celebrate the outcome of the fight?

Strategies and Structures

1. When and where is dialogue used in this narrative? What is its purpose? What would this narrative ac-

count lose if no dialogue had been included? Why?

2. What type of sentence pattern helps Angelou build suspense in this narrative? In what way do observations of those around her echo the author's own feelings? How do we know for sure?

3. What sort of details does Angelou offer her readers so they can visualize the scene she describes? Without rereading the narrative, jot down as many details as you can remember.

4. What images in the opening paragraph create an atmosphere of suspense and anticipation?

Language and Vocabulary

1. Vocabulary: Go through this descriptive narrative and locate any unfamiliar words. Write them down on a piece of paper, along with their dictionary definitions. Continue to add to your personal vocabulary list throughout the semester.

2. What instances of nonstandard English did you notice in this essay? What purpose does such language serve?

Group Activities

1. Go back through the essay and select four or five descriptive phrases. When you assemble in groups, share three of the phrases you wrote down on a separate piece of paper, stating the descriptive phrase you liked best and why. Using a different subject with different modifying words, rewrite each group member's favorite descriptive phrase twice.

2. Spend five minutes or so discussing what you think Uncle Willie's store looks like based upon the concrete details provided by Angelou (refer to your response to question 3 under Strategies and Structures). Next, locate a video copy of *I Know Why the Caged Bird Sings,* a television movie, in your college's audiovisual center, and watch the film. Pay particular attention to the sequence where everybody gets together at Uncle Willie's store to listen to the Joe Louis fight on the radio. Finally, compare and contrast the way your group pictured the occasion based upon Angelou's written

description to the way the film presented (1) the store, and (2) the gathering of people on the night of the Joe Louis fight. (*Note:* Though Angelou adapted *I Know Why the Caged Bird Sings* for television, she was not the set designer.)

Writing Activities

1. Describe an incident that gave you a feeling of pride in your family, culture, nation, religious group, political group, or gender.
2. Construct a thesis that says something about afterthoughts, the things we think about after saying or not saying something. Then, develop your thesis by describing a recent argument or two you've had with another person, noting what you did *not* say or think about until after the argument (perhaps you wish you had said something but neglected to do so). Include dialogue in your descriptive essay to show rather than just tell your reader what you said and did.

Russell C. Leong

Notes from a Son to His Father

A fourth-generation Chinese American, Russell C. Leong writes poetry and fiction as well as expository essays. His work has appeared in such anthologies as Aiiieeeee!: An Anthology of Asian American Writers *and* Charlie Chan is Dead: An Anthology of Contemporary Asian American Fiction, *and he has edited works such as* Los Angeles—Struggle Towards Multiethnic Community: Asian-American, African-American, and Latino Perspectives *(1995),* Asian American Sexualities: Dimensions of the Gay & Lesbian Experience *(1995), and* Asian Americans on War and Peace *(2002). He has also published his own book of poetry,* The Country of Dreams and Dust *(1993). Leong is currently the editor of* Amerasia Journal *at the Asian American Studies Center, UCLA.*

Pre-reading Questions

1. Cluster the word *father*. What images, emotions, and ideas do you associate with the word?
2. Write a letter to your father. Explain memories and feelings about the past. Describe the image you had of him when you were young.

---

1 There is nothing good about being a son. I know; I am a son. When you have to admit that you have a father, allowing people to think that you are a father and son, as if any relation existed between those two terms, when there is really nothing to say.

2 And yet I usually find myself talking about my father, telling my friends and any strangers what he does and where he has

been, trying to describe with exactness his activities, trying to grasp his life through what little information I have of him. Doing this, I feel like a small child pressing a string of hard beads to my chest, a rosary of sorts, chanting the same phrases and images a thousand times in order to derive an order, a strength out of them. But the polished beads do not yield a thing: it is a repetition of uselessness. Nothing comes out of them.

3   I know my father like this. I see him working in his white apron, flashing and sharpening his cleaver on the back rim of a white Chinese pottery bowl. Zhap zhap zhap, the gray steel cleaver on the sturdy bowl. After arranging different vegetables on the table, I see him grasping the handle of the cleaver firmly, then nudging the jade bitter melon under the blade, at a slant, so that the pieces come out in even green crescents, like perfect waves of a green sea, at the same angle, and then the carrots, in thin narrow ovals, cut and dropped to boil lightly in a pot a while, and then the green bell peppers, the seeds and pale green mulch scooped out with a spoon, then cut in quarters and sliced. Then all the vegetables are arranged in neat piles on a large plate, ready to be cooked; the hardest, fibrous vegetables to be cooked first in a dash of oil, and then the more delicately flavored ones, with purple and orange-tipped spears of heat, sizzling them in the heart, while all along the rice is boiling on another part of the stove, each white grain destined to be firm and separate from his brother.

4   My father's hands were always busy preparing food and papers, writing and touching inanimate and ultimately useful things such as pencils and knives. Yet I do not know the real strength of my father's arm, I have never been lifted on his hand, brought up to see any life outside of my own. As a child I dreamed of my father.

5   Was this true, could he see his father dancing, away from the stiff and solemn pace of himself as father, provider, and businessman? Was it true, his father strong and bare, bravely dancing, using the wind as rope to catch all the worlds, flinging his arms and legs?

6   No, that is not him at all; his motions are never quick or free, but formal, stern, and placid for every emotion except rage.

7   At the door to my room, my father is glittering in anger, a knife poised in his hand. His face is pulsing pink, the once pale cauliflower flesh tinged with color and rage, and he is on one side of the room, about to throw the knife into me. I am just standing there, cringing; how can I defend myself against this

violence, this dark pearl which I have struck? So this is what is beneath my father's calmness, his layered dispassion, his view of my foolishness and ignorance and youth, it is this seething fury, not really his, but an inherited bitterness from some vague source, from a life not his, a frustration that has finally found its point in a knife, a silver gleaming tooth that will draw blood from my chest. My father, I screamed inside, but outside I tried to remain calm and rather disinterested in any personal aspect of the situation, as if his piercing my body was an event apart from the two of us, beyond any relation of father and son, as if my death or any son's death could happen like this, if the son did not observe and obey the rules—the correct way of doing things. During these moments I appeared calm, waiting for the blade to fall, and I despised him even more when his arm suddenly dropped down and the knife fell to the floor; he was not strong enough to go through with his convictions—he could not even kill his own son. I had heard the story about Abraham and Isaac, how Abraham would have killed his own son for God, because of his trust in God, but my father was not as good as that, because he does not believe in God in the first place. He will just kill me for no god at all.

8   At a later age, when one is a little older, one begins to strike back against his father with a vengeance, with a force akin to hatred or love, with the urge utterly to destroy all images of men or seek all images of them wherever and whenever possible.

9   Because one is a son himself he must realize his peculiar tendency to be i.e. manly and so he searches. I went out into the streets to look for this, this peculiar stuff of which pictures, pride, and parades are made of. Now I am in the middle of it, sunk into it. With love to the Father and to the Son.

Post-reading Questions

Content

1. Why do you feel Leong says, *"There is nothing good about being a son"*? Does he clearly explain this statement or must you infer its meaning from the context of the opening paragraphs? Could we also say there is nothing good about being a daughter?

2. What frustrations does Leong feel when he attempts to describe his father? How does he try to recall the image of his father?

3. What are the two primary images Leong has of his father? What do these two descriptions suggest about his father's character?
4. What does Leong suggest a son must do when he is older? Why must a son do this? Is this a natural stage in a parent-and-child relationship? Explain your opinion.

Strategies and Structures

1. What is the purpose of Leong's opening paragraphs? How do they introduce the topic of this descriptive essay and imply some of its themes?
2. Where does Leong create a vivid description of his father cooking? What images create this vivid description? Which of the five senses does he appeal to? Which images appeal to which senses?
3. What images in paragraph 7 create a vivid description of the scene in Leong's childhood bedroom? How does he combine a physical description of the scene with an emotional description as well? What effect does combining the two have on the reader?
4. Leong unifies the essay by using similar images in both descriptions. What images in paragraph 3 foreshadow the mood of paragraph 7?
5. Which images appear in the last paragraph that appear in the earlier descriptions of Leong's father? What themes are repeated?

Language and Vocabulary

1. Vocabulary: *fibrous, delicately, inanimate, pulsing, dispassion, seething, disinterested, despised, vengeance. In-* and *dis-* both mean "not." How would the elimination of such prefixes change the meaning of the sentence in which they appear? Could you change the meaning of any of the other vocabulary words by adding *in-* or *dis-* to them? What prefixes can you think of that could change the meanings of the other vocabulary words?
2. Leong vividly describes action. Imitate the following sentences describing an action with which you are familiar.
   a. "I see him working in his white apron, flashing and sharpening his cleaver on the back rim of a white Chinese pottery bowl."

   b. "After arranging different vegetables on the table, I see him grasping the handle of the cleaver firmly, then nudging the jade bitter melon under the blade, . . ."

   c. "My father's hands were always busy preparing food and papers, writing and touching inanimate and ultimately useful things such as pencils and knives."

   d. "During these moments I appeared calm, waiting for the blade to fall. . . ."

Group Activities

1. Discuss the impact of the allusion to Abraham and Isaac. Where does this allusion come from? What is the complete story of Abraham and Isaac? And what does it suggest about the relationship between fathers and sons? What does his comment, "He will just kill me for no god at all," suggest about his father's character, in particular, and the relationship between Leong and his father, in general?

2. Leong makes his narrative exposition come alive through the use of descriptive words and vivid language. Pick a paragraph from this essay and rewrite it without the use of any descriptive language. What is lost in doing so? Next give your rewritten paragraph to another group and have it rewrite the paragraph, making your group's initial rewrite vivid and descriptive once again. (Use your own descriptions, not Leong's.)

Writing Activities

1. Write a clear description of a relative, describing the performance of an action which you associate with him or her. For example, you may describe your father gardening or your aunt cleaning. Use vivid images and sentence patterns that will aid you in describing the action. As Leong does in paragraph 3, use the five senses as much as possible to heighten your description.

2. Relate a conflict you had with your parent(s). How was it resolved: Physically? Intellectually? How did you grow or learn from the situation? Did the conflict change your relationship with your parents? How? Why?

Katherine Barrett

Old Before Her Time

Katherine Barrett is a contributing editor at Financial World *and has received numerous awards, including the New York State Society of CPA's Award for Excellence in Financial Journalism. She is also a contributing editor at* The Ladies' Home Journal *and a monthly columnist for* Glamour. *Her articles and columns have appeared in* Newsweek, Readers' Digest, Harper's, Better Homes and Gardens, Self, Redbook, *and* Working Woman. *Barrett co-authored* The Man Behind the Magic *(1991), a biography of Walt Disney, with her husband Richard Green and* Investigating Artifacts: Making Masks, Creating Myths, Exploring Middens *(2002) with Linda Lipner and Gigi Dornfest. The following essay originally appeared in the August 1983 issue of* The Ladies' Home Journal.

Pre-reading Questions

1. What do you think when you see old people on the street? Do you talk with them or ignore them? Why? Would the way elderly people dress (e.g., well, modestly) influence your willingness to talk to them?

2. When an old person is on the bus, do you offer him or her your seat? Do you open doors for elderly people? Do you make fun of them? Do you ever think about what it will be like when you grow old—or do you think you'll never age?

---

1   This is the story of an extraordinary voyage in time, and of a young woman who devoted three years to a singular experiment. In 1979, Patty Moore—then aged twenty-six—transformed herself for the first of many times into an eighty-five-year-old woman. Her object was to discover firsthand the problems, joys

and frustrations of the elderly. She wanted to know for herself what it's like to live in a culture of youth and beauty when your hair is gray, your skin is wrinkled and no men turn their heads as you pass.

2   Her time machine was a makeup kit. Barbara Kelly, a friend and professional makeup artist, helped Patty pick out a wardrobe and showed her how to use latex to create wrinkles, and wrap Ace bandages to give the impression of stiff joints. "It was peculiar," Patty recalls, as she relaxes in her New York City apartment. "Even the first few times I went out I realized that I wouldn't have to *act* that much. The more I was perceived as elderly by others, the more 'elderly' I actually became . . . I imagine that's just what happens to people who really are old."

3   What motivated Patty to make her strange journey? Partly her career—as an industrial designer, Patty often focuses on the needs of the elderly. But the roots of her interest are also deeply personal. Extremely close to her own grandparents— particularly her maternal grandfather, now ninety—and raised in a part of Buffalo, New York, where there was a large elderly population, Patty always drew comfort and support from the older people around her. When her own marriage ended in 1979 and her life seemed to be falling apart, she dove into her "project" with all her soul. In all, she donned her costume more than two hundred times in fourteen different states. Here is the remarkable story of what she found.

4   **Columbus, Ohio, May 1979.** Leaning heavily on her cane, Pat Moore stood alone in the middle of a crowd of young professionals. They were all attending a gerontology conference, and the room was filled with animated chatter. But no one was talking to Pat. In a throng of men and women who devoted their working lives to the elderly, she began to feel like a total nonentity. "I'll get us all some coffee," a young man told a group of women next to her. "What about me?" thought Pat. "If I were young, they would be offering me coffee, too." It was a bitter thought at the end of a disappointing day—a day that marked Patty's first appearance as "the old woman." She had planned to attend the gerontology conference anyway, and almost as a lark decided to see how professionals would react to an old person in their midst.

5   Now, she was angry. All day she had been ignored . . . counted out in a way she had never experienced before. She didn't understand. Why didn't people help her when they saw her struggling to open a heavy door? Why didn't they include her in conversations? Why did the other participants seem almost embarrassed by her presence at the conference—as if it

were somehow inappropriate that an old person should be professionally active?

6   And so, eighty-five-year-old Pat Moore learned her first lesson: The old are often ignored. "I discovered that people really do judge a book by its cover," Patty says today. "Just because I looked different, people either condescended or they totally dismissed me. Later, in stores, I'd get the same reaction. A clerk would turn to someone younger and wait on her first. It was as if he assumed that I—the older woman—could wait because I didn't have anything better to do."

7   **New York City, October 1979.** Bent over her cane, Pat walked slowly toward the edge of the park. She had spent the day sitting on a bench with friends, but now dusk was falling and her friends had all gone home. She looked around nervously at the deserted area and tried to move faster, but her joints were stiff. It was then that she heard the barely audible sound of sneakered feet approaching and the kids' voices. "Grab her, man." "Get her purse." Suddenly an arm was around her throat and she was dragged back, knocked off her feet.

8   She saw only a blur of sneakers and blue jeans, heard the sounds of mocking laughter, felt fists pummeling her—on her back, her legs, her breasts, her stomach. "Oh, God," she thought, using her arms to protect her head and curling herself into a ball. "They're going to kill me. I'm going to die. . . ."

9   Then, as suddenly as the boys attacked, they were gone. And Patty was left alone, struggling to rise. The boys' punches had broken the latex makeup on her face, the fall had disarranged her wig, and her whole body ached. (Later she would learn that she had fractured her left wrist, an injury that took two years to heal completely.) Sobbing, she left the park and hailed a cab to return home. Again the thought struck her: What if I really lived in the gray ghetto . . . what if I couldn't escape to my nice safe home . . . ?

10   Lesson number two: The fear of crime is paralyzing. "I really understand now why the elderly become homebound," the young woman says as she recalls her ordeal today. "When something like this happens, the fear just doesn't go away. I guess it wasn't so bad for me. I could distance myself from what happened . . . and I was strong enough to get up and walk away. But what about someone who is really too weak to run or fight back or protect herself in any way? And the elderly often can't afford to move if the area in which they live deteriorates, becomes unsafe. I met people like this and they were imprisoned by their fear. That's when the bolts go on the door. That's

when people starve themselves because they're afraid to go to the grocery store."

11   **New York City, February 1980.** It was a slushy, gray day and Pat had laboriously descended four flights of stairs from her apartment to go shopping. Once outside, she struggled to hold her threadbare coat closed with one hand and manipulate her cane with the other. Splotches of snow made the street difficult for anyone to navigate, but for someone hunched over, as she was, it was almost impossible. The curb was another obstacle. The slush looked ankle-deep—and what was she to do? Jump over it? Slowly, she worked her way around to a drier spot, but the crowds were impatient to move. A woman with packages jostled her as she rushed past, causing Pat to nearly lose her balance. If I really were old, I would have fallen, she thought. Maybe broken something. On another day, a woman had practically knocked her over by letting go of a heavy door as Pat tried to enter a coffee shop. Then there were the revolving doors. How could you push them without strength? And how could you get up and down stairs, on and off a bus, without risking a terrible fall?

12   Lesson number three: If small, thoughtless deficiencies in design were corrected, life would be so much easier for older people. It was no surprise to Patty that the "built" environment is often inflexible. But even she didn't realize the extent of the problems, she admits. "It was a terrible feeling. I never realized how difficult it is to get off a curb if your knees don't bend easily. Or the helpless feeling you get if your upper arms aren't strong enough to open a door. You know, I just felt so vulnerable—as if I was at the mercy of every barrier or rude person I encountered."

13   **Ft. Lauderdale, Florida, May 1980.** Pat met a new friend while shopping and they decided to continue their conversation over a sundae at a nearby coffee shop. The woman was in her late seventies, "younger" than Pat, but she was obviously reaching out for help. Slowly, her story unfolded. "My husband moved out of our bedroom," the woman said softly, fiddling with her coffee cup and fighting back tears. "He won't touch me anymore. And when he gets angry at me for being stupid, he'll even sometimes . . . " The woman looked down, embarrassed to go on. Pat took her hand. "He hits me . . . he gets so mean." "Can't you tell anyone?" Pat asked. "Can't you tell your son?" "Oh, no!" the woman almost gasped. "I would never tell the children; they absolutely adore him."

14   Lesson number four: Even a fifty-year-old marriage isn't necessarily a good one. While Pat met many loving and devoted elderly couples, she was stunned to find others who had stayed
together unhappily—because divorce was still an anathema in
their middle years. "I met women who secretly wished their
husbands dead, because after so many years they just ended
up full of hatred. One woman in Chicago even admitted that
she deliberately angered her husband because she knew it
would make his blood pressure rise. Of course, that was pretty
extreme. . . . "

15   Patty pauses thoughtfully and continues. "I guess what really made an impression on me, the real eye-opener, was that
so many of these older women had the same problems as
women twenty, thirty or forty. Problems with men . . . problems
with the different roles that are expected of them. As a 'young
woman' I, too, had just been through a relationship where I
spent a lot of time protecting someone by covering up his problems from family and friends. Then I heard this woman in
Florida saying that she wouldn't tell her children their father
beat her because she didn't want to disillusion them. These issues aren't age-related. They affect everyone."

16   **Clearwater, Florida, January 1981.** She heard the children laughing, but she didn't realize at first that they were
laughing at her. On this day, as on several others, Pat had shed
the clothes of a middle-income woman for the rags of a bag
lady. She wanted to see the extremes of the human condition,
what it was like to be old and poor, and outside traditional society as well. Now, tottering down the sidewalk, she was most
concerned with the cold, since her layers of ragged clothing did
little to ease the chill. She had spent the afternoon rummaging
through garbage cans, loading her shopping bags with bits of
debris, and she was stiff and tired. Suddenly, she saw that four
little boys, five or six years old, were moving up on her. And
then she felt the sting of the pebbles they were throwing. She
quickened her pace to escape, but another handful of gravel hit
her and the laughter continued. They're using me as a target,
she thought, horror-stricken. They don't even think of me as a
person.

17   Lesson number five: Social class affects every aspect of an
older person's existence: "I found out that class is a very important factor when you're old," says Patty. "It was interesting.
That same day, I went back to my hotel and got dressed as a
wealthy woman, another role that I occasionally took. Outside

the hotel, a little boy of about seven asked if I would go shelling with him. We walked along the beach, and he reached out to hold my hand. I knew he must have a grandmother who walked with a cane, because he was so concerned about me and my footing. 'Don't put your cane there, the sand's wet,' he'd say. He really took responsibility for my welfare. The contrast between him and those children was really incredible. The little ones who were throwing the pebbles at me because they didn't see me as human. And then the seven-year-old taking care of me. I think he would have responded to me the same way even if I had been dressed as the middle-income woman. There's no question that money does make life easier for older people, not only because it gives them a more comfortable life-style, but because it makes others treat them with greater respect."

18   **New York City, May 1981.** Pat always enjoyed the time she spent sitting on the benches in Central Park. She'd let the whole day pass by, watching young children play, feeding the pigeons and chatting. One spring day she found herself sitting with three women, all widows, and the conversation turned to the few available men around. "It's been a long time since anyone hugged me," one woman complained. Another agreed. "Isn't that the truth. I need a hug, too." It was a favorite topic, Pat found—the lack of touching left in these women's lives, the lack of hugging, the lack of men.

19   In the last two years, she had found out herself how it felt to walk down Fifth Avenue and know that no men were turning to look after her. Or how it felt to look at models in magazines or store mannequins and *know* that those gorgeous clothes were just not made for her. She hadn't realized before just how much casual attention was paid to her because she was young and pretty. She hadn't realized it until it stopped.

20   Lesson number six: You never grow old emotionally. You always need to feel loved. "It's not surprising that everyone needs love and touching and holding," says Patty. "But I think some people feel that you reach a point in your life when you accept that those intimate feelings are in the past. That's wrong. These women were still interested in sex. But more than that, they—like everyone—needed to be hugged and touched. I'd watch two women greeting each other on the street and just holding onto each other's hands, neither wanting to let go. Yet, I also saw that there are people who are afraid to touch an old person . . . they were afraid to touch me. It's as if they think old age is a disease and it's catching. They think that something might rub off on them."

21   **New York City, September 1981.** He was a thin man, rather nattily dressed, with a hat that he graciously tipped at Pat as he approached the bench where she sat. "Might I join you?" he asked jauntily. Pat told him he would be welcome and he offered her one of the dietetic hard candies that he carried in a crumpled paper bag. As the afternoon passed, they got to talking . . . about the beautiful buds on the trees and the world around them and the past. "Life's for the living, my wife used to tell me," he said. "When she took sick she made me promise her that I wouldn't waste a moment. But the first year after she died, I just sat in the apartment. I didn't want to see anyone, talk to anyone, or go anywhere. I missed her so much." He took a handkerchief from his pocket and wiped his eyes, and they sat in silence. Then he slapped his leg to break the mood and change the subject. He asked Pat about herself, and described his life alone. He belonged to a "senior center" now, and went on trips and had lots of friends. Life did go on. They arranged to meet again the following week on the same park bench. He brought lunch—chicken salad sandwiches and decaffeinated peppermint tea in a thermos—and wore a carnation in his lapel. It was the first date Patty had had since her marriage ended.

22   Lesson number seven: Life does go on . . . as long as you're flexible and open to change. "That man really meant a lot to me, even though I never saw him again," says Patty, her eyes wandering toward the gray wig that now sits on a wig-stand on the top shelf of her bookcase. "He was a real old-fashioned gentleman, yet not afraid to show his feelings—as so many men my age are. It's funny, but at that point I had been through months of self-imposed seclusion. Even though I was in a different role, that encounter kind of broke the ice for getting my life together as a single woman."

23   In fact, while Patty was living her life as the old woman, some of her young friends had been worried about her. After several years, it seemed as if the lines of identity had begun to blur. Even when she wasn't in makeup, she was wearing unusually conservative clothing, she spent most of her time with older people and she seemed almost to revel in her role— sometimes finding it easier to be in costume than to be a single New Yorker.

24   But as Patty continued her experiment, she was also learning a great deal from the older people she observed. Yes, society often did treat the elderly abysmally . . . they were sometimes ignored, sometimes victimized, sometimes poor and frightened,

but so many of them were survivors. They had lived through two world wars, the Depression and into the computer age. "If there was one lesson to learn, one lesson that I'll take with me into *my* old age, it's that you've got to be flexible," Patty says. "I saw my friend in the park, managing after the loss of his wife, and I met countless other people who picked themselves up after something bad—or even something catastrophic—happened. I'm not worried about them. I'm worried about the others who shut themselves away. It's funny, but seeing these two extremes helped me recover from the trauma in my own life, to pull *my* life together."

25   Today, Patty is back to living the life of a single thirty-year-old, and she rarely dons her costumes anymore. "I must admit, though, I do still think a lot about aging," she says. "I look in the mirror and I begin to see wrinkles, and then I realize that I won't be able to wash *those* wrinkles off." Is she afraid of growing older? "No. In a way, I'm kind of looking forward to it," she smiles. "I *know* it will be different from my experiment. I *know* I'll probably even look different. When they aged Orson Welles in *Citizen Kane* he didn't resemble at all the Orson Welles of today."

26   But Patty also knows that in one way she really did manage to capture the feeling of being old. With her bandages and her stooped posture, she turned her body into a kind of prison. Yet, inside she didn't change at all. "It's funny, but that's exactly how older people always say they feel," says Patty. "Their bodies age, but inside they are really no different than when they were young."

Post-reading Questions

Content

1. What is the controlling idea of this essay?
2. How many times did Patty Moore dress as an elderly woman? In how many different states did she conduct her *experiment*?
3. Why did Moore want to "transform herself" into an "eighty-five-year-old woman"?
4. How did Moore's relationships with elderly people help her to pull the pieces of her life together?

Strategies and Structures

1. What are the seven lessons about life Patty Moore learned, and how did Barrett use them to unify the content of her essay?

2. Why do the first few words in some lines appear in boldface type? What do they signal to the reader?
3. In your opinion, how well does Barrett's narrative of Patty Moore's experiences illustrate the broader theme of her essay?
4. What strategies does Barrett use to keep her readers interested in her rather long essay?

Language and Vocabulary

1. Vocabulary: *condescending, audible, deteriorate, disillusion, revel, abysmal.* Use the following suffixes to change the above words from one word form to another: *-ly, -ment, -tion.* (For example, one could change *friend,* a noun, to *friendly,* an adjective.) Use both word forms in a sentence.
2. A lot of the dialogue in this essay is not really addressed to a particular person; rather, it's like a person thinking out loud. Analyze how the author's use of dialogue is appropriate to the theme of her essay.

Group Activities

1. Role-playing: Assume a role that definitely is not you or any member of your group. For example, you could dress as a street person or a business executive. Make sure you notice how people judge and treat you. Then dress exactly the opposite and see if people react differently towards you. Afterward, meet with your group and discuss the different reactions.
2. Semester Project: Keep a running journal account of role-playing you have done for the duration of this class, making sure to record the lessons you've learned, much as Moore did in this essay. After condensing your material, construct a unified composition in which you use the lessons you've learned to guide you in proving your thesis.

Writing Activities

1. Take one of the lessons in life (the issue or moral it offers) Moore experienced and use it as an essay

topic. Take a definite position on the issue and argue/describe why it is true or untrue, using specific details drawn from personal experience.

2. Describe a situation where you learned something by role-playing (acting like another person, talking like another person, thinking like another person). Lead your readers through a sequence of narrated events to help them understand how role-playing in itself taught you a lesson. You might draw on your role-playing experiences from the second group activity.

N. Scott Momaday

From The Way to Rainy Mountain

A member of the Kiowa tribe, N. Scott Momaday has spent his life telling the history and the tales of his people. He has published such books as the Pulitzer Prize–winning The House Made of Dawn *(1968),* The Way to Rainy Mountain *(1969),* The Gourd Dancer *(1976),* The Names: A Memoir *(1976),* The Ancient Child *(1989),* In the Presence of the Sun: Stories and Poems, 1961–1991 *(1992),* Circle of Wonder: A Native American Christmas *(1993), and* More Than Bows and Arrows: The Legacy of the American Indians *(1994). In addition to being a well-respected author, Momaday also is an accomplished artist and has won several awards for both his paintings and drawings. His artistic sensitivity seems to transfer quite naturally into his writings, and as shown in the following descriptive excerpt from the introduction to* The Way to Rainy Mountain, *he often uses symbols and images to paint pictures with words.*

Pre-reading Questions

1. What does the title suggest will be the topic of this essay? Make a list of some of the possible things you think the author will write about.

2. The name of the mountain—Rainy Mountain—has several connotations. What connotations (feelings and/or images) do you associate with the words *rainy* and *mountain*?

---

1   A single knoll rises out of the plain in Oklahoma, north and west of the Wichita Range. For my people, the Kiowas, it is an old landmark, and they gave it the name Rainy Mountain. The

hardest weather in the world is there. Winter brings blizzards, hot tornadic winds arise in the spring, and in summer the prairie is an anvil's edge. The grass turns brittle and brown and it cracks beneath your feet. There are green belts along the rivers and creeks, linear groves of hickory and pecan, willow and witch hazel. At a distance in July or August the steaming foliage seems almost to writhe in fire. Great green and yellow grasshoppers are everywhere in the tall grass, popping up like corn to sting the flesh, and tortoises crawl about on the red earth, going nowhere in plenty of time. Loneliness is an aspect of the land. All things in the plain are isolate; there is no confusion of objects in the eye, but *one* hill or *one* tree or *one* man. To look upon the landscape in the early morning, with the sun at your back, is to lose the sense of proportion. Your imagination comes to life, and this, you think, is where Creation was begun.

2   I returned to Rainy Mountain in July. My grandmother had died in the spring, and I wanted to be at her grave. She had lived to be very old and at last infirm. Her only living daughter was with her when she died, and I was told that in death her face was that of a child.

3   I like to think of her as a child. When she was born, the Kiowas were living the last great moment of their history. For more than a hundred years they had controlled the open range from the Smoky Hill River to the Red, from the headwaters of the Canadian to the fork of the Arkansas and Cimarron. In alliance with the Comanches, they had ruled the whole of the southern Plains. War was their sacred business, and they were among the finest horsemen the world has ever known. But warfare for the Kiowas was preeminently a matter of disposition rather than survival, and they never understood the grim, unrelenting advance of the U.S. Cavalry. When at last, divided and ill-provisioned, they were driven onto the Staked Plains in the cold rains of autumn, they fell into panic. In Palo Duro Canyon they abandoned their crucial stores to pillage and had nothing then but their lives. In order to save themselves, they surrendered to the soldiers at Fort Sill and were imprisoned in the old stone corral that now stands as a military museum. My grandmother was spared the humiliation of those high gray walls by eight or ten years, but she must have known from birth the affliction of defeat, the dark brooding of old warriors.

4   Her name was Aho, and she belonged to the last culture to evolve in North America. Her forebears came down from the high country in western Montana nearly three centuries ago. They were a mountain people, a mysterious tribe of hunters

whose language has never been positively classified in any major group. In the late seventeenth century they began a long migration to the south and east. It was a journey toward the dawn, and it led to a golden age. Along the way the Kiowas were befriended by the Crows, who gave them the culture and religion of the Plains. They acquired horses, and their ancient nomadic spirit was suddenly free of the ground. They acquired Tai-me, the sacred Sun Dance doll, from that moment the object and symbol of their worship, and so shared in the divinity of the sun. Not least, they acquired the sense of destiny, therefore courage and pride. When they entered upon the southern Plains they had been transformed. No longer were they slaves to the simple necessity of survival; they were a lordly and dangerous society of fighters and thieves, hunters and priests of the sun. According to their origin myth, they entered the world through a hollow log. From one point of view, their migration was the fruit of an old prophecy, for indeed they emerged from a sunless world.

5   Although my grandmother lived out her long life in the shadow of Rainy Mountain, the immense landscape of the continental interior lay like memory in her blood. She could tell of the Crows, whom she had never seen, and of the Black Hills, where she had never been. I wanted to see in reality what she had seen more perfectly in the mind's eye, and traveled fifteen hundred miles to begin my pilgrimage.

6   Yellowstone, it seemed to me, was the top of the world, a region of deep lakes and dark timber, canyons and waterfalls. But, beautiful as it is, one might have the sense of confinement there. The skyline in all directions is close at hand, the high wall of the woods and deep cleavages of shade. There is a perfect freedom in the mountains, but it belongs to the eagle and the elk, the badger and the bear. The Kiowas reckoned their stature by the distance they could see, and they were bent and blind in the wilderness.

7   Descending eastward, the highland meadows are a stairway to the plain. In July the inland slope of the Rockies is luxuriant with flax and buckwheat, stonecrop and larkspur. The earth unfolds and the limit of the land recedes. Clusters of trees, and animals grazing far in the distance, cause the vision to reach away and wonder to build upon the mind. The sun follows a longer course in the day, and the sky is immense beyond all comparison. The great billowing clouds that sail upon it are shadows that move upon the grain like water, dividing light. Farther down, in the land of the Crows and Blackfeet, the plain

is yellow. Sweet clover takes hold of the hills and bends upon itself to cover and seal the soil. There the Kiowas paused on their way; they had come to the place where they must change their lives. The sun is at home on the plains. Precisely there does it have the certain character of a god. When the Kiowas came to the land of the Crows, they could see the dark lees of the hills at dawn across the Bighorn River, the profusion of light on the grain shelves, the oldest deity ranging after the solstices. Not yet would they veer southward to the caldron of the land that lay below; they must wean their blood from the northern winter and hold the mountains a while longer in their view. They bore Tai-me in procession to the east.

8   A dark mist lay over the Black Hills, and the land was like iron. At the top of a ridge I caught sight of Devil's Tower upthrust against the gray sky as if in the birth of time the core of the earth had broken through its crust and the motion of the world has begun. There are things in nature that engender an awful quiet in the heart of man; Devil's Tower is one of them. Two centuries ago, because they could not do otherwise, the Kiowas made a legend at the base of the rock. My grandmother said:

> Eight children were there at play, seven sisters and their brother. Suddenly the boy was struck dumb; he trembled and began to run upon his hands and feet. His fingers became claws, and his body was covered with fur. Directly there was a bear where the boy had been. The sisters were terrified; they ran, and the bear after them. They came to the stump of a great tree, and the tree spoke to them. It bade them climb upon it, and as they did so it began to rise into the air. The bear came to kill them, but they were just beyond its reach. It reared against the tree and scored the bark all around with its claws. The seven sisters were borne into the sky, and they became the stars of the Big Dipper.

From that moment, and so long as the legend lives, the Kiowas have kinsmen in the night sky. Whatever they were in the mountains, they could be no more. However tenuous their well-being, however much they had suffered and would suffer again, they had found a way out of the wilderness.

9   My grandmother had a reverence for the sun, a holy regard that now is all but gone out of mankind. There was a wariness in her, and an ancient awe. She was a Christian in her later years, but she had come a long way about, and she never forgot her birthright. As a child she had been to the Sun Dances; she had taken part in those annual rites, and by them she had learned the restoration of her people in the presence of Tai-me.

She was about seven when the last Kiowa Sun Dance was held in 1887 on the Washita River above Rainy Mountain Creek. The buffalo were gone. In order to consummate the ancient sacrifice—to impale the head of a buffalo bull upon the medicine tree—a delegation of old men journeyed into Texas, there to beg and barter for an animal from the Goodnight herd. She was ten when the Kiowas came together for the last time as a living Sun Dance culture. They could find no buffalo; they had to hang an old hide from the sacred tree. Before the dance could begin, a company of soldiers rode out from Fort Sill under orders to disperse the tribe. Forbidden without cause the essential act of their faith, having seen the wild herds slaughtered and left to rot upon the ground, the Kiowas backed away forever from the medicine tree. That was July 20, 1890, at the great bend of the Washita. My grandmother was there. Without bitterness, and for as long as she lived, she bore a vision of deicide.

10   Now that I can have her only in memory, I see my grandmother in the several postures that were peculiar to her: standing at the wood stove on a winter morning and turning meat in a great iron skillet; sitting at the south window, bent above her beadwork, and afterwards, when her vision failed, looking down for a long time into the fold of her hands; going out upon a cane, very slowly as she did when the weight of age came upon her; praying. I remember her most often at prayer. She made long, rambling prayers out of suffering and hope, having seen many things. I was never sure that I had the right to hear, so exclusive were they of all mere custom and company. The last time I saw her she prayed standing by the side of her bed at night naked to the waist, the light of a kerosene lamp moving upon her dark skin. Her long, black hair, always drawn and braided in the day, lay upon her shoulders and against her breasts like a shawl. I do not speak Kiowa, and I never understood her prayers, but there was something inherently sad in the sound, some merest hesitation upon the syllables of sorrow. She began in a high and descending pitch, exhausting her breath to silence; then again and again—and always the same intensity of effort, of something that is, and is not, like urgency in the human voice. Transported so in the dancing light among the shadows of her room, she seemed beyond the reach of time. But that was illusion; I think I knew then that I should not see her again.

11   Houses are like sentinels in the plain, old keepers of the weather watch. There, in a very little while, wood takes on

the appearance of great age. All colors wear soon away in the wind and rain, and then the wood is burned gray and the grain appears and the nails turn red with rust. The window-panes are black and opaque; you imagine there is nothing within, and indeed there are many ghosts, bones given up to the land. They stand here and there against the sky, and you approach them for a longer time than you expect. They belong in the distance; it is their domain.

12   Once there was a lot of sound in my grandmother's house, a lot of coming and going, feasting and talk. The summers there were full of excitement and reunion. The Kiowas are a summer people; they abide the cold and keep to themselves, but when the season turns and the land becomes warm and vital they cannot hold still; an old love of going returns upon them. The aged visitors who came to my grandmother's house when I was a child were made of lean and leather, and they bore themselves upright. They wore great black hats and bright ample shirts that shook in the wind. They rubbed fat upon their hair and wound their braids with strips of col-ored cloth. Some of them painted their faces and carried the scars of old and cherished enmities. They were an old council of warlords, come to remind and be reminded of who they were. Their wives and daughters served them well. The women might indulge themselves; gossip was at once the mark and compensation of their servitude. They made loud and elaborate talk among themselves, full of jest and ges-ture, fright and false alarm. They went abroad in fringed and flowered shawls, bright beadwork and German silver. They were at home in the kitchen, and they prepared meals that were banquets.

13   There were frequent prayer meetings, and great nocturnal feasts. When I was a child I played with my cousins outside, where the lamplight fell upon the ground and the singing of the old people rose up around us and carried away into the darkness. There were a lot of good things to eat, a lot of laugh-ter and surprise. And afterwards, when the quiet returned, I lay down with my grandmother and could hear the frogs away by the river and feel the motion of the air.

14   Now there is funeral silence in the rooms, the endless wake of some final word. The walls have closed in upon my grand-mother's house. When I returned to it in mourning, I saw for the first time in my life how small it was. It was late at night, and there was a white moon, nearly full. I sat for a long time

on the stone steps by the kitchen door. From there I could see out across the land; I could see the long row of trees by the creek, the low light upon the rolling plains, and the stars of the Big Dipper. Once I looked at the moon and caught sight of a strange thing. A cricket had perched upon the handrail, only a few inches away from me. My line of vision was such that the creature filled the moon like a fossil. It had gone there, I thought, to live and die, for there, of all places, was its small definition made whole and eternal. A warm wind rose up and purled like the longing within me.

15   The next morning I awoke at dawn and went out on the dirt road to Rainy Mountain. It was already hot, and the grasshoppers began to fill the air. Still, it was early in the morning, and the birds sang out of the shadows. The long yellow grass on the mountain shone in the bright light, and a scissortail hied above the land. There, where it ought to be, at the end of a long and legendary way, was my grandmother's grave. Here and there on the dark stones were ancestral names. Looking back once, I saw the mountain and came away.

Post-reading Questions

Content

1. Why does Momaday return to Rainy Mountain? What effect does this trip have on him?
2. Who is the central character in Momaday's essay? What traits make up her character?
3. What is the history of the Kiowas? How did they come to reside below Rainy Mountain?
4. What journey does Momaday make? Where does he begin his essay? Where does he say he is going? Where does he end the essay?

Strategies and Structures

1. Momaday opens his essay with a description. What is the primary "mood" (see Glossary) of this description? What images create this mood? What images are most vivid? How does this description set up the tone for the rest of the essay?
2. Why does Momaday tell the story of the Kiowas? How is their story similar to the story of his grandmother?

3. In paragraph 10, what senses—sight, sound, smell, taste, and touch—does he use to describe his grandmother?

4. Momaday writes two descriptions of his grandmother's house—paragraphs 12–13 and 14. What are the two distinct differences between the descriptions? What images does Momaday use to create the two distinct moods?

5. What is the mood of the final paragraph? Is it different from the opening paragraph? What images create the mood?

Language and Vocabulary

1. Vocabulary: *knoll, range, plain, fork, canyon, highland meadows, caldron.* All of these vocabulary words are used to specify or explain geographical areas or features. After you look up the dictionary definition of the words, go back and see where and how Momaday uses them to describe the area around Rainy Mountain. Then, write a paragraph or so describing a geographical area you are familiar with (or an imaginary place), using at least five of the eight vocabulary words.

2. Momaday enables the reader to "relive" his trip to Rainy Mountain because he connects the different parts of his journey. What sorts of transitions and linking devices help the reader follow Momaday?

Group Activities

1. As a group, take a walk around the campus. As you walk, write down all that you can see, smell, taste, touch, and hear. After you finish your walk, decide on a dominant impression the campus projects: old, friendly, traditional, modern, busy, and so on. After you determine the dominant impression of the campus, decide which details from your notes illustrate this impression best.

2. Write a collaborative essay describing the classroom you are sitting in. Make sure everyone in your group contributes information and impressions. In addition to details which help a reader to visualize the room, your essay should create a dominant mood.

Writing Activities

1. Write a description of a close relative. Include the history of the relative's heritage, the relative's past, and the relative's present.
2. Write a description of your hometown or homeland. In the same manner as Momaday, try to create a mood by careful use of details and images.

Barbara Graham

Confessions of a Quit Addict

*Barbara Graham is a journalist, playwright, and author of such
works as* Jacob's Ladder *(1987),* Women Who Run with the Poodles
*(1994), a book whose title takes a lighthearted response to Clarissa
Pinkola Etés's more serious book,* Women Who Run with the Wolves:
Myths and Stories of the Wild Woman Archetype, *a book examining
the "historical woman of progress" in a male-dominated society. Her
great use of irony in the following essay not only highlights her
human folly in moving from one fantasy world to another, but it also
describes the pilgrimage of her chronic addiction—quitting—from
the moment she decided to drop out of college to the time she decides
it may be time to become a "recovering quitter."*

Pre-reading Questions

1. How do you feel about quitting? What negative feelings (if
   any) come to your mind when you hear the word? How
   were you raised to think about this concept?

2. Have you—or anyone you know—ever quit a job or school
   and gone off to seek your (their) fortune or explore the
   world with little or no money? What happened to you or
   the other person? If you've never done this, how do you
   feel about a person who has? Do you consider him or her
   brave, crazy, or stupid?

1   By the time I heard Timothy Leary chant "Turn on, tune in,
drop out" from the stage of New York's Fillmore East, I had already quit college. The year was 1967, and Leary's battle cry
was for me more a confirmation of what I already believed
than a call to action.

2   I had never been much good at doing things that didn't arouse my passion. Even when I was a young girl, it was obvious that I had been born without the stick-to-it, nose-to-the-grindstone gene. I was stubborn, tenacious in my devotion to the people and things I loved, disdainful of everything else. There was no in-between. In high school I got straight A's in English and flunked math. When it came time for college, I enrolled at NYU because it was the only way I could think of to live in Greenwich Village and get my parents to pick up the tab. But I rarely made it to classes and dropped out one month into my sophomore year.

3   That was the first time I felt the rush of quitting, the instant high of cutting loose, the biochemical buzz of burning my bridges. The charge had to do not with leaving college for something else, but with leaving, period—the pure act of making the break. Suddenly it seemed possible to reinvent myself, to discard my old life like last year's outfit and step into a new one—free from the responsibilities and relationships that had dragged me down. I got an unlisted telephone number and warned my parents to stay away. "When one jumps over the edge, one is bound to land somewhere," wrote D. H. Lawrence, and for a long time this was my mantra.

4   It didn't take long for me to find a collaborator, a master of disappearing acts who made me look like a rookie. Brian was ready to morph one life into the next on the turn of a dime. I became his loyal apprentice, and during the summer of 1968, shortly after Bobby Kennedy and Martin Luther King Jr. were gunned down, we sold everything we owned and quit our jobs, our friends, our apartment, the urban jungle, America and blight of Vietnam, and fled to Europe. But our new life didn't quite match our dreams: As winter neared, we found ourselves living in a rusty old van on the outskirts of Rome, hungry and cold and hard up for cash. From there, we boarded a freighter for Puerto Rico—which turned out not to be the nirvana we'd imagined, either—especially after the little episode with customs officials over a speck of hashish. Still, a pattern had been set: living in one place, dreaming of another, working at odd jobs (mine included secretary, salesgirl, cocktail waitress, draft counselor, nude model, warehouse clerk, candle maker), earning just enough money to get us to the next destination. We crisscrossed the United States, went north to British Columbia, and lived in every conceivable sort of dwelling from tenements and tents to farmhouses and plywood shacks. Sometimes I'd

grow attached to a place and plant a garden, thinking that *this* time things would work out and we'd stay forever—or at least long enough to see the flowers bloom. But something always went wrong: It rained too much (British Columbia), the cost of living was too high (Colorado), the air wasn't pure enough (Southern California), or we couldn't find work that was meaningful, not to mention lucrative enough for us (everywhere).

5   For a long time it didn't matter that we weren't happy anywhere, because the rush of heading off into the unknown and starting over was more potent and trippy than anything we smoked, and we just kept going—even after our son, Clay, was born. But one day, in the mountains of Northern California, when our latest scheme for finding True Happiness—living close to nature, in a house we built, near another family—fell apart, I just snapped. In that moment I knew that I no longer had it in me to continue feeding on fantasies of a future that inevitably turned to dust. That night I made this entry in my journal: "I'm so sick of listening to ourselves talk about what's going to be—plans, plans, plans. I want to live in the present for once, not in the future. I mean *live,* settle down, make a home for my son." I had understood finally that the problem wasn't in the places we went or the people we found there but in ourselves. We could shed our surroundings but not our own skin. No matter who or what we left behind, our private demons followed, and our differences with one another erupted like a sleeping volcano the minute we stopped running. In the end, there was nowhere left to go, no place left to leave behind, no one left to say good-bye to except each other.

6   It had taken thousands of miles and one child for me to understand that the quitting I took for freedom was as much of a trap as the social conventions we were trying to escape. Together, Brian and I had been so busy saying no to everything that might limit our options that, except for Clay, we'd neglected to say yes to anything. We had no careers, few friends, and no place to call home. Moreover, what had begun as a journey to find our "true" selves, independent of other people's expectations, had turned into an addictive cycle of fantasy and failure, followed by another stab at redemption. After seven years, I felt sad, spent, and more alienated than ever—from Brian, from the rest of the world, and, most frighteningly, from myself. More than anything, I longed to land *somewhere.*

7   Still, I don't consider myself a "recovering" quitter. That would put too negative a spin on an act that is sometimes the

best, most honest, and most creative response to a life situation, as well as a tremendous source of energy and power. What's more, in the years since Brian and I went our separate ways, I've walked away from a marriage and a number of significant relationships, bailed out of college a second time (just a few credits shy of getting my degree), and moved back and forth across the country twice. As for my relationship to the workforce, it officially ended 15 years ago when I left a long-term (for me—it lasted all of eight months) position as the publicist for a hospital specializing in unusual diseases. I simply could not deal with a life in which I was expected to show up at the same place at the same time five days a week and not take frequent naps. So I did what any self-respecting jobaphobic would do: I became a writer.

8   But, paradoxically, knowing that I'll always have it in me to be a quit artist has in recent years made me want to hunker down, dig deeper, stick around long enough to watch the garden bloom. (I've even gone so far as to plant perennials.) This change has come gradually, on tiptoes, without the fanfare or splash of the Big Quit. Looking back at my current marriage of 12 years, I see that the constancy my husband and I have maintained despite our share of hard times would have, in the past, sent me scrambling in search of higher drama. For me, the act of staying put has required far more courage and humility than it once took to let go. This is somewhat ironic, considering that I used to believe that my capacity to turn my back and walk away from almost anyone or anything was a sure sign of bravery.

9   Over the years, I've also come to understand that even if I don't go chasing after change, it will do a perfectly good job of finding me. Upheavals, startling turns, and unpredictable shifts have all come unbidden—especially when I've been at my most settled. Besides, I've watched enough people I love die to know that no matter how hard we try to be the sole authors of our own stories, life itself will eventually have its way and quit *us*.

10   And though sometimes I miss the rush of cutting loose—and, God knows, the impulse still arises—I've learned that, for the most part, it's impossible to travel deep and wide at the same time. Now it's simply more interesting, more richly satisfying, to mine my life just as it is, with all of its wild imperfections and—superficially, at least—lack of conspicuous drama. My family, my home, close friendships, the natural world, and the

worlds conjured in my work constantly surprise me with their nourishment—a thick and complex root system I might never have known if I hadn't stopped severing the ties that bind.

Post-reading Questions

Content

1. Why is it so easy for the author to adopt Timothy Leary's chant, "Turn on, tune in, drop out," in 1967? What makes her a good candidate for taking his advice and what emotions come into play when she does?

2. Who becomes her collaborator, and how do they spend their lives? What pattern is soon established in their day-to-day living?

3. What causes her to realize that she no longer has it in her to live in a fantasy world? What discovery does she make about the future at the same time? More importantly, what does she finally come to realize that she needs?

4. Why, however, doesn't she consider herself a "recovering quitter"? What has she done in the 15 years since she left the father of her son, Clay?

5. What has she learned from her family, her home, close friendships, and the natural world?

Strategies and Structures

1. What is the purpose of beginning this essay with Timothy Leary's statement in 1967? What does this tell the reader about the author? How does she further this opinion in the next three paragraphs?

2. There are essentially two parts to this essay. How is this division advantageous to the author's purpose and for the reader's perception? How does the author's realization that the problem wasn't in the places they went or with people they met but in themselves contribute to this division?

3. What is the reason for the author's telling the reader that in no way is she a "recovering" quitter? Why does she not want us to jump to conclusions about her?

4. Although the author begins the essay by telling us that she is a quitter, how does she end the essay?

What has she learned over the years? Is there a purpose in this revelation? How does it enhance the process of writing an essay?

Language and Vocabulary

1. Vocabulary: *tenacious, disdainful, collaborator, morph, nirvana, lucrative, redemption, paradoxical, upheaval, superficial.* After looking up the words that you do not know, use them in a paragraph or two to establish a sequence describing how the author first felt about being a quitter and what she has learned from her experiences.
2. Compose your own vocabulary list and use the words in a few paragraphs to describe what it is like to be addicted to success rather than quitting.

Group Activities

1. Gather into two or three groups and research the "Hippie Revolution" of the late 1960s and early 1970s. Who is Timothy Leary, and how did he and this era contribute to the author's desire to "quit"? After completing your research, form into two groups and debate the advantages and/or disadvantages of *dropping out* or *quitting*.
2. Assemble into groups and discuss the effects of the lifestyle portrayed in Graham's essay on the children who were born to these people. Do some research on this in the library and save your information to use in a future essay.

Writing Activities

1. Write a composition in which you describe what it would be like if you suddenly quit school and/or your job. You should include how your parents and friends would accept this, and how you would defend yourself and justify your decision.
2. Using the information you obtained in number two of the Group Activities, write an essay in which you describe what it would be like to be a child born to parents who have no roots. A topic you might deal with could be: Does this lifestyle in any way affect a

child's self-esteem? You might decide whether this lifestyle would be harmful or helpful.

Additional Topics and Issues for Descriptive Essays

1. Describe a place or thing that you fear. What is it that you fear, and when do you fear it most? What sorts of steps do you take to try and overcome your fear?

2. Write a description of your favorite place. Use specific details to make your essay vivid. You may want to answer some of the following questions: Where is this place? What kinds of things are there? Why do you like this place? When do you go there? How did you find this place? Who else goes there?

3. Write a visual portrait of what you perceive to be the youth of America. What or who are they? How do they dress, eat, and think? What sort of music do they listen and dance to? Try to avoid stereotypes when dealing with this subject.

4. Describe your favorite or ideal meal. Use adjectives and adverbs to help your reader smell, taste, and visualize the meal spread before him or her.

5. Compose an essay describing a place usually considered undesirable to visit; for example, you may want to write about a trip to the local garbage dump, slaughterhouse, or cannery. Make sure to include all the unpleasant sights, sounds, and smells. After all, the purpose for using description in this sort of essay is to enable the reader to share in your experience.

6. Describe a sporting or social event which you attended and felt was quite significant in one way or another. Be sure to include the sounds, the sights, and any other sensual imagery that impressed you.

7. Using figurative language, describe two unlike objects, showing how they can be compared with each other by using similes and/or metaphors. (You may wish to review the chapter introduction, particularly if you intend to use an extended metaphor.)

8. Describe a meeting that you have had with a particularly colorful character, integrating dialogue exchanged between the two of you to add variety and interest to your essay.

9. Describe an area considered hostile to life that you know well from personal experience and that you feel has been given an unfair reputation. What is it about this area that most people do not realize but you are aware of?

10. Based on personal experiences, observations, and findings from interviews and readings, write an essay describing what you think it will be like growing old in America and why you think it will be that way.

4

Illustration and Example

Supporting a statement through the use of specific examples is essential to good, clear expository and argumentative writing. We illustrate what we claim with personal experiences, observations, and readings. Citing statistics can also support our examples. When we omit information that will help our reader to visualize our observations, we reduce our arguments to generalizations or simply reinforce stereotypes. In essence, writers use illustrations and examples like artists use brushes and paint; authors paint pictures with words for their readers.

Developing Your Thesis

After writing the thesis paragraph, writers then offer the reader detailed evidence to explain and support material. Where do writers gather their examples? Many authors illustrate their points using personal experience. For instance, in the essay "My Own Style," Nikki Giovanni states that she likes *"useful things"* like candles and then explains (illustrates) why by using reasoning and examples: She keeps candles around the house just in case it *"gets hit by lightning"* and her electrical power is lost; with candles she'll have a sure source of light.

Observations, like personal experiences, can also vividly explain a point in an essay or other form of literature. By watching and listening to what others do and say, we gather a valuable reserve of material, material we can use in everyday conversations as well as essays. (This is one reason many writers keep diaries or journals of what they see.) A fine example of supporting a point with observations is Philip K. Chiu's mention of Chinese stereotypes in "The Myth of the Model Minority." Chiu illustrates a Chinese stereotype by referring to a film character, *"the insidious"* Fu Manchu, followed by a positive— but nonetheless inaccurate—Chinese stereotype: Charlie Chan. His specific examples illustrate general points.

In a similar manner, Ann Scheid uses specific examples of pollution and destruction to animal and plant life to illustrate her thesis that the human race eagerly tries to demonstrate "its superiority to Mother Nature, usually with disastrous results." Additionally, her historical and biblical references provide timelines of human relationships toward nature—adding depth and dimension to her discussion points.

If you are writing an essay on contemporary American culture, you might cite Mark Katz's article, "Power Children"—an article examining the role and economic power of youth in modern society. In fact, referring to books, articles, or reports (especially for statistics) written by authorities in a given field can make your examples more convincing than if you rely solely on your own experience to illustrate a theory or point. Initially citing an authoritative study on *why* more Americans are involved in some sort of physical fitness program today than 30 years ago, for instance, supports what *you may believe* with verifiable evidence.

Creating Vivid Examples

Simply supplying examples to support your points will not be enough to engage actively your reader's imagination, however. To hook your reader's interest and spark his or her imagination, you should make your examples specific and detailed, using concrete nouns and active verbs. Nouns are concrete when they create unmistakable images. Nouns like *things* and *stuff* are vague, imprecise words and may mislead or confuse your reader. Therefore, rather than writing, "Place your *things* on the counter," you would replace the vague word *things* with a word like *clothes, tools,* or *books*—a concrete noun!

Stephanie Ericsson's selected examples in "The Ways We Lie" tend to be vivid, memorable, and concrete. She goes into depth illustrating the lie of *deflecting,* showing how Clarence Thomas, accused of sexual harassment, testified that the

Senate Committee hearings for his Supreme Court nomination were a *high-tech lynching: "Rather than defending himself, he took the offensive and accused the country of racism."* She also makes use of personal experience to illustrate the *out-and-out* lie, relating how her nephew blamed *"the murderers"* when he broke her fence.

Active verbs will also keep your reader involved in your essay. Often overlooked by the inexperienced writer, verbs can be the most powerful tool an author has for showing us what is happening as opposed to telling us. One way of making your essay vivid is to replace verbs that merely link ideas with verbs that indicate action. *Robert is angry at us* would be more effective written as *Robert scowled at us.* Why? The linking verb *is* links the subject, *Robert,* with the adjective, *angry.* The verb *scowl* shows the reader Robert's mood instead of just telling us what he is: angry.

Tips on Writing Illustration and Example Essays

1. The best use of illustration and example occurs when a writer has a clear idea of *what* he or she is trying to explain to the reader. To arrive at this point, you may want to freewrite, cluster, or use any method you find effective in generating ideas and limiting your thesis.

2. After you select a topic to write on, determine what sort of illustrations or examples would help to clarify your points and support them. Draw your examples from personal experiences, observations, and readings.

3. Whenever possible, use specific, concrete nouns so your reader will be able to picture vividly what you intend.

4. Complement your use of concrete nouns with verbs expressing action and mood. Again, this will enable you to *show* rather than simply *tell* your reader about your topic.

5. In most compositions, transitional words and phrases that indicate relationships between words, clauses, and entire paragraphs will help to lead your reader from one idea to the next, unifying the sections of your essay. To introduce an example in an illustration essay, use transitions such as *for instance* or *for example.*

Mark Katz

"Power Children"

A *humorist and popular essayist, Mark Katz's articles have appeared in numerous magazines, including* Time—*the source of the following essay—and* The New Yorker. *His tongue-in-cheek approach, such as the death-bed wishes of a flu patient (had he succumbed to the disease), are at once amusing yet quite telling about people, their values, and the society in which we live.*

Pre-reading Questions

1. Jot down a few sentences noting how and why America could be considered *a land of the young*.

2. In your opinion, what is the relationship between youth and popular culture? How would you define each? When do people cease to be youthful in spirit—if ever—and why?

---

1   I mean, it's like, today's teens, they just don't get it! Sure, for them, life is totally phine—er, phat. They are coming of age in an age that celebrates the coming of age. For every standard-issue adolescent yearning, there is a show that explores it on the WB. For each of life's clichéd ironies encountered for the first time, there is a chat room to lament it on http://TeenGripe.com. For every pimply punk buying a pop CD, another kid with a good complexion has just released a debut album. Being a teenager these days is as effortless as being a Renaissance man during the Renaissance. These kids have no idea how hard it is living in an era that has outgrown grown-ups. They just . . . I dunno. Forget it. Whatever.

2   It's been 20 years since I was a teenager, but if memory serves, my adolescent experience took place in an environment very different from today's. Certainly, I struggled with the

same dilemmas that still define this realm: Who am I? Where will my life take me? When will I get naked with a girl? Like everyone else, I had to solve the riddle of defying my elders while conforming to my peers. Until we find a cure for puberty, there will always be young adults fixated upon these questions. What's new is an entire culture fixated upon those who fixate upon these questions.

3   The irony, of course, is that the affliction of adolescence is traditionally marked by a pronounced sense of isolation. At some critical moment in every proto-adult life comes a lonely, anguished, heartfelt plea: "Nobody understands me!" How can today's teens truly experience this tortured rite of passage when marketers seek them out relentlessly and programmers understand them so well? And with all those Hollywood talent scouts and Silicon Valley headhunters hunting them down and signing them up, why would they even care if their parents understand them at all? Even the lonely losers of yesteryear are no longer locked in suburban basements playing Dungeons & Dragons; they are in downtown lofts uploading Web pages and concocting e-business ventures. There's hardly anyone left in our work force to mow the lawns and flip the burgers. Today's teenagers hold such a commanding position in our economy, it's only a matter of time before antiquated child-labor laws are inverted to establish a maximum wage and minimum hours. (In fact, the better question may be, is it even fair to keep these kids stuck at home or in a classroom during their peak earning years?) These are the odd socioeconomic circumstances that place me among the first generation of Americans who strive to do better than their children.

4   When I came of age, teenagers were not celebrated, only tolerated, as though society said to us, "Come back to us when your skin clears up and you've shaved that cheesy mustache off your face." Out of ideas about how to deal with us, well-meaning adults herded us into "rap sessions" on the off-chance that we might console ourselves. I spent a good part of my teenage years hoping only to outlive the awkward indignities of adolescence. I prayed for the day when I'd be older—and, please God, taller—so I might assume the full status of a human being endowed by my Creator with certain unalienable rights, not least among these was staying out past 11 and entering bars at will. I endured my teenage years by placing faith in the future, only to look back and realize that I managed to miss Woodstock not once but twice.

5   Maybe you can argue that teens should not be shunted aside, but I am curious to know how they've come to be worshipped instead. Now that I am fully grown, I sense two prevailing cultural obsessions that ignore me once again. In American culture, there is potential and nostalgia; we are fascinated by prodigies first and has-beens second. Stuck in the middle are millions like me, living in those awkward years between promising potential and ironic demise. And the parameters of the present keep pushing in. To the tune of discarded disco anthems, our eyes pan slowly from one Gap-clad teen to another, and for 30 seconds we cannot bring ourselves to blink. The teens stare back at us brimming with serene self-assurance, mocking anyone who ever made the mistake of turning 22 and blissfully unaware that 10 years from now, they will be 10 years older.

6   We've come to worship this false god of youth just as wayward, ancient Hebrews once knelt at the hooves of a golden calf. But perhaps there's a lesson there as well. Once the world's darling, that golden calf later found herself a tarnished cow, reduced to flashing her sagging udders at circus sideshows. Over time, self-loathing made her lactose-intolerant, and she died too young from an overdose of prescription-strength Dairy Ease™. How do I know this? I just watched the whole sad aftermath during teen-idols week on VH1's *Where Are They Now?*

7   Britney Spears: Consider yourself warned.

Post-reading Questions

Content

1. What seems to be the controlling idea or thesis in Katz's essay?
2. What are some of the questions and concerns Katz cites as universal dilemmas faced by teenagers? What dilemmas would you add to his examples?
3. Why is it ironic that the "affliction of adolescence" is "marked by a pronounced sense of isolation"? What happens?
4. Katz asserts that "Hollywood talent scouts and Silicon Valley headhunters" track down teenagers and elevate their visibility in society because they are mass consumers—individuals with *buying power*. In part, how might this explain why Americans seem to "worship the false god of youth"?

5. Now a fully grown man, Katz senses that "two prevailing cultural obsessions" are ignoring him once again. What are these two "cultural obsessions" to which he refers, and where does he believe he and millions of other people like him feel stuck? Why?

Strategies and Structure

1. How does the author draw on memories of his own teenage years in order to bridge gaps between his adult self and today's youth?
2. Explain the rhetorical function of the first paragraph in Katz's essay. How is it more than simply an introduction to a topic? Why do you imagine Katz used slang words like "phine" and "phat" in the first sentence of the essay?
3. Characterize the *tone* of "Power Children." What seems to be Katz's attitude toward his subject?
4. How does Katz draw his essay to a close? Where does he bring his readers? Why do you imagine he wrote the single sentence "Britney Spears: Consider yourself warned" as a paragraph in itself?
5. In what way do specific, concrete references and allusions throughout Katz's essay relate to some aspect of popular culture, past and present?

Language and Vocabulary

1. Vocabulary: *adolescent, cliché, renaissance, dilemmas, fixate, venture, socioeconomic, unalienable, prodigies, demise, anthems, parameters, blissfully, lactose intolerant, nostalgia.* Go through the above vocabulary words, check their dictionary definitions, and then place them in one of two columns:
   1) Words associated with youth and renewal, and
   2) Words suggesting the passing of time and adulthood. In view of your list, what can you conclude about the appropriateness and effectiveness of the author's word choice?
2. Reexamine today's vocabulary words. Which words have the richest connotations (associations)? Briefly explain the connotations of at least ten words on the vocabulary list.

Group Activities

1. Divide the class into groups, and have each group select a different commercial television channel to research "youth culture" and "youth appeal" in advertising. Determine whether group members would like to watch blocks of television individually, in pairs, or as an entire group. Regardless of your method of observation, get back together in class as a group to discuss observations and plan a presentation. Then all groups should share all findings. To what extent did the class as a whole reach similar conclusions? Did they concur or differ from Katz's article? How? Why?

2. Get into small groups and discuss how each person imagines him or herself in ten years. In what ways do members believe they will change, and to what extent will they remain the same? Why? Have the recorder jot down the group's projections. If your group had written "Power Children" as a collaborative exercise, how might it revise the content and focus of Katz's essay?

Writing Activities

1. Is the author correct in his assumption that "an entire culture [is] fixated upon" teenagers and what they think about? Write an essay in which you agree or disagree with Katz. If you disagree, tell the reader what teenagers truly believe and practice and what they believe the future holds for them.

2. Brainstorm the word "youth"; what patterns emerge from your responses? Compose an essay explaining whether or not America is a society that worships youth and the importance of staying young. Support your essay with examples drawn from personal experience, observations, or readings.

Nikki Giovanni

My Own Style

Nikki Giovanni, who currently teaches at Virginia Polytechnic and State University, is not only a fine essayist but also a prolific poet. Her works include Black Talk, Black Feeling *(1967),* Black Judgment *(1968),* Spin a Soft Black Song: Poems for Children *(1971),* My House: Poems *(1972),* Cotton Candy on a Rainy Day *(1978),* Those Who Ride in the Night Winds *(1983),* Sacred Cows . . . and Other Edibles *(1988),* Love Poems *(1997), and* Blues: For All Changes: New Poems *(1999). In 1994, Giovanni published* Knoxville, Tennessee, *an illustrated children's book;* Racism 101, *a collection of essays; and* A Multicultural Anthology of Poems, Reminiscences, and Short Stories about the Keepers of Our Traditions. The* Selected Poems of Nikki Giovanni *appeared in 1996. An early influence on her works was her maternal grandmother, Louvenia Terrell Watson, with whom she lived for two years during high school. She instilled Giovanni with a sense of African-American consciousness which would become a guiding force in Giovanni's poetry during the '60s and '70s. Experiences always helped shape Giovanni's works, and by the time* The Women and the Men *(1983) was published, her work had moved from black nationalism to a more humanist world view, partially due to her international travels.*

Pre-reading Questions

1. What is style? How does style influence actions or reactions?
2. What do you associate with uniformity? How might you conform to a uniform way of doing things while developing individual style? Is it possible?

1 I want to be a modern woman. I still have a nostalgic Afro, though it's stylishly short. I apologize to the hair industry, but frankly, I like both my kinks and my gray strands. Plus, being a sixties person, glowing in the dark carries negative implications for me. Most of my friends do wear base, pancake, powder, eye make-up, lipstick and always keep their nails in perfectly ovaled shapes with base, color, sealer and oil for the cuticles. Do I use these things? No. But neither do I put them down nor try to make my friends feel guilty for not being natural. There is something to be said for improvement. I've been known to comment: "Wow, you look really good. Who does your nails?" Why, I even have a dear friend who is a few months younger than I and uses a night cream to guard against wrinkles. Do I laugh? No, ma'am. I say: "Well, your face is very, very smooth," which (1) makes her feel good about her efforts and (2) keeps the friendship intact.

2 My major contribution to cosmetics is soap. I love soap . . . in pretty colors . . . hand milled . . . in interesting shapes . . . with the names of good perfumers on them . . . preferably French. I use it to bathe, of course, but it's also so pretty on my open shelves. Plus it smells good and when properly arranged, is more or less sculpture. No one in my immediate family, and few who have ever used my bathroom, ever wonders what to give me for my birthday, Christmas, Valentine's Day, Mother's Day, the Fourth of July, Labor Day, Martin Luther King Jr.'s Birthday or Lincoln Heights Day. The way I figure, ask for what you want.

3 I really like useful things. You never know. Take candles. I really like a candle. I'm a Democrat, so I have a donkey. I'm a Delta, so I have an elephant. I'm a woman, so I have an apple. (Well, maybe I don't have to justify that.) I also have candle candles. Just tall, pretty candles in little holders. If the house gets hit by lightning, I'm ready. Like all modern women, I like to be ready.

4 Without raising a hair on my chinny-chin-chin I can turn three cans of anything and a quarter cup of dry white wine into a gourmet meal in 15 minutes flat. Give me an ounce of cognac and I really raise hell. I've been known to make the most wicked bean soup with warm croutons and garlic zwieback (the secret is a dabble of sherry) the world has known. People say: "How can you be a full-time mother, full-time professional, and still cook like this?" I smile sweetly, indicating that perhaps the very best is yet to come. Or as the old folks liked to say: "It ain't what you do; it's the way you do it."

5   In observing the younger women, that seems to be the one thing that they are missing: the ability to take nothing and make everybody think that something is there. Know what I mean? The younger women like to brag that they can't cook, as if that makes them modern. What is really modern is that you can throw it together from cans and frozen food and pretend that it was easy. Half of life is not avoiding what you don't like but doing it with no sweat.

6   I must congratulate the twentieth-century woman on her internationalism. You go into practically any house these days and they have Nigerian art, Egyptian cotton throws, French water, Hawaiian fruit, Japanese televisions, California wines, Polish crystal, Haitian lace curtains, Lesothoan rugs and Dutch flowers sitting on grandmother's handmade quilts draped across an Early American table. I remember when you could go by the apartment of any guy and find stale beer in the refrigerator. Nowadays even *their* places are perking up. Everybody wants to make a statement.

7   Oh sure, I've heard all the jokes about BUMP's (Black Upwardly Mobile Professionals), but I like a BUMP. Hell, I am one. The modern woman is a BUMP who is not a grind. And we could use a little ambition in our community. Every time somebody wants to trade their Toyota for a BMW, it means they have to have more people to supervise, a bigger budget to spend. If they're in business for themselves, they have to sell more, do more, 'cause everybody knows you don't get big in business by saving; you get big by spending, by expansion.

8   We are only 15 years away from the twenty-first century! The Black community is 40 percent teenage unemployed, social security froze, Medicaid stopped, unwed, underemployed, unpromoted and generally a not-appreciated-at-all community in America. Who we gonna call—Honkeybusters? No! We're gonna climb out on the BUMP's. We can do it 'cause we've done everything else. And hey, even though my body will be old, sitting on a porch in some home (unless I can convince my son, now 15, to let me live with him), I'll be surrounded by the good feeling that I am a modern woman, 'cause even if I'm old, I'm sure to be positive—and that's our ace in the hole.

Post-reading Questions

Content

1. What does Giovanni observe about younger professional women? Why does the author "congratulate"

them? Do they deserve her congratulations? Why or why not?

2. How is the author different from other professional women?

3. In paragraph 8, Giovanni states, "We're gonna climb out on those BUMP's." What is she referring to here?

Strategies and Structures

1. Why does Giovanni spend the first paragraph establishing differences between herself and many other "modern women"?

2. Throughout the essay, the author shows the reader that she never sacrificed individual identity or style to get ahead in the world. How do her illustrations and examples reinforce her controlling idea—captured by the essay's title?

3. How does the tone of this essay suit Giovanni's ultimate purpose?

Language and Vocabulary

1. Vocabulary: *implications, croutons, honkey, zwieback.* Giovanni's use of language is rather simple. The style of her prose is appropriate for the general audience she is writing for. Write a paragraph or so in your notebook, reflecting on what you presently consider your writing style. How does your style of writing change when you write for different people? Why?

2. Cite two instances in Giovanni's essay where she uses "acronyms" (see Glossary). Also, write down as many acronyms in your notebook as you can. What do the acronyms represent? Translate them.

Group Activities

1. Have a ten-minute panel discussion wherein you examine Giovanni's reference to "Honkeybusters." The preceding phrase, "Who we gonna call?" came from a movie called *Ghostbusters,* which involved four men who claimed to be specialists in getting rid of ghosts. How might the allusion to *Ghostbusters* suit Giovanni's purpose in her essay? What is she trying to accomplish?

2. As a group, carefully go over Giovanni's essay and discuss it regarding her style of communication. What do you find particularly effective about her prose and the essay? How do the particular qualities that you have found work together to make up an identifiable style? What is the role of humor in this essay? Why does she use so many "clichés" (see Glossary) and trendy phrases?

Writing Activities

1. Giovanni says that "Everybody wants to make a statement." Based on personal observation and experience, write an essay proving or disproving what she states. Extensive use of examples will be essential to build a strong expository essay.

2. After summing up and illustrating how *most* people would approach or perform a task, meet new people, or visit new places, include in an expository essay— making ample use of illustration and example— how your individual style is responsible for the way in which you do things.

Philip K. Chiu

The Myth of the Model Minority

Chinese-American freelance writer Philip K. Chiu's works have
appeared in many publications in the United States, including U.S.
News & World Report, *where this essay originally appeared in the*
"Rostrum" column. Chiu presently lives and writes in Carlsbad,
California. In the following essay, Chiu discusses how stereotyping
Asians—the model minority—has been somewhat oppressive;
however, times have changed and so has society's perception of "the
model minority."

Pre-reading Questions

1. What Chinese-American stereotypes are you familiar
with? Make a list of the qualities you associate with people of Chinese ancestry.

2. How does the word *myth* affect the meaning of the essay
title? What does it suggest about Chinese Americans being *the model minority*?

---

1   For years, Chinese Americans have been labeled a model minority. We read in the newspapers how diligently they have worked
and saved. We see on television how quietly they obey the laws
and how conscientiously they stay clear of crime. We learn in
magazines how they climb the economic ladder and how much
better than the Caucasian kids their children do in school.

2   But of late, we have been reading about a different side of Chinese American life. In January, *U.S. News* reported on Chinese
gangs and their criminal activities. Not long afterward, a gun
battle in the quiet streets of Pasadena, Calif., left two federal

drug agents and two Chinese drug dealers dead. Now, the press is reporting on rising Chinese organized crime on the West Coast and citing the Pasadena incident as the latest manifestation.

3   What has happened to that law-abiding, humble Chinese American we have heard so much about? Have the media been wrong all these years? The answer is a complex one.

4   About 60 years ago, the silver screen gave us the insidious Fu Manchu and the ever inscrutable Charlie Chan. We heard about the dim opium dens and the filthy gambling halls. We saw slant-eyed, ever obedient little men toiling about with their pigtails freshly cut off. And we wondered just what kind of expression was "long time no see."

5   Then came World War II, and the Chinese became our allies. The pictures of a smiling, beautiful Madame Chiang Kai-Shek appeared in every newspaper. And we read about clean, amiable, upright and industrious Chinese Americans who, nearly a century before, had contributed to winning the American West by working day and night in the mines, on the farms and on the railroads.

6   The Korean War brought a picture of ferocious Chinese hordes marching to conquer Asia. And we learned that the Chinese spoke with forked tongues. They felt no pain when you stuck a needle in their tummies. They ate from their rice bowls with disgusting noises and giggled with delight when they stabbed you in the back.

7   The 1972 Nixon visit to China ushered in an era of high praise for anything Chinese. The newly discovered extraordinary accomplishments of Chinese Americans in the face of prejudice sent social scholars scrambling for answers. And it was in the late '70s and the early '80s that the scholars told the world that the Chinese Americans were the model minority.

8   Is the wind changing its direction again in 1988? I don't know for sure, but I do know that as a Chinese American I am glad to see reporting on the underside of Chinese American life. In part, I am tired of hearing how miraculously the well-behaved Chinese Americans have been doing, and I'm sick of reading about those bespectacled teenage bookworms who have contributed to exceptionally low juvenile-delinquency rates among Chinese American kids. But mostly I am fed up with being stereotyped as either a subhuman or superhuman creature.

9   Certainly, I am proud of the academic and economic successes of Chinese Americans and proud that many of us have excelled in science, the arts, law, medicine, business, sports

and other endeavors. But it's important for people to realize that there is another side.

10   A few Chinese Americans steal when they are desperate; a few rape when nature overwhelms them; a few sell drugs when they see an easy way to make a buck; a few embezzle when instant fortunes blind them; a few murder when passions overtake them; and a few commit crimes simply because they are wicked.

11   It is about time for the media to report on Chinese Americans the way they are. Some are superachievers, most are average citizens, and a few are criminals. They are only human—no more and no less.

Post-reading Questions

Content

1. Why were Chinese Americans labeled the *model minority* in the late 1970s and the early 1980s? Who or what was responsible for furthering this stereotype?
2. What are some of the stereotypes Chinese Americans have been labeled with over the past 60 years?
3. Why does Chiu feel it is important for people "to realize that there is another side" to Chinese Americans, a side not associated with a model human being?
4. What does Chiu request that the media do? Why?

Strategies and Structures

1. Chiu begins and concludes his essay with references to the media. How does this frame his essay as a whole?
2. How successfully does Chiu illustrate the "superhuman" and the "subhuman" character traits of the Chinese? Why is a discussion of the two extremes of strategic importance to his essay's concluding paragraph?
3. Chiu provides a brief history of the stereotypes— including the model minority—placed on Chinese people by other members of American society, prior to answering the rhetorical question, "Have the media been wrong all these years?" What is the purpose of the history? What does it show the reader?

Language and Vocabulary

1. Vocabulary: *diligently, conscientiously, Caucasian, manifestation, insidious, inscrutable, opium, amiable,*

bespectacled, embezzle, endeavors. Once you have looked up the meanings of these words, decide which of them fit your definition of a model minority. What makes these words positive, in your opinion? The remaining words should be looked over carefully. Why didn't you choose them? Do they have a negative meaning to you, or are they merely part of each human's reality?

2. Does Chiu's word usage reflect what we would expect of a writer from the model minority? What effect does Chiu's casual reference to crimes such as rape, robbery, drug use/sales, embezzlement, and murder—and the motivation behind each crime—have on a reader? Explain your position on Chiu's word use thoroughly.

Group Activities

1. Write a collaborative essay showing how the dominant stereotypes attributed to an ethnic group may never have been more than myths. Begin by brainstorming to come up with specific ethnic or gender stereotypes. Next, have each group member research a stereotype from a specific time period (like the 1940s), share his or her findings, and assemble the group essay.

2. Briefly share your knowledge about people like Charlie Chan, Fu Manchu, Madame Chiang Kai-Shek, as well as events like the Chinese Cultural Revolution, the student uprising at Tiananmen Square, the Korean War, and the Vietnam War. After your initial discussion, list other Chinese people who personify stereotypes of a given era. Also, try to think of one or two events involving people of Chinese origin in the last century, events which have prejudiced or typecast our perception of them.

Writing Activities

1. This article was written several years ago. At the time, Chiu asked, "Is the wind changing its direction again in 1988?" Here he was referring to the numerous stereotypes placed on the Chinese during

the past 60 years. Write an essay in which you devise a thesis that answers Chiu's question. Use illustrations and examples to support what you say.

2. Is there a model social, political, or religious minority in the United States today? What is it? Compose an original thesis on this issue and demonstrate the truth of it through the use of illustration and example.

Ann Scheid

Where Have All the Flowers Gone?: Is the Human Race Its Own Worst Enemy?

A Pittsburgh native, Scheid grew up in a family dedicated to letters and was constantly distressed about the environment in that area. After moving to California, she received a BA and MA in English and taught writing at several local two- and four-year colleges. A social and environmental activist since the 1960s, Scheid has written extensively on social matters ranging from overpopulation to the destruction of the rainforest. In the following essay, Scheid paints an apocalyptic picture of life on earth for future generations.

Pre-reading Questions

1. What do you consider "pollution"? Jot down as many types of pollution as you can, and share your list with your classmates. How were your responses similar and yet different?

2. Do you believe that the human race is capable of preserving this planet or destined to destroy it? Why?

---

1   Human beings are an irritant to Mother Nature, and in spite of the fact that it took their brains five million years to evolve, She can rid Herself of them in an instant. This, however, may not be necessary, since humans seem to be racing to see if they can save Her the trouble. They behave so arrogantly, contending they are superior to Nature. Rain forests are being cut down or burned—not only polluting the air but also causing a drop in oxygen levels. The love affair people have with their automobiles, especially "gas hog" SUV's, adds to the pollutants in the air and is, yet, another

nail in their coffins. Since prehistoric times, humans have been stalking and killing animals, causing many, beginning with the mastodon and saber-toothed tiger, to become extinct. Modern civilization is rushing headlong to slaughter animals in wholesale lots, all the while trying to prove its superiority to Mother Nature, usually with disastrous results.

2   For thousands of years, humans also have been defacing the earth, making scars upon the land. The Vikings overpopulated their own lands and thus depleted the natural resources, which caused them to look for new areas to take advantage of. They then moved on to Iceland, Greenland, and the New World. Also, the throngs of people who responded to the lure of gold in the Yukon, totally stripped mountainsides of trees above the Yukon River, to make rafts in order to sail 500 miles to Dawson. Forty percent never made it! In the populated areas of the Himalayas very few trees remain since the citizens have cut them down for cooking and heating fires. With most of the trees gone, erosion occurs on a large scale, washing away most of the topsoil, making food production difficult. Even more disturbing is the fact that, due to large-scale cutting, the famous cedars of Lebanon, mentioned in the Bible, no longer exist. Along the same lines, so much of the rain forest in Panama is being destroyed that scientists are predicting the Panama Canal could fill with silt, thus prohibiting ships from crossing the isthmus, due to the effects of deforestation.

3   Deforestation and erosion, along with changing weather patterns, have led to the fastest-growing regions on this planet—deserts. All the while, populations are exploding worldwide and the proliferation of deserts means there is less arable land to feed the increasing number of people. Starvation on a massive scale will run rampant, and whenever a noted ecologist or environmentalist sends out warnings about such dangers to human life, very few consider giving up any of their conveniences. For instance, the holes in the ozone layer are getting larger, allowing more ultraviolet rays to hit the Earth, which often leads to skin cancer. Knowing this fact, many people still do nothing about the emissions that cause this to happen. They insist on using aerosols and traveling one-to-a-car, thus adding to the emissions, which cause the ozone holes to expand, leading to more cases of skin cancer—a vicious cycle, indeed.

4   To make matters even more critical, global warming is becoming an ever-increasing threat to the existence of humans and animals. Polar icecaps are melting, and sections the size of the state of Rhode Island are breaking off. Traveling toward the Temperate Zones, they begin to melt, placing an inordinate

amount of fresh water into the oceans and causing an imbalance. In the North Atlantic, this would affect the Gulf Stream, which warms the British Isles. The fresh water would force the salt water to greater depths and inhibit the flow of the Gulf Stream. Great Britain would be plunged into an ice age, killing many animals and, undoubtedly, causing a mass exodus south. Sea levels also would rise; countries, such as The Netherlands and Bangla Desh would be flooded since both of them are at exactly sea level or below. The people who flee from these areas, along with those from the British Isles, would further crowd the remaining lands. It is predicted that sea level could rise 200 feet in the future, thus wiping out all coastal areas around the world, forcing more people to move inland.

5   Humans further complicate their lives by allowing businesses to release pollutants in urban areas, in the name of profit. "Accidents" often take place at refineries where toxic fumes are released into the air that people and animals breathe. Pesticides are so widely used and pose such a threat that it is amazing all of them haven't been banned. When DDT was sprayed on plants, many birds died as a result. It was taken out of circulation, but even more powerful ones have been developed. The farming industry uses great amounts of pesticides. The toxins leach into the soil and contaminate the ground water. In California's Central Valley farm workers and their families have a higher rate of birth defects and cancer than areas not using pesticides. Chemical companies beside rivers are allowed to release their toxins into the water. In Southwestern Pennsylvania, it was discovered that the temperature of the water below such a factory was 183 degrees—in January! Another time that same river was so polluted that the chemicals on the surface caught fire! Even more disastrous is the fact that the area uses water from that river for drinking.

6   Governments, anxious to appease money-hungry corporations and their stockholders, have allowed timber companies into National Forests to cut virgin-growth trees. Most of these businesses clear cut vast areas and often wait an inordinate amount of time to replant. Clear cutting leaves another scar upon the land in their most treasured and scenic areas and also leads to erosion. At the same time, the government is also considering giving permission for oil companies to drill in those sacred lands. Their rigs are hideously ugly and will mar the views for every visitor. Clear cutting and oil drilling also will interfere with the habitats of animals which inhabit our National Parks and Forests.

7   Experts have estimated that 200 species of plants and animals become extinct each day. This, for instance, can be caused by over fishing, either by enormous processing ships that scoop up thousands of fish at a time and freeze them at sea, or by fishing fleets. The U.S. Navy has contributed to the deaths of whales and dolphins with its new sonar. Marine biologists have examined the dead animals, and their ears had hemorrhaged, making them deaf and killing most of them. In the past, ranchers and farmers have contributed to the demise of the wolf in the lower 48 states when they were offered money for each wolf carcass produced. One of the most shameful acts committed by humans was the killing of millions of buffalo in the mid-1800's—for sport. People would shoot them from trains, and the animals would rot by the tracks. No one used the animals for clothes or food.

8   One hundred fifty years later, there are only a few buffalo alive, and coral reefs, which are composed of skeletons secreted by certain marine polyps, are beginning to experience the same fate. Due to a change in temperature in the oceans, pollutants, and the looting of coral by "collectors," ten percent of the reefs are now dead. By 2020, fifty percent will have died if nothing is done, yet divers think only of the profit they will make from the coral jewelry, and polluters think only of the money they will save by not disposing of toxics properly, and factories think only of not having to spend money to purify the emissions.

9   Burning questions never cease: When will governments— local, state, and federal—corporations, and the rest of the human race realize what is happening to this planet? When will the race for profit cease to consume them? Perhaps it will come about when there is no land left to farm and feed the burgeoning population, or there is no clean water left to drink, or wildlife to balance the ecosystem, or, more importantly, when their children start dying. By that time, however, it probably will be too late.

Post-reading Questions

Content

1. Identify the thesis in Scheid's essay. How does it provide the guiding focus for her discussion?
2. How have humans defaced the earth and destroyed its life forms? How long has this been a pattern of human behavior toward Nature? What examples does Scheid use to illustrate her argument?

   3. To whom does the author seem to be appealing?
   4. What could happen as a result of global warming and melting polar icecaps?
   5. According to the author, how many species of plant and animal life become extinct each day?

Strategies and Structures

   1. Explain the strategic purpose and ultimate effect of capitalizing the "m" and "n" in Mother Nature, as well as Scheid's upper case pronoun references such as "She" and "Her."
   2. Scheid cites several authorities, facts, and statistics as she presents her argument. Which supporting information do you find most and least convincing? Why?
   3. Scheid writes her essay using third person point of view; why is this most appropriate to her subject matter and objective for writing her essay? What might have been lost if she had chosen to write the same essay from a first or second person point of view? Explain your reasoning.
   4. How does the author create and re-enforce the believability of her thesis through the extensive use of historical and current examples of the human race's interaction with the environment and its creatures?
   5. Why do you imagine that Scheid decided to offer her readers two rhetorical questions in the final paragraph before the concluding remarks to her essay? What is she inviting the reader to do?

Language and Vocabulary

   1. Vocabulary: *apocalyptic, irritant, inordinate, ecosystem, arrogantly, depleted, erosion, isthmus, deforestation, arable, ultraviolet rays, exodus, pollutants, burgeoning, proliferation, rampant, ozone, aerosol.* Most of the vocabulary words for this essay fall into one of two categories: general vocabulary words, and those words which specifically illustrate and explain the topic at hand: threats to the environment. After looking up the vocabulary words in your dictionary, separate them into the appropriate groups, and write one pro and one con (if possible) paragraph about the threat to the environment.

2. Write a one-page summary of Scheid's essay using the vocabulary words listed in the Language and Vocabulary exercise number one.

Group Activities

1. Visit your college or university's Department of Environmental Studies, Natural Sciences, or Anthropology in small groups and interview faculty members. Prior to your visit, however, prepare a list of scripted interview questions or follow the advice of Kathleen Hudson in her essay, "Interviews: Stories That Make a Difference" (Chapter 6—Process Analysis). Present your findings to the rest of the class in an oral presentation.

2. Go to a computer-assisted classroom, pair off, and research one aspect of an environmental problem facing modern society. Before engaging in research, make sure that every pair in class explores a different issue. For example, one pair might research the issue of global warming; another pair might look into articles on the dwindling Amazon rainforests, and so on. Print your findings and write a collaborative essay with your partner, citing sources when appropriate. Finally, staple all your printed articles to your collaborative essay, and submit it to your instructor.

Writing Activities

1. Using illustration and example, develop an essay showing what readers can do to become environmentally conscientious.

2. Write a letter to a local or federal government official using illustration and example to argue how and why he/she is or is not doing a good job fighting for issues that affect the world around us (e.g., promoting bills encouraging practices to decrease the greenhouse effect, to safeguard wildlife habitats, to protect the planets from needless destruction, and so on), or to point out a clear need for immediate actions.

Stephanie Ericsson

The Ways We Lie

Excerpts from Stephanie Ericsson's works have frequently appeared in such magazines as the Utne Reader. *Her books include* Companion Through the Darkness: Dialogues on Grief *(1993) and* Companion into Dawn: Inner Dialogues on Loving *(1997). The following essay was composed from notes of the latter text.*

Pre-reading Questions

1. Before reading this essay, jot down what you consider to be a lie. How do you or someone you know justify lying? Is a lie ever preferable to the truth? When? Where? Explain.

2. Make a list of all the "little lies" people use throughout their daily lives—such as "I'm busy for lunch" or "I love your hair"—in order to avoid conflicts or confrontations.

---

1   The bank called today and I told them my deposit was in the mail, even though I hadn't written a check yet. It'd been a rough day. The baby I'm pregnant with decided to do aerobics on my lungs for two hours, our three-year-old daughter painted the living-room couch with lipstick, the IRS put me on hold for an hour, and I was late to a business meeting because I was tired.

2   I told my client the traffic had been bad. When my partner came home, his haggard face told me his day hadn't gone any better than mine, so when he asked, "How was your day?" I said, "Oh, fine," knowing that one more straw might break his back. A friend called and wanted to take me to lunch. I said I was busy. Four lies in the course of a day, none of which I felt the least bit guilty about.

3   We lie. We all do. We exaggerate, we minimize, we avoid confrontation, we spare people's feelings, we conveniently forget,

we keep secrets, we justify lying to the big-guy institutions. Like most people, I indulge myself in small falsehoods and still think of myself as an honest person. Sure I lie, but it doesn't hurt anything. Or does it?

4 I once tried going a whole week without telling a lie, and it was paralyzing. I discovered that telling the truth all the time is nearly impossible. It means living with some serious consequences: The bank charges me $60 in overdraft fees, my partner keels over when I tell him about my travails, my client fires me for telling her I didn't feel like being on time, and my friend takes it personally when I say I am not hungry. There must be some merit to lying.

5 But if I justify lying, what makes me different from slick politicians or the corporate robbers who raided the S & L industry? Saying it's okay to lie one way and not the other is hedging. I cannot seem to escape the voice deep inside me that tells me: When someone lies, someone loses.

6 What far-reaching consequences will I, or others, pay as a result of my lie? Will someone's trust be destroyed? Will someone else pay *my* penance because I ducked out? We must consider the *meaning of our actions.* Deception, lies, capital crimes, and misdemeanors all carry meanings. *Webster's* definition of a *lie* is specific: *1: a false statement or action especially made with the intent to deceive; 2: anything that gives or is meant to give a false impression.*

7 A definition like this implies that there are many, many ways to tell a lie. Here are just a few.

8 **The White Lie:** The white lie assumes that the truth will cause more damage than a simple, harmless untruth. Telling a friend he looks great when he looks like hell can be based on a decision that the friend needs a compliment more than a frank opinion. But, in effect, it is the liar deciding what is best for the lied to. Ultimately, it is a vote of no confidence. It is an act of subtle arrogance for anyone to decide what is best for someone else.

9 Yet not all circumstances are quite so cut-and-dried. Take, for instance, the sergeant in Vietnam who knew one of his men was killed in action but listed him as missing so that the man's family would receive indefinite compensation instead of the lump-sum pittance the military gives widows and children. His intent was honorable. Yet for twenty years this family kept their hopes alive, unable to move on to a new life.

10 **Facades:** We all put up facades to one degree or another. When I put on a suit to go to see a client, I feel as though I am

putting on another face, obeying the expectation that serious businesspeople wear suits rather than sweatpants. But I'm a writer. Normally, I get up, get the kid off to school, and sit at my computer in my pajamas until four in the afternoon. When I answer the phone, the caller thinks I'm wearing a suit (though the UPS man knows better).

11   But facades can be dangerous because they are used to seduce others into an illusion. For instance, I recently realized that a former friend was a liar. He presented himself with all the right looks and the right words and offered lots of new consciousness theories, fabulous books to read, and fascinating insights. Then I did some business with him, and the time came to pay me. He turned out to be all talk and no walk. I heard a plethora of reasonable excuses, including in-depth descriptions of the big break around the corner. In six months of work, I saw less than a hundred bucks. When I confronted him, he raised both eyebrows and tried to convince me that I'd heard him wrong, that he'd made no commitment to me. A simple investigation into his past revealed a crowded graveyard of disenchanted former friends.

12   **Ignoring the Plain Facts:** In the '60s, the Catholic Church in Massachusetts began hearing complaints that Father James Porter was sexually molesting children. Rather than relieving him of his duties, the ecclesiastical authorities simply moved him from one parish to another between 1960 and 1967, actually providing him with a fresh supply of unsuspecting families and innocent children to abuse. After treatment in 1967 for pedophilia, he went back to work, this time in Minnesota. The new diocese was aware of Father Porter's obsession with children, but they needed priests and recklessly believed treatment had cured him. More children were abused until he was relieved of his duties a year later. By his own admission, Porter may have abused as many as a hundred children.

13   Ignoring the facts may not in and of itself be a form of lying, but consider the context of the situation. If a lie is a false action done with the intent to deceive, then the Catholic Church's conscious covering for Porter created irreparable consequences. The church became a coperpetrator with Porter.

14   **Deflecting:** I've discovered that I can keep anyone from seeing the true me by being selectively blatant. I set a precedent of being up-front about intimate issues, but I never bring up the things I truly want to hide; I just let people assume I'm revealing everything. It's an effective way of hiding.

15   Any good liar knows that the way to perpetuate an untruth is to deflect attention from it. When Clarence Thomas exploded

with accusations that the Senate hearings were a "high-tech lynching," he simply switched the focus from a highly charged subject to a radioactive subject. Rather than defending himself, he took the offensive and accused the country of racism. It was a brilliant maneuver. Racism is now politically incorrect in official circles—unlike sexual harassment, which still rewards those who can get away with it.

16 Some of the most skillful deflectors are passive-aggressive people who, when accused of inappropriate behavior, refuse to respond to the accusations. This you-don't-exist stance infuriates the accuser, who, understandably, screams something obscene out of frustration. The trap is sprung and the act of deflection successful, because now the passive-aggressive person can indignantly say, "Who can talk to someone as unreasonable as you?" The real issue is forgotten and the sins of the original victim become the focus. Feeling guilty of name-calling, the victim is fully tamed and crawls into a hole, ashamed. I have watched this fighting technique work thousands of times in disputes between men and women, and what I've learned is that the real culprit is not necessarily the one who swears the loudest.

17 **Omission:** Omission involves telling most of the truth minus one or two key facts whose absence changes the story completely. You break a pair of glasses that are guaranteed under normal use and get a new pair, without mentioning that the first pair broke during a rowdy game of basketball. Who hasn't tried something like that? But what about the omission of information that could make a difference in how a person lives his or her life?

18 For instance, one day I found out that rabbinical legends tell of another woman in the Garden of Eden before Eve. I was stunned. The omission of the Sumerian goddess Lilith from Genesis—as well as her demonization by ancient misogynists as an embodiment of female evil—felt like spiritual robbery. I felt like I'd just found out my mother was really my stepmother. To take seriously the tradition that Adam was created out of the same mud as his equal counterpart, Lilith, redefines all of Judeo-Christian history.

19 Some renegade Catholic feminists introduced me to a view of Lilith that had been suppressed during the many centuries when this strong goddess was seen only as a spirit of evil. Lilith was a proud goddess who defied Adam's need to control her, attempted negotiations, and when this failed, said adios and left the Garden of Eden.

20 This omission of Lilith from the Bible was a patriarchal strategy to keep women weak. Omitting the strong-women archetype of Lilith from Western religions and starting the story

with Eve the Rib helped keep Christian and Jewish women believing they were the lesser sex for thousands of years.

21   **Stereotypes and Clichés:** Stereotype and cliché serve a purpose as a form of shorthand. Our need for vast amounts of information in nanoseconds has made the stereotype vital to modern
communication. Unfortunately, it often shuts down original
thinking, giving those hungry for the truth a candy bar of misin-
formation instead of a balanced meal. The stereotype explains a
situation with just enough truth to seem unquestionable. All the
"isms"—racism, sexism, ageism, et al.—are founded on and fueled by the stereotype and the cliché, which are lies of exaggeration, omission, and ignorance. They are always dangerous. They
take a single tree and make it a landscape. They destroy curiosity. They close minds and separate people. The single mother on
welfare is assumed to be cheating. Any black male could tell you
how much of his identity is obliterated daily by stereotypes. Fat
people, ugly people, beautiful people, old people, large-breasted
women, short men, the mentally ill, and the homeless all could
tell you how much more they are like us than we want to think. I
once admitted to a group of people that I had a mouth like a
truck driver. Much to my surprise, a man stood up and said, "I'm
a truck driver, and I never cuss." Needless to say, I was humbled.

22   **Groupthink:** Irving Janis, in *Victims of Group Think,*
defines this sort of lie as a psychological phenomenon within
decision-making groups in which loyalty to the group has become more important than any other value, with the result
that dissent and the appraisal of alternatives are suppressed.
If you've ever worked on a committee or in a corporation,
you've encountered groupthink. It requires a combination of
other forms of lying—ignorance of facts, selective memory,
omission, and denial, to name a few.

23   The textbook example of groupthink came on December 7,
1941. From as early as the fall of 1941, the warnings came in,
one after another, that Japan was preparing for a massive military operation. The Navy command in Hawaii assumed Pearl
Harbor was invulnerable—the Japanese weren't stupid
enough to attack the United States' most important base. On
the other hand, racist stereotypes said the Japanese weren't
smart enough to invent a torpedo effective in less than 60 feet
of water (the fleet was docked in 30 feet); after all, U.S. technology hadn't been able to do it.

24   On Friday, December 5, normal weekend leave was granted to
all the commanders at Pearl Harbor, even though the Japanese
consulate in Hawaii was busy burning papers. Within the tight,

good-ole-boy cohesiveness of the U.S. command in Hawaii, the myth of invulnerability stayed well entrenched. No one in the group considered the alternatives. The rest is history.

25   **Out-and-Out Lies:** Of all the ways to lie, I like this one the best, probably because I get tired of trying to figure out the real meanings behind things. At least I can trust the bald-faced lie. I once asked my five-year-old nephew, "Who broke the fence?" (I had seen him do it.) He answered, "The murderers." Who could argue?

26   At least when this sort of lie is told it can be easily confronted. As the person who is lied to, I know where I stand. The bald-faced lie doesn't toy with my perceptions—it argues with them. It doesn't try to refashion reality, it tries to refute it. *Read my lips . . .* No sleight of hand. No guessing. If this were the only form of lying, there would be no such thing as floating anxiety or the adult-children of alcoholics movement.

27   **Dismissal:** Dismissal is perhaps the slipperiest of all lies. Dismissing feelings, perceptions, or even the raw facts of a situation ranks as a kind of lie that can do as much damage to a person as any other kind of lie.

28   The roots of many mental disorders can be traced back to the dismissal of reality. Imagine that a person is told from the time she is a tot that her perceptions are inaccurate: *"Mommie, I'm scared."* "No you're not, darling." *"I don't like that man next door, he makes me feel icky."* "Johnny, that's a terrible thing to say, of course you like him. You go over there right now and be nice to him."

29   I've often mused over the idea that madness is actually a sane reaction to an insane world. Psychologist R. D. Laing supports this hypothesis in *Sanity, Madness & The Family,* an account of his investigation into the families of schizophrenics. The common thread that ran through all of the families he studied was a deliberate, staunch dismissal of the patient's perceptions from a very early age. Each of the patients started out with an accurate grasp of reality, which, through meticulous and methodical dismissal, was demolished until the only reality the patient could trust was catatonia.

30   Dismissal runs the gamut. Mild dismissal can be quite handy for forgiving the foibles of others in our day-to-day lives. Toddlers who have just learned to manipulate their parents' attention sometimes are dismissed out of necessity. Absolute attention from the parents would require so much energy that no one would get to eat dinner. But we must be careful and attentive about how far we take our "necessary" dismissals. Dismissal is a dangerous tool, because it's nothing less than a lie.

31   **Delusion:** I could write a book on this one. Delusion, a cousin of dismissal, is the tendency to see excuses as facts. It's a powerful lying tool because it filters out information that contradicts what we want to believe. Alcoholics who believe the problems in their lives are legitimate reasons for drinking rather than results of the drinking offer the classic example of deluded thinking. Delusion uses the mind's ability to see things in myriad ways to support what it wants to be the truth.

32   But delusion is also a survival mechanism we all use. If we were to fully contemplate the consequences of our stockpiles of nuclear weapons or global warming, we could hardly function on a day-to-day level. We don't want to incorporate that much reality into our lives because to do so would be paralyzing.

33   Delusion works as an adhesive to keep the status quo intact. It shamelessly employs dismissal, omission, and amnesia, among other sorts of lies. Its most cunning defense is that it cannot see itself.

34   These are only a few of the ways we lie. Or are lied to. As I said earlier, it's not easy to entirely eliminate lies in our daily lives. No matter how pious we may try to be, we will still embellish, hedge, and omit to lubricate the daily machinery of living. But there is a world of difference between telling functional lies and living a lie. Martin Buber once said, "The lie is the spirit committing treason against itself." Our acceptance of lies becomes a cultural cancer that eventually shrouds and reorders reality until moral garbage becomes as invisible to us as water is to a fish.

35   How much do we tolerate before we become sick and tired of being sick and tired? When will we stand up and declare our *right* to trust? When do we stop accepting that the real truth is in the fine print? Whose lips do we read this year when we vote for president? When will we stop being so reticent about making judgments? When do we stop turning over our personal power and responsibility to liars?

36   Maybe if I don't tell the bank the check's in the mail I'll be less tolerant of the lies told me every day. A country song I once heard said it all for me: "You've got to stand for something or you'll fall for anything."

Post-reading Questions

Content

1. According to Ericsson, what are the kinds of lies we all tell?

2. What does Ericsson assume about the "white lie"?
3. Why are facades destructive?
4. Why does she say, "Of all the ways to lie I like this one [the out-and-out lie] the best . . . "?
5. What is the author's definition of delusion?

Strategies and Structures

1. What is the purpose of Ericsson's anecdote at the beginning of the essay?
2. Ericsson divides lies into several categories. In what way do her topic sentences frame her discussion of each type of lie? How does she illustrate the different categories of lies that she has devised?
3. There are three major parts to this essay. Identify them and explain their strategic purposes.
4. An author oftentimes uses a rhetorical question when he or she wishes to present an idea for consideration with no intention of receiving an answer from the readers. What are some of the rhetorical questions Ericsson uses in this essay, and how does she answer them?

Language and Vocabulary

1. Vocabulary: *haggard, pittance, facade, plethora, dioceses, perpetuate, harassment, Sumerian, Genesis, renegade, negotiations, patriarchal, psychological phenomenon, adhesive, staunch, amnesia, embellish, gamut.* Oftentimes when we write, word choices can indicate or suggest meaning or meanings beyond their literal definition. Go through the list of words above and show how the words you selected go beyond the dictionary meaning. Explain how these words give additional insight that just a dictionary could not provide.
2. Write a definition of each of the lies that Ericsson presents in this essay without referring back to the essay or to a dictionary or thesaurus.

Group Activities

1. In small groups, brainstorm your own categories of lies and then provide examples of each type of lie you come up with.

2. Divide into pairs and write a brief skit—a dialogue between two people dramatizing some "common lies" that people tell on a daily basis. Draw on personal experience and readings for additional material. Finally, after you present your skit to the rest of the class and get feedback from your classmates, write a collaborative paper with your partner analyzing the nature and effects of telling extemporaneous or premeditated lies. (You may have ended up using both in your sketch!)

Writing Activities

1. Have you ever been a victim of a lie of "delusion" at school, at work, or at home? What occurred? How did you come to terms with the lie? Write a short essay in which you reflect back and examine your experience. Use specific examples to illustrate how and why lies of "delusion" have been harmful to you.

2. Write an essay in which you offer your own categories of lies, providing examples to support your thesis. Use Group Activity 1 to generate ideas. You may wish to construct your paper much like Ericsson's with a definite introduction, the body consisting of your lies and an analysis of the lies you have categorized, and a conclusion wherein you reach some insight into the entire nature of lying.

Additional Topics and Issues for Illustration and Example Essays

1. Painters or sketchers often are called illustrators. Find a painting or drawing, either in a museum or a book, and in an essay describe what the artist is attempting to illustrate.

2. Attend a meeting of the student government body on your campus or a city council meeting where you live and, through illustration and example, write a composition showing what issues were discussed and how they were resolved. Show how the interactions among the members of the council contributed to the resolutions.

3. Illustrate what it is like (or what you believe it would be like) to work in a fast-food restaurant. Remember your ob-

jective: You want to paint a vivid picture using words so your reader will be able to visualize what you are saying.

4. More and more frequently, people do not want to go out at night since they are afraid of being attacked. To what extent is this fear justified? Using examples and observations drawn from personal experience, develop a thesis supporting your point of view on this issue.

5. Illustrate the differences between what we refer to as "civilized" societies and those which are "underdeveloped" or "primitive." In order to avoid stereotyping, support every general point with at least two specific examples.

6. Construct an essay wherein you illustrate the benefits of using animals, instead of humans, to test the effects of new drugs, wonder cures, and cosmetics. If you believe such a practice is inhumane, illustrate the negative side of this issue. Make sure you illustrate what you believe using specific examples; do not just tell your reader what you think.

7. Construct a paper illustrating and exemplifying the reasons one should pursue higher education, a corporate management position, or a political office. Be sure to supply readers with plenty of representative examples that demonstrate and support each discussion point.

8. Providing illustrations and examples drawn from personal experiences, observations, and readings, write an essay demonstrating how human beings can be insensitive and indifferent to the wants and needs of others. A variation of this same assignment might be to show how most people are compassionate and caring rather than cold and indifferent.

9. Illustrate what people can do to help stop the extinction of plants and animals by showing what will come about in the absence of them. If need be, do some research on the internet, or at your college library. To add greater authority to your essay, be sure to cite reputable sources of information, using parenthetical footnotes, as well as a list of Works Cited, see the end of Mark Charles Fissel's essay, "Online Learning and Student Success" pp. 445.

10. Write an essay in which you illustrate the realities—both good and bad—of the mall culture, freeway culture, hiphop culture, and so on. Provide a wide variety of examples, followed by an analysis to thoroughly explain each subpoint of your thesis.

5

Definition

Definition plays an important part in the development of most
expository essays. Why? Without a clear definition of terms, a
reader will have only a vague idea of what you are writing
about. Specifically defining whom and what you are explaining
will help you, the writer, focus on your goals, giving you less
opportunity to digress and wander.

Often writers define a problem, a group or subgroup, a concept, a place, another person, or themselves. By defining these
things, writers may wish to call certain problems or concepts to
the reader's attention or to dispel a currently popular definition and supply his or her own definition. For example, Jo Goodwin Parker defines "poverty" in order to call the reader's
attention to the problems of the poor: hunger, dirt, and despair.
On the other hand, Isaac Asimov writes his essay "What Is Intelligence, Anyway?" to dispel the myth that all intelligence
can be measured and evaluated in an academic setting. To Asimov, a person's intelligence is based on the situation (e.g., the
author is intelligent at the university but not at the auto repair shop).

For whatever reasons you define something, you should be
careful and concerned about how you define. For example,
people often define themselves cautiously so as to be perceived in positive ways. In the 1987 campaign for the presi-
dency, George Bush did not originally want to use the line
"Read my lips" because no previous U.S. president had ever
mentioned parts of the human body in a debate or campaign
speech. Because of this, he did not want to be defined as peculiar or immoral.

Writers have many techniques available to them when they create a definition; that is, they can arrange and develop their definitions in a variety of ways. However, all good writers realize that definition essays require them to do a considerable amount of research and prewriting before they can even begin to organize their thoughts in a coherent fashion. Once the preliminary steps have been completed, the writer is ready to organize his or her major discussion points: supporting material that helps define the topic or issue. Some of the most common techniques writers use when they create definitions are discussed next.

Definition by Example

Often authors will offer a definition of a term, issue, or topic by giving examples and descriptions. For example, in her essay "What Is Poverty?" Parker explains poverty to us by offering examples of her own poverty-stricken life. *"Let me explain about housekeeping with no money. For breakfast I give my children grits with no oleo or cornbread without eggs and oleo. This does not use up many dishes. What dishes there are, I wash in cold water and with no soap. . . . Look at my hands, so cracked and red."* These examples solidify the definition of poverty in a graphic way for the reader.

Definition by History

Another technique that will aid in creating a definition is to offer the history of the term, issue, or topic being defined. By creating a historical context, the writer establishes where a term, issue, or topic has come from and how it has developed, what its uses have been throughout history, and how it has evolved. Historically, to explain how the perpetuation of a clear and present danger can unify people, Gard E. Norberg notes that if one substituted 'Athenians' for 'Americans,' in the quote, *"'People grow angry when they suffer things that they are unused to, and plunge into action on the spur of their impulse. [Americans] are especially likely to act this way, since they think they have a right to supremacy and are more used to destroying other people's land than seeing this happen to their own,'"* he or she *"might recognize the quote from Thucyldides'* History of the Peloponnesian War. *As that macho Florentine,*

Niccolo Machiavelli, observed some 2000 years later, there is nothing like fear to unite a people behind their Prince."

Definition by Comparison or Contrast

It is often useful to define an unknown term, issue, or concept by comparing or contrasting it with a known term, issue, or concept. The writer will take advantage of what the audience knows already to create a clear definition of what it may not know. Guillermo Gómez-Peña in his essay "Documented/ Undocumented," contrasts his definition of himself and his culture with the definitions found in other cultures. *"I am Mexican but I am also Chicano and Latin American. At the border they call me* chilango *or* mexiquillo; *in Mexico City, it's* pocho *or* norteño; *and in Europe it's* sudaca. *The Anglos call me 'Hispanic' or 'Latino'. . . ."*

Definition by Negation

Another way to write a definition paper, though a bit more difficult, is through negation, which is explaining what something is *not*. (This sometimes proves useful in developing an argumentative essay, too.) By clearly stating what qualities, characteristics, or concepts something lacks, a writer can create a clear picture of what something is. Often writers will disprove a popular definition, notion, or myth about something as they set up a different definition of their own. For example, in "Does America Still Exist?" Richard Rodriguez argues that the "ideal" America is *not* what Americans believe it is.

In whatever way you decide to develop your definition, remember that definitions are a way to clarify your ideas, concepts, and issues. Writers often use a definition to call the reader's attention to a problem or to offer a counter-definition to a popular notion.

Tips on Writing Definition Essays

1. First, ask yourself questions to limit your topic. What do you want to define? Why do you want to define it? Freewrite about your topic or issue in order to focus on what you want to define. Remember, an unfocused topic or issue will lead to a vague or unclear definition.

2. Next, gather information from a variety of sources that will aid in the development of your definition.

3. Organize your definition paper so that it has a clear pattern. If the reader must guess at what you are attempting to define and how you will define it, he or she may become confused or misinterpret your purpose.

4. Fully develop your definition with examples and specifics. You may find the strategies for development listed above useful.

5. As you proofread your essay prior to writing the final copy, ask yourself, "What is my purpose for writing this paper? Do my examples clearly illustrate the term, concept, or issue that I am defining? Where would additional examples strengthen my definition?"

6. Keep in mind that you are writing for a reader who may not be familiar with the term, topic, or issue you are defining. Your development with examples will create concrete meaning for the reader.

Isaac Asimov

What Is Intelligence, Anyway?

Born in the Soviet Union, Isaac Asimov immigrated with his parents to the United States in 1923 and earned a doctorate from Columbia University. A well-respected writer on general science, Asimov has published numerous books and is one of the most prolific science-fiction writers of the twentieth century. His works of fiction and nonfiction include I, Robot *(1950),* The Foundation Trilogy *(1951–53),* The Stars in Their Courses *(1976),* The Gods Themselves *(1977),* Isaac Asimov: The Complete Stories *(1990),* The Best Science Fiction of Isaac Asimov *(1991),* Isaac Asimov's Guide to Earth and Space *(1992),* Asimov Laughs Again: More Than 700 Favorite Jokes, Limericks, and Anecdotes *(1993), and* The Exploding Suns: The Secrets of Supernovas *(1996), to name a few.*

Pre-reading Questions

1. What qualities do you associate with intelligence? If you have trouble thinking of specific things, freewrite or cluster the word.

2. What is a fair test of intelligence? Should people who work in different occupations take different tests to measure their knowledge?

---

1   What is intelligence, anyway? When I was in the army I received a kind of aptitude test that all soldiers took and, against a normal of 100, scored 160. No one at the base had ever seen a figure like that, and for two hours they made a big fuss over me. (It didn't mean anything. The next day I was still a buck private with KP as my highest duty.)

2   All my life I've been registering scores like that, so that I have the complacent feeling that I'm highly intelligent, and I expect other people to think so, too. Actually, though, don't such scores simply mean that I am very good at answering the type of academic questions that are considered worthy of answers by the people who make up the intelligence tests— people with intellectual bents similar to mine?

3   For instance, I had an auto-repair man once, who, on these intelligence tests, could not possibly have scored more than 80, by my estimate. I always took it for granted that I was far more intelligent than he was. Yet, when anything went wrong with my car I hastened to him with it, watched him anxiously as he explored its vitals, and listened to his pronouncements as though they were divine oracles—and he always fixed my car.

4   Well, then, suppose my auto-repair man devised questions for an intelligence test. Or suppose a carpenter did, or a farmer, or, indeed, almost anyone but an academician. By every one of those tests, I'd prove myself a moron. And I'd *be* a moron, too. In a world where I could not use my academic training and my verbal talents but had to do something intricate or hard, working with my hands, I would do poorly. My intelligence, then, is not absolute but is a function of the society I live in and of the fact that a small subsection of that society has managed to foist itself on the rest as an arbiter of such matters.

5   Consider my auto-repair man, again. He had a habit of telling me jokes whenever he saw me. One time he raised his head from under the automobile hood to say: "Doc, a deaf-and-dumb guy went into a hardware store to ask for some nails. He put two fingers together on the counter and made hammering motions with the other hand. The clerk brought him a hammer. He shook his head and pointed to the two fingers he was hammering. The clerk brought him nails. He picked out the sizes he wanted, and left. Well, doc, the next guy who came in was a blind man. He wanted scissors. How do you suppose he asked for them?"

6   Indulgently, I lifted my right hand and made scissoring motions with my first two fingers. Whereupon my auto-repair man laughed raucously and said, "Why, you dumb jerk, he used his voice and asked for them." Then he said, smugly, "I've been trying that on all my customers today." "Did you catch many?" I asked. "Quite a few," he said, "but I knew for sure I'd catch you." "Why is that?" I asked. "Because you're so goddamned educated, doc, I *knew* you couldn't be very smart."

7   And I have an uneasy feeling he had something there.

Post-reading Questions

Content
1. According to Asimov, what is intelligence?
2. What sort of intelligence does Asimov, an academic, have? Is it any better than the intelligence of the auto mechanic or blue-collar worker? Why?
3. How did Asimov value IQ tests at the start of his essay, and what made him reconsider his position?

Strategies and Structures
1. Why does Asimov include several short episodes in this paper (e.g., time in the army, a trip to an automobile mechanic)? How do they assist him in defining *intelligence?*
2. What would happen if Asimov placed his trip to the automobile mechanic prior to his discussion of his performance on IQ tests? Why do you think he arranged his material as he did?
3. What might have been Asimov's strategic purpose for concluding his essay with a one-sentence paragraph?

Language and Vocabulary
1. Vocabulary: *KP, complacent, indulgently.* Outside of KP (*kitchen police*), the other two vocabulary words deal with qualities associated with someone who is lacking intelligence. What other characteristics do you associate with an unintelligent person? Write a list of them, and, through repeated usage for at least three days, make them a part of your everyday speech.
2. How many of Asimov's words *sound* intelligent? Make some sort of chart of important-sounding or scholastic words (be sure you know their definitions) and spend a day consciously using them whenever you have an opportunity. How did others react to your use of words? Did using *big* words make you feel more or less intelligent? Why?

Group Activities
1. In pairs, in much the same way as Asimov reported his conversations with his mechanic, visit a person who runs a business neither of you knows anything

about and, together, write a summation of this person's intelligence. In what areas do you feel superior to this person, and in what ways is his or her intelligence superior to your own?

2. After the class has been divided into four or five groups, have each group member write down three things he or she knows little about as well as three things he or she knows much about. Compare notes and find a common element of expertise in your group (e.g., math, "street smarts," science, philosophy). Next, make up an intelligence quiz based on questions from your group's area of expertise (ten questions), and make copies of it for the rest of the class. Finally, with the exception of your own, take each group's intelligence quiz, correct them all as a class, and graph the results for each test. What do the results imply about intelligence tests? Did the outcome of the class exercise confirm Asimov's conclusions about IQ tests? How?

Writing Activities

1. Write an essay defining your own conception of intelligence. As Asimov has done, cite some specific instances that demonstrate how and why your definition is valid. Feel free to refer to Group Activity 2.

2. Make up a list of the qualities you associate with stupidity, lunacy, or another human characteristic. Focus on a recurring theme from your list and use it as the controlling idea in an essay defining your topic.

Jo Goodwin Parker

What Is Poverty?

*When Jo Goodwin Parker originally published this article, she
preferred that the editor present no byline. In keeping with the spirit
of its initial publication, we have decided to reprint Parker's article
without any biographical data about its author.*

Pre-reading Questions

1. Write a three-sentence definition of *poverty*. Who are the
poor? Why are they poor? Where do the poor usually live?
What problems must poor people overcome?

2. What are your feelings about poor people? Do you feel superior to them? Do they make you feel angry? Do they
make you feel despair? Do you try to help them? If so,
why? If not, why not?

---

1   You ask me what is poverty? Listen to me. Here I am, dirty,
smelly, and with no "proper" underwear on and with the stench
of my rotting teeth near you. I will tell you. Listen to me. Listen without pity. I cannot use your pity. Listen with understanding. Put yourself in my dirty, worn out, ill-fitting shoes,
and hear me.

2   Poverty is getting up every morning from a dirt- and illness-
stained mattress. The sheets have long since been used for diapers. Poverty is living in a smell that never leaves. This is a
smell of urine, sour milk, and spoiling food sometimes joined
with the strong smell of long-cooked onions. Onions are cheap.
If you have smelled this smell, you did not know how it came.
It is the smell of the outdoor privy. It is the smell of young children who cannot walk the long dark way in the night. It is the
smell of the mattress where years of "accidents" have happened. It is the smell of the milk which has gone sour because

the refrigerator long has not worked, and it costs money to get it fixed. It is the smell of rotting garbage. I could bury it, but where is the shovel? Shovels cost money.

3   Poverty is being tired. I have always been tired. They told me at the hospital when the last baby came that I had chronic anemia caused from poor diet, a bad case of worms, and that I needed a corrective operation. I listened politely—the poor are always polite. The poor always listen. They don't say that there is no money for iron pills, or better food, or worm medicine. The idea of an operation is frightening and costs so much that, if I had dared, I would have laughed. Who takes care of my children? Recovery from an operation takes a long time. I have three children. When I left them with "Granny" the last time I had a job, I came home to find the baby covered with fly specks, and a diaper that had not been changed since I left. When the dried diaper came off, bits of my baby's flesh came with it. My other child was playing with a sharp bit of broken glass, and my oldest was playing alone at the edge of a lake. I made twenty-two dollars a week, and a good nursery school costs twenty dollars a week for three children. I quit my job.

4   Poverty is dirt. You can say in your clean clothes coming from your clean house, "Anybody can be clean." Let me explain about housekeeping with no money. For breakfast I give my children grits with no oleo or cornbread without eggs and oleo. This does not use up many dishes. What dishes there are, I wash in cold water and with no soap. Even the cheapest soap has to be saved for the baby's diapers. Look at my hands, so cracked and red. Once I saved for two months to buy a jar of Vaseline for my hands and the baby's diaper rash. When I had saved enough, I went to buy it and the price had gone up two cents. The baby and I suffered on. I have to decide every day if I can bear to put my cracked sore hands into the cold water and strong soap. But you ask, why not hot water? Fuel costs money. If you have a wood fire it costs money. If you burn electricity, it costs money. Hot water is a luxury. I do not have luxuries. I know you will be surprised when I tell you how young I am. I look so much older. My back has been bent over the wash tubs every day for so long, I cannot remember when I ever did anything else. Every night I wash every stitch my school age child has on and just hope her clothes will be dry by morning.

5   Poverty is staying up all night on cold nights to watch the fire knowing one spark on the newspaper covering the walls means your sleeping child dies in flames. In summer poverty is watching gnats and flies devour your baby's tears when he

cries. The screens are torn and you pay so little rent you know they will never be fixed. Poverty means insects in your food, in your nose, in your eyes, and crawling over you when you sleep. Poverty is hoping it never rains because diapers won't dry when it rains and soon you are using newspapers. Poverty is seeing your children forever with runny noses. Paper handkerchiefs cost money and all your rags you need for other things. Even more costly are antihistamines. Poverty is cooking without food and cleaning without soap.

6   Poverty is asking for help. Have you ever had to ask for help, knowing your children will suffer unless you get it? Think about asking for a loan from a relative, if this is the only way you can imagine asking for help. I will tell you how it feels. You find out where the office is that you are supposed to visit. You circle that block four or five times. Thinking of your children, you go in. Everyone is very busy. Finally, someone comes out and you tell her that you need help. That never is the person you need to see. You go see another person, and after spilling the whole shame of your poverty all over the desk between you, you find that this isn't the right office after all— you must repeat the whole process, and it never is any easier at the next place.

7   You have asked for help, and after all it has a cost. You are again told to wait. You are told why, but you don't really hear because of the red cloud of shame and the rising cloud of despair.

8   Poverty is remembering. It is remembering quitting school in junior high because "nice" children had been so cruel about my clothes and my smell. The attendance officer came. My mother told him I was pregnant. I wasn't, but she thought that I could get a job and help out. I had jobs off and on, but never long enough to learn anything. Mostly I remember being married. I was so young then. I am still young. For a time, we had all the things you have. There was a little house in another town, with hot water and everything. Then my husband lost his job. There was unemployment insurance for a while and what few jobs I could get. Soon, all our nice things were repossessed and we moved back here. I was pregnant then. This house didn't look so bad when we first moved in. Every week it gets worse. Nothing is ever fixed. We now had no money. There were a few odd jobs for my husband, but everything went for food then, as it does now. I don't know how we lived through three years and three babies, but we did. I'll tell you something, after the last baby I destroyed my marriage. It had been a good one, but could you keep on bringing children in this dirt? Did you ever

think how much it costs for any kind of birth control? I knew my husband was leaving the day he left, but there were no good-byes between us. I hope he has been able to climb out of this mess somewhere. He never could hope with us to drag him down.

9   That's when I asked for help. When I got it, you know how much it was? It was, and is, seventy-eight dollars a month for the four of us; that is all I ever can get. Now you know why there is no soap, no needles and thread, no hot water, no aspirin, no worm medicine, no hand cream, no shampoo. None of these things forever and ever and ever. So that you can see clearly, I pay twenty dollars a month rent, and most of the rest goes for food. For grits and cornmeal, and rice and milk and beans. I try my best to use only the minimum electricity. If I use more, there is that much less for food.

10   Poverty is looking into a black future. Your children won't play with my boys. They will turn to other boys who steal to get what they want. I can already see them behind the bars of their prison instead of behind the bars of my poverty. Or they will turn to the freedom of alcohol or drugs, and find themselves enslaved. And my daughter? At best, there is for her a life like mine.

11   But you say to me, there are schools. Yes, there are schools. My children have no extra books, no magazines, no extra pencils, or crayons, or paper and most important of all, they do not have health. They have worms, they have infections, they have pink-eye all summer. They do not sleep well on the floor, or with me in my one bed. They do not suffer from hunger, my seventy-eight dollars keep us alive, but they do suffer from malnutrition. Oh yes, I do remember what I was taught about health in school. It doesn't do much good. In some places there is a surplus commodities program. Not here. The country said it cost too much. There is a school lunch program. But I have two children who will already be damaged by the time they get to school.

12   But, you say to me, there are health clinics. Yes, there are health clinics and they are in the towns. I live out here eight miles from town. I can walk that far (even if it is sixteen miles both ways), but can my little children? My neighbor will take me when he goes; but he expects to get paid, *one way or another.* I bet you know my neighbor. He is that large man who spends his time at the gas station, the barbershop, and the corner store complaining about the government spending money on the immoral mothers of illegitimate children.

13   Poverty is an acid that drips on pride until all pride is worn away. Poverty is a chisel that chips on honor until honor is worn away. Some of you say that you would do *something* in my situation, and maybe you would, for the first week or the first month, but for year after year after year?

14   Even the poor can dream. A dream of a time when there is money. Money for the right kinds of food, for worm medicine, for iron pills, for toothbrushes, for hand cream, for a hammer and nails and a bit of screening, for a shovel, for a bit of paint, for some sheeting, for needles and thread. Money to pay in *money* for a trip to town. And, oh, money for hot water and money for soap. A dream of when asking for help does not eat away the last bit of pride. When the office you visit is as nice as the offices of other governmental agencies, when there are enough workers to help you quickly, when workers do not quit in defeat and despair. When you have to tell your story to only one person, and that person can send you for other help and you don't have to prove your poverty over and over and over again.

15   I have come out of my despair to tell you this. Remember I did not come from another place or another time. Others like me are all around you. Look at us with an angry heart, anger that will help you help me. Anger that will let you tell of me. The poor are always silent. Can you be silent too?

Post-reading Questions

Content

1. What does Parker claim poverty is? Look at the beginning of each paragraph for some specific definitions. Next, jot down her definitions of poverty and compare them to the list you wrote as a pre-reading activity.

2. How is poverty difficult for Parker's children? List some specific examples.

3. In what ways does Parker try to obtain help, and what problems does she encounter?

4. Why are people's opinions and prejudices her greatest obstacles?

Strategies and Structures

1. What writing strategy does the author use at the beginning of most paragraphs? Do you notice a recurring pattern? What is it?

2. How does Parker develop each paragraph? What details make each paragraph memorable?
3. How does Parker defend her inability to get help? How does she discount the usual solution society has for poverty (e.g., welfare, education, and health clinics)? In the final paragraph, how does the author use questions to involve the reader in the issue of poverty?

Language and Vocabulary

1. Vocabulary: *chronic, immoral, illegitimate, antihistamines, enslaved.* Which of these words tend to produce a negative feeling in you? Why? Pick one of the negative words and cluster the feelings the word evokes. Save your list.
2. Note the author's use of adjectives to describe the subhuman conditions in which her family lives. For instance, instead of writing "Poverty is looking into a future," she writes, "Poverty is looking into a black future." How many other such adjectives can you find?

Group Activities

1. In small groups, go to one of the charity or social-welfare organizations in town and interview a social worker about the life of the poor. After this, determine whether Parker was exaggerating the problem.
2. As a group, create a realistic list of possible solutions to Parker's problem: poverty. Consider the possible role of government programs, charity organizations, and individual participation in your solution.

Writing Activities

1. Define a social problem (homelessness, sexism, racism) imitating Parker's style, beginning several of your paragraphs with "*your topic is . . .*" to define your topic or issue.
2. Using adjectives to highlight the futility of the situation, write a short definition essay on *Growing Up in Poverty.*

Guillermo
Gómez-Peña

Documented/Undocumented

*Besides writing, Guillermo Gómez-Peña works as a visual artist and
frequently dramatizes the dilemma of the "border-crosser" in the theater, on the radio, and through the cinema.* Gómez-Peña edited Made
in Aztlan: Centro Cultural de Raza *(1987), and his other works
include* Warrior for Gringostroika *(1993),* The New World Border:
Prophecies, Poems, & Loqueras for the End of the Century *(1996),*
Dangerous Border Crossers: The Artist Talks Back *(2000) and—
along with Enrique Chagoya—*Friendly Cannibal *(1996).* Temple of
Confessions: Mexican Beasts and Living Santos, *written with
Roberto Sifuentes, was published in November 1996. The following
essay, which initially appeared in the* L.A. Weekly *in 1988, was
translated by Ruben Martínez.*

Pre-reading Questions

1. What images of Mexican Americans do we find on television and in the newspapers? Who are they? Where are
they from? What is their history? When did they become a
part of American history? How are they perceived by the
rest of society? As a class, share your perceptions of this
culture. Remember these are only perceptions and not
hard-and-fast definitions.

2. In the essay you are about to read, Gómez-Peña defines himself as "a border-crosser." What do you think—without reading the essay—are the characteristics of a border-crosser?

1   I live smack in the fissure between two worlds, in the infected
wound: half a block from the end of Western Civilization and four
miles from the start of the Mexican–American border, the north-
ernmost point of Latin America. In my fractured reality, but a re-

ality nonetheless, there cohabit two histories, languages, cosmologies, artistic traditions, and political systems which are drastically counterposed. Many "deterritorialized" Latin American artists in Europe and the U. S. have opted for "internationalism" (a cultural identity based upon the "most advanced" of the ideas originating out of New York or Paris). I, on the other hand, opt for "borderness" and assume my role: My generation, the *chilangos* [slang term for a Mexico City native], who came to "el norte" fleeing the imminent ecological and social catastrophe of Mexico City, gradually integrated itself into otherness, in search of that other Mexico grafted onto the entrails of the et cetera . . . became Chicano-ized. We de-Mexicanized ourselves to Mexi-understand ourselves, some without wanting to, others on purpose. And one day, the border became our house, laboratory, and ministry of culture (or counterculture).

2   Today, eight years after my departure (from Mexico), when they ask me for my nationality or ethnic identity, I can't respond with one word, since my "identity" now possesses multiple repertories: I am Mexican but I am also Chicano and Latin American. At the border they call me *chilango* or *mexiquillo;* in Mexico City it's *pocho* or *norteño;* and in Europe it's *sudaca.* The Anglos call me "Hispanic" or "Latino," and the Germans have, on more than one occasion, confused me with Turks or Italians. My wife Emilia is Anglo-Italian, but speaks Spanish with an Argentine accent, and together we walk amid the rubble of the Tower of Babel of our American post-modernity.

3   The recapitulation of my personal and collective topography has become my cultural obsession since I arrived in the United States. I look for the traces of my generation, whose distance stretches not only from Mexico City to California, but also from the past to the future, from pre-Columbian America to high technology and from Spanish to English, passing through "Spanglish."

4   As a result of this process I have become a cultural topographer, border-crosser, and hunter of myths. And it doesn't matter where I find myself, in Califas or Mexico City, in Barcelona or West Berlin; I always have the sensation that I belong to the same species; the migrant tribe of the fiery pupils.

Post-reading Questions

Content

   1. What does Gómez-Peña mean when he begins his essay by writing, "I live smack in the fissure between two worlds, in the infected wound"? How might this

explain his sense of "fractured reality"? What do the
words "fractured reality" suggest?

2. What is the history of *chilangos?* Where are they
   originally from and where did they flee? Finally,
   why did they flee?

3. What names do others use when defining Gómez-
   Peña? What does he use when defining himself?

4. How does Gómez-Peña's definition of himself explain why he has "become a cultural topographer,
   border-crosser, and hunter of myths"?

Strategies and Structures

1. How does the opening sentence set the theme of the
   essay? What tension does it create? How does it
   limit the scope of the essay?

2. Gómez-Peña defines his "self" in two ways. What are
   they? How does he organize the essay around these
   two ways of defining one's self?

3. How does the title of Gómez-Peña's essay define his
   topic as a whole?

Language and Vocabulary

1. Vocabulary: *fissure, cohabit, cosmologies, counterposed, deterritorialized, ecological, post-modernity,
   recapitulation, topography.* After looking up the
   definitions in the dictionary, reread the essay. Does
   the topic take on a new meaning for you? Explain.

2. Using the word *topography,* make an essay map
   (see Glossary) of your own cultural background.

Group Activities

1. As a group, research one culture or social segment in
   the United States. What is its history? How have
   others used names to define this group? What
   names have members of this group used to define
   themselves? Be prepared to present your findings to
   the rest of the class.

2. Create a collage that defines your group. Use magazine photos, newspaper headlines, and so on. Finally,
   translate (define) your visual collage into the written
   language.

Writing Activities

1. Write a short essay in which you define yourself by providing the history of your family and by stating the perceptions others have of you. Here you might mention names and categories others use to label you.
2. Compose an essay in which you explain what you feel it means to grow up caught between two cultures, two realities.

Gard E. Norberg

Jingo Bells, Jingo Bells

After the September 11, 2001, attack on the World Trade Center in New York, the media fed United States citizens a steady diet of articles on moral indignation, patriotism, nationalism, determinism, and even militarism as the answer to world democracy. Gard E. Norberg looks beyond the popular rhetoric of the moment, appeals to his audience with a "voice of reason," and asks them to place "loss of life" into perspective—now and in the future. Norberg's following article originally appeared in the February 2002 issue of Ecologist.

Pre-reading Questions

1. What does it mean to be patriotic? What is the difference between being patriotic and being nationalistic? Locate all of the information you can about the words jingo or jingoism. How does this word (and/or these terms) affect your perception of true nationalism or patriotism? You might want to check the dictionary definition for each word.

2. What were your feelings following the attack on the World Trade Center in New York on September 11, 2002? If, as many have said, the event has altered Americans' lives forever, exactly what did it change? How? Why?

---

1   I wouldn't say that my wife is a psychic, because the word has a certain con-artist connotation. Let's just say she's prescient. She tells me not to worry about the fact that world population has more than tripled in my lifetime, polluting the environment and imposing an unbearable burden on the earth's finite and renewable resources. "Nature will take care of it," she says. "You'll see." If she were religiously inclined, she could have substituted "God" for "Nature." For more people

have been killed in religious wars than in any other kind of conflict. And just one week before the surprise attack on the World Trade Center, she casually advised me that "Armageddon is coming." It remains to be seen whether this terrorist act was a precursor to the Apocalypse.

2   As terrible as the events of 11 September 2001 were, we should put the loss of life in the proper perspective. Every day 40,000 children worldwide succumb to starvation and disease, because most religions oppose the abortion of unwanted fetuses, and in many cases prohibit the use of contraceptives. Conception is considered sacrosanct per se, even if it is the biproduct of unbridled lust, and the fetus doesn't stand a chance of surviving. Perhaps if we were to stuff a few thousand of these innocents into some tower of Babel and blow it up on live television, the world would take notice of their appalling predicament.

3   In Afghanistan, which has one of the world's highest birth rates and its second highest maternal mortality rate—17 in 1,000 births—85,000 children die each year from drinking polluted water. Ironic as it may seem, perhaps their adoptive Saudi father figure did them a service by bringing their desperate plight to the world's attention. Because of his dastardly deed, we in the West have literally overnight been made aware of the fact that millions of people in their homeland are starving. And, if the twin towers in Manhattan had not been knocked over, I bet few people would ever have heard about the four-year Afghan drought. Welcome as this sudden attention to the sufferings of the Afghanis may be, the opportune timing of the revelation smacks of hypocrisy.

4   A wise man once observed that: "People grow angry when they suffer things that they are unused to, and plunge into action on the spur of their impulse. [Americans] are especially likely to act this way, since they think they have a right to supremacy and are more used to destroying other people's land than seeing this happen to their own." If you substitute "Athenians" for "Americans," you might recognize the quote from Thucydides' *History of the Peloponnesian War*. As that macho Florentine, Niccolo Machiavelli, observed some 2000 years later, there is nothing like fear to unite a people behind their Prince. Thus the junior Bush, thanks to the acts of Muslim fanatics, saw his approval rating jump from 50 to 90 per cent as the WTC walls came tumbling down, shattering forever the U.S. illusion of being untouchable.

5   Not one to pass up a golden opportunity, the president, backed by his Republican party, lost no time in pushing through Congress a series of corporate tax breaks, totaling $1.4 trillion and including thank-you gifts of $600 million each to two of his biggest election contributors in his home state of Texas. Predictably, the rationale for this fiscal largesse was that old canard from the glory-days of Reaganomics: the trickle-down theory. Meanwhile, more than one million working stiffs lost their jobs last year to Asian sweatshops and Mexican maquiladores, while the Federal Reserve shaved points off the interest rate, a fraction at the time, instead of devaluing the over-inflated dollar to stimulate exports.

6   Taking a cue from his boss, Attorney General John Ashcroft rounded up more than 1,000 Arab-Americans and locked them up for an indefinite period without charging them with any crime—a blatant violation of the U.S. Constitution, and a victory of sorts for enemies of those democratic principles which he was elected to protect. To make matters worse, he forbade his minions at the FBI to ascertain whether these "suspects" had a license to carry arms. This seeming contradiction was motivated by the fact that over his political career, Ashcroft, a staunch defender of the right to bear arms, had received a total of $340,000 from the National Rifle Association—and you don't bite the hand that feeds you!

7   As the taxpayers' civil rights were being severely circumscribed in the interests of national security, the Interior Department lost the right to veto mining projects on public land, and the Bureau of Land Management altered its rules so global mining corporations wouldn't have to worry about the pollution they inflicted on the environment, making this the first casualty of 'America's New War.' One is reminded of the comment made by the then Speaker of the House about one of president Reagan's financial schemes: "We can't fix the economy by selling pizzas to one another."

8   Nor can we do it by abusing our environment. As Ed Ayres, editor of World Watch, sums it up in a recent editorial: "Lives are lost regularly in dismaying numbers . . . not from evil intent but from human [upsetting] of natural balances. As biodiversity loss and climate disruption [increase], we need to understand that the measure of a threat is not whether it is made on purpose, but how much loss it may cause." Well said, but who will heed the voice of reason? Much easier to chime in with the *jingo* bells. For, as the radical American writer, Randolph Bourne, observed during WWI: "War is the health of the state."

Post-reading Questions

Content

1. What is the controlling idea in Norberg's essay?

2. Why does Norberg say we should put the terrible events of September 11, 2001, in proper perspective?

3. What was the "first casualty of *"America's New War"*?

4. Why do you imagine Norberg refers to both the Greek writer, Thucydides, and the Italian political essayist, Niccolo Machiavelli? How did the situation in Athens and Florence, mirror some of the reactions and behaviors of Americans following the September 11 attack on the World Trade Center? (You may want to do this activity together with Group Activity 1.)

5. What do the National Rifle Association, taxpayers' civil rights, and abuse of the environment have in common with the rest of Norberg's essay?

Strategies and Structures

1. Norberg opens his essay with an anecdote about his wife, written in the first person singular point of view. What strategic purpose does it serve? How might it draw even a reluctant reader into his essay?

2. When Norberg discusses the fact that Afghanistan has one of the world's highest birth and "second highest maternal mortality rate," he alludes to Osama bin Laden as "their adoptive Saudi father figure." What might have been Norberg's strategic purpose for not directly referring to bin Laden?

3. How or in what way does the author define war from a historical perspective as well as definition by contrast and example with modern wars? What does he accomplish?

4. What is the effect of Norberg first telling his readers about the president giving "thank-you gifts of $600 million each to two of his biggest election contributors in his home state of Texas" and then informing us more than one million lost their jobs to "Asian sweatshops and Mexican maquiladores"?

5. Discusss the implicit irony in the title of Norberg's essay, "Jingo Bells, Jingo Bells." What does it call to mind?

Language and Vocabulary

1. Vocabulary: *jingo, psychic, prescient, Armageddon, Apocalypse, succumb, sacrosant, predicament, dastardly, macho, rationale, largesse, canard, maquiladores, blatant, minions, circumscribed, biodiversity.* Go through each of today's vocabulary words, refresh your knowledge of their definitions, and then list any connotation (associated meaning) that an individual word might carry.
2. Write an original paragraph or so on patriotism or nationalism, incorporating at least five vocabulary words from this essay into your brief composition.

Group Activities

1. Return to Content question number four, and in small groups you may want to visit the library or explore online informational resources concerning Thucydides and Niccolo Machiavelli. For what are these two men best known, how did they influence political and social thought during their lifetimes, and are they still influential today? Compare and contrast your research results with the rest of the class.
2. Putting political and religious beliefs aside, in small groups, investigate as objectively as you can the economic and environmental practices of G. W. Bush and Ronald Reagan. Each member in every group should re-examine the findings to reassess the subjective or objective source of information.

Writing Activities

1. Using the data collected in Group Activity 2, in a manner different than or similar to Norberg's essay, write an essay using definition by history to explain a current social, economic, religious, or environmental issue. Make sure you use specific, concrete examples to illustrate your discussion points.
2. During World War I, according to Randolph Bourne, an American writer cited in Norberg's essay, "War is the health of the state." To what extent do you agree or disagree with his statement? Write an essay fully defending your point of view with details and examples drawn from personal experiences, observations, and readings.

Richard Rodriguez

Does America Still Exist?

A San Francisco native, Richard Rodriguez is the son of Mexican immigrants. His articles frequently appear in Change, The American Scholar, *and* The Saturday Review. *His works include* Hunger of Memory *(1982), which relates the conflict of ethnic identification and American cultural assimilation,* Days of Obligation: An Argument with My Mexican Father *(1992),* King's Highway *(2000), and* Brown: The Last Discovery of America *(2002). In the following essay, Rodriguez develops his definition of America by arguing what the country "is not."*

Pre-reading Questions

1. What are some traditional symbols and words associated with America? What do they stand for?

2. Who are Americans? Is America a common culture or a diverse culture? Are all its citizens truly equal in the eyes of society?

3. Is there a common "American Dream"? If so, what is it?

1   For the children of immigrant parents the knowledge comes easier. America exists everywhere in the city—on billboards, frankly in the smell of French fries and popcorn. It exists in the pace: traffic lights, the assertions of neon, the mysterious bong-bong-bong through the atriums of department stores. America exists as the voice of the crowd, a menacing sound— the high nasal accent of American English.

2   When I was a boy in Sacramento (California, the fifties), people would ask me, "Where you from?" I was born in this country, but I knew the question meant to decipher my darkness, my looks.

3   My mother once instructed me to say, "I am an American of American descent." By the time I was nine or ten, I wanted to say, but dared not reply, "I am an American."

4   Immigrants come to America and, against hostility or mere loneliness, they recreate a homeland in the parlor, tacking up postcards or calendars of some impossible blue—lake or sea or sky. Children of immigrant parents are supposed to perch on a hyphen between two countries. Relatives assume the achievement as much as anyone. Relatives are, in any case, surprised when the child begins losing old ways. One day at the family picnic the boy wanders away from their spiced food and faceless stories to watch other boys play baseball in the distance.

5   There is sorrow in the American memory, guilty sorrow for having left something behind—Portugal, China, Norway. The American story is the story of immigrant children and of their children—children no longer able to speak to grandparents. The memory of exile becomes inarticulate as it passes from generation to generation, along with wedding rings and pocket watches—like some mute stone in a wad of old lace. Europe. Asia. Eden.

6   But, it needs to be said, if this is a country where one stops being Vietnamese or Italian, this is a country where one begins to be an American. America exists as a culture and a grin, a faith and a shrug. It is clasped in a handshake, called by a first name.

7   As much as the country is joined in a common culture, however, Americans are reluctant to celebrate the process of assimilation. We pledge allegiance to diversity. America was born Protestant and bred Puritan, and the notion of community we share is derived from a seventeenth-century faith. Presidents and the pages of ninth-grade civics readers yet proclaim the orthodoxy: We are gathered together—but as individuals, with separate pasts, distinct destinies. Our society is as paradoxical as a Puritan congregation: We stand together, alone.

8   Americans have traditionally defined themselves by what they refused to include. As often, however, Americans have struggled, turned in good conscience at last to assert the great Protestant virtue of tolerance. Despite outbreaks of nativist frenzy, America has remained an immigrant country, open and true to itself.

9   Against pious emblems of rural America—soda fountain, Elks hall, Protestant church, and now shopping mall—stands the cold-hearted city, crowded with races and ambitions, curious laughter, much that is odd. Nevertheless, it is the city that has most truly represented America. In the city, however, the millions of singular lives have had no richer notion of wholeness to describe them than the idea of pluralism.

10   *"Where you from?" the American asks the immigrant child. "Mexico," the boy learns to say.*

11   Mexico, the country of my blood ancestors, offers formal contrast to the American achievement. If the United States was formed by Protestant individualism, Mexico was shaped by a medieval Catholic dream of one world. The Spanish journeyed to Mexico to plunder, and they may have gone, in God's name, with an arrogance peculiar to those who intend to convert. But through the conversion, the Indian converted the Spaniard. A new race was born, the *mestizo,* wedding European to Indian. José Vasconcelos, the Mexican philosopher, has celebrated this New World creation, proclaiming it the "cosmic race."

12   Centuries later, in a San Francisco restaurant, a Mexican-American lawyer of my acquaintance says, in English, over *salade niçoise,* that he does not intend to assimilate into gringo society. His claim is echoed by a chorus of others (Italian-Americans, Greeks, Asians) in this era of ethnic pride. The melting pot has been retired, clanking, into the museum of quaint disgrace, alongside Aunt Jemima and the Katzenjammer Kids. But resistance to assimilation is characteristically American. It only makes clear how inevitable the process of assimilation actually is.

13   For generations, this has been the pattern. Immigrant parents have sent their children to school (simply, they thought) to acquire the "skills" to survive in the city. The child returned home with a voice his parents barely recognized or understood, couldn't trust, and didn't like.

14   In Eastern cities—Philadelphia, New York, Boston, Baltimore— class after class gathered immigrant children to women (usually women) who stood in front of rooms full of children, changing children. So also for me in the 1950s. Irish-Catholic nuns. California. The old story. The hyphen tipped to the right, away from Mexico and toward a confusing but true American identity.

15   I speak now in the chromium American accent of my grammar school classmates—Billy Reckers, Mike Bradley, Carol Schmidt, Kathy O'Grady. . . . I believe I became like my classmates, became German, Polish, and (like my teachers) Irish. And because assimilation is always reciprocal, my classmates got something of me. (I mean sad eyes; belief in the Indian Virgin; a taste for sugar skulls on the Feast of the Dead.) In the blending, we became what our parents could never have been, and we carried America one revolution further.

16   "Does America still exist?" Americans have been asking the question for so long that to ask it again only proves our continuous link. But perhaps the question deserves to be asked with urgency—now. Since the black civil rights movement of the

1960s, our tenuous notion of a shared public life has deteriorated notably.

17   The struggle of black men and women did not eradicate racism, but it became the great moment in the life of America's conscience. Water hoses, bulldogs, blood—the images, rendered black, white, rectangular, passed into living rooms.

18   It is hard to look at a photograph of a crowd taken, say, in 1890 or in 1930 and not notice the absence of blacks. (It becomes an impertinence to wonder if America *still* exists.)

19   In the sixties, other groups of Americans learned to champion their rights by analogy to the black civil rights movement. But the heroic vision faded. Dr. Martin Luther King, Jr., had spoken with Pauline eloquence of a nation that would unite Christian and Jew, old and young, rich and poor. Within a decade, the struggles of the 1960s were reduced to a bureaucratic competition for little more than pieces of a representational pie. The quest for a portion of power became an end in itself. The metaphor for the American city of the 1970s was a committee: one black, one woman, one person under thirty. . . .

20   If the small town had sinned against America by too neatly defining who could be an American, the city's sin was a romantic secession. One noticed the romanticism in the antiwar movement—certain demonstrators who demonstrated a lack of tact or desire to persuade and seemed content to play secular protestants. One noticed the romanticism in the competition among members of "minority groups" to claim the status of Primary Victim. To Americans unconfident of their common identity, minority standing became a way of asserting individuality. Middle-class Americans—men and women clearly not the primary victims of social oppression—brandished their suffering with exuberance.

21   The dream of a single society probably died with *The Ed Sullivan Show*. The reality of America persists. Teenagers pass through big-city high schools banded in racial groups, their collars turned up to a uniform shrug. But then they graduate to jobs at the phone company or in banks, where they end up working alongside people unlike themselves. Typists and tellers walk out together at lunchtime.

22   It is easier for us as Americans to believe the obvious fact of our separateness—easier to imagine the black and white Americas prophesied by the Kerner report (broken glass, street fires)—than to recognize the reality of a city street at lunchtime. Americans are wedded by proximity to a common culture. The panhandler at one corner is related to the pamphleteer at the

next who is related to the banker who is kin to the Chinese old man wearing an MIT sweatshirt. In any true national history, Thomas Jefferson begets Martin Luther King, Jr., who begets the Gray Panthers. It is because we lack a vision of ourselves entire—the city street is crowded and we are each preoccupied with finding our own way home—that we lack an appropriate hymn.

23   Under my window now passes a little white girl softly rehearsing to herself a Motown obbligato.

Post-reading Questions

Content

1. Where does Rodriguez claim America exists? What does he feel symbolizes America?
2. What is more important in America, individuality or membership? According to Rodriguez, where do we stand in relationship to each other?
3. Why does Rodriguez feel the 1960s were so important to American history? What has happened since that era?
4. According to Rodriguez, did the dream of a single society probably die? What proof does he offer?

Strategies and Structures

1. Rodriguez develops his definition of America by stating what it is *not* (arguing through negation). How effective is this strategy? If the author had reversed his strategy and told us what America is, would this have inspired any creative or critical thinking on the part of the reader? Why or why not?
2. How does Rodriguez explain his definition of America? Through abstract discussion or concrete examples? Why does he choose one over the other?
3. In what other ways does the author develop his definition?

Language and Vocabulary

1. Vocabulary: *assimilation, reciprocal, inarticulate, congregation, gringo, chromium, bureaucratic, metaphor, exuberance.* Read the sentences in which these words are found and try to determine their definitions. Then look up each one in the dictionary and see how accurate your determinations were. What does

this exercise show you about reading words in context? What did you discover about dictionary use?

2. Without looking up their definitions, use the following words in a paragraph: *conscience, secession, secular, beget, pamphleteer, allegiance, plunder.* As you did in the previous exercise, check your usage in the dictionary after you draft your paragraph, noting how context assisted you in using words you were not too familiar with. Then, rewrite your paragraph, making changes to improve the sense and to eliminate faulty usage.

Group Activities

1. If possible, get into culturally diverse groups and discuss what you have in common. For instance, do you eat foods, listen to music, or enjoy the sports of another culture? What are the greatest differences among the members of your group? Have you ever wanted to attend social functions of a different culture but were afraid to? What information have you always wanted to ask about another culture?

2. In a group forum analyze precisely what America is. Begin by asking yourselves what is and is not American? What historical facts can your group brainstorm supporting your position? Do people have a tendency to stereotype Americans? Why? You may want to save the information that you've collected for Writing Activity 2, below.

Writing Activities

1. Compose an original essay wherein you define a concept, a country, or a person through *negation.* That is, focus your attention on arguing what someone or something *is not* to define your topic. Make sure you use specific examples to illustrate what you claim.

2. Write an argument of fact, defining and defending your concept of America. Consider what you were taught when you were little about the United States (e.g., land of the free where everyone has an equal

opportunity to achieve—where everything is fair).
Does your personal experience support what you
were told? How? Why?

Additional Topics and Issues for Definition Essays

1. Write an essay in which you compare and contrast Asimov's definition of human intelligence with your own definition of artificial intelligence.

2. Write an essay in which you define one of the following: love, hate, peace, loneliness, or happiness. Since such qualities are difficult to measure, you'll want to provide several representative examples to win your reader over to your viewpoint.

3. Define "elevator music." What is it? Where is it heard most? Need a person be in an elevator to experience such music? After your initial definition, illustrate the effects of this music on people who, unwillingly, are subjected to it.

4. What does it mean to be an independent or a dependent person? Compose an essay in which you define yourself as one of the above, supporting your ideas with examples drawn from personal experience.

5. Define the concepts of liberalism and conservatism. Which is better? Do you consider yourself a liberal or a conservative? Why? Integrate information from recent news articles that justifies the concept you have chosen.

6. Write an essay defining "success." Is it being well paid for your work? Is it being happy or content with what you do? Is it joy in helping others? Use specific examples and references to illustrate your definition.

7. In a well-developed essay, define the rights and privileges of a sovereign nation. In these times, why might respecting the rights of sovereign nations and their people be crucial in establishing and maintaining a peaceful coexistence?

8. Define the steps a person might take to survive the trauma of being a victim of a mean practical joke, a violent crime (rape or battery), or a bad, though unearned, reputation?

9. Write a definition essay about positive parent-teenager relationships, by illustrating what they should not be (definition by negation).

10. Go on the internet and look up the key term "Farm Aid," reading as many articles as you can on the subject. Then freewrite until arriving at an original thesis. Compose a definition essay explaining the mission and objectives of Farm Aid. What is its history, and what are its prospects for the future? Support your essay using information gleaned from personal experience, interviews, and readings, such as those you did online.

6

Process Analysis

What is process analysis? In contrast to narration, which relates *what* happens, or cause and effect, which explains *why* something occurs, process analysis addresses the question of *how*. Of crucial importance in explaining *how* is carefully organizing materials and marking them with time transitions (first, second, third). Such linking devices help a reader follow a process from start to finish. When do we use process analysis? Usually, process analysis explains one of two things: *how* to do something (directive process analysis) or *how* something is or was done (informative process analysis).

Directive Process Papers: How to Do Something

Like most expository strategies, process analysis explains. We are all familiar with the process of explaining how to do something; if we aren't explaining to others how to do something, then others may be explaining to us how to do something. Think for a moment about the last time you gave another person directions on how to get somewhere. What did you do? Undoubtedly, you told the person which direction to go and where and when to make left or right turns. In doing so, you were actively involved with a process; you were analyzing the possibilities and determining what a person had to do in order to reach a desired destination.

The "how to" essay is deceptively simple. That is, while an author may have no trouble explaining how to read a book, how to mow a lawn, or how to ride a bike, he or she may find it difficult to "hook" the interest of the intended audience. Why? The topics sound rather dull and will be just as dull as their titles promise when fully written unless the writer creates a reason—real or contrived—such a topic is relevant and therefore *meaningful* to its reader. In "How to Write a Personal Letter," Garrison Keillor begins his essay with: *"We shy persons need to write a letter now and then, or else we'll dry up and blow away."* Here the author identifies his intended audience, shy people, points out that he himself is a shy person, and proceeds to explain how writing letters will fulfill an important void in the lives of shy people. By the end of the introductory paragraph, Keillor has established a reason why the reader, shy or aggressive, should be interested in learning how to write a personal letter: A letter is better than a telephone call.

Informational Process Essays: How Something Is/Was Done

Process analysis can also be an effective way of informing someone how a process occurs. Informative process analysis explains topics like how a tree grows, how a gas engine runs, or how a worm regenerates itself. Such information is usually expressed in some sort of logical sequence process. Joyce Jarrett, for example, informs readers of the sequential turn of events on her first day at school—events that propelled her to *"new liberty more out of curiosity than mission,"* in her essay "Freedom." Other times the division between directive and informative process analysis papers overlaps to some extent. A prime example would be Kathleen Hudson's "Interviews: Stories That Make a Difference." Though her essay predominantly focuses on informative process analysis—how she interviews people—Hudson also provides readers with tips that they can use for the same purpose; in other words, she offers directive as well as informative information.

Informative process analysis is not limited to investigative reporting or to the natural sciences, of course. Rather than explaining a natural relationship, Malcolm X discusses the strategy (process) he used to increase his "word base" in "A Homemade Education." Like Jarrett, Malcolm X uses process analysis to inform us rather than direct us (tell us how to do something). Granted, it is possible to imitate what another person did in hopes of achieving the same results; we see this in the acting world and political arena daily. Nonetheless, there is an unmistakable difference between imitating to achieve an end (informative process analysis) and following directions to accomplish a task (directive process analysis).

One might say that Luis M. Valdez actually blends informative with directive process analysis in his essay called "Perspectives on 'Borders.'" Indeed, early in the essay he uses informational process analysis to explain how something was done (the Mayan achievements). His essay could also be directive in that he specifically suggests what must be acknowledged for harmony and pluralism in the diverse societies of the Americas.

Tips on Writing Process Analysis Essays

1. Have a clear sense of the process, whether it is informative or directive, you plan to explain. When in doubt, check a reliable source; don't try to bluff your way through an introduction and assume your reader will perceive the controlling idea of your composition.

2. Use transitional and linking devices indicating *time* in order to lead your reader from step to step, point to point.

3. Bear in mind that as with any expository essay, your goal in writing is to *explain how* to do something (directive process analysis) or how something is or was done (informative process analysis). Avoid getting sidetracked on issues that would only confuse your reader.

4. Make sure to use key words and specific references. These will help your reader remain focused on the controlling idea or purpose of your essay.

5. Go over your rough draft and carefully check your work for omitted steps in a process, adding them as necessary. Sometimes it is helpful to continuously ask yourself Who? What? When? Where? Why? and, of course, How?

Garrison Keillor

How to Write a Personal Letter

Born in 1942, author/humorist Garrison Keillor began his successful writing and broadcasting career after graduating from the University of Minnesota. Keillor received nationwide attention for his radio program, Prairie Home Companion, *broadcast every Saturday evening on National Public Radio. His printed works include* Happy to Be Here *(1982),* Lake Wobegon Days *(1985),* Leaving Home: A Collection of Lake Wobegon Stories *(1987),* We Are Still Married *(1989),* WLT: A Radio Romance *(1992),* The Book of Guys *(1993),* Me: by Jimmy (Big Boy) Valente *(1999) and* Pretty Good Joke Book *(2000). Keillor offers audiences a rarified style of homespun humor, frequently distinguished by tongue-in-cheek remarks, understatement, and irony. He wrote the following process essay as an advertisement for the International Paper Company.*

Pre-reading Questions

1. How often do you write a personal letter to family or friends? Do you think you should write more often? Why or why not?

2. What do you consider *personal?* What do you find *impersonal?* After briefly considering these questions, freewrite for ten minutes and attempt to answer each with as many examples as you can think of.

1   We shy persons need to write a letter now and then, or else we'll dry up and blow away. It's true. And I speak as one who loves to reach for the phone, dial the number, and talk. I say,

"Big Bopper here—what's shakin', babes?" The telephone is to shyness what Hawaii is to February, it's a way out of the woods, *and yet:* a letter is better.

2   Such a sweet gift—a piece of handmade writing, in an envelope that is not a bill, sitting in our friend's path when she trudges home from a long day spent among wahoos and savages, a day our words will help repair. They don't need to be immortal, just sincere. She can read them twice and again tomorrow: *You're someone I care about, Corinne, and think of often and every time I do you make me smile.*

3   We need to write, otherwise nobody will know who we are. They will have only a vague impression of us as A Nice Person, because frankly, we don't shine at conversation, we lack the confidence to thrust our faces forward and say, "Hi, I'm Heather Hooten, let me tell you about my week." Mostly we say "Uh-huh" and "Oh really." People smile and look over our shoulder, looking for someone else to talk to.

4   So a shy person sits down and writes a letter. To be known by another person—to meet and talk freely on the page—to be close despite distance. To escape from anonymity and be our own sweet selves and express the music of our souls.

5   Same thing that moves a giant rock star to sing his heart out in front of 123,000 people moves us to take ballpoint in hand and write a few lines to our dear Aunt Eleanor. *We want to be known.* We want her to know that we have fallen in love, that we quit our job, and we're moving to New York, and we want to say a few things that might not get said in casual conversation: *thank you for what you've meant to me, I am very happy right now.*

6   The first step in writing letters is to get over the guilt of *not* writing. You don't "owe" anybody a letter. Letters are a gift. The burning shame you feel when you see unanswered mail makes it harder to pick up a pen and makes for a cheerless letter when you finally do. *I feel bad about not writing, but I've been so busy,* etc. Skip this. Few letters are obligatory, and they are *Thanks for the wonderful gift* and *I am terribly sorry to hear about George's death* and *Yes, you're welcome to stay with us next month,* and not many more than that. Write those promptly if you want to keep your friends. Don't worry about the others, except love letters, of course. When your true love writes *Dear Light of My Life, Joy of My Heart, O Lovely Pulsating Core of My Sensate Life,* some response is called for.

7   Some of the best letters are tossed off in a burst of inspiration, so keep your writing stuff in one place where you can sit down for a few minutes and *Dear Roy, I am in the middle of an*

essay for International Paper but thought I'd drop you a line. Hi to your sweetie too dash off a note to a pal. Envelopes, stamps, address book, everything in a drawer so you can write fast when the pen is hot.

8   A blank 8″ × 11″ sheet can look as big as Montana if the pen's not so hot—try a smaller page and write boldly. Or use a note card with a piece of fine art on the front; if your letter ain't good, at least they get the Matisse. Get a pen that makes a sensuous line, get a comfortable typewriter, a friendly word processor—whichever feels easy to the hand.

9   Sit for a few minutes with the blank sheet in front of you, and meditate on the person you will write to, let your friend come to mind until you can almost see her or him in the room with you. Remember the last time you saw each other and how your friend looked and what you said and what perhaps was unsaid between you, and when your friend becomes real to you, start to write.

10   Write the salutation—*Dear You*—and take a deep breath and plunge in. A simple declarative sentence will do, followed by another and another and another. Tell us what you're doing and tell it like you were talking to us. Don't think about grammar, don't think about lit'ry style, don't try to write dramatically, just give us your news. Where did you go, who did you see, what did they say, what do you think?

11   If you don't know where to begin, start with the present moment: *I'm sitting at the kitchen table on a rainy Saturday morning. Everyone is gone and the house is quiet.* Let your simple description of the present moment lead to something else, let the letter drift gently along.

12   The toughest letter to crank out is one that is meant to impress, as we all know from writing job applications; if it's hard work to slip off a letter to a friend, maybe you're trying too hard to be terrific. A letter is only a report to someone who already likes you for reasons other than your brilliance. Take it easy.

13   Don't worry about form. It's not a term paper. When you come to the end of one episode, just start a new paragraph. You can go from a few lines about the sad state of rock'n roll to the fight with your mother to your fond memories of Mexico to your cat's urinary tract infection to a few thoughts on personal indebtedness to the kitchen sink and what's in it. The more you write, the easier it gets, and when you have a True True Friend to write to, a *compadre,* a soul sibling, then it's like driving a car down a country road, you just get behind the keyboard and press on the gas.

14   Don't tear up the page and start over when you write a bad line—try to write your way out of it. Make mistakes and plunge

on. Let the letter cook along and let yourself be bold. Outrage, confusion, love—whatever is in your mind, let it find a way to the page. Writing is a means of discovery, always, and when you come to the end and write *Yours ever* or *Hugs and Kisses,* you'll know something you didn't when you wrote *Dear Pal.*

15   Probably your friend will put your letter away, and it'll be read again a few years from now—and it will improve with age. And forty years from now, your friend's grandkids will dig it out of the attic and read it, a sweet and precious relic of the ancient Eighties that gives them a sudden clear glimpse of you and her and the world we old-timers knew. You will then have created an object of art. Your simple lines about where you went, who you saw, what they said, will speak to those children and they will feel in their hearts the humanity of our times.

16   You can't pick up a phone and call the future and tell them about our times. You have to pick up a piece of paper.

Post-reading Questions

Content

1. Why does Keillor say people should write personal letters once in a while? As a means of communication, what advantages do letters have over phone calls?
2. According to Keillor, when are the best letters written? Why?
3. How does Keillor recommend you *prepare* to write a personal letter?
4. Once you begin to write, what special advice does he offer regarding the format of your letter? Explain his reasoning.

Strategies and Structures

1. In your opinion, why does the author spend five paragraphs leading up to his directions on *how* to write a personal letter? What does he achieve?
2. How does referring to a personal letter as a gift clearly indicate the author's attitude toward his subject in this essay?
3. Why does Keillor spend more time exploring ways to avoid the common problems people encounter when they write letters than leading the reader through the writing process step by step?
4. In paragraph 15, Keillor makes some predictions about the future of letters you write. How does this

paragraph directly relate to the opening paragraph
and reinforce the controlling idea of the essay?

Language and Vocabulary
1. Vocabulary: Outside of *wahoos* (any of various
   American trees or shrubs), *obligatory* (legally, ethically, or morally binding), and *anonymity* (the state
   of having or giving no name), how and why does
   Keillor's simple choice of vocabulary words suit the
   purpose of his essay?
2. To create a clear, down-to-earth tone, Keillor often
   uses slang words and informal language. List at least
   five instances of informal language in his essay and
   explain how they reinforce the tone that a writer uses
   for personal letters. Then go back over your list; what
   formal words or phrases would express the same information? How is each use of language (informal and
   formal) appropriate to a different audience?

Group Activities

1. Write a collaborative personal letter to your college
   president or local government officials using directive process analysis to explain how to solve a current problem. While you will want to ultimately
   type (and have everyone sign) the letter, you'll want
   to avoid extremely formal language in order to per-
   sonalize what you say.
2. Personality can often be expressed through language (words and phrases), and this exercise
   demonstrates (1) the power of personality (word
   choice) in writing and (2) the ways we can use
   process analysis to explain how something is done.
   In small groups, go somewhere on campus to observe how something is done (e.g., how books are
   collected, sorted, and reshelved in the library). Take
   notes and, individually, write short *personal* (informal) essays explaining the process your group observed. Next, have members share (1) their
   definitions and examples of what is personal and
   what is impersonal and (2) their informally written
   observations. How well did group members person-
   alize their writing?

Writing Activities

1. Write an *informative* process analysis paper explaining the origin or demise of subcultures or countercultures in America (e.g., surfers, rednecks, and/or punk rockers).
2. Compose an essay which provides *directions* on how to eat a formal dinner served at a very refined restaurant.

Kathleen Hudson

Interviews: Stories that Make a Difference

Kathleen Hudson, Ph.D., completed a dissertation for her degree at TCU in Fort Worth in 1984. Her title was "Writers on Writing: An Eclectic Approach to Teaching Composition." In 1997 she had a book manuscript accepted by University of Texas Press titled In Their Own Words: Texas Songwriters Tell Their Stories *(2000). As a trainer in an educational program called "The Past is Prologue," she uses the Native American learning story as a tool in the classroom and in her life. She teaches writing and literature at Schreiner College. She is also the founder/director of the Texas Heritage Music Foundation, home for her oral history archives—a collection of 300 interviews with Texas songwriters and musicians. Other projects that come from her interest in stories include a weekly newspaper column, a freshman seminar based on the power of the story, a coffeehouse series, a series of house concerts, and a living history day in Kerrville, Texas. In the following essay, Hudson explains how interviews provide a fertile basis for generating writing ideas.*

Pre-reading Questions

1. Have you ever interviewed a person? How did (or would) you prepare to do so?
2. How might interviewing someone uncover ideas, facts, and details that you could use to illustrate, explain, and argue discussion points in writing?

---

1   Stories hold people together. I began collecting the stories of Texas musicians in 1986 at the Memphis Blues Awards. Willie

Nelson and B. B. King were co-hosting the event. Both men shared their stories with me, one during a press conference and one at the party after the show. With both men I talked about "Night Life," a classic hit written by Willie and transformed into a blues classic by B. B. I knew at that moment that I wanted to continue collecting the stories songwriters and musicians have to tell. In fact, I wanted to document the entire Texas music scene, in the field, gathering the stories on my little tape recorder. I really wanted to collect the stories all creative people have. Stop! That's the way my mind works; things just keep getting bigger. The vision keeps expanding. Regardless of who tells the story, an interview captures the moment.

2   Soon the judge, the editor, had to take over. The project called for discrimination, choosing. So I created the Texas Heritage Music Foundation in 1987, an organization to preserve and perpetuate the traditions in Texas music. My ever-growing collection of interviews became the heart of an organization committed to the possibility that telling stories and singing songs make a difference in the world.

3   After years of collecting these stories, these "interviews," I began to reflect on the source of my success in each conversation. First, I broke a few rules. Since I didn't have a background in journalism, I hadn't read the part about keeping myself, the interviewer, out of the interview. I began each interview with a comment about myself, a way for the artist to see a connection with me. Then we were off and running.

4   Prior to an interview, I often generate a list of interesting questions, and then I throw the list away during the conversation. A good interview is like a jazz performance; neither depends on scripted material. Instead, the saxophone player responds to the band even while leading the band. In a similar manner, I just listen to the response I receive, and then I respond to the person in front of me. The worst scene for an interviewer is to just go down a list of questions, regardless of the response. For example, consider what is missing in the following:

Hudson: Tell me about your most profound experience that led to a song.

Interviewee: Oh, my dad died when I was a teenager, and I was devastated. I wrote about it in school, and one day I tried a song. It all just came out, in one piece. When I was about 30, my mom was in a wreck. She was left without her legs.

Hudson: Now tell me about your most successful
             moment on stage.

That's not a conversation! Instead of such predictable or
canned questions and answers, I keep my attention on the
other person and respond to the words I hear. True, I often feel
like that trapeze artist flying without a net, but I trust my own
years of experience, my own intuition, my own listening to generate the interview I'm seeking.

5   Once I interviewed blues musician Stevie Ray Vaughan
when he had just gotten out of rehab and did not want to talk
about music. He told me how it felt to be whole and healthy. He
told me how much he loved his life. He told me he wanted to
warn other young musicians about the tragedies of drug addiction. As I put down the phone, I thought at first that I had
missed the chance to really interview him. Then I realized that
by allowing him to tell the story, which mattered most to him,
I did, indeed, have a great interview.

6   Research before the interview enriches the possibilities of a
great conversation. I'd listen to the entire Leonard Cohen album, drawn over and over to "The Ballad of the Absent Mare."
I raise and train horses, and I've often perceived of myself as
one running free. Therefore, when I walked into the backstage
area of the Austin Opry House, I began the interview saying, "I
am the original absent mare. Where did you get that horse imagery?" I began the interview stating something about myself,
something true for me. Leonard took over from that point,
telling me all about watching his own horses at a place he once
owned in Tennessee.

7   My advice to those choosing the interview as a way to generate writing, a way to conduct research, or a way to collect important information is to trust your own vision, your own life.
Trust what you bring to the interview, whether it's years of experience or an hour's worth of research.

8   Listen carefully and look deeply into the lives of those you interview. Only then will the true dimension of one's story surface.
For instance, I looked deeply at the literary interests inherent in
Texas songwriting and came upon information I would never
have guessed. In our first interview, Joe Ely wanted to talk about
reading Allen Ginsberg. I knew we might share other literary interests, so I went down that road. Cormac McCarthy and Clive
Barker surfaced as other common interests. Robert Earl Keen
also mentioned Cormac McCarthy. I discovered another blues
artist, Steve Earl, is writing short stories and that Keen wants to

write a novel. By delving deeply and listening carefully to the multiple interests expressed by musicians—or anyone you interview—the interview reveals the complexity and richness of stories that matter to them and, by extension, to us.

9   Pay attention, and always be ready to throw down the script. Go down new roads and explore. Every conversation between two people creates a new world, one which both inhabit for a short time. Johnny Winter and I were scheduled for a twenty-minute interview. We quit talking when it was time to get more tattoos (I got Pegasus on my shoulder) about two hours later. My script did not cover this conversation.

10   A journalist may set out with certain goals in mind, certain questions to answer. As a feature writer, I decide to explore. Once, when I was interviewing Townes Van Zandt, I heard myself coming up with questions I'd never asked before. Townes told me about the blues scene in Houston, about Lightnin' Hopkins and about women with short hair. Lightnin' said, "I don't want no woman whose hair is shorter than mine." Townes told me about haircuts. He told me about the voices he often heard and had to drown out. He told me about his deep friendship with Choctaw writer, Roxy Gordon. "We were born on the same day, March 7," Townes explained. "We're blood brothers."

11   The interviewer works as a tool; the desired end results can shape the questions being asked. I always prefer to let language be that tool that carves out meaning, not just a bridge to convey ideas. For instance, an editor looking over my manuscript, *33 Interviews with Texas Songwriters*, commented, "The one with Townes is a bit disjointed." How could it be otherwise? I didn't need to shape the conversation to sound like all the other interviews I've done in my life. It needed to sound like Townes.

12   I'm a collector. I collect rocks, Belle Starr stories, writers' stories, friends' stories and the stories of many other cultures (to use in my mythology class at Schreiner College). As such, I believe Paula Underwood, founder of the Past is Prologue and author of *The Walking People*, who said, "Story can create the space in which new and necessary thinking can occur. It can be the process through which we build increasing awareness of life and its many options, through which we show ourselves—in time—the many paths that lie open to us."

13   Stories capture moments; stories stimulate thinking; and stories open entire worlds with which many of us may connect. The interview process inspired me to continue collecting stories,

spaces where new thinking can occur. I find myself inviting all I meet to "Tell me your story."

Post-reading Questions

Content

1. What does Hudson imply when she explains that as she interviews people, she often feels "like that trapeze artist flying without a net . . . "?
2. Explain what Hudson says should be the most important objective of an interview. Why would you agree or disagree with her?
3. What does Hudson graphically illustrate with her anecdote about a twenty-minute interview with guitarist Johnny Winters?
4. Why does the author suggest doing some research on a person before an interview?
5. What inspired her to gather stories on the "entire Texas music scene"?

Strategies and Structures

1. Outside of general research, Hudson suggests preparing a "list of interesting questions" before an interview and then throwing them away. Why? What is often the end result of such a strategy?
2. According to Hudson, in what way will *listening carefully* and *responding deeply* to a person being interviewed produce the best results?
3. How do the first and last paragraphs provide Hudson with a framing device for discussing interview techniques? Why do you imagine she stresses "the story" as the "big picture" and the interview as part of it?
4. Hudson drops a lot of concrete references to legendary Texas songwriters and rhythm-and-blues icons such as B. B. King. How do such references add authority to her exposition? What might have been lost without them and why?
5. Explain the strategic purpose—and the ultimate effect—of "anaphora," the repetition of the first word at the *beginnings* of successive clauses, prior to the final paragraph in Hudson's essay: "Stories capture moments; stories stimulate thinking; sto-

ries open entire worlds from which to connect"?

Language and Vocabulary

1. The vocabulary tends to be straightforward and easily accessible in Hudson's essay. To gain a full appreciation of her analogy (extended comparison), however, look up *jazz* in the dictionary or on the Internet. Then, discuss its characteristics in a brief paragraph. In your opinion, how might an interview be appropriately—or inappropriately—explained as jazz performance?

2. Language often reflects an author's attitude toward his or her subject. What sorts of words or word groups seem to indicate her attitude toward interviewing people?

Group Activities

1. Gather in groups and identify three or four major problems in your community. Then, prepare a list of questions as a group, a list each member will then use to interview people in the community who can address your concerns (e.g., If your concern is water pollution, you might talk to people who work at water treatment plants).

2. Have a member of your college community come to class and pretend he or she is a candidate interviewing for the position he or she presently holds. Prior to the class visitation, generate a list of questions that the group's members in general, and the class as a whole, believe would be important to ask. Then, have each class member take a turn asking a question. Following the interview, break into smaller groups and share your feelings about the person just interviewed. Then, based on everyone's input, write a collaborative composition arguing why the person deserves to be an employee of your district. An alternate approach to this activity would be to explain how and why the formal interview procedure used in class was or was not an adequate process to assess the candidate's strengths and weaknesses.

Writing Activities

1. Interview a local musician, actor, actress, or comedian, and then use their responses to your questions
   (planned ahead of time or otherwise) as the basis for
   a process essay explaining how you ultimately
   "learned someone's story."
2. Write an "informational" process essay explaining
   how knowledge of past events or experiences in your
   life have served as "a prologue" for the present.
   How, for instance, has scientific, technological, and
   medical achievements in your lifetime shaped the
   last part of the twentieth century and set the stage
   for changes—positive or negative—as we move into
   the new millennium? In this essay, you will explain
   how something was done, concluding with a speculation on what may happen as a result of it.

Joyce M. Jarrett

Freedom

*Joyce M. Jarrett, associate professor of English at Hampton
University, has authored many creative works, all of which she notes
have grown out of her African-American experience. She has also co-
authored* Pathways: A Text for Developing Writers *(1990) and*
Heritage: African American Readings for Writing *(1996). The
following essay in which Jarrett reflects on one of her struggles
during the civil rights movement was originally published in*
Between Worlds *(1986).*

Pre-reading Questions

1. Brainstorm and write a journal about personal freedom.
   What would you require to be free? What would make
   you feel restrained or imprisoned?

2. If you had been born without freedom (as you define it),
   how would it affect your daily interaction with others, your
   education, your employment, and possibly your future?

---

*"Born free, as free as the wind blows, as free as the grass
grows, born free to follow your heart." (Don Black)*

1   My first illusion of freedom came in 1966, many years following the Supreme Court's decision on school desegregation. Of
course to a fifteen-year-old girl, isolated, caged like a rodent in
the poverty-stricken plains of the Magnolia State,[1] Brown vs.
the Board of Education had no meaning. Though many must
have thought that my decision to attend the all-white city high
school that fall, along with 49 other blacks, was made in protest
or had evolved from a sense of commitment for the betterment

[1]Magnolia State   Mississippi.

of my people, nothing could have been further from the truth. Like a rat finding a new passageway, I was propelled to my new liberty more out of curiosity than out of a sense of mission.

2   On the first day of school, I was escorted by hordes of national guardsmen. Like a funeral procession, the steady stream of official-looking cars followed me to the campus. Some patrolmen were parked near campus gates, while others, with guns strapped to their sides, stood near building entrances. Though many of my escorts had given me smiles of support, still I was not prepared for what I encountered upon entering *my* new school.

3   There, I had to break through lines of irate white protestors, spraying obscenities at me while carrying their denigrating signs: "KKK Forever," read one; "Back to Africa," said another. And as I dashed toward the school door, blinded with fear, I nearly collided with another sign that screamed, "Nigger Go Home."

4   Once inside the fortress, I was ushered by school administrators and plain-clothes police to and from my respective classes. The anger and fear that I had felt outside of those walls were numbed by the surprisingly uneventful classroom experiences— until I went to geometry, my last scheduled class for that day.

5   As I sauntered into the classroom and took a seat, there was a flurry of activity. When everyone had settled, I sat in the center of the class, surrounded by empty desks—on each side, and in front and back.

6   "We have a nigger in the class," someone shouted.

7   "Let's get quiet and make the best of it," Mr. Moore smugly replied. Then he proceeded with the course orientation.

8   Near the end of the class, I mustered up enough courage to ask a question, so, nervously, I raised my hand. Keeping silent, Mr. Moore stared, and stared, and stared at me until my arm grew heavy and began to tremble. My heart sank, and my picture of freedom shattered in infinite pieces as he said, "I see that there are no questions. Class dismissed."

9   I have always blamed myself for that crushing moment. Why did I allow myself to be overlooked? Why did I not feel free? That painful, dehumanizing incident within itself did not provide any answers, though it signaled the beginning of my search. And finally, through years of disappointments, I discovered the truth—the truth that had evaded me during those high school years.

10   Freedom is not a gift, but a right. Officials did not, could not, award "freedom." It had to be something that I wanted,

craved, demanded. The Supreme Court had liberated me of many external restrictions, but I had failed to liberate myself. In some instances internal constraints can be more binding than the overt ones. It is impossible to enslave one who has liberated oneself and futile to pry off the external chains of an internally bound person. Only when there is emancipation of both body and soul are any of us truly *free* to follow our hearts.

Post-reading Questions

Content

1. What does the narrator mean when she writes about her "first illusion of freedom"? How does her curiosity contribute to that first illusion?

2. Outside of the school, the narrator encountered crowds of angry white "integration" protestors. Once within the school, why was she lulled into a false sense of security? In what way was her geometry class a "wake-up call"?

3. How does the geometry teacher demonstrate his racism? In what way does he make the author feel invisible?

4. Why does Jarrett blame herself for the "crushing moment" in the geometry classroom? Do you think she had any accurate conception of freedom?

Strategies and Structures

1. Explain how and why the scene in the geometry classroom provides the climatic moment in Jarrett's essay. Would it have been appropriate earlier in the essay? Why or why not? How does this incident signal the beginning of her "search" for freedom?

2. Jarrett begins her essay mentioning her "first illusion of freedom"; how does she conclude her piece? In what way does her introductory paragraph look forward to her concluding paragraph—and how does her concluding paragraph look back at her introductory paragraph?

3. In ten compact paragraphs, how does the author lead her readers from teenage innocence, believing that desegregation had no meaning for her, to the mature conclusion that "Only when there is emancipation of

both body and soul are any of us truly *free* to follow our hearts"?

4. An important part of writing is maintaining a sensitivity to the reader. Bearing this in mind, how does Jarrett convey her experience with racism and prejudice without alienating her readers?

Language and Vocabulary

1. Vocabulary: *desegregation, futile, horde, irate, denigrating, saunter, dehumanizing, crave, emancipation.* After you look up the vocabulary words, write a paragraph explaining how the words help to capture the intensity of her realizations as she moved from innocence to enlightenment.

2. Discuss the denotation and connotation of words in this essay. What connotations, for instance, does *fortress* carry? How might reference to a fortress reinforce the theme of false security?

Group Activities

1. In small groups, go to your college library and investigate the Supreme Court's decision, *Brown* v. *Board of Education.* How did it provide for the desegregation of schools? To what extent did this ruling succeed in its intentions? Share your findings in a class forum.

2. Why do people allow themselves to be overlooked in painful, dehumanizing situations? Get into groups, assign a recorder, and brainstorm as many answers to this question as you can. What do your answers suggest about human nature? State your group's major insights and analyze them both in context to Jarrett's essay and the world you live in today.

Writing Activities

1. Write an essay in which you defend the notion that "freedom is not a gift, but a right." Support your composition with facts, details, and examples drawn from observations, personal experiences, and readings.

2. Brainstorm the idea of freedom (you might look back to your pre-reading responses for Jarrett's essay). Then construct a paper detailing an incident where, like the narrator in "Freedom," you moved from an innocent sense of the world to the harsh realities provided by that experience.

Malcolm X

A Homemade Education

*Born in Omaha, Nebraska, in 1925, Malcolm X, the son of a black
separatist preacher, spent his early childhood in middle America.
When his father died, Malcolm X became involved with life on the
streets, which ultimately led to his imprisonment for burglary.
Denouncing his Christian name—his slave name—he took the name
"X" and became devoted to the Black Muslim movement which was
headed by the honorable Elijah Muhammad. Malcolm X began to
correspond with Elijah Muhammad while still in prison, and
Malcolm X's desire to further his writing skills was directly
responsible for the "Homemade Education" discussed in the following
essay, an excerpt from* The Autobiography of Malcolm X. *Malcolm X's
relationship to Elijah led him to become a militant leader of the black
revolution. Ironically, he was preaching the brotherhood of man when
assassinated in 1965.*

Pre-reading Questions

1. What are the denotations and connotations (see Glossary)
   of the word *homemade?* How would you personally relate
   the word *homemade* to the educational process?

2. List the steps you would take if your education were left
   entirely up to you, without the aid of teachers or parents.
   What would you do to build your vocabulary, how would
   you empower yourself as a writer, and how would you develop a thorough knowledge of the world around you?

1   It was because of my letters that I happened to stumble
upon starting to acquire some kind of homemade education.

2   I became increasingly frustrated at not being able to express
what I wanted to convey in letters that I wrote, especially

those to Mr. Elijah Muhammad. In the street, I had been the most articulate hustler out there—I had commanded attention when I said something. But now, trying to write simple English, I not only wasn't articulate, I wasn't even functional. How would I sound writing in slang, the way I would *say* it, something such as, "Look, daddy, let me pull your coat about a cat, Elijah Muhammad—"

3   Many who today hear me somewhere in person, or on television, or those who read something I've said, will think I went to school far beyond the eighth grade. This impression is due entirely to my prison studies.

4   It had really begun back in Charlestown Prison, when Bimbi first made me feel envy of his stock of knowledge. Bimbi had always taken charge of any conversation he was in, and I had tried to emulate him. But every book I picked up had few sentences which didn't contain anywhere from one to nearly all of the words that might as well have been in Chinese. When I just skipped those words, of course, I really ended up with little idea of what the book said. So I had come to the Norfolk Prison Colony still going through only book-reading motions. Pretty soon, I would have quit even these motions unless I had received the motivation that I did.

5   I saw that the best thing I could do was get hold of a dictionary—to study to learn some words. I was lucky enough to reason also that I should try to improve my penmanship. It was sad. I couldn't even write in a straight line. It was both ideas together that moved me to request a dictionary along with some tablets and pencils from the Norfolk Prison Colony school.

6   I spent two days just riffling uncertainly through the dictionary's pages. I'd never realized so many words existed! I didn't know *which* words I needed to learn. Finally, just to start some kind of action, I began copying.

7   In my slow, painstaking, ragged handwriting, I copied into my tablet everything printed on that first page, down to the punctuation marks.

8   I believe it took me a day. Then, aloud, I read back, to myself, everything I'd written on the tablet. Over and over, aloud, to myself, I read my own handwriting.

9   I woke up the next morning, thinking about those words—immensely proud to realize that not only had I written so much at one time, but I'd written words that I never knew were in the world. Moreover, with a little effort, I also could remember what many of these words meant. I reviewed the

words whose meanings I didn't remember. Funny thing, from the dictionary's first page right now, that "aardvark" springs to my mind. The dictionary had a picture of it, a long-tailed, long-eared, burrowing African mammal, which lives off termites caught by sticking out its tongue as an anteater does for ants.

10   I was so fascinated that I went on—I copied the dictionary's next page. And the same experience came when I studied that. With every succeeding page, I also learned of people and places and events from history. Actually the dictionary is like a miniature encyclopedia. Finally the dictionary's A section had filled a whole tablet—and I went on into the B's. That was the way I started copying what eventually became the entire dictionary. It went a lot faster after so much practice helped me to pick up handwriting speed. Between what I wrote in my tablet, and writing letters, during the rest of my time in prison I would guess I wrote a million words.

11   I suppose it was inevitable that as my word-base broadened, I could for the first time pick up a book and read and now begin to understand what the book was saying. Anyone who has read a great deal can imagine the new world that opened. Let me tell you something: from then until I left that prison, in every free moment I had, if I was not reading in the library, I was reading on my bunk. You couldn't have gotten me out of books with a wedge. Between Mr. Muhammad's teachings, my correspondence, my visitors—usually Ella and Reginald—and my reading of books, months passed without my even thinking about being imprisoned. In fact, up to then, I had never been so truly free in my life.

Post-reading Questions

Content

1. What led Malcolm X to improve his vocabulary? That is, what were the initial problems that he had with reading, and how did these lead to his desire to build his vocabulary?

2. What steps did Malcolm X take to build his vocabulary?

3. What were his emotional responses after he copied the first page of the dictionary?

4. How did reading affect Malcolm X's outlook on life?

Strategies and Structures

1. Malcolm X starts many of his paragraphs with the first-person pronoun "I." What effect does this have on the essay, and what does it suggest about the results of education?
2. Malcolm X concludes paragraph 11 by writing "In fact, up to then, I had never been so truly free in my life," referring to his ability to read. How does this concluding statement sum up the value of a homemade, personally tailored education as opposed to the rigid learning methods often used in schools?
3. What transitions lead the reader from one step in Malcolm X's educational process to the next?
4. What phrases does Malcolm X use to keep his writing conversational? Which phrases does he use to suggest he is educated? What is the effect of balancing these two styles? What does it suggest about the author's personality?

Language and Vocabulary

1. Vocabulary: *articulate, hustler, emulate, riffling, inevitable, bunk.* As Malcolm X did, write down the entire dictionary definitions of the aforementioned words and bring them with you to your group activity.
2. In paragraph 2, Malcolm X suggests that slang cannot be written. Brainstorm a list of your own slang. Why is slang more effective on the streets or among your peers than it is in an academic setting?

Group Activities

1. Devise some homemade, as opposed to traditional, methods for learning the above vocabulary words. Also devise some homemade study techniques that you can use in your other classes.
2. Today there is much debate over the education of prisoners. How do you feel about this issue? Should prisoners be educated or simply be punished? In groups, prepare to debate both sides of this issue in a seminar situation.

Writing Activities

1. Write a process essay wherein you explain how to acquire and use common sense to resolve the majority of the problems you encounter in daily life. Make sure you present your material in clear, sequential steps.

2. Research a current educational program in a local prison. Describe the program in detail, answering such questions as who is involved, what are the benefits and problems, where does the program take place, when is a prisoner or instructor eligible for such a program, why is such a program in place, and how does the program work? Your job is to inform your readers about this program. (Your local research librarian can help you find out where to get such information.)

Luis M. Valdez

Perspectives on "Borders"

Luis M. Valdez is well known for his work with the Chicano Theater and for founding the Teatro Capisino. *A graduate in English of San Jose State University, Valdez writes his plays, called* actos, *in both English and Spanish; they deal with issues of social importance and are meant as much to inform as to entertain. His dramas include* The Shrunken Head of Pancho Villa *(1963),* The Sellouts *(1967),* Dark Root of a Scream *(1971),* Zoot Suit *(1978),* Luis Valdez's Early Works: Actos, Bernabe, and Pensamiento *(1990), and* Taking It to the Streets: The Social Protest Theater of Luis Valdez and Amiri Baraka *(1997). Valdez's other credits include the movie* La Bamba *(1987), which he wrote and directed, and the Peabody Award-winning* Corridos: Tales of Passion and Revolution *(1982), which he produced for PBS (1987). The following essay was taken from a talk Valdez presented at a public humanities lecture in 1986. It appeared in its present form in* Columbus & After: Rethinking the Legacy *(A Touring Chautauqua Program of the California Council for the Humanities and the Oregon Council for the Humanities).*

Pre-reading Questions

1. What purpose do borders serve? Are they always visible to the naked eye?

2. What symbols (a token of identity or something that stands for or represents something else) do you identify with and why?

1   It's curious that Amerigo Vespucci lent his name to the continent. There's a tremendous coincidence here because this

place, this Western Hemisphere, this America, had another ancient name before the coming of the Europeans. The Mayans used to call it "Amaruca." "Amaruca" means the land of the feathered serpent. Mexico means feathered serpent. Boundaries, borders between the material and the spiritual. Mysteries of this gigantic part of the world, this place that was new and old at the same moment, this place that was a place of endless fascination and endless mystery. And yet it had a map that was sketched in the *Popol Vuh,* which is the book of the ancient Quiché Maya, the Mayan Bible if you will. It survived as creation stories for the children so the priests didn't completely destroy it. It was an oral tradition anyway, and was finally transferred to print in the 18th century. So it has come down to us as a damaged fragment, but nevertheless enough is there for us to be able to see this map of ancient America and the promise. Because you see if there's anything that ancient America understood, it was time. The functioning of time. The Mayans were able to predict the future—360,000 years ahead. They predicted the conquest of America by men who came dressed in armor on these creatures that came to be known as horses. One of the South American pre-Columbian leaders had a dream, and he had one of his artists sketch and eventually sculpt a figure that he had dreamed, that he had seen in this vision. And it was the image of a Conquistador, in armor, 200 years before the coming of the Spanish.

2   The Mayans were mathematicians. I never tire of saying they invented zero along with other people, but they had zero a long time. The circle. That's what zero is, the circle, cero. They understood the workings of time, and there are books of prophecy—if you know how to read them—they predict our time. I'm not claiming that the Mayans knew everything. They made a few mistakes in their time. But it's a piece of human knowledge that whether we know it or not, we have been fusing together for 500 years. This hemisphere and that hemisphere, opposites that unite. Thirteen colonies. Thirteen colonies united. According to some kind of plan.

3   Did you know that the early Americans who arrived here from Europe studied the Indian tribes and what they saw were plans, methods of being together that they had never encountered before? Confederacies. The confederacy of the Iroquois led to a concept of United States, which was still a very new and fresh concept in Europe. The confederacy of Mayapan in the Yucatan Peninsula. There was stuff seeping up from the land. There was a spirit here, this fresh new world, and that seduc-

tion of America has been irresistible. There's more to America than just transplanted European culture. The destiny of America is greater than any of us can possibly imagine. I'm a cockeyed optimist, ok? Because I believe that the strength of our humanity lies in our infinite and spiritual potential. I believe that at the heart of all material being is energy, is spirit, is belief. And so that makes me very optimistic about America in spite of the whips and the lashes and the deaths and the killings. I believe that we will get by, that we will evolve, that America will complete her destiny, and it is going to take all of us to be able to do it.

4   Let's go back to the *Popol Vuh.* We're talking about borders now. There is a border that defines the human being as a material and spiritual being. We have all learned that we're *Homo sapiens,* wise monkeys. The monkey is a symbol of intelligence in the *Popol Vuh,* and in the classic Chinese novel *Monkey.* The wise monkey is a symbol for humanity. Now let me offer you another symbol for our human being—the feathered serpent. You are a feathered serpent that is evolving and crawling out of the seeds of your being. And once in awhile you get caught up in the dead skins of your life. You know biologically we go through a complete cellular change every seven to nine years. We're totally renewed. So in one sense, biologically, you crawl out of a dead skin. You evolve out of yourself. The feathers are necessary because they represent our spiritual being.

5   Now the Spanish Conquistadors and the missionaries who came to the New World didn't understand that these pre-Columbian cultures were infatuated with the devil. They didn't understand Earth symbols. And yet it continues to be present in our American mentality. The symbol of the rattlesnake is an early North American symbol. "Don't tread on me." You don't step on a rattlesnake. Those little rattlers are symbols of time, and so like a snake, America continues to crawl out of itself and evolve. And the dead skins fall away as we emerge clean and fresh with a new skin, so new, so fresh, that at times it is painful. And these times that we are going through right now are precisely like that.

6   These are painful times, and yet they are very exciting times. Many people in this country are intimidated and frightened by the brown hordes pouring across the border, the non-border, this border that cannot hold. And so they want to declare English the official language of the United States. But I tell you that you cannot keep something natural from

happening. The evolution of America has always involved north and south migration. It was the Europeans who gave it east and west. And we're happy to have it because what that did is to set up the four directions. Another ancient symbol, the Christian cross. The cross represents four directions, and in the *Popol Vuh* they speak of the upper world and the lower world and right at the point where the two worlds meet there is a crossroads that leads from one to the other. It's like the belly-button of the world. Right at that intersection, four roads meet—the white road, the black road, the yellow road, and the red road. What they represent to me is the promise of America— that four roads will meet and will bear new fruit in this ancient land. You can represent it any way that you like—racially, culturally.

7   The representations of what these people mean to each other ultimately represents a whole, that sphere, the power of the sun, the power of the planet that pulls from within to hold it together in space. And so we, our humanity, is a humanity that must pull from within and hold us together, but not without recognizing the four corners of the universe, certainly the four human corners of human civilization. It is important that Europe came to these shores. It is important that Asia came to these shores. It is important that there was a pre-Columbian America here waiting to blend and to create something greater than the parts. A whole vision of humanity.

Post-reading Questions

Content

1. What does the author mean when he talks about the "brown hordes pouring across the border, the nonborder, this border that cannot hold"?

2. What is the controlling idea or thesis of this essay? Where does it appear?

3. In your opinion, what is the most striking image Valdez presents in this essay? Why do you find it particularly powerful?

4. Earlier in this text, Gómez-Peña dealt with the issue of "crossing borders" in his essay "Documented/Undocumented." How does Valdez's essay compare with Gómez-Peña's tone and content?

5. What symbols of wholeness which come from different cultures does the author present?

Strategies and Structures

1. How does the author structure the material in this essay? (Does his composition consist of one or more parts?)
2. In what way is Valdez's essay an example of informational process analysis? What other rhetorical strategies are at work here?
3. Why do you think Valdez uses so many similes in this essay? Do they serve a strategic purpose? Explain your answer.
4. How persuasive is the author's account of history? Why? Do you agree with his vision of the possibilities of the future? Why or why not?
5. "Perspectives on 'Borders'" was taken from a public humanities lecture presented in 1986. What characteristics of spoken English are evident in this transcription of his talk? How do or don't they interfere with clearly written communication?

Language and Vocabulary

1. Vocabulary: *hemisphere, confederacy, seduction, irresistible, Homo sapiens, serpent, intimidate.* Look up the definitions in the dictionary and write the words you did not know on your permanent vocabulary list. Many of these words begin with prefixes (one or more sounds or letters placed before a word to indicate a derivative meaning). Carefully go over each of the words, checking your dictionary, to see which words begin with prefixes. Then list the meaning of the prefix and state how the prefix has changed the meaning of the root word.
2. Valdez uses symbols from many cultures throughout this essay. For instance, he points out that monkeys are symbols of intelligence in the Mayan bible *Popol Vuh*. Go through the essay and list the other symbols that Valdez uses. How do these contribute to Valdez's idea of "a whole vision of humanity"?

Group Activities

1. In small groups, create a list of as many cultures in the United States as you can think of. Then focus on the four or five of these cultures that you know best,

listing and discussing the contributions each has made to American society.

2. Borders tend to confine and restrict people. Sometimes they are erected for positive purposes. Discuss the following with your group: What are some of the positive purposes of borders? What are the effects of borders? How do cultures create "borders" which keep others out and their own people in? As a society, how can we dismantle the negative borders and promote cultural pluralism?

Writing Activities

1. Beginning with historical background, write an essay persuading someone that his or her worldview—including the borders that define this worldview—does him or her more harm than good. Incorporate informational process analysis in this effort to persuade someone to change his or her worldview.

2. Valdez calls for a multicultural American society. What steps can we take to create such a society—one in which people are appreciative of individuals from diverse cultures? Write a process analysis essay explaining how this goal realistically can be achieved.

Additional Topics and Issues for Process Analysis Essays

1. Compose a process paper explaining how to make work easier. Begin by limiting your focus a bit so your reader has a pretty good idea of what you mean by work (e.g., physical labor or mental labor). Then explain your "how to" process, illustrating each step with specific examples.

2. Write an informative process analysis explaining how you would raise a child compared with how you were raised. What would be the advantages of your method of child rearing? Why do you think your parents raised you the way they did?

3. Making sure that you develop each discussion point, write an essay explaining one of the following topics:

a. How to enjoy studying and still be popular
b. How to earn A's without studying
c. How to embarrass your friends in public and still maintain your dignity
d. How to research your family roots or chart a family tree

4. Write a *directive* process analysis explaining how you would overhaul our present educational system (either high school or college). What can parents, teachers, and students do?

5. What sorts of things have you witnessed in your life that you consider meaningful and important? Select one particular incident, such as your graduation from high school or your wedding day, and trace the process you went through from start to finish.

6. Write a paper explaining how you learned to sing, dance, or play a musical instrument, or tell someone else how to do it.

7. Write an original directive process analysis paper explaining how to thoroughly relax after work or school, how to make other people miserable and remain happy yourself, or how to enjoy living with several people in a very small apartment or house. Your paper may have either a serious or humorous tone.

8. Write an informational process essay in which you describe the burial practices of a culture other than your own. (This may necessitate some research on your part.) What do these practices suggest about the culture's attitude toward life as well as toward death?

9. Select a topic or field of interest after watching one of the home improvement or cooking shows on television. At the end of the show, get the information that is usually provided on how to acquire a copy of the show's transcript, and send for it. In your own words, relate how to do or how something was done, based on the transcript.

10. Write a humorous or satirical paper in which you explain how to run a company into the ground and end up being a billionaire.

7

Comparison and Contrast

We compare and contrast every day of our lives, so much so that some psychologists believe that it is our most elemental thinking strategy. When we compare, we look at the similarities between two or more things. When we contrast, we look at the differences between them. Think about a trip to the grocery store. What types of things do we compare and contrast as we shop? We may compare the usefulness of items. We may compare and contrast the quality of items. We may contrast the prices of two items. When we write, we often compare and contrast also. In school, we may compare and contrast two different points of view on a topic. At work, we may write a report comparing and contrasting two competitors. Michael Segell uses comparison and contrast in *The Politics of Greeting* to showcase the similar yet different body language exhibited by men and women. Then he employs the same method of development to draw *"corollaries among our primate relatives."* In Cobie Kwasi Harris's essay *River of Memory: The Ebb and Flow of Black Consciousness Across the Americas,* he uses the rhetorical mode of Comparing and Contrasting to reveal information about customs, religions, belief systems, and individuals. Additionally, his comparative exposition highlights differences between slaves in the United States and those in the Caribbean and South America.

In "American SF and The Other," Ursula Le Guin takes a comparative look at *The Other*—the sexual alien, the social alien, the cultural alien, and the racial alien—to explain and support her thesis that people are not portrayed realistically in science fiction. Instead, science fiction writers focus on differences and create barriers. Using comparison and contrast, Le Guin argues that *"If you deny affinity with another person or kind of person, if you declare it to be totally different than yourself—as men have done to women, and class has done to class, and nation has done to nation—you may hate it or defy it; but in either case you have denied its spiritual equality and human reality. You have made it into a thing to which the only possible relationship is a power relationship."*

Successful writers know that when they compare and contrast, the most important step is gathering as much information as possible about the two items or ideas being compared and contrasted. Many of the prewriting strategies mentioned in the opening chapter on writing can help you gather the necessary information. One way that is most effective is to make a similarities list and a differences list: First, list all the similarities between the two items or ideas; next, list all the differences between them.

After a writer has gathered enough information and begins to write, he or she will often clearly introduce the items or ideas to be analyzed in the opening paragraph. For example, Suzanne Britt, in "Neat People vs. Sloppy People," introduces her topic in the opening sentence of her essay: *"I've finally figured out the difference between neat people and sloppy people."*

Many writers choose to use thesis statements. For instance, in E. B. White's essay, "Education," he states his thesis at the beginning of his second paragraph: *"The shift from city school to country school was something we worried about quietly all last summer."* He creates tension—although with ironic examples—between his son's present way of life (and schooling) and what it will be like at a country school; White wonders if his son will be able to adapt to the new environment.

Developing Essays Using Comparison and Contrast

How you structure a comparison/contrast essay depends on the intended audience (reader), the subject matter, and your purpose for writing. There are two basic methods for organizing comparison and contrast essays: the *point-by-point method* and the *block method.*

In the point-by-point method, the author considers one point of comparison or contrast at a time, analyzing the two subjects in alternate sentences or paragraphs. In "They Shut

My Grandmother's Room Door," Andrew Lam frequently uses the point-by-point technique of development to compare and contrast American and Vietnamese cultural attitudes: *"But if agony and pain are part of Vietnamese culture, pleasure is at the center of America's culture. While Vietnamese holidays are based on death anniversaries, birthdays are celebrated here* [the United States]."

In the block method, the author first analyzes one item or idea completely and then analyzes the second item or idea, being sure to compare and contrast the same points in the same order as the first. White uses a modified block format to structure his composition; an outline of White's essay would look something like this:

I. The country school
II. The city school (paragraphs 2 & 3)
  • clothes
  • transportation
  • the school
  • instructors/caregiver
  • actual education
III. The country school (paragraphs 4 & 5)
  • clothes
  • transportation
  • the school
  • instructors/caregiver
  • actual education
IV. Conclusion: The better school

Many, if not most, essays do not strictly follow a single pattern. An author may mix and blend strategies as he or she feels necessary to give the reader a clear explanation of the topics. For example, notice how Andrew Lam mixes both methods in "They Shut My Grandmother's Room Door," where the first part of his composition is primarily block and the latter part tends to develop his material using the point-by-point method. Regardless of what strategy you use, remember that comparing and contrasting people, places, and things is a means to an end (proving or supporting a thesis)—not an end in itself.

Tips on Writing Comparison and Contrast Essays

1. Select topics that offer a clear basis for comparison and contrast. That is, make sure your items for comparison are closely enough related to make a meaningful analysis. (Avoid comparing apples with oranges.)

2. Use an effective prewriting activity to gather as much information as possible, keeping in mind that you are looking for similarities and differences.

3. Write a thesis statement that clearly explains whether you will be analyzing differences and/or similarities and that introduces the two items or ideas of your essay.

4. Decide on a clear organizational pattern for your essay, either the point-by-point method, the block method, or a blend of the two patterns.

5. As you edit, be sure that you compared and contrasted the same points for each item or idea, preferably in the same order.

Andrew Lam

They Shut My Grandmother's Room Door

*Andrew Lam is a Vietnamese immigrant who currently resides in
San Francisco, where he is the associate editor for the Pacific News
Service. His articles have appeared in* Nation, Mother Jones, *and the*
Washington Post—*as well as many anthologies—and his work has
been acknowledged by many prestigious organizations. Lam won the
Thomas Stock Award for Excellence in International Journalism
(1991), a Rockefeller Fellowship (1992 / 93) and, most recently, the
Asian American Journalism Award for Commentary. Along with De
Tran and Hai Dai Nguyen, Lam edited* Once upon a Dream . . . : The
Vietnamese-American Experience *(1995).*

> ### Pre-reading Questions
>
> **1.** What holidays, customs, or rituals do you associate with
> death?
> **2.** Answer this question before reading the following essay:
> Where do you imagine you'll end up in your old age?
> (Write your answer in your notebook.)

1   When someone dies in the convalescent home where my
grandmother lives, the nurses rush to close all the patient's
doors. Though as a policy death is not to be seen at the home,
she can always tell when it visits. The series of doors being
slammed shut remind her of the firecrackers during Tet.

2   The nurses' efforts to shield death are more comical to my
grandmother than reassuring. "Those old ladies die so often,"
she quips in Vietnamese, "everyday's like new year."

3   Still, it is lonely to die in such a place. I imagine some wasted old body under a white sheet being carted silently through the empty corridor on its way to the morgue. While in America a person may be born surrounded by loved ones, in old age one is often left to take the last leg of life's journey alone.

4   Perhaps that is why my grandmother talks now mainly of her hometown, Bac-Lieu: its river and green rich rice fields. Having lost everything during the war, she can now offer me only her distant memories: Life was not disjointed back home; one lived in a gentle rhythm with the land; people died in their homes surrounded by neighbors and relatives. And no one shut your door.

5   So it goes. The once gentle, connected world of the past is but the language of dreams. In this fast-paced society of disjointed lives, we are swept along and have little time left for spiritual comfort. Instead of relying on neighbors and relatives, on the river and land, we deal with the language of materialism: overtime, escrow, stress, down payment, credit cards, tax shelter. Instead of going to the temple to pray for good health we pay life and health insurance religiously.

6   My grandmother's children and grandchildren share a certain pang of guilt. After a stroke which paralyzed her, we could no longer keep her at home. And although we visit her regularly, we are not living up to the filial piety standard expected of us in the old country. My father silently grieves and my mother suffers from headaches. (Does she see herself in such a home in a decade or two?)

7   Once, a long time ago, living in Vietnam we used to stare death in the face. The war in many ways had heightened our sensibilities toward living and dying. I can still hear the wails of widows and grieving mothers. Though the fear of death and dying is a universal one, the Vietnamese did not hide from it. Instead we dwelt in its tragedy. Death pervaded our poems, novels, fairy tales and songs.

8   But if agony and pain are part of Vietnamese culture, pleasure is at the center of America's culture. While Vietnamese holidays are based on death anniversaries, birthdays are celebrated here. American popular culture translates death with something like nauseating humor. People laugh and scream at blood and guts movies. The wealthy freeze their dead relatives in liquid nitrogen. Cemeteries are places of big business, complete with colorful brochures. I hear there are even drive-by funerals where you don't have to get out of your own car to pay your respects to the deceased.

9   That America relies upon the pleasure principle and happy endings in its entertainments does not, however, assist us in evading suffering. The reality of the suffering of old age is apparent in the convalescent home. There is an old man, once an accomplished concert pianist, now rendered helpless by arthritis. Every morning he sits staring at the piano. One feeble woman who outlived her children keeps repeating, "My son will take me home." Then there are those mindless, bedridden bodies kept alive through a series of tubes and pulsating machines.

10   But despair is not newsworthy. Death itself must be embellished or satirized or deep-frozen in order to catch the public's attention.

11   Last week on her 82nd birthday I went to see my grandmother. She smiled her sweet sad smile.

12   "Where will you end up in your old age?" she asked me, her mind as sharp as ever.

13   The memories of monsoon rain and tropical sun and relatives and friends came to mind. Not here, not here, I wanted to tell her. But the soft moaning of a patient next door and the smell of alcohol wafting from the sterile corridor brought me back to reality.

14   "Anywhere is fine," I told her instead, trying to keep up with her courageous spirit. "All I am asking for is that they don't shut my door."

Post-reading Questions

Content

1. What does the door symbolize in Lam's essay?
2. How is *the grandmother's* life in America different than in Vietnam? Why?
3. What are the most striking differences between American and Vietnamese culture presented in this essay?
4. How do people deal with their fear of death?

Strategies and Structures

1. In what way do Lam's first and last paragraphs "frame" the real point of this composition? What image appears in both paragraphs and how does it function as a unifying device?
2. Where does Lam gather information to illustrate his essay? How is it effective?

3. Reread this article, omitting the initial sentence in each paragraph. How do the essay's clarity and meaning change? What does this suggest to us about the importance of opening sentences?

4. What specific examples does the author provide to illustrate his ideas? How is the comparison and contrast strengthened by his use of specific examples? What is the overall effect?

Language and Vocabulary

1. Vocabulary: *convalescent, morgue, disjointed, pang, filial, pervaded, liquid nitrogen, arthritis, monsoon.* Many of the words in this list deal with suffering and death. Using the antonyms (see Glossary) to those words, write a short paragraph or two dealing with Lam's subject. Does the meaning change? What does this suggest to you about proper word selection for your essays?

2. Lam frequently makes use of alliteration (see Glossary) in this composition. Why might a writer use alliteration? What is the effect of such phrases as "last leg of life's journey," "rich rice fields," and "wails of widows"? What other examples of alliteration can you find in his essay?

Group Activities

1. Get into groups and compare and contrast your responses to Pre-reading Question 2: "Where do you imagine you'll end up in your old age?" Has reading this essay changed your response? In what way did reading this essay sharpen your focus on where you want to be when you are old?

2. Brainstorm different ways that one can take care of an elderly relative. What are the advantages and disadvantages to each solution? What are the benefits and problems of each solution?

Writing Activities

1. Compare and contrast how you plan to take care of your parents to Lam's description of American elderly care practices today. Comparison and contrast

should be used here as the means of explaining your points as effectively as possible. Be sure to use specific examples.

2. Model an essay after Lam's composition, using the introductory and closing paragraphs as a framing device. Write a comparative paper explaining why you are for or against placing elderly people in rest homes. As you compare, you should make sure that your position on the issue is clear; however, make sure that you carefully consider both sides of the issue prior to making your conclusion.

Suzanne Britt

Neat People vs. Sloppy People

Suzanne Britt is a journalist and essayist whose articles have appeared in a wide range of news magazines, journals, and newspapers: the Dickens Dispatch, Newsweek, *the Des Moines* Register *and* Tribune, *the* Baltimore Sun, Newsday, *and the* New York Times. *Her books include* Skinny People Are Dull and Crunchy Like Carrots *(1982) and* Show and Tell *(1983). Britt often develops her satirical essays by using some form of comparison and contrast. She particularly enjoys exposing the follies of human behavior and the absurdity of stereotypes. As Britt said in the preface to* A Writer's Rhetoric *(1988), "Competent writers are imitators; compelling writers are original." The following essay illustrates how one's natural voice can be a "compelling" rhetorical tool.*

Pre-reading Questions

1. What negative things do you associate with neatness?
2. What are some positive qualities you associate with sloppiness?

1   I've finally figured out the difference between neat people and sloppy people. The distinction is, as always, moral. Neat people are lazier and meaner than sloppy people.

2   Sloppy people, you see, are not really sloppy. Their sloppiness is merely the unfortunate consequence of their extreme moral rectitude. Sloppy people carry in their mind's eye a heavenly vision, a precise plan, that is so stupendous, so perfect, it can't be achieved in this world or the next.

3   Sloppy people live in Never-Never Land. Someday is their métier. Someday they are planning to alphabetize all their books and set up home catalogues. Someday they will go through their wardrobes and mark certain items for tentative mending and certain items for passing on to relatives of similar shape and size. Someday sloppy people will make family scrapbooks into which they will put newspaper clippings, postcards, locks of hair, and the fried corsage from their senior prom. Someday they will file everything on the surface of their desks, including the cash receipts from coffee purchases at the snack shop. Someday they will sit down and read all the back issues of *The New Yorker.*

4   For all these noble reasons and more, sloppy people never get neat. They aim too high and wide. They save everything, planning someday to file, order, and straighten out the world. But while these ambitious plans take clearer and clearer shape in their heads, the books spill from the shelves onto the floor, the clothes pile up in the hamper and closet, the family mementos accumulate in every drawer, the surface of the desk is buried under mounds of paper and the unread magazines threaten to reach the ceiling.

5   Sloppy people can't bear to part with anything. They give loving attention to every detail. When sloppy people say they're going to tackle the surface of the desk, they really mean it. Not a paper will go unturned; not a rubber band will go unboxed. Four hours or two weeks into the excavation, the desk looks exactly the same, primarily because the sloppy person is meticulously creating new piles of papers with new headings and scrupulously stopping to read all the old book catalogs before he throws them away. A neat person would just bulldoze the desk.

6   Neat people are bums and clods at heart. They have cavalier attitudes toward possessions, including family heirlooms. Everything is just another dust-catcher to them. If anything collects dust, it's got to go and that's that. Neat people will toy with the idea of throwing the children out of the house just to cut down on the clutter.

7   Neat people don't care about process. They like results. What they want to do is get the whole thing over with so they can sit down and watch the rasslin' on TV. Neat people operate on two unvarying principles: Never handle any item twice, and throw everything away.

8   The only thing messy in a neat person's house is the trash can. The minute something comes to a neat person's hand, he

will look at it, try to decide if it has immediate use and, finding none, throw it in the trash.

9   Neat people are especially vicious with mail. They never go through their mail unless they are standing directly over a trash can. If the trash can is beside the mailbox, even better. All ads, catalogs, pleas for charitable contributions, church bulletins and money-saving coupons go straight into the trash can without being opened. All letters from home, postcards from Europe, bills and paychecks are opened, immediately responded to, then dropped in the trash can. Neat people keep their receipts only for tax purposes. That's it. No sentimental salvaging of birthday cards or the last letter a dying relative ever wrote. Into the trash it goes.

10   Neat people place neatness above everything, even economics. They are incredibly wasteful. Neat people throw away several toys every time they walk through the den. I knew a neat person once who threw away a perfectly good dish drainer because it had mold on it. The drainer was too much trouble to wash. And neat people sell their furniture when they move. They will sell a La-Z-Boy recliner while you are reclining in it.

11   Neat people are no good to borrow from. Neat people buy everything in expensive little single portions. They get their flour and sugar in two-pound bags. They wouldn't consider clipping a coupon, saving a leftover, reusing plastic non-diary whipped cream containers or rinsing off tin foil and draping it over the unmoldy dish drainer. You can never borrow a neat person's newspaper to see what's playing at the movies. Neat people have the paper all wadded up and in the trash by 7:05 A.M.

12   Neat people cut a clean swath through the organic as well as the inorganic world. People, animals, and things are all one to them. They are so insensitive. After they've finished with the pantry, the medicine cabinet, and the attic, they will throw out the red geranium (too many leaves), sell the dog (too many fleas), and send the children off to boarding school (too many scuffmarks on the hardwood floors).

Post-reading Questions

Content

1. What is the point of this essay? Upon what do you base your conclusions?

2. Why does Britt compare neat people with sloppy people?

3. What group of people does Britt identify with? How do you know for sure?
4. Why are neat people poor people to borrow things from?

Strategies and Structures

1. What is the tone or mood of Britt's essay, and what is the function of its humor?
2. Explain the effect of opening several consecutive paragraphs with the same phrase.
3. What impact do Britt's generalizations have on her essay as a whole? Why does she dwell on extreme notions of neatness and sloppiness?
4. How could such liberal use of generalizations be deadly in the hands of an inexperienced writer? Do generalizations undermine the quality of Britt's essay? Justify your opinion.
5. Why does Britt focus on contrasts—differences— rather than mention things that neat and sloppy people have in common?

Language and Vocabulary

1. Vocabulary: *rectitude, distinction, stupendous, métier, mementos, excavation, meticulously, scrupulously, organic.* Write down a synonym—a word that has the same (or nearly the same) meaning as another word—for as many of the vocabulary words as you can. When you are finished or can't think of any more words, find a synonym for the unknown words by asking your classmates; likewise, share your work with others.
2. When Britt writes about people, places, or things that are opposite in nature, she often reinforces this sense of opposition through her word choice. Go back over the essay and make a list of words associated with neatness and words associated with sloppiness.

Group Activities

1. Rent the Neil Simon film *The Odd Couple* and watch it in a relaxing environment (there is no need to take notes). After the film, discuss the extent to which Oscar Madison (the sloppy character) and Felix Unger

(the neat character) illustrate the theme of Britt's essay. Also, talk about the parts of the film you could refer to if you were using it to exemplify a point about neat and sloppy people. In part, this activity is an exercise in learning how to use your observations to your best advantage when you write. What you see can be valuable information!

2. For a group project, locate a copy of one of Britt's best-known essays, "That Lean and Hungry Look." Compare the techniques she employs in this essay when contrasting fat and thin people to those used when she contrasts neat and sloppy people in "Neat People vs. Sloppy People." What patterns exist in her writing style? How are they identifiable?

Writing Activities

1. Using a mixture of humor and seriousness similar to Britt's, write an essay comparing and contrasting two people, places, or things to demonstrate the stupidity and/or reliability of stereotypes.

2. Write an essay in which you try to rigidly categorize two types of people (e.g., young/old, rich/poor, coordinated/awkward) and thereby illustrate a controlling idea or thesis on the nature of stereotypes.

Cobie Kwasi Harris

River of Memory: The Ebb and Flow of Black Consciousness Across the Americas

Cobie Kwasi Harris, Associate Professor of Political Science, San Jose State University, San Jose, California, is an editor and author of one of the essays for Readings in Black Political Economy, *published in 1999. He has lived and taught in Africa for three years, hosts several radio programs on station KPFA, Berkeley, California, as well as a weekly program for three years at the same station, sponsored by Pacific News Service. He also has written several articles on civil and military relations in Africa, and is a noted lecturer and speaker on democratization in Africa and race relations in the United States.*

Pre-reading Questions

1. What does it mean to be enslaved? What do you think dignity means to enslaved people?
2. Get into groups of two or three and discuss how hope can spring from terrible circumstances. Write your responses in a journal entry.

Defir a la Force
(Defiance to Violence)

You who stop, you who weep,
You who one day die without knowing why,
You who fight, who watch while Another sleeps,
You who no longer laugh with your eyes,
You, my brother, full of fear and anguish,
Raise yourself and cry *No!*

David Diop

1   One of the most compelling stories of the modern period is the inability of slave masters to crush the Black spirit to be free. It is also how African peoples kept afire the embers of liberty and dignity while enduring the terrors of slavery. The indomitable spirit of Black people has led them to continue to struggle for freedom, despite enduring unspeakable crimes, such as, the raping of their mothers, the selling of their children like potatoes, or the killing of their fathers in front of them, and endless other humiliations. It is the mystery of this spirit of resistance against all odds that makes the Black liberation struggle for honor and justice one of the defining activities of modern times.

2   The struggle began in Africa when Europeans tried to extract humanity from the indigenous people, in hope of creating a human animal devoid of reason and spirit. They then objectified Africans' status by calling them chattel. In so doing, Europeans were able to steal African lands by enslaving the people who lived on them. The struggle of African people in their quest for freedom is best represented by the metaphor of a river because rivers twist and turn, and when a river's path is blocked, it finds another way to flow. Religion, rebellion, and arts and culture, which slaves encoded as a way to keep the flames of independence and honor alive, will help relate the story.

3   Just as African people were regarded as inferiors, so too were their religions. Their slave masters insisted that they adopt Christianity instead of keeping their African beliefs. The main difference between the African and European/Semitic idea of God is the role of Spirits in the world. In the African tradition, it is commonly believed that Spirits exist between God and human beings. There are essentially five Spirits: Nature and Human Spirits are the major ones. Nature Spirits are divided into two parts: sky and earth. Human Spirits also are divided into two parts: long-deceased (ancestors) and the recently deceased (living dead). These forces, which may be described as "Divinities" or "Deities," serve as a bridge connecting living and deceased members of a family and community. They also connect the living to the inanimate spheres, and animate spheres to humanity.

4   The preceding brief description illustrates how different African religious thought is from the stereotypes slave traders used to justify enslaving the Africans. What is important is that Africans, in turn, used European religious stereotypes as a cover to practice their own religions. The Europeans believed that Africans had no notion of a transcendental God and only prayed to rocks, trees, and rivers. This belief allowed the slaves to preserve their religious traditions and practices,

which came to be known as Candomble in Brazil, Santeria in Cuba, and Voodoo in Haiti. Another tradition that facilitated the fusion of African religious practice was the use of ancestor worship. Catholics make pilgrimages to places where earlier Church leaders lived and died, they pray for their patron saint to intervene in their lives, and they ask saints to bless their animals and crops. They also have a ritualistic blood sacrifice every communion where they symbolically eat the body and drink the blood of Jesus as a way to obtain everlasting life. Of course, the role of the saints in the Catholic Church is the role that ancestors play in African religion. Hence, slaves were able to preserve their dignity in South and Central America and the Caribbean because they were able to fuse their belief structure with that of European Christianity.

5   The preservation and integrity of the African religious system directly led to revolt throughout the Americas. In short, there is a direct correlation between the retention of African religion and culture, and insurrection. Haiti, which developed Voodoo, the most overt and institutional system in the Americas, was the scene of the only slave revolt in recorded history that successfully overthrew slavery. As a result, in the eighteenth century Haiti became the first free republic in the world, but revolts by African people also occurred throughout the modern slave world. In the case of slaves in the U. S., although they revolted, they did not have any of the major results that occurred throughout the rest of the modern slave world. This was due to the fact that they retained the least amount of their African religion.

6   This tragedy occurred for several reasons: the U. S. was a latecomer to plantation agriculture, and the mining of gold and silver was not as extensive as it was in Latin America. Perhaps the most important reason was that the U. S. did not have a constant influx of new Africans because Britain began prohibiting ships on the high seas, and laws were passed in the U. S. to stop the importing of slaves. Hence the U. S. slave owners were forced to breed slaves as they did horses and cows. This, in turn, meant that every succeeding generation of slaves bred in America would have less and less of the African material culture, such as rituals, cosmologies, secret societies, and naming ceremonies.

7   Even though the U. S.'s enslaved Africans did not retain as many memories as those in other pars of the Americas, they still retained enough to incorporate the African call-and-response tradition into their Christianity. Slaves in the U. S. immediately

began to identify more with the Old Testament than the New because in the Old Testament is the story of the liberation of an enslaved people from Egypt and the wicked Pharaoh. For enslaved Blacks, the U. S. was Egypt, and the slave master was the contemporary Pharaoh. The greatest slave revolt in the U. S. was led by Nat Turner, a self-taught minister who stated that he had visions similar to those that Moses had. Both had visions that prophesized death as a just punishment against a land and its people that had held others in bondage. Whereas Moses served as God's messenger to inform the Pharaoh that all Egyptian first-born sons would be killed by his God, Nat Turner claimed that God told him to act as the Angel of Death himself and to kill each white man, woman, and child. Moses, of course, is considered a hero who liberated his people by warning them how to avoid being slaughtered. In contrast, people judged Turner insane, tortured, and lynched him. As a result of that incidence, the river of African consciousness was diverted and slowed in the U. S., but it never stopped.

8   One of the best examples of how Africans combined their beliefs with those of Western religions is seen in the name of one of the first Black churches in the U. S., the African Methodist Episcopalian Church. The Black church essentially was the only place that slaves could gather collectively without disturbing their masters and their families. This church space and places in wooded areas and swamps were named "hush spaces" where slaves could nurture the desire for freedom and justice. They also were places where slaves would meet to determine who could be trusted to travel on the Underground Railroad to gain their independence. The indomitable spirit that enslaved Africans had for liberty and equality would flow in those "hush spaces."

9   Another major dimension that nurtured and cultivated the spirit of Black resistance against becoming the imagined stereotype of the slave master was brought about through the arts, such as: sculpture/painting, textiles, dance, singing/dancing, drumming, and story telling. Fortunately for the slaves, the slave masters were blinded by their belief that they were the superior race and that the Africans were devoid of the consciousness that would allow them to create art. Ironically, the masters' belief in their own supremacy provided a "hush space" right under their eyes, which allowed the slaves to maintain the embers of freedom and justice and keep them aglow in their souls.

10   The arts and religion took shape because they were fused together in traditional African beliefs and served as an incubator that prevented the slave master from destroying the cultural

memory of Africa. In African religion and art, dance, music, and story telling are indispensable parts of ritual and practice. Masks and sculptures are designed in ways to show the elemental forces of good and evil. Other dimensions of life are evident in uses of the body. For example, white is the color of mourning in some African religions; therefore, if people cover their bodies with white chalk, it is a sign of grief. Music was also a powerful means of communication for the scattered villages within a region. The drum was especially effective since it was used like a telephone. In fact, in New Orleans, in an area of the city called "Conga Square," a traitor informed the masters to stop slaves from playing drums since they were using them to mobilize people for a slave revolt. The drums also kept the Black consciousness flowing.

11   The first recorded revolt of an enslaved African occurred in 1502 on the island of Hispaniola when an escaped slave joined the indigenous people's rebellion against the Spanish. It still continues today—five hundred years later. There also were revolts in Santa Domingo, Mexico, Puerto Rico, Cuba, Venezuela, Honduras, and Colombia. In Colombia and Cuba, the liberated villages were called Palenques, and in Venezuela they were known as Cumbes. In the U. S., a significant contribution of the slaves was to join the Underground Railroad and flee to Canada. Perhaps their greatest contribution to their liberation struggle, however, was when they stopped working and producing food to support the Confederate Army. Instead, they joined Sherman's march to the sea, seized territory and developed communities that were self-sustaining.

12   The failure of slavery to actually transform Black people into beasts of burden without souls or minds serves as a torchlight for all those who suffer. Further, the Europeans' unsuccessful attempt to crush Black's consciousness and their driving spirit for liberty and dignity demonstrates that anyone and everyone can say "no" to the oppressor. Any individual can choose to submit to domination or can resist by saying "no!" Black people never have accepted the ideal that the slave master has always hoped that they would—a docile and happy slave.

Post-reading Questions

Content

1. What metaphor does Harris use to express "the struggle of African people in their quest for freedom"?

How and why does the metaphor capture the spirit of the paper?

2. According to Harris what is "one of the best examples of how Africans combined their beliefs with those of Western religions"?

3. Explain what Harris describes as a "hush space"? How did this "hush space" allow Africans to cultivate and nurture indigenous art forms?

4. What is the "main difference between the African and European/Semitic idea of God…"? How did the African slaves provide a cover "to practice their own religions"?

5. Where did the first revolt of an enslaved African occur according to Harris? What followed and continues today?

Strategies and Structures

1. What does Harris achieve through his analogy between the visions of Nat Turner and Moses?

2. How does Harris' introductory paragraph lead to the thesis "It is the mystery of this spirit of resistance against all odds that makes the Black liberation struggle for honor and justice one of the defining activities of modern times"?

3. What was a drum comparable to? Why did some slave masters stop their slaves from playing drums?

4. Why is comparison and contrast the most effective method that Harris could employ to develop his essay?

5. How does the quote at the beginning of Harris' essay anticipate or foreshadow the concluding paragraph?

Language and Vocabulary

1. Vocabulary: *dignity, indomitable, indigenous, devoid, objectify, chattel, Semitic, inanimate, transcendent, facilitated, fusion, patron, intervene, dimension, cultivated, liberation.* After reviewing the definitions of each vocabulary word, determine which words have negative or positive connotations. How did selection of words carrying connotative meanings add depth to Harris' discussion?

2. Look for any words that deal with enslavement in this essay. First write a paragraph using these words.

Next look up the antonyms (opposite meanings) in a thesaurus and write a contrasting paragraph dealing with the opposite of enslavement.

Group Activities

1. Go to the library or an electronic classroom and look up the word slavery. Then look up three to five incidents in history where men have enslaved fellow human beings. What were the justifications? Did the slaves rebel or give in to oppression? As slaves how were men and women treated differently? In the twenty-first century are we still in the business of slavery, skillfully cloaked by politicians as legal, ethical behavior? Share your findings and take notes for a subsequent writing assignment.
2. Divide the class into two diverse groups and prepare for a debate. One side will favor the use of slavery and the benefits derived from it, and the other, of course, will take the opposite point of view, being in favor of permanently abolishing slavery.

Writing Activities

1. Return to the information collected in the first group activity and write an essay in which you compare and/or contrast the methods that two of the societies you investigated used to enslave people, stating the reasons each group used to justify the treatment of these people.
2. Again referring to the information collected in the first group activity, compare and/or contrast how separate enslaved peoples reacted to bondage. What happened when the slaves rebelled? Did they gain freedom or were they imprisoned? Also what happened to the slaves who gave into repression? How long were they enslaved, and how did they gain their freedom? Finally, how did each oppressor treat men and women?

Ursula Le Guin

American SF and The Other

*An author of over thirty books, Ursula K. Le Guin, a native of
Berkeley, California, received her Bachelor's of Arts from Radcliffe
and her Master's of Arts from Columbia University. When she
received a Fulbright Scholarship, she moved to Paris, France, where
she met and married her future husband, Charles Le Guin, a
historian. After publishing* Rocannon's World *(1964), Le Guin wrote
a succession of books for all age groups. She became particularly
well known for her science fiction and fantasy stories. Some of her
science-fiction novels include* Planet of Exile *(1966),* City of
Illusions *(1967),* The Left Hand of Darkness *(1969),* The
Dispossessed *(1974),* Very Far from Anywhere Else *(1976), and* The
Water Is Wide. *Her works of fantasy include* A Wizard of Earthsea
(1968), The Tombs of Atuan *(1972),* The Farthest Shore *(1972),*
Malafrena *(1979),* The Beginning Place *(1980), and* Always Coming
Home *(1985). Le Guin also has written three volumes of short
fiction:* The Wind's Twelve Quarters *(1975),* Orsinian Tales *(1976),
and* The Compass Rose *(1982).* The Language of the Night: Essays
on Fantasy and Science Fiction *(1979) and* Dancing on the Edge of
the World: Thoughts on Words, Women, and Places *(1989) represent
her two collections of essays. In the following essay, taken from* The
Language of the Night, *Le Guin examines "The Other," the being
different from the true self. In science fiction, Le Guin contends the
people—especially women—are not portrayed as real people;
instead, "they are masses, existing for one purpose: to be led by their
superiors [usually male elitists]."*

Pre-reading Questions

1. To what extent have the film industry, comic books, television, short stories and novels shaped your perception of *science fiction* as opposed to *science fact?*

2. What do you consider a typical storyline in science fiction? How are women often depicted in science fiction? Jot down a few representative examples to illustrate your answer.

---

1   One of the great early socialists said that the status of women in a society is a pretty reliable index of the degree of civilization of that society. If this is true, then the very low status of women in SF should make us ponder about whether SF is civilized at all.

2   The women's movement has made most of us conscious of the fact that SF has either totally ignored women or presented them as squeaking dolls subject to instant rape by monsters—or old-maid scientists desexed by hypertrophy of the intellectual organs—or, at best, loyal little wives or mistresses of accomplished heroes. Male elitism has run rampant in SF. But is it only male elitism? Isn't the "subjection of women" in SF merely a symptom of a whole which is authoritarian, power-worshiping and intensely parochial?

3   The question involved here is the question of The Other—the being who is different from yourself. This being can be different from you in its sex; or in its annual income; or in its way of speaking and dressing and doing things; or in the color of its skin, or the number of its legs and heads. In other words, there is the sexual Alien, and the social Alien, and the cultural Alien, and finally the racial Alien.

4   Well, how about the social Alien in SF? How about, in Marxist terms, "the proletariat"? Where are they in SF? Where are the poor, the people who work hard and go to bed hungry? Are they ever *persons,* in SF? No. They appear as vast anonymous masses fleeing from giant slime-globules from the Chicago sewers, or dying off by the billion from pollution or radiation, or as faceless armies being led to battle by generals and statesmen. In sword and sorcery they behave like the walk-on parts in a high-school performance of *The Chocolate Prince.* Now and then there's a busty lass amongst them who is honored by the attentions of the Captain of the Supreme Terran Command, or in a spaceship crew there's a quaint old cook, with a Scots or Swedish accent, representing the Wisdom of the Common Folk.

5   The people, in SF, are not people. They are masses, existing for one purpose: to be led by their superiors.

6   From a social point of view most SF has been incredibly regressive and unimaginative. All those Galactic Empires, taken straight from the British Empire of 1880. All those planets— with 80 trillion miles between them!—conceived of as warring nation-states, or as colonies to be exploited, or to be nudged by the benevolent Imperium of Earth toward self-development— the White Man's Burden all over again. The Rotary Club on Alpha Centauri, that's the size of it.

7   What about the cultural and the racial Other? This is the Alien everybody recognizes as alien, supposed to be the special concern of SF. Well, in the old pulp SF, it's very simple. The only good alien is a dead alien—whether he is an Aldebaranian Mantis-Man or a German dentist. And this tradition still flourishes: witness Larry Niven's story "Inconstant Moon" (in *All the Myriad Ways,* 1971), which has a happy ending—consisting of the fact that America, including Los Angeles, was not hurt by a solar flare. Of course a few million Europeans and Asians were fried, but that doesn't matter, it just makes the world a little safer for democracy, in fact. (It is interesting that the female character in the same story is quite brainless; her only function is to say Oh? and Ooooh! to the clever and resourceful hero.)

8   Then there's the other side of the same coin. If you hold a thing to be totally different from yourself, your fear of it may come out as hatred, or as awe—reverence. So we get all those wise and kindly beings who deign to rescue Earth from her sins and perils. The Alien ends up on a pedestal in a white nightgown and a virtuous smirk—exactly as the "good woman" did in the Victorian Age.

9   In America, it seems to have been Stanley Weinbaum who invented the sympathetic alien, in *A Martian Odyssey.* From then on, via people like Cyril Kornbluth, Ted Sturgeon and Cordwainer Smith, SF began to inch its way out of simple racism. Robots—the alien intelligence—begin to behave nicely. With Smith, interestingly enough, the racial alien is combined with the social alien, in the "Underpeople," and they are allowed to have a revolution. As the aliens got more sympathetic, so did the heroes. They began to have emotions, as well as rayguns. Indeed they began to become almost human.

10   If you deny any affinity with another person or kind of person, if you declare it to be wholly different from yourself—as men have done to women, and class has done to class, and nation has done to nation—you may hate it or deify it; but in either case

you have denied its spiritual equality and its human reality. You have made it into a thing, to which the only possible relationship is a power relationship. And thus you have fatally impoverished your own reality. You have, in fact, alienated yourself.

11   This tendency has been remarkably strong in American SF. The only social change presented by most SF has been toward authoritarianism, the domination of ignorant masses by a powerful elite—sometimes presented as a warning, but often quite complacently. Socialism is never considered as an alternative, and democracy is quite forgotten. Military virtues are taken as ethical ones. Wealth is assumed to be a righteous goal and a personal virtue. Competitive free-enterprise capitalism is the economic destiny of the entire Galaxy. In general, American SF has assumed a permanent hierarchy of superiors and inferiors, with rich, ambitious, aggressive males at the top, then a great gap, and then at the bottom the poor, the uneducated, the faceless masses, and all the women. The whole picture is, if I may say so, curiously "un-American." It is a perfect baboon patriarchy, with the Alpha Male on top, being respectfully groomed, from time to time, by his inferiors.

12   Is this speculation? Is this imagination? Is this extrapolation? I call it brainless regressivism.

13   I think it's time SF writers—and their readers!—stopped daydreaming about a return to the age of Queen Victoria, and started thinking about the future. I would like to see the Baboon Ideal replaced by a little human idealism, and some serious consideration of such deeply radical, futuristic concepts as Liberty, Equality and Fraternity. And remember that about 53 per cent of the Brotherhood of Man is the Sisterhood of Woman.

Post-reading Questions

Content

1. Who or what is the most recognizable form of "The Other"?
2. Explain what Le Guin means when she writes, "From a social point of view, most SF has been incredibly regressive and unimaginative."
3. What is the mood or tone of Le Guin's essay?
4. What occurs, according to Le Guin, when people "deny any affinity" with other "kinds of people"?
5. Why might a person consider the social change (or lack thereof) in SF so "un-American"?

Strategies and Structures

1. How does Le Guin express her thesis, and in what way does her presentation of it suit the overall purpose of her essay?
2. Why do you imagine that Le Guin chooses to refer to *science fiction* as SF?
3. Strategically, how and why does Le Guin analyze different types of Aliens—manifestations of "The Other"?
4. Why does Le Guin refer to several representative writers of science fiction? Briefly list a few of the authors (and their works, if provided) that she mentions.
5. How does the author draw her essay to a satisfactory conclusion, one that echoes her thesis?

Language and Vocabulary

1. Vocabulary: *socialists, hypertrophy, elitism, subjection, authoritarianism, parochial, Marxist, proletariat, anonymous, regressive, benevolent, myriad, affinity, complacently, hierarchy, patriarchy, Alpha Male, extrapolation, fraternity.* Le Guin's rich use of vocabulary may first require you to look up the meaning for words you are unfamiliar with and to refresh your memory about the appropriate use of words you do know. Next, create two lists, one with the header "types of people," and the second with the header "types of power (or words denoting power). How do both lists relate to Le Guin's discussion of the many types of Aliens, particularly in regard to science fiction?
2. What is meant by the phrase, "White Man's Burden"? What does this so-called burden justify, and how does Le Guin relate it to the nature of most science fiction?

Group Activities

1. After you get together with three or four other students, write down your personal definition for *alien.* Then compare and contrast your personal definition of "alien" to that of your peers. In what ways are

your definitions alike and how do they differ? Have your group recorder fold a sheet of paper into two columns, and make a list of common definitions in one column and dissimilar definitions (those carrying different connotative meanings) in another. Review both lists, and then write a single, unified, collaborative definition for the word "aliens."

2. How and why might stories about *paranormal* experiences be considered a form of science fiction? By the same token, how and why might some individuals believe that psychic phenomena or paranormal experiences should more properly be labeled *science fact?* Divide the class into two groups, and assign each group a position to take on paranormal experiences. After a brief discussion with the rest of your peers, prepare a five-minute class presentation. (Suggestion: Allow each group to make a position statement about paranormal experiences before debating them.)

Writing Activities

1. Brainstorm the term "alien" in reference to yourself. Then, develop a thesis based on a recurring theme or issue which arose in your pre-writing exercise. Using the technique of comparison and contrast, illustrate the different ways individuals perceive you and why. You might, for instance, compare your actual and idealized self, as seen through the eyes of others, drawing some conclusions about a particular aspect of your personality (e.g., I am an Alien to myself—I am "The Other").

2. Go to the college library and look up a representative collection of Le Guin's fiction, as well as a few science-fiction stories by authors you are familiar with or by authors she mentions in her essay (e.g., Larry Niven, Cyril Kornbluth, Ted Sturgeon, or Cordwainer Smith). After reading at least one piece of science fiction by Le Guin and one by another author, construct an essay where you compare and contrast how each author characterizes people in his or her story.

Michael Segell

The Politics of Greeting

Is everything in life a matter of politics? In the following article that initially appeared in the July 1997 issue of Esquire, *Segell discusses the difference in body language practiced by men and women, including greeting rituals.*

Pre-reading Questions

1. Traditionally, how do you greet women? How do you greet men? Do you find that you greet your own sex significantly different from others?

2. Have you ever felt uncomfortable because you were out of touch with a particular culture or gender's way of greeting one another properly? What did you do, if anything, to overcome your discomfort?

Do you want to diddle me—or are you just saying hi?

1   HEY. WHEN IT COMES to greeting each other, men are famously economical. And with the NBA playoffs fresh in mind, this is a good time of year to appreciate the most highly evolved—that is to say, minimalist—form of male body language. Like the somewhat passé high and low fives, the chest bump involves only fleeting physical contact but trumps the hand slap by adding a welcome frisson of violence. Plus, it's sanitary. Its concussive effects upon the retinal rods also preclude any lengthy eye contact—for eons one of the requisites of any politic manly salutation. Like our primate cousins and many other animals, we still perceive direct eyeballing from another male as a threat.

2   The body language women use with each other, by contrast, is so elaborate, it should be considered a discrete dialect. For

starters, they have no qualms about gawking at each other—perhaps because they smile so much. They begin soon after birth, weeks before infant guys, and over a lifetime beam about 30 percent more than men. They're also adept at what psychologists call, stroking—a highly nuanced style of social interaction, not always physical, that promotes and maintains interpersonal harmony (high on their agenda). During a conversation, or whenever they feel the emotional pitch flagging, women console each other with pats, nod encouragingly, knit their brows sympathetically, emit glissandos of emotional reassurance. How are you?

3   It must be exhausting.

4   Men, on the other hand, stroke each other just enough to get down to the business at hand—poker, say—or to acknowledge each other without seeming rude or as if they're toting a grudge. Good to see ya. We can also tell a lot from each other's handshake. The dead hand bespeaks passive hostility and conceit; the Vulcan death grip—a two-fisted simultaneous wrist cruncher and shoulder massage deployed by ad execs and party hosts—superiority. We picked up this handshaking ritual from chimpanzees, for whom a little digital press confers blessing of sorts. When a lower-ranking chimp wants to pass by a higher one, he holds out his mitt, hoping the dominant ape will give it a reassuring squeeze. Without it, he's wise to watch his back, as is a man whose proffered hand has been refused.

5   Still, body language was a lot easier to decode when we had furry coats and a rival's fear or anger was signaled by the horripilating hedgerow at the nape of his neck. But our modern clean-shaven circumspection may be more a reaction to the intimate physical language we were required to speak in our human past. Biblical figures, for instance, swore oaths by placing their hands under each other's "loins" or "thigh"—euphemisms for the scrotum or penis. Hence the common Latin root of the words testament, testify, and testicle. Feudal lords mercifully reduced the familiarity of this act by demanding that a vassal swear his fealty upon the landowner's sword.

6   Again, there are corollaries among our primate relatives. Rivalrous vervet monkeys often threaten each other by flashing their erect penises. Even when extending friendly greetings, male baboons jostle and mount each other to establish dominance. But older male baboons who have been greeting each other for years have devised a particularly effective form of negotiation—a series of intimate, carefully balanced greetings intended to communicate their mutual

support and neutralize any rivalry. One animal will approach his pal and present his rump. The other will smack his lips, then tickle the other's scrotum and pull on his penis. Primatologists call this "diddling," and it's thought to be a sign of trust. The monkeys then reverse roles to keep their relationship perfectly in balance.

7   According to primatologist Barbara Smuts of the University of Michigan and anthropologist J. M. Watanabe of Dartmouth College, diddling carries all the power of the covenant of Abraham, into which many of us are initiated eight days after birth by sacrificing our foreskin. "Genital touching . . . perhaps serves to enhance the truth value of whatever these males are 'saying' to each other," they write in The International Journal of Primatology. "Lacking articulate speech, and unable to swear oaths, perhaps male baboons make a gestural equivalent by literally placing their future reproductive success in the trust of another male."

8   How they hangin'? Only the baboon in me really wants to know.

Post-reading Questions

Content

1. What does the semi-humorous tone of Segell's essay add to his discussion? What might have been lost without it?

2. According to the author, what can we tell from a person's handshake? How do men and women greet each other differently?

3. Why was "body language easier to decode when we had furry coats..."?

4. What does the author identify as the minimalist of male body language? Would you or someone you know fit his description?

5. Do you think that the author was fair when he stated that women, "have no qualms about gawking at each other—perhaps because they smile so much"? Why? Why not?

Strategies and Structures

1. Why do you imagine Segell decided to structure his essay using block format rather than point-by-point? What did the block format enable him to do?

2. Why does he spend the first three paragraphs detailing the body language between men and women before introducing primates into the discussion? What could have been his strategic purpose?

3. Why does the author quote a noted primatologist and anthropologist in his essay?

4. What may the author's reason be for citing the corollaries between humans and their primate relatives when focusing on an essay that deals with body language?

5. Why might the manner in which animals greet each other, as described in the essay, be embarrassing for men and women to talk about? Here you might consider the difference between deviant and instinctual behavior.

Language and Vocabulary

1. *Vocabulary: diddle, minimalist, fleeting, frisson, primate, discreet, interpersonal, glissandos, proffered, horripilating, hedgerow, circumspection, euphemisms, vassal, fealty, negotiations, covenant, gestural, equivalent.* Review the definitions for today's vocabulary. Then, take a walk across campus and notice "body language" at work. Next, using a minimum of six of the above vocabulary words, describe what you witnessed.

2. How would you describe Segell's language choice in "The Politics of Greeting"? Does it seem to suit the subject? How? Why?

Group Activities

1. In small groups, discuss the way different people—not simply gender—greet each other throughout the world. If you have access to a computer-assisted classroom, meet there and then look up "greeting rituals" on various research engines. Finally, share what you uncover with the rest of the class.

2. As a follow-up to Strategies and Structures question #5, break into small groups and examine how and why people react to natural animal behavior as if it should follow some sort of ethical social code when in the presence of human beings. What conclusion can your group agree upon as to why we try

to distance human interactive tradition from that of our primitive ancestors?

Writing Activities

1. Using comparison and contrast and your dominant method of developing and explaining points, write an essay wherein you analyze a social custom from two points of view. What did you conclude?
2. Write an essay wherein you compare and contrast something to argue for a particular action. For example, you might advocate a certain type of dress, language, or behavior over another.

E. B. White

Education

Elwyn Brooks White (1899–1985) was a well-known essayist and
contributing editor for The New Yorker. *In collaboration with author*
James Thurber, White wrote the satire Is Sex Necessary? *(1929).*
White's other works include The Lady Is Cold *and various books for*
children including Stuart Little *(1945),* Charlotte's Web *(1952), and*
The Trumpet of the Swan *(1970). White also revised William Strunk's*
The Elements of Style. *His essays frequently appeared in magazines,*
including The New Yorker *and* Harper's Magazine. *The following*
essay first appeared in the March 1939 issue of Education.

Pre-reading Questions

1. What does it mean to "get an education"? How can anyone
   tell if another has truly been educated?

2. Freewrite on the topic of *American* education. What meanings, ideas, and opinions do you associate with it?

---

1   I have an increasing admiration for the teacher in the country school where we have a third-grade scholar in attendance.
She not only undertakes to instruct her charges in all the subjects of the first three grades, but she manages to function quietly and effectively as a guardian of their health, their clothes,
their habits, their mothers, and their snowball engagements.
She has been doing this sort of Augean task for twenty years,
and is both kind and wise. She cooks for the children on the
stove that heats the room, and she can cool their passions or
warm their soup with equal competence. She conceives their
costumes, cleans up their messes, and shares their con-
fidences. My boy already regards his teacher as his great
friend, and I think tells her a great deal more than he tells us.

2   The shift from city school to country school was something we worried about quietly all last summer. I have always rather favored public school over private school, if only because in public school you meet a greater variety of children. This bias of mine, I suspect, is partly an attempt to justify my own past (I never knew anything but public schools) and partly an involuntary defense against getting kicked in the shins by a young ceramist on his way to the kiln. My wife was unacquainted with public schools, never having been exposed (in her early life) to anything more public than the washroom of Miss Winsor's. Regardless of our backgrounds, we both knew that the change in schools was something that concerned not us but the scholar himself. We hoped it would work out all right. In New York our son went to a medium-priced private institution with semi-progressive ideas of education, and modern plumbing. He learned fast, kept well, and we were satisfied. It was an electric, colorful, regimented existence with moments of pleasurable pause and giddy incident. The day the Christmas angel fainted and had to be carried out by one of the Wise Men was education in the highest sense of the term. Our scholar gave imitations of it around the house for weeks afterward, and I doubt if it ever goes completely out of his mind.

3   His days were rich in formal experience. Wearing overalls and an old sweater (the accepted uniform of the private seminary), he sallied forth at morn accompanied by a nurse or a parent and walked (or was pulled) two blocks to a corner where the school bus made a flag stop. This flashy vehicle was as punctual as death: seeing us waiting at the cold curb, it would sweep to a halt, open its mouth, suck the boy in, and spring away with an angry growl. It was a good deal like a train picking up a bag of mail. At school the scholar was worked on for six or seven hours by half a dozen teachers and a nurse, and was revived on orange juice in mid-morning. In a cinder court he played games supervised by an athletic instructor, and in a cafeteria he ate lunch worked out by a dietitian. He soon learned to read with gratifying facility and discernment and to make Indian weapons of a semi-deadly nature. Whenever one of his classmates fell low of a fever the news was put on the wires and there were breathless phone calls to physicians, discussing periods of incubation and allied magic.

4   In the country all one can say is that the situation is different, and somehow more casual. Dressed in corduroys, sweatshirt, and short rubber boots, and carrying a tin dinner-pail, our scholar departs at the crack of dawn for the village school, two and a half miles down the road, next to the cemetery.

When the road is open and the car will start, he makes the journey by motor, courtesy of his old man. When the snow is deep or the motor is dead or both, he makes it on the hoof. In the afternoons he walks or hitches all or part of the way home in fair weather, gets transported in foul. The schoolhouse is a two-room frame building, bungalow type, shingles stained a burnt brown with weather-resistant stain. It has a chemical toilet in the basement and two teachers above the stairs. One takes the first three grades, the other the fourth, fifth, and sixth. They have little or no time for individual instruction, and no time at all for the esoteric. They teach what they know themselves, just as fast and as hard as they can manage. The pupils sit still at their desks in class, and do their milling around outdoors during recess.

5   There is no supervised play. They play cops and robbers (only they call it "Jail") and throw things at one another— snowballs in winter, rose hips in fall. It seems to satisfy them. They also construct darts, pinwheels, and "pick-up sticks" (jackstraws), and the school itself does a brisk trade in penny candy, which is for sale right in the classroom and which contains "surprises." The most highly prized surprise is a fake cigarette, made of cardboard, fiendishly lifelike.

6   The memory of how apprehensive we were at the beginning is still strong. The boy was nervous about the change too. The tension, on that first fair morning in September when we drove him to school, almost blew the windows out of the sedan. And when later we picked him up on the road, wandering along with his little blue lunch-pail, and got his laconic report "All right" in answer to our inquiry about how the day had gone, our relief was vast. Now, after almost a year of it, the only difference we can discover in the two school experiences is that in the country he sleeps better at night—and *that* probably is more the air than the education. When grilled on the subject of school-in-country vs. school-in-city, he replied that the chief difference is that the day seems to go so much quicker in the country. "Just like lightning," he reported.

Post-reading Questions

Content

1. What is the controlling idea in this essay?
2. In paragraph 3, although White says that at the city school, his son's "days were rich in formal experiences," the images, examples, and diction he chooses

to back up that statement seem to indicate otherwise. What is the true nature of his son's experiences? Explain your answer using specific details from White's essay to illustrate what you say.

3. What does White's son wear when he goes to school in the city? How does his choice of clothing change when he attends school in the country? Is one mode of dress more appropriate than another? Explain.

4. Contrast White's depictions of city school teachers to country school teachers. As human beings, how are they different and how are they alike?

5. What vivid details and examples in this essay help you to envision the distinct differences (at least, according to White's experience) between education at *city schools* and education at *country schools?*

Strategies and Structures

1. How does the tone of this essay reflect the author's attitude toward city (private) schools and country (public) schools?

2. Why do you think that White admits his bias toward public schools in the second paragraph? How might this lighthearted examination of the origins of his bias serve a larger purpose in his essay?

3. How does White use irony in this essay? How, for instance, do the things you relate to the word *scholar* contrast with the sort of learning White's son receives in the city school?

4. Which method of structuring comparative essays tends to be *predominant* in this essay? Why do you imagine White selected one method of organization over another?

5. In the final paragraph, White informs us that his son initially thinks that education at the country school is just "all right," but later states that days go by quickly—"just like lightning." How does the final sentence sum up White's general attitude toward country schools?

Language and Vocabulary

1. Vocabulary: *Augean, regimented, gratifying, discernment, bungalow, milling, laconic.* Write down each of the above words on a sheet of paper and locate the dictionary definition for each. Next, determine

what an antonym (word that carries an opposite meaning) for each word might be. You may use your own intuition and experience to predict an appropriate antonym for *Augean.*

2. White frequently uses figurative language such as metaphors (direct comparison) and similes (comparisons with the use of *like* or *as*) in this essay—as well as hyperbole (exaggeration of a point for emphasis). Search through the essay and locate as many examples of each type of figurative language as you can. (Suggestion: highlight the metaphors, similes, and so on, in your textbook.) Then write a brief paragraph—possibly using figurative language yourself—explaining what effect the use of figurative language had on you as a reader.

Group Activities

1. Divide into groups and select a "group recorder" to write down the material other members generate. Brainstorm the words *natural* versus *clinical education.* Make a separate list for each. Attempt to match every *natural* method of education with its corresponding *clinical* or artificial counterpart. Make copies of the list for all group members, and then for homework, have each person draft a comparative essay on the topic. Finally, assemble once again with your group and blend your individual insights into one collaborative essay.

2. Many educational practices today differ from educational practices of the past. For a group assignment, explore the similarities and differences between the past and present. First have each member of the group interview either his or her parents or grandparents about educational practices in their day. (Before your interview, you may want to brainstorm a series of appropriate questions as a group.) Next, do an individual freewriting on educational practices today; try to draw comparisons and contrasts with your parents' or grandparents' experiences. Finally, get together with your group, share your findings, and then draw some general conclusions about the similarities and differences between the two dif-

ferent generations. (It might be interesting to note whether those you interview went to country schools or city schools.)

Writing Activities

1. Write an essay in which you compare and contrast high school with college, a city school with a country school, or a private school with a public school. How are they similar yet different? What are the differences? What specific experiences have you had which illustrate these differences? Which do you prefer, and why do you prefer it?

2. Compose an essay in which you compare and/or contrast the American educational system with an educational system from another country. You may gather the needed information in several ways: Interview someone who has been educated in another country, interview a teacher who has taught in another system, research another system in the library, and/or watch a documentary on another educational system. As you gather your information, take notes on the similarities and differences between the other system and the American educational system.

Additional Topics and Issues for Comparison and Contrast Essays

1. Compare and contrast the most popular social activities in your parents' or grandparents' day to the most popular social activities of today.

2. Using the strategy of comparison and contrast, develop an essay in which you argue that one car, sport, movie star, sports hero (or team) is better than another.

3. Compare two very different magazines, like *People* and *Time;* discuss their different characteristics (e.g., the sort of ads, number of pictures, and choice of subjects). How does the intended audience for each magazine determine its characteristics?

4. Compare two places that you have visited (e.g., countries, restaurants, parks).

5. Contrast two likely candidates for public office in an upcoming election. Consider their qualifications for the office they seek. A variation of this assignment would be to compare dirty campaign tactics (which often ignore issues of public concern) to dignified ones.

6. Compare two characters in a novel, short story, or play you have read, or two people in a television show or movie you have seen.

7. Compare and contrast stereotypes between two cultures or between males and females for an ultimate purpose, determined by your thesis statement.

8. Write an essay in which you contrast the portrayal of a particular ethnic group on television and/or movies with your knowledge of and experiences with that particular culture.

9. Compare and contrast two sides of a current social issue in your community (e.g., banning smoking in all public areas). Your strategy of comparison/contrast should ultimately lead your reader to a sound conclusion.

10. Compare and contrast countercultures or subcultures (surfers, hippies, beatniks, bikers, yuppies) in America from different eras. This topic may require a little bit of research, but most of your information can be gathered by talking to people who lived during different time periods.

8

Division and Classification

When we divide and classify, we take a large and complicated subject and break it into smaller parts more easily handled by the writer and more easily grasped by the reader. Sometimes the smaller parts, or categories, are readily apparent, but at other times, we must carefully analyze our larger subject in order to discover how it breaks apart. As with other strategies, division and classification can be seen and used in everyday life. For instance, your college is more than likely divided into schools, divisions, and/or departments. You probably have a school of humanities which contains an art department, an English department, a humanities department, a speech and communications department, and a philosophy department.

When we write, we divide and classify in order to make a subject clear to the reader. We may hope that by clarifying an issue or subject like racism, as Martin Luther King, Jr., does in his essay, "The Ways of Meeting Oppression," our reader will be motivated to take some sort of action. Or we may hope to bring to the forefront some forgotten points about a certain issue or subject as Gary Tewalestewa does in "American Indians: Homeless in Their Own Homeland." For whatever reason we divide and classify a subject, we usually follow a few basic steps.

When we start to divide and classify a subject, we need to clearly divide it into recognizable parts. We should analyze our subject from several points of view until we feel that we have found the clearest and most appropriate categories in which to break it. Obviously, Robertson Davies in his essay "A Few Kind

Words for Superstition" carefully considered the many forms of superstition found in his community before he divided it into four forms: Vain Observances, Divination, Idolatry, and Improper Worship of a True God.

After you have carefully analyzed your subject and divided it into parts, it may help to create a rough outline or some other form of notes to help guide you as you write. A rough set of notes for Constance García-Barrio's essay "Creatures That Haunt the Americas" might look like this:

I. Creatures from Africa that stalk children
- Hairy Man
- guije
- Tunda
- deformed woman

II. Creatures from Africa that haunt adults
- Ciguapa
- Lobisón
- the ghost of the slave owner

As you write, you should feel free to revise or delete certain parts of your outline, but as a general rule, an outline will help keep you from wandering off the subject and into less important or irrelevant points.

As in most of your essays, use clear transitions to help guide your reader. Simple transitions such as *first, second,* and *third* can be very helpful. Often by simply keeping your points clearly separated (divided), you can write an essay that is easy to follow. What is an excellent film, and when do movies amount to little more than *mind candy?* Bill Swanson examines this topic and reveals some interesting answers— including the fact that *"filmmaking is both an art form and a business"* by dividing and classifying films as well as film viewers. Though he claims that *"the effect a film has, though, has as much to do with the film viewer as the film itself,"* he also illustrates that *"the best films make for a cinematic diet that enhances the psychological sinews and synapses that are life sustaining."*

After you have written your rough draft, you should go back over your essay and ask yourself if you have achieved your purpose. How do your categories help achieve your original goal— possibly to persuade your audience into a certain action or possibly to reveal a hidden truth about your subject? If a category does not ultimately contribute to your goal, you should delete it from your essay.

Tips on Writing Division and Classification Essays

1. Decide why you are classifying and dividing this subject. Keep this purpose in mind as you analyze your subject and compose your essay.

2. Carefully analyze your subject from many different points of view, looking for clear dividing lines.

3. Make some rough notes or an outline to help guide you during your writing. (Feel free to make alterations to your outline as necessary; it may be necessary to revise your outline several times.)

4. Use clear transitions to guide your reader and unify the parts of your essay.

5. Use controlling ideas and/or topic sentences to make your divisions clear. Then use specifics and details to help illustrate your divisions.

6. Carefully reread your rough draft, looking for inappropriate and irrelevant points or categorizations and eliminating them.

Martin Luther King, Jr.

The Ways of Meeting Oppression

Martin Luther King, Jr., a Baptist minister and civil rights leader during the 1950s and 1960s, preached nonviolence when advocating civil disobedience and sought to end segregation. His writings include Stride Toward Freedom *(1958) and the highly anthologized "Letter from the Birmingham Jail." On August 28, 1963, King led over 200,000 blacks and whites to the Lincoln Monument in Washington, D.C. There he delivered his renowned speech, "I Have a Dream," during the centennial of Abraham Lincoln's Emancipation Proclamation which freed the slaves in the United States. In 1964 at the age of 35, King became the youngest person ever to receive the Nobel Peace Prize. Four years later on April 4, 1968, he was assassinated in Memphis, Tennessee.*

Pre-reading Questions

1. What is oppression? What freedoms does an oppressor deny another person?
2. Have you ever been oppressed? What did you do to try and change the situation you were in? Was your method of overcoming oppression successful? How?

1   Oppressed people deal with their oppression in three characteristic ways. One way is acquiescence: the oppressed resign themselves to their doom. They tacitly adjust themselves to oppression, and thereby become conditioned to it. In every movement toward freedom some of the oppressed prefer to remain oppressed. Almost 2800 years ago Moses set out to lead the children of Israel from the slavery of Egypt to the freedom of

the promised land. He soon discovered that slaves do not always welcome their deliverers. They become accustomed to being slaves. They would rather bear those ills they have, as Shakespeare pointed out, than flee to others that they know not of. They prefer the "fleshpots of Egypt" to the ordeals of emancipation.

2 There is such a thing as the freedom of exhaustion. Some people are so worn down by the yoke of oppression that they give up. A few years ago in the slum areas of Atlanta, a Negro guitarist used to sing almost daily: "Been down so long that down don't bother me." This is the type of negative freedom and resignation that often engulfs the life of the oppressed.

3 But this is not the way out. To accept passively an unjust system is to cooperate with that system; thereby the oppressed become as evil as the oppressor. Noncooperation with evil is as much a moral obligation as is cooperation with good. The oppressed must never allow the conscience of the oppressor to slumber. Religion reminds every man that he is his brother's keeper. To accept injustice or segregation passively is to say to the oppressor that his actions are morally right. It is a way of allowing his conscience to fall asleep. At this moment the oppressed fails to be his brother's keeper. So acquiescence— while often the easier way—is not the moral way. It is the way of the coward. The Negro cannot win the respect of his oppressor by acquiescing; he merely increases the oppressor's arrogance and contempt. Acquiescence is interpreted as proof of the Negro's inferiority. The Negro cannot win the respect of the white people of the South or the peoples of the world if he is willing to sell the future of his children for his personal and immediate comfort and safety.

4 A second way that oppressed people sometimes deal with oppression is to resort to physical violence and corroding hatred. Violence often brings about momentary results. Nations have frequently won their independence in battle. But in spite of temporary victories, violence never brings permanent peace. It solves no social problem; it merely creates new and more complicated ones.

5 Violence as a way of achieving racial justice is both impractical and immoral. It is impractical because it is a descending spiral ending in destruction for all. The old law of an eye for an eye leaves everybody blind. It is immoral because it seeks to humiliate the opponent rather than win his understanding; it seeks to annihilate rather than to convert. Violence is immoral because it thrives on hatred rather than love. It destroys community and

makes brotherhood impossible. It leaves society in monologue rather than dialogue. Violence ends by defeating itself. It creates bitterness in the survivors and brutality in the destroyers. A voice echoes through time saying to every potential Peter, "Put up your sword." History is cluttered with the wreckage of nations that failed to follow this command.

6   If the American Negro and other victims of oppression succumb to the temptation of using violence in the struggle for freedom, future generations will be the recipients of a desolate night of bitterness, and our chief legacy to them will be an endless reign of meaningless chaos. Violence is not the way.

7   The third way open to oppressed people in their quest for freedom is the way of nonviolent resistance. Like the synthesis in Hegelian philosophy, the principle of nonviolent resistance seeks to reconcile the truths of two opposites—the acquiescence and violence—while avoiding the extremes and immoralities of both. The nonviolent resister agrees with the person who acquiesces that one should not be physically aggressive toward his opponent; but he balances the equation by agreeing with the person of violence that evil must be resisted. He avoids the nonresistance of the former and the violent resistance of the latter. With nonviolent resistance, no individual or group need submit to any wrong, nor need anyone resort to violence in order to right a wrong.

8   It seems to me that this is the method that must guide the actions of the Negro in the present crisis in race relations. Through nonviolent resistance the Negro will be able to rise to the noble height of opposing the unjust system while loving the perpetrators of the system. The Negro must work passionately and unrelentingly for full stature as a citizen, but he must not use inferior methods to gain it. He must never come to terms with falsehood, malice, hate, or destruction.

9   Nonviolent resistance makes it possible for the Negro to remain in the South and struggle for his rights. The Negro's problem will not be solved by running away. He cannot listen to the glib suggestion of those who would urge him to migrate en masse to other sections of the country. By grasping his great opportunity in the South he can make a lasting contribution to the moral strength of the nation and set a sublime example of courage for generations yet unborn.

10   By nonviolent resistance, the Negro can also enlist all men of good will in his struggle for equality. The problem is not a purely racial one, with Negroes set against whites. In the end, it is not a struggle between people at all, but a tension between

justice and injustice. Nonviolent resistance is not aimed against oppressors but against oppression. Under its banner consciences, not racial groups, are enlisted.

Post-reading Questions

Content

1. What are the three ways "oppressed people deal with their oppression"?
2. According to King, why do some people prefer to remain oppressed? How do such people undermine the quest for equality and reinforce injustice?
3. Explain why King says that "violence as a way of achieving racial justice is both impractical and immoral."
4. What are the advantages of nonviolent resistance over both acquiescence and violence to cause change? How does King argue this point?

Strategies and Structures

1. How does King strategically use historical instances of oppressed people to illustrate each of the three ways of dealing with oppression?
2. In what way does King's division/classification of material help a reader to read, comprehend, and evaluate the merit of each type of resistance to oppression?
3. King presents the three ways of dealing with oppression (acquiescence, violence, and nonviolence) in a particular order. What would have happened if he had reversed or mixed his present sequence of material? What does your conclusion point out about the importance of organizing the parts of an essay?

Language and Vocabulary

1. Vocabulary: *acquiescence, tacitly, corroding, annihilate, desolate, synthesis, sublime.* Denotation is the dictionary definition of a word; connotations are the associated meanings of the word (see Glossary). Reread through the first two ways of dealing with oppression, acquiescence, and violence—noting King's choice of vocabulary. Make a list of the words

you encounter which have negative connotations (e.g., acquiescence suggests giving in, laziness). Then read through the last part of King's essay where he discusses nonviolence (peaceful resistance), making a list of words that have positive connotations. Overall, how does King use "connotations" to win his readers over to his point of view?

2. King refers to African Americans as Negroes several times in his essay. How do such references and similar references in other compositions indicate the time period when something was written? Why might knowledge of when something was written be of interest to a reader?

Group Activities

1. Divide into three groups, review all content and strategy questions, and then study in greater detail one way King mentions of resisting oppression. Each group will be responsible for a different strategy for overcoming oppression. Your group will ultimately *teach* to the rest of the class the section of King's essay dealing with the type of resistance you studied.

2. Go to your learning resource center on campus and locate some recordings or videotapes of King. In particular, search for his famous "I Have a Dream" speech. (After listening to his speech, you may also want to get a copy of it from the library and reread it.) Discuss the impact King's speech had on group members and then reevaluate each of the ways of fighting oppression in view of his ultimate goal.

Writing Activities

1. Write an essay wherein you classify and divide one of the following topics in order to explain it: ways of making friends, ways of reacting to aggressive people, ways of influencing people with the language that you use (e.g., big or dirty words), or ways of dealing with fame, racism, or sexism.

2. Leaving the method you agree with until last, write an essay explaining the ways people deal with *stress* or *depression*. (When writing about ways to overcome oppression, King structured his discussion of nonviolence this way.)

Constance García-Barrio

Creatures That Haunt the Americas

Constance García-Barrio is a widely published author, with articles appearing in such magazines and newspapers as Essence *and the* Philadelphia Inquirer. *She speaks English, Spanish, and Chinese and has received her doctorate in Romance languages. Currently, García-Barrio is writing a novel and teaching at West Chester University, West Chester, Pennsylvania.*

Pre-reading Questions

1. What are some of the scary creatures, ghosts, and/or monsters that are common in the stories of your culture? When did you hear about these creatures? What do they do that makes them frightening?

2. Brainstorm the word *haunt.* What do you associate with the word *haunt?* What is its dictionary definition? What kinds of creatures do you think García-Barrio will be describing?

1   When Africans were forced into slaving ships, the creatures, invisible, slipped in with them. A witch's brew of supernatural beings, these were creatures remembered from stories from the homeland. When Africans reached the New World, the creatures stepped ashore with them.

2   The supernatural beings made their homes in the mountains, rivers, and forests of the Americas, wherever the Africans went. The Hairy Man, for example, has the run of Georgia's woods, according to a story told by a former slave from that state. The Hairy Man is a fat, ugly little man with more hair all over than hell has devilment. Tricky as he is

hairy, he can shrink or swell at will. He's afraid of dogs and is most at home near rivers. The Hairy Man spends his time capturing careless children.

3   The guije seems to be a Caribbean cousin of the Hairy Man, the way the late Cuban centenarian Esteban Montejo tells it in *The Autobiography of a Runaway Slave*. The guijes, or jigues, are mischievous little black men who wear no clothes and live near rivers. Their heads are like a frog's. Black people have a natural tendency to see them, according to Montejo. Guijes pop out of the river to admire a señorita as she bathes, especially during Holy Week. The guijes are also known to carry off children.

4   The Tunda looms large in the folklore of Esmeraldas, a predominantly black province on the northern coast of Ecuador, notes Afro-Ecuadorian writer Adalberto Ortiz. Local legend has it that in the 1530s a ship whose cargo included twenty-three enslaved blacks was traveling from Panama to Peru. As it skirted Ecuador's northern coast, the ship struck a reef. In the confusion that followed, the blacks scrambled from the vessel, swam ashore, and fought with Indians occupying the land.

5   After one especially fierce battle, dying blacks and Indians moaned so much that the noise reached hell and disturbed the devil. He decided he'd have to exterminate both sides if he wanted peace and quiet. So the devil went to Esmeraldas disguised as an African prince, Macumba. But before he could carry out his plan, a lively, buxom Esmeraldeña caught his fancy. He married her and settled down, as much as the Devil can ever settle.

6   One of the creatures born from their union is the Tunda, a deformed black woman with huge lips and clubfoot. As a child of the devil, the Tunda can't have children, so she's taken to carrying off those of black folk in Esmeraldas. The Tunda can make herself look like a member of the potential victim's family. She lures people into the forest, then stuns them by breaking wind in their faces. After this they lose their will power and are easily led to her lair, usually a place in or near water.

7   Adalberto Ortiz mentioned that there are similarities between the Tunda, a character in Afro-Colombian stories and the Quimbungo from Bantu folklore.

8   If some creatures pursue black children, others stalk adults. The Afro-Dominican Ciguapa is a gorgeous but strange being who lives in the island's forests. She comes out at night to steal food but is never caught since she escapes by jumping from tree to tree. Her beauty has won many hearts, but she uses her

magic to destroy men. Wise to her ways, they try to avoid her. But she can fool them. The Ciguapa's feet are on backward, so they think she's going when she's coming.

9   Tales of the Lobisón, or Wolfman, made many an Afro-Uruguayan peasant cringe. Legend has it that every Friday night at midnight the seventh consecutive son in a family turns into an animal. This animal has a wolf's body and a mis-shapen pig's head. It commits acts too horrible to tell. It has great supernatural powers, and only by wounding the Lobisón and drawing its blood can it be made to return to human form.

10   The old and new worlds blend in the Lobisón legend. The story shows the influence of Bantu, European, and certain South American Indian cultures.

11   Some tales of the supernatural arose from historic events in which blacks took part. Such was the case with Spanish America's struggle for independence from Spain from 1810 to 1822. One Afro-Uruguayan story tells of a rich but miserly man who treated his slaves cruelly. Emancipated before the wars of in-dependence, the newly freed blacks demanded money with which to start a new life. They knew their former master had gold nuggets hidden in the house. When he refused to give them anything, they killed him.

12   The money remained hidden after the murder until a pla-toon of black soldiers camped near the old house during the wars of independence. The location of the treasure was re-vealed to them by the ghost of a black who had remained with the master even after emancipation. The soldiers divided the cache, each receiving a nice sum. The ghost had waited years but finally saw that his black countrymen got the money.

13   Like the ghost who showed the soldiers the treasure, black folktales bring to light sometimes forgotten cultural treasures Africans brought to the Americas.

Post-reading Questions

Content

1. Where do the creatures that García-Barrio de-scribes originate? How did they get here?
2. García-Barrio describes the actions of these crea-tures. What are some actions or deeds common to them all? What do these common elements suggest about the creatures?
3. Why did the devil decide to exterminate the "blacks and Indians"? What happened to him on his way to

exterminate them? What creature was the end result of the devil's actions?
4. García-Barrio claims, "As a child of the devil, the
Tunda can't have children. . . . " What characteristics
do you associate with the devil and his offspring?
How might these characteristics prevent them from
having children?

Strategies and Structures
1. What is the thesis of this essay? Is it stated directly
or implied? What is the purpose of the opening
paragraph?
2. García-Barrio writes vivid descriptions of the different creatures which "haunt the Americas." What
are some of the images she uses to create vivid
physical descriptions? What is the purpose of these
vivid descriptions?
3. How is this essay organized? What general categories do the different creatures fit into? Why might
García-Barrio divide the essay in such a way?
4. What is the purpose of the last paragraph? Aside
from summarizing the essay, what might be some of
its other purposes?

Language and Vocabulary
1. García-Barrio uses many unfamiliar geographical
names: *Georgia's woods, Caribbean, Esmeraldas,
Ecuador, Panama, Peru, Colombian, Uruguayan.*
Where are these different places located? What are
the unique geographical characteristics of these regions? What makes them particularly suitable to
tales about frightening creatures?
2. García-Barrio uses the prefix *Afro-* before many
words: *Afro-Colombian, Afro-Dominican, Afro-
Uruguayan.* (1) Write a definition for the prefix
Afro-. (2) Write a definition for each of the root
words. (3) Write a definition for the word made
when the prefix and roots are combined.

Group Activities

1. In groups, discuss the following questions: Who
usually passes on the stories of creatures such as

ghosts or monsters? Who are these stories often told to? When are they often told? What are the purposes of such frightening folktales about creatures? What is the function of such imaginative creatures in our culture? What specifics in the stories García-Barrio retells illustrate your ideas?

2. It has been suggested that stories about creatures and monsters are really imaginative representations of our individual and cultural fears. (1) What do the creatures in García-Barrio's essay suggest about the fears of their creators? In other words, what might their fears be? (2) Create a list of some of the creatures and monsters in the different cultures your group represents and then, next to each creature's name, list the fears it represents. (3) According to your analysis, what fears do most cultures have in common? Why do we have these common fears?

Writing Activities

1. García-Barrio divides and classifies the creatures of African Americans: those that haunt children, those that haunt adults, those that came to America from Africa, and those that are a hybrid of African and European culture. Write an essay in which you classify the creatures and monsters of your own culture. First, brainstorm a list of creatures. Second, divide these creatures into general categories (e.g., creatures associated with holidays, creatures associated with certain regions, creatures associated with certain historical events). Finally, write your essay to clearly illustrate your division, using transitions and vivid descriptions.

2. Write an essay in which you explain the origin of a specific folktale, ghost story, or myth from your culture. It may be useful to divide your topic into smaller units (paragraphs) as you develop your ideas.

Robertson Davies

A Few Kind Words
for Superstition

*A novelist, playwright, and scholar, Robertson Davies remains one of
Canada's best-known authors. Novels* Fifth Business *(1970),* The
Manticore *(1972),* World of Wonders *(1975),* The Rebel Angels *(1983),*
What's Bred in the Bone *(1985),* The Lyre of Orpheus *(1989),* Voice
from the Attic: Essays on the Art of Reading *(1990),* Murther and
Walking Spirits *(1991),* Reading and Writing *(1993),* The Cunning
Man *(1996),* The Merry Heart: Reflections on Reading, Writing, and
the World of Books *(1998) and* High Spirits: A Collection of Ghost
Stories *(2002) are among the more than two dozen books Davies has
to his credit.*

Pre-reading Questions

1. What is a superstitious person? Do you consider yourself
superstitious? Why or why not?

2. If superstition is folly, why don't airplanes have a row 13?
Why don't most business buildings have a floor 13 indi-
cated on the elevator panel?

3. What part does superstition play in your daily life? What
cultural roots lie behind your superstitions?

---

1   In grave discussions of "the renaissance of the irrational" in
our time, superstition does not figure largely as a serious challenge to reason or science. Parapsychology, UFOs, miracle cures,
transcendental meditation, and all the paths to instant enlightenment are condemned, but superstition is merely deplored. Is
it because it has an unacknowledged hold on so many of us?

2   Few people will admit to being superstitious; it implies naiveté
or ignorance. But I live in the middle of a large university, and I

see superstition in its four manifestations, alive and flourishing among people who are indisputably rational and learned.

3   You did not know that superstition takes four forms? Theologians assure us that it does. First is what they call Vain Observances, such as not walking under a ladder, and that kind of thing. Yet I saw a deeply learned professor of anthropology, who had spilled some salt, throwing a pinch of it over his left shoulder; when I asked him why, he replied, with a wink, that it was "to hit the Devil in the eye." I did not question him further about his belief in the Devil: But I noticed that he did not smile until I asked him what he was doing.

4   The second form is Divination, or consulting oracles. Another learned professor I know, who would scorn to settle a problem by tossing a coin (which is a humble appeal to Fate to declare itself), told me quite seriously that he has resolved a matter related to university affairs by consulting the *I Ching*. And why not? There are thousands of people on this continent who appeal to the *I Ching*, and their general level of education seems to absolve them of superstition. Almost, but not quite. The *I Ching*, to the embarrassment of rationalists, often gives excellent advice.

5   The third form is Idolatry, and universities can show plenty of that. If you have ever supervised a large examination room, you know how many jujus, lucky coins, and other bringers of luck are placed on the desks of the candidates. Modest idolatry, but what else can you call it?

6   The fourth form is Improper Worship of the True God. A while ago, I learned that every day, for several days, a $2 bill (in Canada we have $2 bills, regarded by some people as unlucky) had been tucked under a candlestick on the altar of a college chapel. Investigation revealed that an engineering student, worried about a girl, thought that bribery of the Deity might help. When I talked with him, he did not think he was pricing God cheap because he could afford no more. A reasonable argument, but perhaps God was proud that week, for the scientific oracle went against him.

7   Superstition seems to run, a submerged river of crude religion, below the surface of human consciousness. It has done so for as long as we have any chronicle of human behavior, and although I cannot prove it, I doubt if it is more prevalent today than it has always been. Superstition, the theologians tell us, comes from the Latin *supersisto*, meaning to stand in terror of the Deity. Most people keep their terror within bounds, but they cannot root it out, nor do they seem to want to do so.

8   The more the teaching of formal religion declines, or takes a sociological form, the less God appears to great numbers of people as a God of Love, resuming his older form of a watchful, minatory power, to be placated and cajoled. Superstition makes its appearance, apparently unbidden, very early in life, when children fear that stepping on cracks in the sidewalk will bring ill fortune. It may persist even among the greatly learned and devout, as in the case of Dr. Samuel Johnson, who felt it necessary to touch posts that he passed in the street. The psycho-analysts have their explanation, but calling a superstition a compulsion neurosis does not banish it.

9   Many superstitions are so widespread and so old that they must have risen from a depth of the human mind that is indifferent to race or creed. Orthodox Jews place a charm on their doorposts; so do (or did) the Chinese. Some peoples of Middle Europe believe that when a man sneezes, his soul, for that moment, is absent from his body, and they hasten to bless him, lest the soul be seized by the Devil. How did the Melanesians come by the same idea? Superstition seems to have a link with some body of belief that far antedates the religions we know— religions which have no place for such comforting little ceremonies and charities.

10   People who like disagreeable historical ceremonies recall that when Rome was in decline, superstition proliferated wildly, and that something of the same sort is happening in our Western world today. They point to the popularity of astrology, and it is true that sober newspapers that would scorn to deal in love philters carry astrology columns and the fashion magazines count them among their most popular features. But when has astrology not been popular? No use saying science discredits it. When has the heart of man given a damn for science?

11   Superstition in general is linked to man's yearning to know his fate, and to have some hand in deciding it. When my mother was a child, she innocently joined her Roman Catholic friends in killing spiders on July 11, until she learned that this was done to ensure heavy rain the day following, the anniversary of the Battle of Boyne, when the Orangemen would hold their parade. I knew an Italian, a good scientist, who watched every morning before leaving his house, so that the first person he met would not be a priest or a nun, as this would certainly bring bad luck.

12   I am not one to stand aloof from the rest of humanity in this matter, for when I was a university student, a gypsy woman

with a child in her arms used to appear every year at examination time, and ask a shilling of anyone who touched the Lucky Baby; that swarthy infant cost me four shillings altogether, and I never failed an examination. Of course, I did it merely for the joke—or so I thought then. Now, I am humbler.

Post-reading Questions

Content

1. What is the ultimate point of this essay? Where does Davies stand on the topic of superstition?
2. Why is "Vain Observances" an appropriate title for the author's first category of superstition? Name a few examples of "Vain Observances" that you can remember from your childhood.
3. Why will few people admit it if they are superstitious? What is superstition generally associated with?
4. How would referring to the *I Ching* (a Chinese book offering general advice on how to act) be similar to consulting an oracle?

Strategies and Structures

1. What kind of superstition do you feel is most common? In what order does Davies divide and classify superstition? What does he talk about first? Second? Third? Fourth?
2. According to Davies, what are the four divisions of superstition? Can you think of any other division he might have made?
3. In the final paragraph, Davies mentions how, during examination week as a student, he spent a shilling to touch a gypsy lady's lucky baby. Why?
4. Davies refers to the reaction of distinguished professors to exemplify the first two kinds of superstitions. Why might professors acting superstitiously be more effective and thought provoking than farmers acting superstitiously?

Language and Vocabulary

1. Vocabulary: *placated, cajoled, minatory, proliferated, philter.* One of the ways to understand words and their meanings better is to learn the origin of the word. Your dictionary is the first tool you should em-

ploy for this task. For instance, the word *expand,* which means to spread out or unfold, is listed as coming from Middle English *expanden,* which comes from the Latin word *expandere: ex-* out + *pandere* to spread. Trace the origins of the above words and use each in a sentence. If you cannot find such explanations in your pocket dictionary, use an etymological dictionary (one that traces the origin and historical development of a word), which can be found in your school library.

2. List the words in your present vocabulary beginning with the prefix *super-.* What common meaning do all of these words share? How do the words on your list change meaning if you eliminate the prefix?

Group Activities

1. Write down two superstitions that came to your mind while reading this essay. Now write down two other superstitions which have their roots in your cultural origins. Next, break into groups and share your various superstitions. Which were most common? Did you find that many superstitions were universal? How? Finally, write a short collaborative essay whose thesis is based on your group's findings.

2. Interview several people one-on-one and as a group; your questions should focus on what the people say they believe and how they behave. You might also ask the people you interview for a sample of the kind of superstitions they grew up with. Have everyone who claims he or she does not believe in superstition give you a definition of the word. What percentage of the people interviewed admitted they believed or reacted to some superstitions? Did group interviews differ significantly from one-on-one interviews? How? Why?

Writing Activities

1. Using some of the material gathered in Group Activity 2, write a thoroughly developed essay in

which you divide and classify superstitions or folk
beliefs.

2. Write an essay in which you defend the importance
of superstition in American society. Make sure you
cite several specific superstitions (other than the
ones mentioned by Davies) and show how their existence often influences our actions.

Gary Tewalestewa

American Indians: Homeless in Their Own Homeland

Gary Tewalestewa, a member of the Alliance of Native-Americans, wrote the following article, which originally appeared in La Gente de Aztlan *in November of 1989. With the winter approaching, Tewalestewa takes a grim look at what the changing seasons mean to thousands of Native Americans. As you read this article, ask yourself whether living conditions have improved for Native Americans, many of whom were homeless when Tewalestewa wrote this.*

Pre-reading Questions

1. How to you feel about homeless people? What influences your attitudes? In your opinion, why are there so many homeless people in America?
2. In what way does independence differ from the confines of homelessness?

1   Where will the American Indian homeless go to avoid freezing to death this winter? Yes, that's right; it's hard for some people to believe, but it's true. There are a lot of American Indians who are homeless; as a matter of fact, 1 out of 18 homeless on skidrow is Indian (Testimony provided at the Los Angeles County Board of Supervisors Budget Hearings, June 5, 1988).

2   The American Indian Studies Center at the University of California at Los Angeles (UCLA) estimates that 90,000 of the country's American Indian population reside in Los Angeles. Through no fault of their own, more than half of those estimated

90,000 Indians living in Los Angeles are one paycheck away from becoming homeless—be it welfare, food rations, unemployment insurance, food stamps, tribal benefits, or unemployment. Homelessness does not discriminate.

3   As programs continue to get cut and budgets of existing programs that target the general homeless population are slashed, groups of homeless Indians standing on street corners grow. Many of these Indians are reluctant to take refuge from the elements mainly because they do not feel accepted.

4   Throughout history, the United States government has successfully isolated Indian people from the general population. Hence, a basic philosophical conflict exists between American Indians and the U.S. capitalist system. American Indian philosophy is based on a cooperative, spiritual, and communal way of life. The capitalist system, on the other hand, is based on accumulation of land wealth, mass profit, and individual competition. The goal of capitalist education for Indian people has always been that of total indoctrination into the American education system. American Indians have been taught that their communal ways are savage and anti-Christian. The worst lesson being taught to American Indians is to hate themselves. It becomes increasingly clear that the conflict existing between the two social systems is manifested in the classrooms, which can be said to have even more devastating results than struggles over land and resources. These two warring systems are the root of the increasing numbers of American Indians becoming homeless.

5   Despite all our efforts to destroy the identity and land base of the American Indian population, Indian people have held on to their spiritual and cooperative cultural forms. A resurgence of Indian spirituality and sobriety is occurring throughout the land. But, Indian people maintain their "walls of silence" and other cultural strategies in order to protect the little they have left.

6   Because there are so few service agencies for the homeless, this winter thousands of homeless people will be forced to compete against each other. A sort of "This is our turf! Keep away!" extortion atmosphere, comparable to the rival street gang dilemma, will intensify. Similar situations in the past have resulted in frustration and anger to those waiting in soup lines, and in many instances, fights break out and killings occur. Thus, battle lines are drawn and in many instances ethnic groupings are formed and intimidate other groups from entering "their territory" for a mere meal. Yet all have one condition in common, homelessness.

7   Despite the fact that American Indians are neglected in general and the condition worsens if they become homeless, President Bush contends that he is taking care of the situation. The U.S. government has taken care of American Indians through the BIA relocation, forced sterilization, broken treaties, political isolation, and House and Senate bills which more often than not take away rights that protect them. Meanwhile, nuclear supplies are stockpiled, and orbiting missiles are fueled which provide substantial profit.

8   American Indians are presently organizing throughout the United States. They see through the lies, tricks, and ploys of the capitalists. Their need for decent housing, education, nutritious food, real jobs, and programs that really work has steadily increased and the demand has not been met. The United States government and the Federal offices that oversee Indian affairs cannot afford to neglect the need of American Indians to live as they were meant to live. American Indians need to be Indian.

Post-reading Questions

Content

1. List some of the causes that contribute to the growing number of "homeless" Native-American Indians.
2. Explain the philosophical conflict between Native-American Indians and the capitalist system.
3. Why does Tewalestewa believe that many Native Americans feel like inferior members of American society? What Native-American "needs" have not been met by the U.S. government?
4. Since this article was written, what headlines have you noticed in the news about the homeless population in America? What have you read about Native Americans?

Strategies and Structures

1. What emotions does the author try to draw out of the reader with his essay's title: "American Indians: Homeless in Their Own Homeland"? What ultimate irony does Tewalestewa express?
2. How could we break down Tewalestewa's essay into four major parts?
3. How does the author use the word *capitalists* in his essay? Why does it create a sense of "us" and "them" (two categories of people)?

Language and Vocabulary

1. Vocabulary: *reluctant, resurgence, relocation.* The prefix *re-* means back to, again. Jot down your understanding of each word's meaning. Then write down what you believe is the root of each word along with its meaning. Finally, write as many words as you can think of that use the prefix *re-*, bearing in mind its meaning.

2. In his second paragraph, Tewalestewa condenses the University of California at Los Angeles with an acronym: UCLA. Often, writers will use acronyms (a group of letters formed by taking the first letters of a compound term and writing them in succession) throughout their papers, but like Tewalestewa, by initially presenting what the capitalized letters represent—complete words—a writer is certain not to assume too much on the part of a reader. Write five sentences using references to businesses or schools followed by their acronyms in parentheses (e.g., My mom attended the University of California at Santa Barbara [UCSB]).

Group Activities

1. Compare your initial responses to the Pre-reading Questions with other members in your group. Then work through the Post-reading Questions together.

2. For a week, collect as many articles as you can find that deal with homeless people. In addition to using daily newspapers, have each group member be responsible for looking up recent "homeless people" articles in magazines like *Time, Newsweek,* and *U.S. News & World Report.* You'll have 15 minutes in class to compare your materials. Then you will do a short individual writing assignment on the topic.

Writing Activities

1. Should Native Americans expect and receive special privileges from the U.S. government? Construct a thesis based on your answer to this question, divide

and classify your material, and develop it into a logically argued, well-supported essay.

2. Write an essay explaining how growing up on a
reservation—isolated from the rest of the world—
would be like aging in a concentration camp. (Consider the fact that after the Native-American tribes
were conquered and placed on reservations, the U.S.
government tried to "Westernize" them, changing
them *culturally* and *spiritually.*)

Bill Swanson

How Films Feed the Mind *or* When I'm Hungry, I Don't Want to Eat Candy

Bill Swanson teaches humanities, writing, and film classes at South Puget Sound Community College in Olympia, Washington, where he is also the advisor of the international students. He co-edited two books with Michael Nagler, including Wives and Husbands: Twenty Stories about Marriage *and* Stolen Moments: Twenty Stories about Desire. *Additionally, he is the coauthor of the college reader* Projections: Brief Readings on American Culture. *In the following essay, Swanson employs the rhetorical mode of division and classification to distinguish and exemplify different types of movies and the criteria we use to judge them.*

> Experience is never limited, and it is never complete;
> it is an immense sensibility,
> a kind of huge spider-web of the finest silken threads
> suspended in the chamber of consciousness,
> and catching every air-borne particle in its tissue.
> It is the very atmosphere of the mind;
> and when the mind is imaginative . . .
> it takes to itself the faintest hints of life,
> it converts the very pulses of the air into revelations.
>
> —*Henry James,* "The Art of Fiction"

1   Author Henry James thought it important to be a person "on whom nothing is lost." He meant the world has a lot to offer if we have the eyes to see it. This applies to everything we perceive, including various types of movies and the effects the movies have on us. Some films help us develop psychologically, help us to become more complete human beings, and other

films are just a way of distracting us from understanding ourselves. The effect a film has, though, has as much to do with the film viewer as the film itself.

2   The mind, Henry James says, is a spider-web that catches even the minutest particles. Nothing really escapes its attention. The bigger the web, the more intricate and complex the design, the more that gets caught in it. Web-making is a metaphor for psychological development. The mind spins out its fine fibers when stimulated to grow, when challenged to think in new ways, when asked to solve new kinds of problems. Any person who has ever seen a spider on a windy day, when the strands of web become detached from the stems of plants or the limbs of a tree, will have an apt analogy for the way the mind scurries about and strives to maintain its mode of perception. The world is constantly changing, and our minds are constantly adapting to the changes by making small modifications in our "web" of understanding. We seek new experiences because they give us new knowledge; they help us to grow. This is one of the reasons we travel, read books, listen to music and go to the movies. It feeds our brain, which is a hungry and busy little spider.

3   When watching a film, images pass by the eyes in a few seconds, but they have an impact; they become part of consciousness, and the imagination goes to work on them trying to find out what they mean. This is how films add to our experience. Our minds take in little bits of information just as they do when we aren't watching a movie, but movies have a way of fooling the mind. We *believe* movies more than we do books because we literally see things happen before our eyes. This is probably why people react so strongly to violence in films. Of course, the violence is all simulated; no one really gets hurt. Still, we often get so caught up in the action, we forget this and cringe and recoil when we see fights and gunplay on the screen. Our consciousness feels the effect even more powerfully than when violence takes place in real life. Our hearts beat faster; our adrenaline rushes. We feel excited. I have always been struck by the strange incongruity of fistfights in real life. The fighters look like bad stuntmen: clumsy and flailing, with punches flying but rarely hitting their mark. The "real" life cannot live up to the choreography of "reel" life. By "real" I mean the actual experiences we have when we are not in a theatre; by "reel" I mean the simulated experiences that take place in movies that resemble actuality but are fabricated in order to create certain psychological effects on the audience. Movie events are constructed to produce calculated effects, and they usually succeed.

4   Around the same time that Henry James wrote his essay on fiction, his brother, William James, founder of the first psychology department in the United States at Harvard, was working on his own book, *The Principles of Psychology*. This was also the era when cinema was invented. It seems unlikely that either William or Henry James saw many films, but their ideas about how the mind works help us understand why we watch movies and how they influence us.

5   William James observed that the mind is a "stream of consciousness," not simply a repository of perceptions, memories, and ideas. The mind is a flow of images constantly moving, like *moving pictures*. This is probably why we enjoy movies so much. They seem to mimic consciousness itself which also has the psychological capacity to make jump cuts, crane shots or close-ups. The mind's eye has a flexible lens and a mobile tripod. A movie doesn't just show us how the world looks; it shows us how a mind works. It jumps around quite a bit to create a coherent narrative out of sense impressions. We "edit" our memories the way a film editor does, creating mental montages used to communicate with ourselves and with others. We can't possibly remember everything we see, so we edit it down into memories we can re-play over and over like our own personal videos. Memories help us to make sense out of our own lives; they become our personal story. The movies we see become part of our memories. Sometimes they have a life-changing impact upon us by giving us insight into our own experience. We carry them around with us in memory, and we can compare them to our own experience and reflect on the differences. If movies weren't meaningful in this way, no one would want to spend time watching them. If we watch films closely, we can glean meaningful information from them, especially if they are constructed in ways that challenge us to pay close attention and to reflect upon what we have seen.

Everyone in a Theatre Watches the Same Film But Not Everyone *Sees* the Same Film

I am not entertained by entertainment.

    —*Cynthia Ozick*, author of *The Shawl*. Her response
to a request from the *New York Times* for her list
of books for summer reading.

6   Each film represents a style of perception, a way of looking at the world. For the time that you are watching a movie, the camera mimics the subjective point of view of a particular person who looks at specific things in specific ways. The camera notices certain things and not others. As we watch, we come to identify with this way of seeing. There are certain conventions of cinematography that we all recognize without even thinking about them—the close-up, the pan, a shot/reverse shot. These methods allow the camera to break down the all-at-once world that surrounds us into a series of shots that create a fluid mosaic of images moving through time. The fragments of the world are edited together and the audience must use its imagination to make sense out of it.

7   If you think of a film as a purely imaginary experience, as a dream created by all the people listed in the credits, then the movie viewer is someone who pays money to inhabit someone else's dream in order to make sense out of it. When we watch a movie, we dream someone else's dream just for a little while. We accept the illusion that we are looking at the real world. We forget, as soon as the lights go down, that we are sitting in a theatre looking at lights and shadows projected on a screen. The real world—the actual world we live in—resides outside the theatre. Audiences experience the *reel* world of fabricated illusions dancing around on a screen accompanied by dialogue and music. Films thus become an interior, psychological experience. They resemble the real world, but they are only analogies for the real world that condense time and experience into a two-hour story. During this time anything can happen. It could be anything, from *Beauty and the Beast* to *A Beautiful Mind*. Whatever it is, we just accept it as real and participate in it by identifying with the characters and the actions they take.

8   Filmmakers have various motives for making films because filmmaking is both an art form and a business. Certain films like *Star Wars* or *Titanic* are blockbusters because they create an easily accessible world with fantasies that appeal to almost any audience. They make it easy to get involved with the story because they simplify human experience into familiar categories of good and evil, and love and death. Films that make it easy for audiences to participate are more immediately entertaining than films that ask audiences to stretch a bit and experience something new and unfamiliar. Every person has a Comfort Zone within which are contained their unquestioned assumptions about the world, their basic beliefs, their familiar ways of thinking about what is natural or normal or right.

Films that reinforce the borders of the Comfort Zone are entertaining. They are "feel good" movies because they make viewers feel more comfortable about themselves and what they believe. Filmmakers who make Comfort Zone films are rewarded by vast profits. For examples of Comfort Zone films, here is a list of the Top Ten Grossing Films World Wide:

1. Titanic (James Cameron, USA, 1997) $1,835,300,000
2. Harry Potter and the Sorcerer's Stone   965,000,000
   (Chris Columbus, USA, 2001)
3. Star Wars: Episode 1: The Phantom   922,000,000
   Menace (George Lucas, USA, 1999)
4. Jurassic Park (Steven Spielberg, USA,   919,700,000
   1993)
5. The Lord of the Rings: The Fellowship   860,200,000
   of the Ring (Peter Jackson, USA, 2001)
6. Independence Day (Roland Emmerich,   811,000,000
   USA, 1996)
7. Star Wars (George Lucas, USA, 1977)   797,900,000
8. Spider-Man (Sam Raimi, USA, 2002)   791,400,000
9. The Lion King (Roger Allers and Rob   767,700,000
   Minkoff, USA, 1994)
10. E.T. The Extra-Terrestrial (Steven   756,700,000
    Spielberg, USA, 1982)

(Source: imdb.com)

9   What do these films have in common? The Comfort Zone movies are children's movies in which human beings behave like cartoon characters. This doesn't apply to *The Lion King* because it *is* a cartoon. Adventure stories with melodramatic villains, elaborate quest journeys and plenty of action, they are spectacles that thrill the eyes and the imagination with threats to the main characters that are always external beings—dinosaurs, dragons, space aliens—or forces of nature—icebergs, predatory animals. The main characters are simply good and innocent. Their motives are child-like (though real children are never this simple). The special effects represent the latest in action film technology. The happy, open-ended endings provide both emotional closure and plot points that allow for continuation, that is, sequels. For the most part, they are very expensive serials. The earliest of these films, *Star Wars*, was made in 1977, but most are more recent. These films have benefited from the movie going habits of young people who like to see a favorite

film several times and from older people who want to return to their Comfort Zone when they see a film. Usually called "escapist" entertainment, they represent an escape from the actual conflicts, frustrations and disappointments of everyday life.

10   In these films the good guys and the bad guys are clearly defined and the good guys win—or at least their values are shown to be true and valid. Values like love, friendship, loyalty, and honesty are shown to be the greatest sources of human fulfillment. Messages like this easily gain universal approval. These values *are* the greatest sources of human fulfillment, but these films do not adequately represent the struggle involved in making conflicting values a functional part of everyday life. It is not a mistake for films to champion these values, but it is a mistake to put them in the pure realm of fantasy, to remove them from the complexity of actual psychological experience. By creating such stark contrast between good and evil these films eliminate mixed motives, difficult choices, and moral ambiguity. The characters rarely have to choose between conflicting ethical values. Designed for maximum international distribution, simple mythic stories communicate to people everywhere because the conflicts are external and don't require conflicted, personal dialogue or special cultural knowledge.

11   Though these films have dialogue in them they might be described as pre-verbal. When I saw *Titanic* (number one on the list), I was struck by how much it resembled a silent film; in fact, it would have probably have been better if it were a silent film. The dialogue was so wooden and predictable most audiences could have imagined better dialogue if they'd been allowed to. *Titanic* uses a plot idea very popular in the silent era: the damsel in distress. In 1914, only two years after the real Titanic went down, an actress named Pearl White starred in a twenty-part serial called *The Perils of Pauline* in which a fair-haired girl must escape from her rich guardian in order to run off with her true love and in the process falls from an air-balloon, escapes a burning house and is nearly run over by a train, among other life-threatening events. Eighty-three years later James Cameron was able to recycle this basic fantasy, add computer graphics, and bring in close to two billion dollars. An old-fashioned tear-jerker, it succeeded so well partly because it adds so little to a formula for sentimentality that is based upon putting virtuous young girls in danger and pinning all their hopes on the redeeming power of love. This was a overworked cliché in 1914! Yet the film had unprecedented success because it was aimed directly at

the center of the Comfort Zone, and it hit its target. The performances of Kate Winslett and Leonardo DiCaprio carried the whole thing off because audiences liked them and believed in their innocence. They were the very image of Young Love. Cooler heads, mostly film critics, snickered and sniffed their noses at the whole thing, but it made little difference.

12   Think of the difference between watching *Titanic* and *Memento*. Christopher Nolan's film literally reverses our expectations by having the story move backward in time. Also, he mixes black and white with color footage, and gives the story a narrator who can't retain short term memories. *Memento* also asks audiences to identify with a character who is not a conventional hero, not even a conventional *film noir* hero. A difficult film, it gets better and better with multiple viewings as various bits of information begin to cohere in your mind. Its tightly constructed and complex story raises questions about the nature of memory, the relation of memory to a sense of self, the necessity of memory in order to have conscience. It is not a simple entertainment in which we can sit back and be amused by special effects and daring actions. Ultimately, films like *Memento* are more involving than merely entertaining because they require us to put the clues together, to perceive the subtle details, and come up with a coherent understanding of the film. Though few people will experience the unusual brain injury depicted in *Memento*, all of us struggle to remember things, and eventually come to realize that the things we remember define who we are. When we lose our memories, we lose a big part of our identity.

Conventional and Unconventional Films

13 We have a spectrum of filmmaking that ranges from the conventional to the unconventional. Conventional films have a comforting psychological effect, even if they are about violent or disturbing things. *Saving Private Ryan*, for example, is full of grisly and horrific violence, but in the end, it reinforces the beliefs that the Nazis were evil, the soldiers who died on D-Day made a heroic sacrifice and that dying for your country is a noble death. These are not new or controversial ideas, and were probably already held by most people in the audience before they came to see the movie. Watching *Saving Private Ryan* was like watching one of the propaganda films made during World War II like *Bataan* or *The Sands of Iwo Jima*, except that *Sav-*

ing Private Ryan was much more technologically sophisticated and explicit about combat and death. If you compare it to an unconventional war film like *Apocalypse Now*, you will see how films can work on a different level of communication. Francis Coppola's 1978 film, not a blockbuster when it was released, failed for several years to turn a profit and made it difficult for Coppola to get financial backing to do another film. With the passing of time (and the invention of the VCR), however, this film has been reconsidered. It now appears on any list that names the best films of the 1970s. Gradually, the complexity of the film revealed itself to audiences. At first audiences found its dark vision of moral ambiguity, political confusion, military betrayal and drug-induced paranoia hard to accept. To put it simply: it is not an entertaining film. It is not easy to figure who the "good guys" are; we're not sure what the main character should do—should an American officer assassinate another American officer? Coppola said in a press conference at the Cannes Film Festival when the film was released that he did not want it to be *about* the Vietnam War but to *be* the Vietnam War. This sounded a bit pretentious to people at the time, but Coppola meant he wanted audiences to come away from the film with the same confusion, dismay and dread that both Vietnam War protesters and veterans struggled to describe and understand. *Apocalypse Now* was no pleasant two hour diversion; it was a filmic descent into hell. And audiences did not enjoy the trip, but they were moved by it.

14   Such films raise questions that movie producers and financiers are inclined to ask: if you're not planning to give audiences what they want, why do you expect anyone to come and see your film? What audiences want, it turns out, is varied. On the one hand, they do want to have a predictable, familiar experience. This explains why sequels and remakes do quite well at the box office even when they don't get good reviews. Many people, for example, went to see *Men in Black II* to find out if they would have the same good time they had watching the first version. Film reviewers mostly mocked it as a not very clever attempt to cash in on reputation of the first film. Audiences went to see it anyway because it was something they knew they could relate to. It didn't become another blockbuster, but it still brought in more profit than the average independent film.

15   Popular taste, however, is not the only criterion for judging films. Since 1952, *Sight and Sound*, a magazine published by the British Film Institute, has been taking a poll of critics and directors that asks them to name the ten best films ever made.

The list below is a sample of the Directors' Poll from 2002. None of the Top Ten Grossing Films was mentioned by any of the critics or directors. Here is the list (I have added annotations to explain why I think they were chosen).

Sight and Sound Directors' Top Ten Poll 2002—The Best Films (108 Directors)
(Actually eleven films because of ties in the voting.)

16 **1. Citizen Kane** (Orson Welles, USA, 1940)

This film is ranked first because of its technical innovations in lighting, framing, editing, sound, and narrative structure. The story of Charles Foster Kane, a power hungry newspaper owner, is narrated from **five different points of view,** and raises questions about how it is possible to know any person completely or to ever know for certain what is true about anything.

17 **2. *The Godfather* and *The Godfather Part II***
(Francis Coppola, USA, 1972/1974)

Like *Citizen Kane*, these films are about the effects of striving for power and wealth. In this case Michael Corleone emerges as the godfather of a Mafia family whose interests he is dedicating to serving and in the process destroys the family. These films reveal **the deep ambivalences** built into the immigrant experience so deeply imbedded in American culture. The values that are necessary for survival have a way of turning on those who adopt them. Both films also contain cinematic innovations in lighting, editing, narrative structure and acting styles.

18 **3. 8 1/2** (Federico Fellini, Italy, 1963)

A film director half-finished with his ninth film experiences a psychological crisis in which his past life passes before his eyes in the form of memories, fantasies, and excerpts from his previous films. This displays **the ever-changing nature of the mind,** that turns around and around in the present like a merry-go-round. This film asks us to reflect upon the nature of the self. It shows how difficult it is to answer the question: Who am I?

19 ## 4. Lawrence of Arabia (David Lean, Britain, 1962)

A wide screen epic shot in the Arabian desert, *Lawrence of Arabia* used color photography with expressive and overpowering vividness. Also, it depicts the life of the real T.E. Lawrence who became a British war hero in World War I fighting for the empire and at the same time allied himself with the indigenous aspirations of the Arabs. As a man caught between his conscience and his loyalty to his country, he symbolizes the **confusion and ambivalence created by political change** in the twentieth century.

20 ## 5. Dr. Strangelove, Or How I Stopped Worrying and Learned to Love the Bomb
(Stanley Kubrick, USA, 1963)

A classic work of satire that rivals the best works of literature, *Dr. Strangelove* reveals the incipient madness built into the Cold War arms race with nuclear weapons. It shows the subversions of **rational policy making by paranoia, patriotism, bureaucracy, secrecy, and megalomania.** One of the most politically influential films ever made.

21 ## 6. Ladri di Biciclette/The Bicycle Thief (Vittorio De Sica, Italy, 1948)

A desperate man on the verge of unemployment and homelessness searches the crowded Roman streets for his stolen bicycle that he must have for work. Like a biblical parable, this film uses simplicity to plumb the depths of despair and conscience. It makes us ask ourselves: **What would you do to survive?**

22 ## 6. Raging Bull (Martin Scorsese, USA, 1980)

The cinematography, camera movement and editing of this film show how technique can create meaning in a film. More than a boxing film, *Raging Bull* is an exploration of rage itself, **the irrational urge to define ourselves by violent acts of control and domination.** This film shows us that love and anger are both attached to passionate urges that are difficult to control. Though apparent opposites, these two emotions are inextricably linked.

23 ## 6. Vertigo (Alfred Hitchcock, USA, 1954)

In Vertigo the power of a sexual and romantic obsession causes a police detective to **re-examine his whole life and his own hidden guilt.** The elaborate plot, disguises and mistaken identities raise fundamental questions about how accurate our perceptions of other people can be. Do we see other people as they are or as we wish they were? How do we see ourselves?

24 ## 9. Rashomon (Akira Kurosawa, Japan, 1950)

Set in medieval Japan, this story of a rape, murder and trial is told from multiple points of view and, like Citizen Kane, **shows how subjective perceptions make it difficult to arrive at objective conclusions.** The testimony here doesn't quite add up to a coherent explanation of the events, and the film asks us to consider whether it is possible to get beyond self-interest when expressing our perception of the world.

25 ## 9. La Règle du jeu/Rules of the Game (Jean Renoir, France, 1939)

A shooting party at a French country house just before World War II provides the setting for a comedy about love, betrayal and reconciliation. Mistaken identities, whispered rumors, class distinctions, marital jealousy, and gunshots in the night bring the whole party to a confused conclusion. Renoir tells us that when it comes to making choices, **"everyone has their reasons."**

26 ## 9. Seven Samurai (Akira Kurosawa, Japan, 1954)

Seven unemployed samurai are hired by farmers to defend their remote village from a marauding band of brigands. Samurai and villagers face the impending battle in several different ways. The film is **a study in the diverse ways individuals find courage in the face of adversity and death.** For the final battle scene, a blur of swords, horses, mud and rain, Kurosawa used ten cameras and put together a masterpiece of film editing.

(Source: www.bfi.org.uk)

27 Some observations:

- These films were made between 1939 and 1980; the blockbusters were made between 1977 and 2002.

- There are five American films; two Italian, two Japanese, one French and one British; all the blockbusters are American films—though some have British actors.

- Eight of the directors' choices are in black and white; all the blockbusters are in color.

- None of the directors' choices have children or teenagers as the central characters; all of the blockbusters have children or teenagers as central characters.

- Both lists contain films with many technical innovations though the blockbusters have more fantasy-related special effects.

- All of the blockbusters, except *Titanic*, contain supernatural phenomena; none of directors' choices contain supernatural phenomena.

The directors' choices represent a range of cultures and time periods. Complex works that utilize multiple narratives and intense interior conflicts and states of mind, they contain extraordinary acting performances that provide insight into ambivalent feelings and mixed motives. The highlighted phrases in the annotations above are meant to emphasize that these films are about human dilemmas that stretch intelligence and feeling to the limits by placing the characters in complex situations where difficult decisions must be made. The heroes (or anti-heroes) are not necessarily noble or courageous; they are flawed, confused, and torn in different directions, but they carry on with their lives. Their conflicts are not between themselves and impersonal aliens or villains or natural forces but arise from profound interior moments when they have to decide who they really are, what they really believe, and what it is really possible for them to accomplish. They learn to accept their own limitations and the limitations of others; they face disappointment, failure and death without illusions. This may sound on the surface like pretty depressing movies, but that is not the effect they have. That is not why they are on the list. These films, serious and genuinely moving, carry the emotional and intellectual weight that ultimately communicates a deeper understanding of what it is to be alive and aware of yourself as a thinking and feeling being. This is how they contribute to psychological growth.

28   As William James argued in *The Principles of Psychology*, psychological development is related to having new perceptions, or seeing familiar situations in fresh ways. These films show us powerful hypothetical scenes that we mentally participate in

and see how the consequences play out in the story. The films on the *Sight and Sound* list create a complex picture of reality that represents an analogy for our own psychological complexity. These directors' films all reflect a multi-faceted reality where several things are going on simultaneously. They imitate the psychological description that James described in words. The films display this restless, complicated consciousness that moves continuously from image to image, moment to moment.

29   Reflection upon powerful and complex films (or other great works of art) encourages the mental focus and tenacity that is related to personal growth. Eye candy—films full of spectacular special effects and saccharine happy endings—cannot generate much growth in viewers. The best films make for a cinematic diet that enhances the psychological sinews and synapses that are life sustaining.

Post-reading Questions

Content

1. What is the difference between conventional and unconventional films? Explain your response with specific examples drawn from Swanson's essay.
2. Why do people react so strongly to violence in films?
3. According to Swanson, what is one of the reasons why we probably "enjoy movies so much?" What relationship exists between the *mind* and *films*?
4. Why do people who watch the same movie in a theater often see a different film?
5. What are some of the characteristics of "comfort zone movies"? Mention a few of the examples Swanson uses to illustrate this film category.

Strategies and Structures

1. How does Swanson divide and classify films? How many times does he do so in his essay and for what purpose?
2. Describe the function of paragraph two in Swanson's essay. With what does it provide his readers?
3. Discuss Swanson's strategic rationale for including film lists in his article. To what extent do they strengthen and clarify his analysis?
4. Why does Swanson mention both Henry James and his brother, William? What does the allusion to

them and their work add to this essay?

5. Why do films like *Star Wars* and *Titanic* become blockbusters? How might this help explain why "filmmaking is both an art form and a business"?

Language and Vocabulary

1. Vocabulary: *minutest, metaphor, detached, apt, incidental, cinema, repository, mimics, subjective, conventions, cinematography, fabricated, stark, predictable, virtuous, cliché, unprecedented, spectrum, propaganda, ambiguity, paranoia, filmic, indigenous, aspirations, incipient, bureaucracy, megalomania, samurai, parable, annotations, dilemmas, hypothetical, analogy.* Review how Swanson used each vocabulary work on this list in context. If uncertain of a word's definition, look it up in a dictionary. Then, write a short paragraph about a recent film you saw, using at least seven of today's vocabulary words.

2. Go over today's vocabulary list, select ten words from it, and then use a dictionary or a thesaurus to locate one synonym (word carrying the same meaning) and one antonym (word carrying an opposite meaning) for at least five words on the list.

Group Activities

1. Gather in groups of four people, brainstorm together, and determine your own definition of (1) entertaining movies, and (2) excellent movies. Then generate a list of films, past and present that might appear on either list. Finally, as a group, divide and classify each other's film choices based on the group's definition of entertaining and excellent movies. When and where did you locate films that fit appropriately on both lists? For subsequent writing assignments, have the group recorder make and copy a master list of films for each group member.

2. Before gathering in small groups, generate your own list of the ten best movies for the previous year (e.g., if you read this essay in 2004, then consider all films from 2003). Include specific reasons, examples, and other criteria you applied to determine

how and why particular films belong on your list. Next, gather in groups, compare lists and justifications for "best films," and arrive at a single list reflecting the collaborative judgment of your group members. Finally, write an original annotation for each film on the list.

Writing Activities

1. Refer to the film list generated in Group Activity 1. Reflect on your personal definition of entertaining and excellent films—the definition you wrote prior to the group activity. Do some prewriting on the issue of what constitutes an entertaining movie versus an excellent film, and arrive at a thesis. Finally, write an essay where you convince readers on the reliability of your entertaining and excellent film definitions. Feel free to directly disagree or agree with Swanson's definition. However, be certain that you offer some original justifications for dividing and classifying films in both categories.

2. Write an essay agreeing or disputing Swanson's contention that "The effect of a film, though, has as much to do with the film viewer as the film itself." Divide your argument into three to five major discussion points that you plan to defend in the body of your essay. Gather examples of several films and film viewers to offer representative support for your claim.

Additional Topics and Issues for Division and Classification Essays

1. Divide and classify different kinds of relationships in order to gain a better insight into your own life.

2. Compose an essay in which you classify the different ways you have noticed that you and others deal with problems. (Some people, for instance, deal with problems by seeking solitude, others by confronting problems head-on, and still others by seeking advice from friends.)

3. After devising a thesis on the issue of racism, divide and

classify the issue in order to develop each part of your topic thoroughly.

4. Compose an essay discussing the different types of fears a child might have which might affect his or her behavior. How do these fears change as the child grows older—or do they?

5. Examine the different careers available to you, dividing them into distinct categories, and conclude your essay with the most likely profession you will pursue in your future.

6. Many people feel art is only decorative, but after careful analysis it becomes apparent that art serves many functions in American society. Write an essay in which you classify and divide the different uses of art in America.

7. We all speak and write in different ways, depending on the situation and audience. Write an essay examining a specific topic and discuss (1) how you would talk to your friends about your subject, (2) how you would inform a professor or government official about your topic, and (3) how you would compose a formal essay on it.

8. Discuss the subject majors available from your college or university. What are the characteristics of each major? What job opportunities can a student look forward to upon graduation?

9. Write an essay wherein you classify and divide your concept of "sloppiness" or "untidiness." Begin your essay with a catchy title. How you divide and classify your topic will largely depend on what you have to say about it.

10. Construct an essay wherein you use the techniques of division and classification to explain gender initiation rites, religious initiation rites, children's initiation rites, academic/social initiation rites, business initiation rites, cultural initiation rites, and so on.

9

Cause and Effect

When we explain the causes and/or the effects of something, we are busy explaining *why* something occurs (cause) and/or *what the consequence of an action is* (effect). There are immediate and secondary (contributing) causes which lead to an effect, as well as immediate and long-range effects from an action. When our stomachs begin to make noises after going without food for two days, we can identify an immediate cause: hunger. However, more often than not, a string of causes leads to an ultimate effect. By the same token, a number of causes can lead to numerous effects—not just one.

Structuring Cause-and-Effect Essays

Usually, a writer will begin to develop a topic using the strategy of cause and effect by stating the effect(s) of something in a thesis paragraph and then examining the cause or multiple causes. For instance, in Carlos Bulosan's "Labor and Capital: The Coming Catastrophe," he cites the fattening of industrialists by profits, their investing profits in idle luxury, their quarreling among themselves, and causing the depression as reasons for discontent among the workers.

In "Growing Up with Two Moms," Megan McGuire demonstrates the second method of organizing a cause-and-effect essay. She focuses her discussion on the *effects* of growing up with gay parents (mother and partner) rather than the *causes* of gay relationships. For instance, early in the essay she states, *"I was afraid everything I had gained socially would disappear if anyone ever found out that while they went home after volleyball practice to their Brady Bunch Mom and Dad, I went home to my two moms."* Ironically, McGuire ultimately points out that her feelings of awkwardness in having two moms had nothing to do with the family unit—but with *"other people's ignorance."* Similarly, Karen Ray structures her essay, "The Naked Face," by initially stating reasons why she does not wear makeup (her *"nakedness is partly pragmatic and partly philosophical"*) and then explaining the effects of wearing or not wearing makeup in society from a historical as well as a personal perspective. While Rose Anna Higashi spends a good deal of time discussing the causes or reasons for her hobby of *"eating with immigrants,"* she spends a larger portion of her essay explaining its positive effects. All in all, *"food is more nourishing eaten in community."*

In yet other instances, your essay may focus as much on the reasons why something occurs (the cause[s]) as the result (effect[s]) of an action. Phillip Persky, for example, cites reasons why his confused sense of pride and shame in his parents (cause) led to feelings of guilt (effect). The fact that his parents were oblivious to his *"shame and, by extension, the resulting guilt,"* only intensified the situation, especially since, as he grew older, he *"became much more appreciative of [his] parents' accomplishments in the United States under extremely difficult conditions."*

Regardless of whether your essay moves from cause to effect(s), from effect to cause(s), or a fairly balanced combination of the two, your explanations should answer the question "why" something has happened.

Cause-and-Effect Fallacies

Post hoc ergo propter hoc: The post hoc fallacy deals with faulty cause-and-effect relationships, something you'll definitely want to avoid when writing any composition. Literally, the Latin phrase translates as: "It happened *after* this; therefore, it happened *because* of this." A good example of the post hoc fallacy would be a sentence like "My sister won a million dollars last night because she found a lucky penny in the morning." In many instances, one event's following another does not produce a cause-and-effect relationship. Thus, in the case of the previous sentence, the person could very well have found a penny and won a million dollars on the same day, but one (finding a penny) did not cause the other (winning a million dollars) to occur.

Tips on Writing Cause-and-Effect Essays

1. While almost any essay may contain an element of causation, for the purpose of this essay select a topic that can be best explained by focusing on causes and/or effects. A discussion of two cars, for instance, would be a poor choice for a cause-and-effect topic; this lends itself to comparison and contrast.

2. After you have selected a topic or issue, prewrite (cluster, freewrite, brainstorm, list) to determine the focus of your composition. Will you initially mention causes and devote the majority of your composition to a discussion of the short-term and long-range effects of your topic? Or will you move from mentioning the results of an action to discussing its causes?

3. Check your work carefully for faulty cause-and-effect relationships. Never mistake coincidence as evidence of a valid cause-and-effect relationship.

4. Ask yourself questions like the following: What sort of evidence have I offered to prove what I say? Are my examples specific and compelling? Would my examples convince even the most doubtful reader? How much do I rely on my reader simply to agree with what I say? And, most importantly, have I thoroughly addressed the question *why?*

Megan McGuire

Growing Up with Two Moms

Megan McGuire, an 18-year-old student at Mills College at the time she wrote this essay for the November 4, 1996 issue of Newsweek *magazine, examines her childhood embarrassment that her mother was a lesbian. She hid the truth from friends and lied about her mother, but in retrospect, she is proud of her family.*

Pre-reading Questions

1. Do you think that gay parents can do as good a job at raising children as straight parents? Why or why not?

2. Did you ever feel you needed to hide the truth about your family from your immediate friends and acquaintances? Jot down your response to this question in your writing log or journal.

---

1   When I was growing up, the words "fag" and "queer" and "dyke" were everywhere, even though we lived in a relatively tolerant community, Cambridge, Mass. I even used them myself to put down someone I didn't like. If you were a fag or a dyke, you were an outcast. All that changed when I was 12. My mother had a friend, Barb, who started spending the night, though she lived minutes away. One night when Barb wasn't there, I asked my mother, "Are you gay?" I can only remember the "yes"—and the crying. All I could think was that she couldn't be gay. It wasn't fair. She was one of "those" people.

2   I always thought my family was normal. By the time I was 5, my mother and father no longer lived together. My brother and I split our time between our parents. My father remarried, and my mother dated men. We assumed our parents were straight. That's all you see on TV.

3   As it turned out, we didn't have a stereotypical family. The years after my mother came out to me were very difficult for me and my brother. We had just moved from Washington, D.C. We had to start over, and at the same time we had to lie about our mom. In school I wanted to be liked, so I laughed at the jokes about gays. I had yet to figure out how to make a friend I could trust with my secret. I wasn't ready to talk about my family because I wasn't ready to deal with it myself.

4   High school was the hardest. I was into all kinds of clubs, but I was afraid everything I had gained socially would disappear if anyone ever found out that while they went home after volleyball practice to their Brady Bunch dinners with Mom and Dad, I went home to two moms. My brother and I would never allow Mom and Barb to walk together or sit next to each other in a restaurant. We wouldn't have people spend the night; if we did have friends over, we would hide the gay literature and family pictures. When a friend asked about the pink triangle on our car, my brother told him it was a used car and we hadn't had time to take the sticker off. We lived like this for three years, until we moved to a house with a basement apartment. We told our friends Barb lived there. It was really a guest room.

5   Ironically, our home life then was really the same as a straight family's. We had family meetings, fights, trips and dinners. My brother and I came to accept Barb as a parent. There were things she could never have with us the way our mother did. But she helped support us while my mother got her Ph.D. in public health. And she pushed my brother and me to succeed in school, just like a mom.

6   With the help of a really great counselor and a friend who had a "it's not a big deal and I knew anyway" attitude, I started to become more comfortable with my two-mom family. The spring of my junior year, a local newspaper interviewed me for an article on gay families. I was relieved, but also afraid. The day the article appeared was incredibly tense. I felt like everyone was looking at me and talking about me. One kid said to my brother, "I saw the article, you fag." My brother told him to get lost. Some people avoided me, but most kids were curious about my family. People asked if I was gay. I chose not to answer; as teenagers, most of us can't explain the feelings in our minds and bodies.

7   Last year, in my final year of high school, I decided to speak at our school's National Coming Out Day. Sitting up front were

my best friend, my mother, my brother and my counselor, Al. That day was the best. I no longer had to laugh at the jokes or keep a secret. I hoped I was making a path for others like me: a kid with a gay parent, scared and feeling alone. After my speech, I lost some friends and people made remarks that hurt. But that only made me stronger. The hardest thing to deal with is other people's ignorance, not the family part. That's just like any other family.

Post-reading Questions

Content

1. What was the cause of McGuire's discomfort and embarrassment as a child?
2. When was her mother's sexual preference hardest on her and why?
3. What was McGuire's home life like? Did it really differ that much from the home life of her friends? Explain.
4. At what point in her life did McGuire come to terms with her "two moms"?
5. After the speech she gave at her school's National Coming Out Day, how did some of her friends treat her? What did McGuire realize about them?

Strategies and Structures

1. In addition to using cause and effect to describe her childhood with "two mothers," what other literary technique does McGuire use to develop her essay?
2. How does the tone reflect the author's attitude, and what purpose does this serve?
3. Why is the testimonial approach to McGuire's essay so appropriate to her subject matter? What might have been lost if she had opted to discuss *growing up with two moms* from a strictly scientific point of view?
4. Explain what you consider the most thought-provoking part of McGuire's essay.
5. To what extent do you believe that the length of McGuire's essay is sufficient to analyze her subject matter? Do you believe more detail or further exposition would have added to her discussion? Why or why not? How?

Language and Vocabulary

1. Vocabulary: *fag, queer, dyke, gay, stereotypical.*
   What is "pejorative language"? Look up the word *pejorative* in your dictionary, as well as in your thesaurus. What are the denotative and connotative meanings of a pejorative word? How are most of the vocabulary terms above pejorative?
2. How does the author's simple word choice lend clarity to the real focus of McGuire's essay (a girl growing up with two mothers)?

Group Activities

1. Break into groups and brainstorm as many pejorative terms for as many groups of individuals as you can. What pejorative terms, for instance, refer to straight people, to men, to women, to people of color, to politicians, and so on?
2. Have all groups go to the library and make a copy of the articles on gay families in the November 4, 1996, issue of *Newsweek* magazine (the source of Megan McGuire's article). After reading each article, do some additional research on (1) what growing up in a gay family can or might be like, and (2) the future probability of the social acceptance of gay families. Finally, divide the class into two groups: those who think that gay couples should "have the right to adopt children" and those who oppose granting gay couples such a right. Debate both sides of the issue, attempting to clearly distinguish between social prejudice, beliefs about traditional families, and the fact that gay people can be as good at parenting as straight people.

Writing Activities

1. Construct an essay where you examine the cause(s) of discomfort for children who grow up in a single-parent, a two-mother, or two-father family, and the positive or negative effect(s) from such an upbringing. Providing plenty of representative examples which justify your claims will be an essential part of your essay.

2. Write a composition explaining the reasons (causes) and results (effects) of taking pride in your family, your career, your physical appearance, your moral character, your personal ethics, and so on. Did you always "take pride" in your topic?

Karen Ray

The Naked Face

Karen Ray is a full-time writer whose articles, columns, and essays have appeared in many magazines and periodicals throughout the nation: Glamour, Science Digest, Working Woman, Christian Science Monitor, *and the* New York Times. *Ray's novels include* The Proposal *(1981),* Family Portrait *(1983),* Come Home to Darkness *(1991), and* The T. F. Letters *(2000). She now lives and writes at home in Arlington, Texas.*

Pre-reading Questions

1. When do you feel "naked" or incomplete in front of other people? Why?
2. Do you like "beauty aids" such as makeup? Who determines what is and what is not beautiful?
3. What is the relationship between fashion and beauty?

---

1   From the neck up, I am a nudist.

2   No mascara for me. No eyeliner, no lipstick, no blush, no powder, foundation, eye shadow, highlighter, lip pencil or concealing stick.

3   My nakedness is partly pragmatic and partly philosophical. Just getting my eyes open in the morning is a feat. I have neither the will nor the ability to apply makeup when I can hardly see straight. At night, the most I can manage is brushing my teeth. I'm afraid that removing makeup would go the same way as scrubbing the sink and cleaning the oven. Also I rub my eyes occasionally, which doesn't help the makeup. Neither does my baby daughter.

4   My philosophical reasons are less defined. I don't like the idea of having to put cosmetics on my face to appear in public.

Many women who wear makeup every day don't look "themselves" without it. I remember running home one long ago Saturday morning to tell my mother that a strange lady had come out of the Johnsons' house and picked up their newspaper. Turned out Mrs. Johnson just hadn't gotten her "face" on yet that morning.

5 My college roommate wouldn't step out the door without her makeup. I've heard sad stories of women who didn't want their husbands to see them as they really are and a pathetic one about a husband who forbade his wife to be seen without makeup. (The latter marriage is no longer intact.)

6 Most people don't go this far. Women use cosmetics to hide imperfections, to accentuate good points, to add drama and to feel polished. Many women in fact look "better" with makeup though, of course, our idea of beauty is tremendously affected by fashion. There are probably millions of men who would look "better" wearing makeup, but I've never met a man who did.

7 Recently a major women's magazine placed various amounts of makeup on a hypothetical job applicant, then asked managers and personnel directors which face they would hire. It should come as no surprise that in a magazine whose major advertisers are cosmetics companies the woman with the naked face was not awarded the job.

8 It has not always been so. During the 19th century, unadorned innocence was the height of fashion. Intricate hairstyles and colors were out of fashion and lip coloring was thought to be downright vulgar. The Roman poet, Ovid, in his famous poem *Ars Amatoria (Art of Love),* criticized Roman women for their excessive use of artifice. At various times Christian leaders have taught that makeup was sinful. A ridiculous attitude, but the opposite stand is equally absurd. To say, in one's mind if not with one's mouth, that a woman is not fully dressed without a full facial complement is crazy.

9 My friend Mary is manager in a technical area at a Fortune 100 company. Not long ago, she was in a business meeting when—in the middle of arguing an especially sticky point—a male superior leaned over and asked, "Why don't you wear makeup?" When she recovered, Mary asked her questioner why he didn't wear makeup. The response, "Because I'm not a girl." Focus on makeup, whether the right amount for the job, the profession or the company, often seems to be just one more excuse for not taking women seriously in the work world.

Much of the worry about makeup is really a worry about being accepted.

10   According to Fenja Gunn's recent history of cosmetics, *The Artificial Face,* makeup has been used throughout history to help create an everchanging ideal of beauty. Prehistoric body painting and tattooing began as pagan ritual, in part to camouflage defenseless man and to help conjure up the fiercer qualities of animals.

11   Later, Egyptian eye paint also helped guard against eye diseases of the region and so children and men, as well as women, were encouraged to use kohl. Fashions changed with the time and geography, reaching a peak of ridiculousness in 18th century England. During that time the fashionable woman (and man, too) wore false eyebrows made of mouseskin. Natural beauty was usually destroyed by about age 30 from the use of lead-based cosmetics. The scarlet or black patch, or *mouche,* originated as a cover for smallpox scars but became a fashion symbol. Lipstick and rouge were popular. Perfume was fashionable, in part, because bathing was not.

12   Modern women, who are glad we have grown past such things, may be surprised to learn that, as in Elizabethan or Egyptian days, talc and rice are still the base of face powders. Waxes, oils and fats are still used as binding agents and as the primary ingredients in lipstick and complexion creams. Red ochre, used as a cosmetic coloring since civilized antiquity, is still used for that purpose. Women who favor pearlized lipstick, however, may be relieved to discover that there is now an artificial substance responsible for the silvery glitter, a role historically filled by fish scales.

13   On a recent dreary afternoon, I decided that a little lipstick might cheer me up. There wasn't much time to be cheered, however, because my baby daughter soon smeared it all over my face, shirt and her clothes. My friend Debbie has two small boys and refuses to give it up: "The lady at the cosmetics counter gets positively gleeful whenever she sees me." Debbie's boys, two and four, have experimented generously with the use of cosmetics on themselves, the walls and furniture.

14   I wash my face with soap that costs $8.50 a bar, even though I am not convinced it's better than hand soap. Occasionally I use the cleansers, toners and scrubs that come along in the bonus package. But when it comes time for the colors and enhancers and concealers, I hesitate. In high-minded moments I like to

think this is because my self-confidence comes from inside, not from a collection of products.

15   At the same time, I admit to being proud of my fingernails. They are naturally strong and hard. Even with housework and baby, it is easy to keep them long. I keep thinking it might be nice to show them off a little more. One of these days I'm going to have a manicure.

Post-reading Questions

Content

1. In what way is Ray's decision not to wear makeup— and thereby remain naked—"partly pragmatic and partly philosophical"?

2. Why does the author spend time discussing the history of cosmetic use? What were some of the historical reasons for wearing rouge and perfume?

3. When did human beings begin to use makeup? In what way did prehistoric humans try to enhance their natural beauty? How do we know?

4. Ray claims that "our idea of beauty is tremendously affected by fashion." What evidence does she offer to support what she says? Do you agree with her? Why?

5. What might modern women be surprised to learn about cosmetics? What might they be "relieved to discover"?

Strategies and Structures

1. What does Ray's one-sentence opening paragraph accomplish? What effect did it have on you, the reader?

2. How does the author's use of specific examples strengthen her essay?

3. Paragraph 2 consists of what we recognize as fragmented sentence structures. However, in context, how do these fragments shed light on the essay's title and initial paragraph, clarifying the focus for the rest of the composition?

4. What is the tone or mood of this essay? Where does it become firmly established? How does the author feel about makeup use?

5. Explain the irony of Ray's final paragraph. Does it call the rest of Ray's attitudes toward makeup or artificial aids to beauty into question? Why or why not?

Language and Vocabulary

1. Vocabulary: *mascara, foundation, highlighter, blush, concealing stick, lipstick, eye liner, lip pencil, cosmetics, artifice, kohl, mouche.* All of these vocabulary words deal with makeup or are some type of makeup. If you are not familiar with the different sorts of makeup discussed, look up their definitions in your dictionary or ask your friends what they are used for. Then write both the makeup and its definition on a sheet of paper. Next, make a list of cosmetics and their uses which were not mentioned by the author of this essay.

2. This essay contains a very *personal* voice. What pronouns, phrases, and specifics contribute to this *personal* voice?

Group Activities

1. Get into groups and brainstorm at least *ten* questions about wearing or not wearing makeup. Next, individually interview friends and strangers, jotting down their responses to your questions. Interview people of all ages, of both genders, and from a wide range of social, economic, and ethnic backgrounds; then write a brief essay on the topic of "beauty aids" in modern society. The next time your group assembles, pass out photocopies of each other's essays and read them. Then, categorize the common uses of cosmetics among men and women in America as a group. Note which categories men do not fall into. Finally, from the viewpoint of advertising executives, how would your group increase the male market for cosmetics? Write a five-point plan.

2. Go to the library after class and have each group member select three different popular magazines (e.g., *People, GQ, Ms.*). Then go through your magazines, noting the number of ads that deal with beauty aids, from eyeliner and lipstick to hair transplants and cologne. Then, get together with your group and make a master list of your findings. You may want to use statistics your group has gathered in one of the following writing assignments.

Therefore, remember to write down the names and issue dates of the magazines you reviewed.

3. Over the weekend, participate in a small group activity that involves makeup. For instance, you might get together with three other people (male or female) who never wear makeup and go somewhere Saturday night outrageously painted like peacocks. Whatever you do, write a brief group summary of your activity, including your initial plans, and what you learned about yourself and others with regard to makeup.

Writing Activities

1. What is the relationship between cosmetic use and sexism in American society? Write an essay explaining how and why the media in America make women feel dependent upon "beauty aids" to be presentable or complete human beings.

2. Compose an essay entitled "The Masked Face," wherein you argue that you have a strong philosophical and logical basis for wearing makeup. Illustrate your material with examples drawn from personal experience, observations, and readings.

Phillip Persky

Guilt

Phillip Persky, Professor of English, San Jose State University, San Jose, California, was also Foreign Student Advisor for nearly twenty-five years at the university. He has taught English in Rome under a Fulbright Award, in Nigeria under the auspices of Southern Illinois University and the Ford Foundation, and in Micronesia through the Pacific Islands Project of SJSU. In the following essay, Persky distinguishes the difference between guilt and shame, drawing from his own personal experiences and observations of others.

Pre-reading Questions

1. When in your life have you experienced guilt, and what happened—if anything—as a result? Did your initial shame in someone or something later become a source of guilt?

2. What is your attitude toward your parents? When have you experienced pride and/or shame because of them? How did you deal with this?

1   Do you know the difference between shame and guilt? A generation ago the distinction was clearer: Shame was private and guilt was public. Today such distinctions are observed less often. The situation I'm writing about took place when I was 14–15 years old—that is over 60 years ago. Yet, I still think about it, occasionally, and I still feel ashamed when I do. It was the way in which my parents spoke English that bothered me so much then. They knew no English when they arrived in the United States as immigrants from Poland and learned English slowly by listening, repeating and just plain trying hard.

2   My parents were oblivious to my shame and, by extension, the resulting guilt. They had come from a small town in Poland,

Harodok, bordering Russia. It was a time of poverty in the ghettos, and those who could tried to come to America: then, as now, a country of promise. They lived first in Canal Fulton, Ohio, and then moved to Southeast Kansas to Caney. In order to support his family—my mother and two brothers—Dad began driving an old horse and cart around town buying junk and old rope. Shortly thereafter, the family moved to Independence, a town a short distance away and somewhat larger by a couple of thousand. There Dad, still with horse and cart, began the Persky Iron and Metal Company. The year was 1914, the year the United States entered World War I.

3   Later, during World War II, I remember well when there was a solemn ceremony of taking a metal statue and an old cannon, which had commemorated World War I, from the front of Memorial Hall downtown and hauling them in a civic procession to the junk yard where they would eventually be used to make ammunition for the military. Three generations later, in 1999, my sister-in-law still lives in Independence, and the company still does business under its fourth ownership, and until recently, under the family name, something of which I am very proud.

4   I remember many things about my childhood and youth in Independence. Those were happy times. My parents worked hard and were devoted to their children. I belonged to the Sea Scouts, a branch of the Boy Scouts, where the emphasis was on water sports—swimming and canoeing. I also worked for a grocery store through the kindness of my father, who, unbeknownst to me, had paid the grocer for hiring me. It wasn't until a week later that the store owner decided that I was worth the quarter an hour and that my father didn't have to pay it. Family was everything; nonetheless, there still was an underlying shame of my parents, and I always felt guilty because of it.

5   At home they spoke Yiddish with each other, an amalgam of many Central and Eastern European languages and German; in the United States it includes a smattering of English. People referred to such languages as "Broken English"—the term used then. It was the language used in business, with friends, and with me. Although I got the gist of what was being spoken in Yiddish, I never learned to speak it—never needed to. While many people confuse Yiddish with Hebrew, the official language of prayer and religious ceremonies, as well as that of modern Israel, I didn't embrace that language either because I had no need for it in my daily life.

6   My parents subscribed to the *Jewish Daily Forward*, a news-paper written in Yiddish and carrying most of the national news of the day. There were also radio and, later, TV. In short, my parents were reasonably well-aware of what was going on in the world. Dad could read English with difficulty and did so with pride; however, Mother could not. If anyone asked her if she had studied English in America, she replied that as a newly-arrived, young woman in this country, she had begun night school. One evening after class, she was sure she was being followed and fearing for her safety, she never returned. Perhaps.

7   Ironically, my guilt stemmed from a confused sense of shame fused with pride in my parents. I knew how hard they worked. I knew how much they loved my brothers and me. Nonetheless, I also knew that I was ashamed of the way they spoke "Broken English"—with its distinctive Yiddish accent. Granted, no one had difficulty understanding my parents' English, and they were well-respected by everyone in the community. However, to me that Yiddish accent seemed to mark them as immigrants—uneducated foreigners. Attempting to distance myself from such social trappings only intensified my feelings of guilt.

8   As I grew older and began teaching English classes for foreign students at the University of Kansas, I became much more appreciative of my parents' accomplishments in the United States under such difficult conditions. This teaching experience motivated me to teach abroad in Italy, Nigeria, Taiwan, and many islands of Micronesia, including Palau and Pohnpei. More and more I have realized that difference is a strength, rather than a liability, and that shame is the result of discomfort and not a viable social construct for guilt. Indeed, I was reminded of a quote from *The Prophet* by Gibran, "Much of your pain is self-chosen." Reflecting to that time, I now realize that perhaps I was more concerned with my own perceived pain and neglected to think of my parents' struggles, achievements, and strides toward dignity.

9   In Santa Clara County, California, where I now live, there are literally hundreds of thousands of immigrants from nearly every country of the world, and I wonder if their second and third generation children also share in my shame and guilt. I hope not. Instead, I would hope that they can appreciate the sacrifices and hardships their parents probably have endured to live here and to adjust to a different culture and a new life. It is a magnificent tribute to this country that so many can become

such successful, devoted Americans. Diversity and culture are ideals which one should be proud of, not ashamed. The United States has gone from being the "melting pot of the world" to a nourishing "mixed salad." For myself, I, too, have come a long way from my childhood, but I still experience feelings of guilt for being ashamed of my parents' "Broken English."

Post-reading Questions

Content

1. What bothered Persky about his parents?
2. Why is guilt a natural consequence of shame? What led the author from one to the other?
3. What does the author remember about his childhood and youth in Independence? Why might his positive memories trigger an occasional sense of guilt?
4. Why does Persky bother to distinguish Yiddish from Hebrew, and what made it unnecessary for him to learn either?
5. The author's teaching experience gave him insight and appreciation of individuals who strive to learn a language other than their native tongue. What did that ultimately motivate him to do?

Strategies and Structures

1. In the opening paragraph, how does Persky clearly establish the point and direction of his essay?
2. Explain the purpose for the author's detailed discussion of his parents' poverty, aspirations, and ultimate accomplishments. How does this information relate to the rest of the essay?
3. Persky concludes paragraph 6 with a rhetorical fragment. What is the effect of this single word following his discussion? What does this insinuate?
4. Toward the end of the essay, the author has moved from shame to appreciation of his parents. However, has this changed his feelings of guilt about the past? Please explain your answer.
5. The concluding paragraph of the essay places the theme into a different perspective of personal guilt. Explain the ethical and emotional strength of his

appeal to the new immigrants who might look at their parents the same way that he did.

Language and Vocabulary

1. Vocabulary: *distinction, oblivious, ghettos, commemorated, civic, underlying, perceived, liability, magnificence.* "Shame" and "guilt" have negative connotations, but many of the above words do not. What might this imply about the author?

2. Identify when and where Persky uses "emotionally charged words" in his essay. What does he accomplish by using them?

Group Activities

1. Get into groups and share experiences wherein you initially felt ashamed and then guilt. How were your experiences similar to, and in what way were they different from the other members of your group? Share your general perceptions of guilt with the rest of the class.

2. Persky seems to indicate that hands-on experiences with teaching English to foreign students gave him a new appreciation of the difficulty in learning a new language. Break up into groups of four or five people and have each member describe his or her experience learning a second language. When did you begin to take pride in your new language, or did you? Ultimately, did your group's attitude toward learning a new language reinforce or weaken the author's argument?

Writing Activities

1. Brainstorm the word *guilt*, making as many associations with the word as you can. Focus on a particular aspect of guilt to explore in detail; state it as the thesis. You might, for instance, analyze four or five motivating factors behind the concept of guilt, as well as people, situations, and institutions that reinforce one's sense of daily understanding of the word.

2. Take the line, "Much of your pain is self-chosen" by Gibran from paragraph 8, and paraphrase the

statement to use as the thesis of an essay. Fully develop your essay with examples drawn from personal experiences, observations, and readings. Strive to move your argument beyond the personal narrative by varying the examples you use and analyze.

Carlos Bulosan

Labor and Capital: The Coming Catastrophe

Carlos Bulosan was born in Luzon in the central Philippines and spent the first seventeen years of his life working in fields with his father or selling fish at the public market with his mother. Bulosan came to America in 1930 and worked as a migrant worker, a union activist, and a writer. Bulosan published several books, including The Laughter of My Father *(1942),* America Is in the Heart *(1977),* The Philippines Is in the Heart: A Collection of Short Stories *(1979), and* If You Want to Know Who We Are: A Carlos Bulosan Reader *(1983). In the following essay, Bulosan expresses his views on the need for unions to protect the laborer from exploitation by an employer.*

Pre-reading Questions

1. Cluster the word *capitalism*. What positive and negative associations do you relate with the word?

2. Who controls most of the money in America? Who is responsible for producing our nation's wealth?

1   Labor is the issue of the day. It has always been the issue. It is high time we should understand why thousands of workers' lives are sacrificed; why millions of dollars' worth of property are destroyed in the name of labor.

2   As in all industrial countries, America's wealth is concentrated in the hands of the few. This wealth is socially produced and privately appropriated. This precisely means that the wealth of the United States is produced by the people, the work-

ers as a whole, and distributed by the industrialists. The contradictions of the social production and the private distribution of wealth [brings about] all social problems.

3 Industrialists are fattened by profits. Profits are sucked from the very blood of the workers. This profiteering scheme is made possible by speed-ups, long hours and brutal methods. It is by driving workers into a most intolerable condition that the profiteers grow impregnable. There is a better term for this condition: barbarism. But do not think they spend their profits in philanthropic ventures. They invest it in the forces of production, machines, etc. They spend it in idle luxury. Have you seen a banker's daughter throwing away thousands of dollars for a sick dog? They pay more attention to animals than to us. Have you seen a manufacturer's machinery housed and guarded by a cordon of armed men? We are nearly [destroyed] in their riot for profits.

4 But the industrialists have also a quarrel among themselves. The bigger ones pool together and drive out the smaller ones. This struggle goes on until only one or two are left to dictate in the market. The bigger the combines they have, the more enormous profits they acquire, which means more exploitation. This goes on until society constricts and workers are thrown into the streets to starve. Do not believe that economic depressions are natural phenomena. All depressions are made, and inevitable when the markets are overflowing with surplus: Crisis is bound to come. The only solution that capitalism could give is war. This is why the coming war is more threatening and dangerous than the previous ones. All wars are fought for profit. That is why we must sacrifice everything for the prevention of war. For war is not only the slaughter of humanity but also the destruction of culture, the barbarization of man. We must die for peace and not for profit.

5 Labor and capital are sharp enemies. There never was any amnesty between them and there shall never be. One or the other stay[s]. The most disastrous proposal is compromise between them. This will never do: it only means the demoralization of the workers, the betrayal of these advanced groups working among the exploited and oppressed.

6 Unionism is one way of fighting for a better living condition. We are lucky to have in this country a considerable strong group which is fighting for us workers. But this is only a stepping-stone available in democracies. Unionism is a way to

economic freedom. But we must have political freedom also. We could have this through unionisms. We must have everything or nothing.

Post-reading Questions

Content

1. What does Bulosan state are the causes of "labor exploitation"? What are the implied effects of such exploitation?
2. According to Bulosan, what are the causes of economic depression?
3. Why does Bulosan say that we must avoid war at all costs? Do you agree with him? Why or why not?
4. Although the author wrote this essay in 1937, much of what he says is true today. What issues discussed in his essay are relevant to our modern workforce? How? Why?

Strategies and Structures

1. Why does Bulosan take a commonly accepted notion like *wars are justified by noble ideals* and claim wars are fought for profit? Which idea about war do you believe? Why?
2. Reread the topic sentences in each of the body paragraphs of the essay; in what way does Bulosan break down his theme? How well does he build upon his previous points?
3. Bulosan concludes his essay talking about the need for unionism to achieve better living. Does his composition logically build up to his conclusion? How? Why?

Language and Vocabulary

1. Vocabulary: *slaughter, amnesty, philanthropic, intolerable, profiteering, impregnable, cordon, exploitation, phenomena*. What do the majority of these words suggest to you? Which do you find more closely associated with labor?
2. The author is quite descriptive in this essay, and most of his descriptions produce a negative feeling in the reader (e.g., "Profits are sucked from the very blood of the workers"). Write two or three

paragraphs in which you present "profits" in a positive way.

Group Activities

1. Discuss capital or money. Is there anything positive that can be said about money other than it can "buy" people, places, and things? Would you change your present opinion about money or the capitalist system if you were a farm laborer picking fruits and vegetables for four dollars an hour?

2. Break the class up into two groups—one group representing the interests of laborers and the other group representing the interests of big business— and prepare a class debate arguing which is more essential to the well-being of a capitalist society. Write a summary of the debate explaining which group presented the best argument (you need not be faithful to your group).

Writing Activities

1. If you were a top industrialist, how would you spend your profits? Would you go out of your way to improve working conditions for your laborers or invest your money in schemes to make you even greater profits? Focusing in on either the causes or the ultimate effects of your actions, write a composition explaining the rationale for what you would do with your money.

2. Write an essay comparing and contrasting the unions mentioned by Bulosan in his article written in 1937 and unions of today. Have people's attitudes changed regarding unions? Are the unions of today more, less, or equally as effective as those of 1937? Are unions necessary today? Why or why not? Make sure you support your statements with verifiable facts and not personal opinions.

Rose Anna Higashi

Eating With Immigrants

A Professor of English, Rose Anna Higashi, specializes in Japanese, English, and Asian literature, as well as composition. Her poems frequently appear in numerous magazines, textbooks, and professional journals. After the publication of her personal journal and poetry collection, Blue Wings *(1995), she wrote the scholarly text,* Finding the Poet *(1996), a book on writing poetry and about self-discovery. Additionally, she has written several novels such as* Waiting for Rain, The Learning Wars *(2000),* Keeping Secrets *(2001), and* Catholic Girls *(2002). Over the years, many people, places, and things have helped shape Higashi's prose and piety: her hometown, Joplin, Missouri; authors Matsuo Basho, Gerard Manley Hopkins, and Robert Browning; and mysticism and spirituality. In the following essay, Higashi takes a critical look at the influence of mass media in American culture, arguing for renewed personal awareness in order to take charge of critical thinking skills—skills too often manipulated by media.*

Pre-reading Questions

1. What sorts of food do you like to eat and why? Do you like to eat at restaurants?
2. How would you characterize the workers at your favorite restaurant or fast food outlet? Describe them using concrete nouns and active verbs.

1   My husband and I share a hobby—eating. Clearly this is not an unusual activity, but we like to specialize. Our interest is in eating in immigrant restaurants, more particularly, places where the owners, cooks, serving staff and customers are all first

generation Americans. Why do we like immigrant restaurants? First of all, the food is good. Real people who grew up eating the food they are cooking prepare it. This is not fast food or food based on chain restaurant formulas. Immigrant food has real ingredients, like fresh ginger, fresh vegetables that didn't come out of a plastic freezer bag, and nutritious elements like tofu, bean sprouts and yogurt. Secondly, immigrant restaurants are sensible. The prices are reasonable and there is no silly pretentiousness. Immigrants are busy people who don't have time to put on airs. Snobbishness is for people who have been in this country for at least two generations. And finally, immigrant restaurants are happy places. Immigrants have hope. They have come to America believing that their lives can be better, and they've brought their families along with them on the greatest, bravest and riskiest adventure of their lives. Along with a good meal, a person who eats in an immigrant restaurant can receive a refresher course in the positive effects that traditional cultures can have on life in America.

2   Last Saturday, while we were eating dim sum at a Chinese immigrant restaurant, my husband and I got a pleasant reminder of the importance of family values and intergenerational respect. As we were nibbling on our fresh broccoli and turnip cakes, a glance around the huge room revealed not a single person eating alone. We noticed large family groups seated together at round tables sharing food from the lazy Susan in the center. Elderly grandparents sat next to young children who refilled the old folks' teacups without being told to do so. Even teenagers seemed unembarrassed by being seen in public with their parents. Attentive family members assisted senior citizens into and out of the restaurant. And children were allowed to be themselves. Babies got to cry and toddlers got to run around under the tables, and no one got angry if the kids spilled their noodles. And there was no "children's menu" nonsense. Everybody ate the same food.

3   There was plenty of evidence of the good old-fashioned work ethic at the dim sum restaurant too. The large staff of hostesses, waiters and waitresses, busboys, women pushing the carts filled with food, cooks and cashiers worked together like bees in a hive. Although each had a specific task to perform, I noticed that they automatically helped each other out when the need arose. When the restaurant got busy, the host himself helped bus tables and set them up for the next customers. When she came to our table with our bill, the cashier noticed that we had leftover food and quickly brought us some boxes rather than waiting for

our server to get them. Not one employee was goofing off or adopting a "that's not my job" attitude. What a painful contrast with some of America's fast food restaurants where the poorly trained help are so busy talking to each other that they can hardly be bothered to wait on a customer.

4   Whether we're eating sushi and soybeans at a little Japanese place where no one speaks English, enjoying freshly made *larb* at our favorite Thai restaurant or snacking on *kim chee* and *bibim bap* at a Korean tofu house, we like to dine with immigrants because of the upbeat ambience. There is no room for boredom and cynicism among first generation Americans. The woman who cooks the fabulous meals at our favorite Indian restaurant always comes out of the kitchen and asks us if we are enjoying the food, and she is genuinely pleased that we are. The owner of our local taqueria calls us "amigos" and actually means it. Immigrants have come from difficult circumstances believing that life is still worth living. They have traveled long distances, suffered culture shock and financial deprivation, and they have observed some of the truths of life along the way. Immigrants know that disrespect and self-centered egotism will not help them succeed. The traditional emphasis on community, combined with excellence in individual effort, treasured historically by both the Native Americans and the founders of the U.S. Constitution, is brought back to us through our immigrants as reminders of what we once valued before selfishness, arrogance and greed became the norm.

I sigh with sadness when I read the predictable letters to
5 the editor of my local newspaper blaming immigrants for such social ills as lack of affordable housing, the deterioration of our educational system and even terrorism. I wish that the people who write these letters would go down to the neighborhood Vietnamese *pho* shop for a simple bowl of noodles elegantly garnished with fresh basil and limes and served with courtesy and respect by a man who suffered horribly in his previous life yet loves his new country and hopes for a better life for his children. Somehow, tea tastes better among people who have left bitterness behind, and food is more nourishing eaten in community.

Post-reading Questions

Content

1. Why does Higashi like "eating in immigrant restaurants . . . where all the owners, cooks, serving staff

and customers are all first generation Americans"?
Does she appear to be a first generation immigrant
herself?

2. What evidence of the "good old fashioned work
ethic" did Higashi encounter at her local "dim sum"
restaurant?

3. Why does the author "sigh with silence" when she
reads letters "to the editor" in her local newspaper?

4. Higashi says that she and her husband enjoy eating
at immigrant restaurants "because of the upbeat
ambiance." What does she imply are the immediate
causes for such positive eating atmospheres?

5. Make a brief list of the representative immigrant
restaurants mentioned by Higashi, as well as any
outstanding details she offers about each.

Strategies and Structures

1. What cause and effect relationship does Higashi
specifically establish in her thesis sentence? How
does it provide a guiding focus for the rest of her
essay?

2. Describe the tone of "Eating With Immigrants."
What does it lend to her discussion?

3. How do Higashi and her husband get a pleasant reminder of family values by eating at a Chinese
restaurant? In what way does their "pleasant reminder" reinforce her essay's thesis?

4. Why do you imagine Higashi strategically selected
cause and effect as the dominant rhetorical method
of development in "Eating With Immigrants"? Cite
at least two examples from the essay to help illustrate and explain your answer.

5. In what way does the last sentence in Higashi's essay tie together all of her discussion points?

Language and Vocabulary

1. Vocabulary: *cuisine, cynicism, deprivation.* Add these
words to your vocabulary log. Then write an original
sentence using each word.

2. Go through Higashi's essay and identify places
where she introduces a word group followed or pre-
ceded by a definition of it. Then, using a similar technique, write a paragraph about foods you eat to an
audience that may not be aware of them. (Example:

Jessica likes to eat *poi*, a tarot root dish with the consistency of pudding.)

Group Activities

1. Pair off in a computer-assisted classroom, and search the Net for information on ethnic foods—particularly those you eat very seldom. Next, research restaurants you and your partner would like to visit. Narrow your list to one restaurants, eat there, and then write a collaborative critique of the establishments, noting such things as food quality, service, atmosphere, and so on.
2. In small groups, go back through Higashi's essay sentence by sentence—paragraph by paragraph, and analyze it in terms of 1) organization, 2) coherence, 3) support, 4) sentence skills, and 5) overall effectiveness. Also, be sure to mention the numerous ways she denotes cause/effect relationships throughout her essay.

Writing Activities

1. Write an essay wherein you argue the American weakness for fast foods curtails or strengthens one's ongoing exploration of restaurants featuring international/immigrant foods. Consider the eating habits of your friends, yourself, and your family as you prewrite on this topic.
2. What hobby or pastime do you enjoy? Using the rhetorical mode of cause and effect, write an essay explaining why you enjoy your chosen hobby, how you were introduced to it, and the consequences of nurturing a hobby in your daily life.

Additional Topics and Issues for Cause-and-Effect Essays

1. Compose an essay regarding the cause(s) and/or effect(s) of watching so much television in American society. You may want to limit your audience to adults, teenagers, or children.

2. Write an essay explaining the effects of growing up in a one-parent family. In developing your essay, try to avoid clichés.

3. Because they often looked so much like real weapons, a few years ago toy guns began to appear in stores in a variety of colors to indicate their nature (a toy versus a threatening weapon). Based on personal observation and readings, compose an essay discussing the effects of this action by toy makers. Has America's interest in firearms decreased? Has it had any effect on crime (formerly people used toy guns to commit robberies and other acts of violence)?

4. Compose a paper explaining how aging affects an animal's temperament, agility, eating habits, and character in general. To begin this assignment, freewrite about the pets you or your family owned or have known over the years.

5. Write about the cause(s) and/or effect(s) of one of the following: role-playing, shoplifting, flirting, stereotyping.

6. What causes pollution and what are the effects of unchecked pollution? Who are the main culprits, and why do they pollute? You will want to incorporate authoritative sources in your essay. (A good source of information would be an environmental studies department. If your college has such a department, consult with professors or majors in that field.)

7. Describe a person who irritates or frustrates you abnormally. What does this person do that frustrates you so? Does this person clean too much, watch television excessively, expect favors, or complain too much? Write an essay in which you concentrate on the causes or the effects of your irritation. Use specific details to demonstrate your point.

8. Write an essay in which you examine either the cause(s) or the effect(s) of owning an exotic animal, bird, reptile, fish, and so on. (Why does one purchase exotic creatures to begin with, and what often becomes of them in the long run?)

9. Write an essay explaining the causes and/or effects of an *injustice*. You could write about social, economic, political, or ecological *injustices* as presented in the news.

10. Based on interviews, observations, experiences, and readings, write an essay describing what you believe it will be like to grow old in America. Make sure to "qualify" how and why multiple causes could lead to an ultimate effect or effects (or vice versa).

10

Combined Strategies

We could have labeled this section "additional essays"; however, there is one point we wanted to emphasize with the title: Essays rarely use only one rhetorical strategy for development—a point that is quite obvious from our selections here. In "Of Pigs and Prigs: Revolution in the Name of Manners," for instance, Martha L. Henning blends description, illustration, process analysis, definition, and argumentation as she takes readers on a journey across a college campus. Along her trek, she stops at an administration building, a classroom and, finally, a publishing house, bringing us full circle with our point of departure. She ultimately concludes that the *various cultural elements that should nourish us—from our college classrooms and textbooks to the articles that fill our homes—reinforce an American sense of 'self' based more on the objects of life—the commodities—and less on living, by doing, with manners.* Coupling descriptive analysis with narration, Frank LaPeña discusses the Native-American oral tradition in his aptly titled essay, "Sharing Tradition." In doing so, he notes the merits of listening to our elders as they share their knowledge, wisdom, and stories with us. In "Curanderismo: A Healing Art," Cynthia Lopez combines narration and description as she explains how Western medical practices have limitations which create barriers between would-be patients and medical practitioners, and that *curanderismo,* the Mexican art of healing, provides those alienated from "high tech" medicine a way to holistically address their needs and *bring a sense of balance to all.*

Woody Allen's satirical essay, "Slang Origins," gives readers another glimpse of combined rhetorical strategies at work in writing. Using illustration and example, along with description, Allen defines the history of numerous slang phrases. "To eat humble pie," for instance, evolved from *jumbo* pie. *"Jumbo pie soon became* jumble *pie and 'to eat a jumble pie' referred to any kind of humiliating act. When Spanish seamen heard the word* jumble, *they pronounced it 'humble,' although many preferred to say nothing and simply grin."*

Jeanne Wakatsuki Houston also uses more than one rhetorical strategy when she develops her recollection of her arrival at Manzanar, a Japanese internment camp, during World War II. On one hand, simple narration provides Wakatsuki Houston with a vehicle to chronologically tell her story. On the other hand, cause and effect strategies are also at work in the essay. While Houston clearly alludes to the reason or cause for her family's move to Terminal Island, Boyle Heights, and ultimately Manzanar (anti-Asian sentiment as a result of the war in the Pacific), her essay deals with the consequences or effects the moves had on her—as well as those around her—as a child.

It may be a good idea to determine the dominant rhetorical strategies at work in the following selections and review the introductory chapters dealing with each. For example, one would review narration, illustration and example, and process analysis after reading Reginald Lockett's "How I Started Writing Poetry." No single rhetorical strategy made this essay work; rather, a mixture of strategies created a coherent composition that (1) explains, in a sense, the *rites of passage* (narration); (2) uses details and references to make people, places, and things come alive (illustration and example); and (3) draws on informational process analysis in order to vividly describe how something was done—how, against the odds, he started to write poetry (process analysis). No new knowledge is required to blend two rhetorical techniques; in fact, it comes quite naturally. For instance, you may begin a process or illustrate something by first defining it or argue for a cause by narrating a story. Still other times in the act of classifying and dividing a subject, you may be using some other rhetorical strategy without being aware of it. Exposition means to expose or explain and is not limited to a single method of development.

Tips on Writing Expository Essays

After prewriting to arrive at a specific focus, answer the following questions:

1. Have you sufficiently narrowed your thesis?

2. What is the point of this expository essay? What are you trying to explain and what rhetorical strategies lend themselves naturally to your objective?

3. Who is your audience? What tone or mood is most appropriate in addressing your audience and your occasion for writing?

4. Does your essay have an interesting introductory paragraph, a thoroughly supported thesis, and a satisfying conclusion?

5. Is there anything that you believe would make your essay more memorable?

6. Did you vary your sentence patterns to add variety and interest?

7. How often did you use transitions and linking devices to establish relationships between words, phrases, clauses, and entire paragraphs?

8. Did you carefully proofread your work for careless spelling, verb tense agreement, pronoun agreement, and subject/verb agreement errors?

9. Did you punctuate all complete ideas with a period, question mark, or exclamation point in order to avoid run-on sentences or comma splices?

10. Were all partial ideas combined with other sentences to avoid fragments?

11. Did you revise awkward, misleading sentences—sentences that forced your audience to read and reread your essay in order to understand what you meant?

12. Did you defend your discussion points or merely make a list of them?

Frank LaPeña

Sharing Tradition

Frank LaPeña is the director of the Native American Indian Studies program at California State University, Sacramento. As suggested by the following article, LaPeña is quite interested in the arts and traditions of Native Americans. He coedited Legends of Yosemite Miwok *(1992) with Craig D. Bates.*

Pre-reading Questions

1. What sort of stories did your parents tell you—rather than read to you—when you were a child? Did they have anything to do with your culture or society in general? Did they deal with values that transcend generations? Explain.

2. When do you tell stories and to whom? What is the purpose behind the stories you relate to others? Did you ever change the details of a story to relate to an audience or suit your purpose? How?

1   I was thinking one day about recent deaths of some of the traditional people and how difficult it is to maintain tradition. I was also thinking how important oral tradition is in helping maintain the values of culture, and how in a sense oral tradition is also an art form. As the elders pass on, the young people fill their places. Even though we know no one lives forever, no one dies if what they have gained by living is carried forward by those who follow—if we as individuals assume the responsibilities. This is easy to talk and write about, but it is hard to practice.

2   Not everyone is capable of fulfilling the roles of the elders. On one hand everyone who lives long enough automatically becomes an elder—it is something that just happens. Yet some elders have enhanced their lives by creating a special "niche,"

and once they have passed on, that niche is hard to fill. Religious obligations for the ceremonies and dance, for example, were reflected in their knowledge and in how those elders lived and how they affected people around them in common everyday activities as well. In fact, after the elders passed away, their knowledge of the culture and the responsibilities they had in their community had to be assumed by several individuals.

3   Because longevity is the guarantor of becoming an elder, the young don't pay too much attention to something that will happen some years down the road, but they regret it later. I have talked to individuals who were seventy years old or older, and even those forty and fifty years old, and they all expressed the feeling that they wished they had listened more, remembered more, or asked more about the things that the elders were willing to share with them.

4   The separation that exists between generations will always be with us. Each generation is faced with new technologies which replace the old; ever-growing populations make necessary new developments that replace fertile land with housing and impact on the natural resources of air and water. Part of tradition is tied to a natural world which is being destroyed. If we are not worried about the apocalypse, getting killed in the streets, or having the drug culture undercut our lives, we might wonder what kind of world it will be in the future. It is hard to live with all the stress, worry, and change that modern technology imposes on people. It is hard to maintain traditions in such circumstances. Our world is not the world of our great-grandparents.

5   So we have to remind ourselves that there are things that transcend generations, and the living force of that truth is carried by the person-to-person confidentiality of oral tradition. A lot depends upon the transmission of information from one person to another. Oral tradition is the educational tool of understanding the natural world.

6   Oral tradition is not, however, the way many people in modern society learn things. The educational process of getting degrees to show how educated we are forces people to do things out of necessity and not necessarily out of interest, passion for the true story, or because it is good for the community. Sometimes modern researchers gathering what they think is "oral" material "in the field" are not always told the truth. I can still see the smile of my friend who used to tell people "whatever they wanted to hear. I let them figure it out later," he said. Or

a person doesn't understand what has been told, so he/she corrects it by modifying the material so it makes sense. The result is that erroneous information is published and falsely validates [sic] one's research. With the printed word there is a tendency to place the author as "someone who knows" what's going on. As "experts," writers and lecturers may be put into a position where they think they must have an answer, so they answer by making something up. We need to learn to say we don't know the answer, and direct the question to someone who might know. We need to learn from the elders who sometimes say "I'll sleep on it," or who approach a problem by having everybody's input come up with an answer—which can be changed. Logistically, it is harder to correct errors in a book if it is already published.

7   A living oral tradition, as opposed to a literary tradition, accommodates corrections, because the stories are "known" by the listeners—although today a story could be someone's fantasy and it might be harder to validate. The source of one's information and how it was given affects how correct it is. Only if one is patient and gains information over a long period of time is it possible to get a proper understanding of one's information. If a person is *one of the group* (an insider), usually the information is given correctly, because it relates to something the speaker and listener have a vested interest in or participate in. It is their life. It is worth doing right.

8   For an artist, the oral tradition has an impact on how one visualizes the stories, the characters, the designs and color for art, the atmosphere, and other information which can be useful to an artist. If I think of these elders whom I respect and love and who were my teachers, I sometimes wonder—as I extend and alter the traditions—if I am somehow not doing right by them. If an artist's work is abstract, is it true to the stories? At what time of doing one's art does the artist begin to relate conceptually instead of representationally to his source, and is that good or bad? Ultimately being good or bad can refer to how we do our art—what's included or left out, and how true the artwork is to the "real" Native American thing. Do our modern life and new things function independently of or holistically with the old ways and symbols? Each of us has choices in the outcome of our lives.

9   As an artist, I won't try to answer these questions because the answers will be reflected in artists' works, and how they explain their work and how they understand their work. Each

of us makes choices in how we work and how we live. If one knows tradition and modifies how he/she presents it, I hope it is not only for one's ego but that more independently we are also paying attention to the source of our inspiration. And if it is tradition, I hope that we honor the elders and think of the responsibility they entrusted to us by sharing the traditions with us.

Post-reading Questions

Content

1. What does LaPeña feel is the importance of the oral tradition? To what extent do you agree with his opinions and why?
2. Who are the people who "preserve and pass on" the oral tradition? What is the danger of not passing on information? (Is there information about life that most likely will never be written down? Why?)
3. What is the difference between oral tradition and literary tradition?
4. How does LaPeña establish a relationship between art and the oral tradition?

Strategies and Structures

1. What is the controlling idea or thesis of this essay?
2. LaPeña develops four major problems with regard to maintaining the oral tradition. What are they, and how are they used to structure the essay?
3. How do topic sentences guide the reader through the essay? What would be lost without them?

Language and Vocabulary

1. Vocabulary: *niche, obligation, longevity, guarantor, apocalypse, confidentiality, erroneous, logistically, validate, holistically.* You may not know many of the above words. Without looking at a dictionary, reread the essay and write down what you think the definitions might be; then verify your guesses by looking up the definitions.
2. Using the words *obligation, longevity, apocalypse,* and *erroneous* from the vocabulary list above, write a story at least three or four paragraphs in length

that resembles one passed down from generation to generation in your culture.

Group Activities

1. Get into groups and share the story you have created or one that you know has been passed down from generation to generation in your culture. Then, choose a story someone else from your group has told and tell it to another group while the original teller listens to your version. Then have the original storyteller point out any differences in the stories and note how much has changed.

2. LaPeña states that the oral tradition helps maintain the values of a culture. Today one might say that movies and television play the same role. Make a list of current popular movies and TV shows. What values are they promoting? Do you think these are the dominant values of our culture? Why or why not?

Writing Activities

1. Write a paragraph or two explaining your attitude toward the oral tradition of passing along information.

2. If you believe that the oral tradition is important, write several paragraphs explaining how you intend to preserve it.

Cynthia Lopez

Curanderismo: A Healing Art

A freelance writer from San Francisco, Cynthia Lopez wrote this essay while completing her master's degree in health administration at the University of Southern California. Lopez was formerly one of the managing editors for Intercambios, *has worked for a civil rights law firm, and is presently active on the San Mateo County AIDS Advisory Committee. The following essay was printed in* Intercambios *in the winter of 1990.*

Pre-reading Questions

1. What *healing arts* do you use for ailments and discomforts— *arts* that are not acknowledged modern medical practices?

2. Cluster the term *folk medicine.* What do you associate with medicine?

1   "Western medicine alone limits people," says Elena Avila, R.N., M.S.N., and practitioner of curanderismo, the art of Mexican folk healing. With origins in pre-Columbian times and influenced by 16th century Spanish health care traditions, curanderismo uses herbs, ritual prayer, music, dance, and massage to cure people.

2   "It's a way of healing," explains Avila, "by seeking balance in all areas of life: social, physical, and spiritual."

3   One need only visit the mercado in almost any Mexican town to find the art of curanderismo in practice. Amid the stalls of modern-day commercial goods one can still find the local *yerbería,* or herb store, specializing in plants, ointments, and incense, designed to aid in the healing process. The dispensers of these cures often practice the medical knowledge

handed down from generations. It's a form of traditional, holistic medicine, not well understood nor accepted in the United States, although some practitioners, like Elena Avila, believe that curanderismo can be practiced alongside modern medicine.

4   Avila began her study of Mexican folk medicine as a nursing student at the University of Texas. A first generation Chicana and native of El Paso, she was asked by an Anglo professor to speak about curanderismo. That request led her to a curandera in the El Paso–Juarez area, and hence initiated her journey into Mexican folk medicine. She was an apprentice for two years, visiting curanderos throughout Mexico and the southwestern United States. She studied Aztec dancing and participated in rituals in many of the "power places" in Mexico.

5   At the same time, she chalked up an impressive list of medical degrees and clinical experience. After earning her registered nurse degree, she was nurse manager of the Psychiatry Department of Thomason General Hospital in El Paso. She later became the hospital's director of maternal/child nursing. In 1981, she made a move to Los Angeles, as clinical coordinator of the UCLA Neuropsychiatric Institute. Two years later, she returned to her native Southwest to direct the Albuquerque Rape Crisis Center. It was a position she held for four years.

6   Avila now has her own private practice at home, where she specializes in resolving emotional problems of adult children of alcoholics, rape survivors, adult incest survivors, and addicts, among others. Business professionals as well as aging Native Americans from the surrounding reservations have sought her counsel. Curanderismo plays an integral part in her practice.

7   "I have altars in my treatment rooms, and I get a lot of my supplies from Mexico," she explains. She uses romero and ruda, both plants, when performing *limpias,* a kind of spiritual cleansing for returning balance to the life of a person. She also treats *susto pasado,* or chronic shock which causes the spirit to hide after a person suffers from trauma. Some patients have sought her help when suffering from *envidia,* a kind of negative energy created when one person is extremely jealous of another.

8   Nevertheless, Avila claims she had to redefine some ideas behind curanderismo to make it powerful for her patients. "When someone tells me *'alguien me hizo mal'* (someone

harmed me) it affirms a belief that people outside of us have more power than ourselves. I work with the opposite idea that what I do empowers people to not become victims of others," she said.

9   While Avila incorporates the tenets of curanderismo into her practice, she won't hesitate to refer patients to a physician if she suspects a medical problem. The many years she spent as a nurse helped hone her ability to spot diseases requiring additional intervention. Perhaps this cooperative relationship between healers and physicians is what could enhance curanderismo's sometimes bad reputation with the medical establishment. Skeptical physicians often blame a misdiagnosed serious disease on curanderismo. The fact remains that for Hispanics, who have always comprised a large part of the uninsured, a visit to the curandero can provide an alternative to no health care at all.

10   An understanding of traditional Mexican medicine can help practitioners of Western medicine earn the confidence of their Mexican patients. Avila is a firm believer in sharing the knowledge she has gained and conducts workshops throughout the country on curanderismo to interested medical practitioners. Health care workers admitted to better cultural understanding once they learned that simply touching a child avoided the magical disease of *mal de ojo* or "evil eye," which makes a child susceptible to illness, or that egg or soap on the head of a baby is treatment for *mollera caido* or fallen fontanel attributed to dislocated internal organs.

11   A tradition of folk medicine is common in cultures throughout Latin America and elsewhere, with practices that may seem very alien to some. Avila acknowledges that some people still liken curanderismo to witchcraft. "The drive in society is to assimilate, to abandon the past, and although I don't deny that there are *brujos* or witches, I consider curanderismo a healing art," she said. And the holistic approach is what more and more people may be looking for as modern medicine becomes more specialized and to many people, alienating. Incorporating the new with the traditional may bring a sense of balance to all.

Post-reading Questions

Content

1. What does curanderismo use to cure people? What are its healing properties?
2. Does the author have a solution for those alienated

by modern medicine? Explain your answer.
3. Make a list of the medical degree and clinical experiences Avila acquired prior to directing the Albuquerque Rape Crisis Center.
4. What did Avila specialize in once she began her private practice at home?
5. Why might understanding "traditional Mexican medicine" help practitioners of Western medicine earn the confidence of their Mexican patients?

Strategies and Structures

1. How do the first and last sentences in this essay frame Lopez's discussion of curanderismo?
2. Why does the author discuss Avila's qualifications and experiences as a practitioner of Western medicine in such detail?
3. The events in this essay follow a chronological progression. Jot down a brief list of transitional words, phrases, and linking devices which move the reader coherently from point to point.
4. Explain the possible reason the author expands her focus on folk medicine in Mexico to folk medicine throughout South America in paragraph 11.
5. Why do you imagine that Lopez frequently uses Spanish words throughout her essay? What does she accomplish by doing so?

Language and Vocabulary

1. Vocabulary: *practitioner, holistic, dispensers, susceptible, fontanel, assimilate.* Use each of these words in a sentence dealing with some aspect of medicine, healing, or illness.
2. What are the denotative meanings of *folk medicine* and *faith healing?* What connotative meaning does each term carry? How might the use of either term prejudice a person who believes in the power of Western medicine? Why?

Group Activities

1. Explore the breadth of folk medicine throughout the world. Begin by breaking the class down into groups of four or five people. Each group should select the

folk medicine from a particular culture to research in detail. Visit the library and gather as much information about your culture's practices as possible; each group member should be responsible for material. Finally, in a class forum, present your group's findings.

2. Assemble into groups and discuss myths surrounding the medical profession. You might consider everyone from dentists and surgeons to general practitioners and chiropractors. Ultimately, write a collaborative paragraph explaining how and why your group feels "health attitudes" are shaped by the medical myths around us.

Writing Activities

1. Write an essay in which you present your own definition of *folk medicine,* using specific, concrete examples to illustrate what you say.
2. Using information drawn from class forums and personal research, compare and contrast the folk medicine practiced by two societies that do not fully embrace Western medicine.

Reginald Lockett

How I Started Writing Poetry

A PEN Oakland, Josephine Miles award *winning poet, Reginald Lockett is a very prolific writer whose poetry, literary reviews, critiques, and prose have appeared in over forty anthologies and periodicals. His collected works of poetry include* Good Time & No Bread *(1978), verse which prompted poet Al Young to comment that "Like a jubilant Saturday night deejay, Lockett spins out one celebration of life after another in a yea-saying street idiom guaranteed to keep listeners turned to his spot on the dial," and* Where the Birds Sing Bass *(1995), acclaimed by Ishmael Reed as possibly "the best book of poetry in 1995. The voice is hip, urban, observant, and nostalgic. Reginald Lockett brings the world home, and in the process tells us about folks who don't make the news." Most recently he publushed* The Party Crashers of Paradise *(2001). As Lockett's essay title suggests, his "informational" process essay explains how he came to write poetry. Currently, Lockett teaches at San Jose City College and lives in Oakland, California and regularly performs with the* Word Wind Chorus.

Pre-reading Questions

1. Was there ever a time in your life when you walked, talked, and acted in a particular way just to be "cool" or "fit in"? Freewrite about the experience in your journal. (This assignment encourages greater creativity and imagination than reflection on an actual event.)

2. Cluster the word *poetry.* What do you associate with a poem? If someone asked you for a definition of a *poem,* what would you say? Do you have any favorite poets?

3. Experiment. Write a poem which illustrates the theme of innocence in your writing log or journal. Then, project

yourself ten years into the future and rewrite the same poem from the point of view of a more experienced person. (This assignment encourages creativity and imagination.)

---

1   At the age of fourteen I was what Richard Pryor over a decade later would call "going for bad" or what my southern-bred folks said was "smellin' your pee." That is, I had cultivated a facade of daring-do, hip, cool, con man bravado so prevalent among adolescent males in West Oakland. I "talked that talk and walked that walk" most parents found downright despicable. In their minds these were dress rehearsals of fantasies that were Popsicles that would melt and evaporate under the heat of blazing hot realities. And there I was doing the pimp limp and talking about nothing profound or sustaining. All I wanted to do was project that image of being forever cool like Billy Boo, who used to wear three T-shirts, two slipover sweaters and a thick Pendleton shirt tucked neatly in his khaki or black Ben Davidsons to give everybody the impression that he was buffed (muscle bound) and definitely not to be messed with. Cool. Real cool. Standing in front of the liquor store on 35th and San Pablo sipping white port and lemon juice, talking smack by the boatloads until some *real* hoodlum from Campbell Village (or was it Harbor Homes?) with the real biceps, the shonuff triceps and sledgehammer fists beat the shirt, both sweaters, the T-shirts and pants right off of Billy Boo's weak, bony body.

2   Herbert Hoover Junior High, the school I attended, was considered one of the toughest in Oakland at that time. It was a dirty, gray, forbidding-looking place where several fights would break out every day. There was a joke going around that a mother, new to the city, mistook it for the Juvenile Detention Center that was further down in West Oakland on 18th and Poplar, right across the street from DeFremery Park.

3   During my seventh-grade year there were constant referrals to the principal's office for any number of infractions committed either in Miss Okamura's third-period music class or Mrs. George's sixth-period math class in the basement, where those of us with behavioral problems and assumed learning disabilities were sent. It was also around this time that Harvey Hendricks, my main running buddy, took it upon himself to hip me to everything he thought I needed to know about sex while we were doing a week's detention in Mrs. Balasco's art class for capping on "them steamer trunks" or "suitcases" under her eyes. As we sat there, supposedly writing "I will not insult the

teacher" one hundred times, Harvey would draw pictures of huge tits and vaginas, while telling me how to rap, kiss, and jump off in some twanks and stroke. Told me that the pimples on my face were "pussy bumps," and that I'd better start getting some trim or end up just like Crater Face Jerome with the big, nasty-looking quarter-size pus bumps all over his face.

4   Though my behavior left a lot to be desired, I managed to earn some fairly decent grades. I loved history, art and English, and somehow managed to work my way up from special education classes to college prep courses by the time I reached ninth grade, my last year at Hoover. But by then I had become a full-fledged little thug, and had been suspended—and damn near expelled—quite a few times for going to knuckle city at the drop of a hat for any real or imagined reason. And what an efficient thief I'd become. This was something I'd picked up from my cousins, R. C. and Danny, when I started hanging out with them on weekends in San Francisco's Haight-Ashbury. We'd steal clothes, records, liquor, jewelry—anything for the sake of magnifying to the umpteenth degree that image of death-defying manhood and to prove I was indeed a budding Slick Draw McGraw. Luckily, I was never caught, arrested and hauled off to Juvenile Hall or the California Youth Authority like so many of the guys I ran with.

5   Probably through pressure from my parents and encouragement from my teachers and counselors, I forced myself to start thinking about pursuing a career after graduation from high school, which was three years away. Reaching into the grab bag of professional choices, I decided I wanted to become a physician, since doctors were held in such high esteem, particularly in an Afro-American community like West Oakland. I'd gotten it in my head that I wanted to be a plastic surgeon, no less, because I liked working with my hands and found science intriguing. Then something strange happened.

6   Maybe it was the continuous violence, delinquency and early pregnancies that made those Oakland Unified School District administrators (more than likely after some consultation with psychologists) decide to put a little Freudian theory to practical use. Just as I was grooving, really getting into this fantastic project in fourth-period art class, I was called up to the teacher's desk and handed a note and told to report to a classroom downstairs on the first floor. What had I done this time? Was it because I snatched Gregory Jones' milkshake during lunch a couple of days ago and gulped it down, savoring every drop like an old loathsome suck-egg dog, and feeling no

pain as the chump, big as he was, stood there and cried? And Mr. Foltz, the principal, was known to hand out mass suspensions. Sometimes fifteen, twenty, twenty-five people at a time. But when I entered the classroom, there sat this tall, gangly, goofy-looking white woman who wore her hair unusually long for that time, had thick glasses and buckteeth like the beaver on the Ipana Toothpaste commercials. Some of the roughest, toughest kids that went to Hoover were in there. Especially big old mean, ugly Martha Dupree who was known to knock out boys, girls, and teachers when she got the urge. If Big Martha asked you for a last-day-of-school kiss, you'd better give it up or make an appointment with your dentist.

7   When Miss Nettelbeck finally got our attention, she announced that this was a creative writing class that would meet twice a week. Creative writing? What the hell is creative writing a couple of us asked. She explained that it was a way to express what was on your mind, and a better way of getting something off of your chest instead of beating up your fellow students. Then she read a few poems to us and passed out some of that coarse school-issue lined paper and told us to write about something we liked, disliked, or really wanted. What I wanted to know was, did it have to be one of "them pomes." "If that's how you want to express yourself, Reginald," she said. So I started racking my brain, trying to think about what I liked, didn't like and what I really wanted. Well, I liked football, track and Gayle Johnson, who would turn her cute little "high yella" nose up in total disgust every time I tried to say something to her. I couldn't stand the sight—not even the thought—of old monkey-face Martha. And what I really wanted was either a '57 Buick Roadmaster or a '56 Chevy with mag wheels and tuck 'n' roll seats that was dropped in the front like the ones I'd seen older dudes like Mack's brother, Skippy, riding around in. Naw, I told myself, I couldn't get away with writing about things like that. I might get into some more trouble, and Big Martha would give me a thorough ass-kicking for writing something about mashing her face in some dough and baking me some gorilla cookies. Who'd ever heard of a poem about cars? One thing I really liked was the ocean. I guess that was in my blood because my father was then a master chief steward in the navy, and, when I was younger, would take me aboard ships docked at Hunter's Point and Alameda. I loved the sea so much that I would sometimes walk from my house on Market and West MacArthur all the way to the

Berkeley Pier or take a bus to Ocean Beach in San Francisco
whenever I wasn't up to no good. So I wrote:

I sit on a rock
  watching
the evening tide
  come in.
The green waves travel
  with the wind.
They seem to carry
  a message of
warning, of plea
  from the dimensions
of time and distance.

8   When I gave it to Miss Nettelbeck, she read it and told me
it was good for a first attempt at writing poetry, and since
there was still some time left in the period, I should go back
to my seat and write something else. Damn! These teachers
never gave you any kind of slack, no matter what you did and
how well you did it. Now, what else could I think of to write
about? How about a tribute to Miss Bobby, the neighborhood
drag queen, who'd been found carved up like a Christmas
turkey a week ago? Though me, Harvey and Mack used to
crack jokes about "her" giving up the boodie, we still liked
and respected "her" because she would give you five or six
dollars to run an errand to the cleaners or the store, never
tried to hit on you, and would get any of the other "girls"
straight real quick if they even said you were cute or something. So I wrote:

Bring on the hustle
In Continental suits
And alligator shoes
Let fat ladies of the night
In short, tight dresses
And spiked heels enter.
We are gathered here
To pay tribute to
The Queen of Drag.

What colorful curtains
And rugs!
Look at the stereo set
And the clothes in the closet.

On the bed, entangled
In a bloody sheet,
Is that elegant one
Of ill repute
But good carriage
Oh yes! There
Was none like her.
The Queen of Drag.

9   When she read that one, I just knew Miss Nettelbeck would immediately write a referral and have me sent back upstairs. But she liked it and said I was precocious for someone at such an innocent age. Innocent! When was I ever innocent? I was guilty of just about everything I was accused of doing. Like, get your eyes checked, baby. And what was precocious? Was it something weird? Did it mean I was queer like Miss Bobby? Was I about to go to snap city like poor Donny Moore had a year ago when he suddenly got up and started jacking off in front of Mr. Lee's history class? What did this woman, who looked and dressed like one of them beatniks I'd seen one night on *East Side, West Side,* mean? My Aunt Audry's boyfriend, Joe, told me beatniks were smart and used a lot of big words like precocious so nobody could understand what they were talking about. Had to be something bad. This would mess with me for the rest of the week if I didn't ask her what she meant. So I did, and she told me it meant that I knew about things somebody my age didn't usually know about. Wow! That could only mean that I was "hip to the lip." But I already knew that.

10   For some reason I wasn't running up and down the streets with the fellas much anymore. Harvey would get bent out of shape every time I'd tell him I had something else to do. I had to, turning punkish or seeing some broad I was too chinchy to introduce him to. This also bothered my mother because she kept telling me I was going to ruin my eyes if I didn't stop reading so much; and what was that I spent all my spare time writing in a manila notebook? Was I keeping a diary or something? Only girls kept diaries, people may start thinking I was one of "them sissy mens" if I didn't stop. Even getting good grades in citizenship and making the honor roll didn't keep her off my case. But I kept right on reading and writing, looking forward to Miss Nettelbeck's class twice a week. I stopped fighting, too. But I was still roguish as ever. Instead of raiding Roger's Men's Shop, Smith's and Flagg Brothers'

Shoes, I was stealing books by just about every poet and writer Miss Nettelbeck read to the class. That's how I started writing poetry.

Post-reading Questions

Content

1. Who got Lockett to consider "pursuing a career after graduation from high school"? What did he plan on becoming and why? What was he referring to when he said, "Then something strange happened" which changed his initial goal and his lifestyle?

2. What academic courses did the author always "love"? In what way did his academic preparation conflict with his social persona?

3. Who was "Big Martha Dupree"? What sort of reputation did she have? Why?

4. What kind of things was the author stealing at the start of the essay? What was he stealing at the end of the essay?

5. In your opinion, what audience would this essay appeal to (1) in general, (2) in particular? Explain how and why you arrived at your conclusions.

Strategies and Structures

1. Why do you imagine the author devotes so much time to providing readers with personal background information before he uses informational process analysis to explain how he became a poet?

2. How does the author's word choice establish and maintain the tone of this essay and reflect his personality?

3. This essay blends many rhetorical strategies which lead to the final sentence: "That's how I started writing poetry." Identify some of the rhetorical modes of development at work and comment on their effectiveness.

4. How does the author create unity and coherence in this personal essay?

5. Assess how well the inclusion of two poems he wrote for Miss Nettelbeck demonstrates his struggle to find topics and a voice for writing poetry. (In what way were the poems different? Which poem was more daring? Why?)

Language and Vocabulary

1. Vocabulary: *infractions, delinquency, referrals, precocious.* With the exception of *precocious,* the above words all deal with some aspect of human conduct and its consequences. Write a single paragraph about a real or imaginary situation in which you use all the above vocabulary words. You might begin your paragraph with something like: "Precociousness frequently leads to disrespect and trouble. . . . "

2. The author uses street talk and African-American idioms in this essay to give it a particular flavor. Go through the essay and identify as many of these idioms as you can. Next, write them down and then offer an informal definition for each one. Make a separate list of idioms you are not familiar with or cannot define. Save both lists for a group activity.

Group Activities

1. Break into groups and exchange your answers to Language and Vocabulary question 2. Spend the majority of your time discussing unfamiliar idioms and, as a group, attempt to arrive at some tentative translations of them.

2. As a group, examine the difference between justifiable causes for doing something and rationalizing one's behavior *after* doing something. What does Lockett do in his essay?

Writing Activities

1. In a manner similar to Lockett's, write a narrative account of a situation that motivated you to do something or that explains how something was done. Use your local dialect and idioms to give your essay a personal flair—a distinct voice—whenever possible.

2. Cluster the term *self-discovery* and carefully consider the free associations you make and their implications. Then, write an expository essay wherein you relate how you or somebody you know came to a greater understanding of someone or something through personal *reflection* and *self-discovery.*

Woody Allen

Slang Origins

Woody Allen, a comedian, actor, screenwriter, and essayist, was born in Brooklyn, New York, in 1935 and began writing jokes when he was a high school student. Early in his career, he wrote for several television programs, including The Tonight Show. *Among the many films Allen has written and directed are* Bananas *(1970),* Play it Again Sam *(1972), the Academy Award–winning* Annie Hall *(1975),* Manhattan *(1979),* The Floating Lightbulb *(1982),* Don't Drink the Water *(1993),* Manhattan Murder Mystery *(1993), and* Deconstructing Harry *(1997). His books and collections of essays include* Getting Even *(1971),* Without Feathers *(1975),* Side Effects *(1980),* The Lunatic's Tale *(1986),* Three Films by Woody Allen *(1987), and* Woody Allen on Woody Allen *(1998). Allen's films, essays, and short fiction tend to be humorous, cynical, and satirical—often poking fun at some type of human folly.*

Pre-reading Questions

1. Based on the title of this essay, "Slang Origins," and your knowledge of the author, what do you expect this essay to be about? (Do not read it before thinking about an answer for this question.)

2. In the essay you're about to read, Allen gives some un-orthodox definitions of slang. Explain the word origins of the following: "eat humble pie," "take it on the lam," and "to look down one's nose." Do not consult a dictionary. Make up your definitions using your imagination and common sense. (Feel free to use humor.)

1   How many of you have ever wondered where certain slang expressions come from? Like "She's the cat's pajamas," or to

"take it on the lam." Neither have I. And yet for those who are interested in this sort of thing I have provided a brief guide to a few of the more interesting origins.

2   Unfortunately, time did not permit consulting any of the established works on the subject, and I was forced to either obtain the information from friends or fill in certain gaps by using my own common sense.

3   Take, for instance, the expression "to eat humble pie." During the reign of Louis the Fat, the culinary arts flourished in France to a degree unequaled anywhere. So obese was the French monarch that he had to be lowered onto the throne with a winch and packed into the seat itself with a large spatula. A typical dinner (according to DeRochet) consisted of a thin crêpe appetizer, some parsley, an ox, and custard. Food became the court obsession, and no other subject could be discussed under penalty of death. Members of a decadent aristocracy consumed incredible meals and even dressed as foods. DeRochet tells us that M. Monsant showed up at the coronation as a wiener, and Étienne Tisserant received papal dispensation to wed his favorite codfish. Desserts grew more and more elaborate and pies grew larger until the minister of justice suffocated trying to eat a seven-foot "Jumbo Pie." *Jumbo* pie soon became *jumble* pie and "to eat a jumble pie" referred to any kind of humiliating act. When the Spanish seamen heard the word *jumble,* they pronounced it "humble," although many preferred to say nothing and simply grin.

4   Now, while "humble pie" goes back to the French, "take it on the lam" is English in origin. Years ago, in England, "lamming" was a game played with dice and a large tube of ointment. Each player in turn threw dice and then skipped around the room until he hemorrhaged. If a person threw a seven or under he would say the word "quintz" and proceed to twirl in a frenzy. If he threw over seven, he was forced to give every player a portion of his feathers and was given a good "lamming." Three "lammings" and a player was "kwirled" or declared a moral bankrupt. Gradually any game with feathers was called "lamming" and feathers became "lams." To "take it on the lam" meant to put on feathers and later, to escape, although the transition is unclear.

5   Incidentally, if two players disagreed on rules, we might say they "got into a beef." This term goes back to the Renaissance when a man would court a woman by stroking the side of her head with a slab of meat. If she pulled away, it meant she was spoken for. If, however, she assisted by clamping the meat to

her face and pushing it all over her head, it meant she would marry him. The meat was kept by the bride's parents and worn as a hat on special occasions. If, however, the husband took another lover, the wife could dissolve the marriage by running with the meat to the town square and yelling. "With thine own beef, I do reject thee. Aroo! Aroo!" If a couple "took to the beef" or "had a beef" it meant they were quarreling.

6   Another marital custom gives us that eloquent and colorful expression of disdain, "to look down one's nose." In Persia it was considered a mark of great beauty for a woman to have a long nose. In fact, the longer the nose, the more desirable the female, up to a certain point. Then it became funny. When a man proposed to a beautiful woman he awaited her decision on bended knee as she "looked down her nose at him." If her nostrils twitched, he was accepted, but if she sharpened her nose with pumice and began pecking him on the neck and shoulders, it meant she loved another.

7   Now, we all know when someone is very dressed up, we say he looks "spiffy." The term owes its origin to Sir Oswald Spiffy, perhaps the most renowned fop of Victorian England. Heir to treacle millions, Spiffy squandered his money on clothes. It was said that at one time he owned enough handkerchiefs for all the men, women and children in Asia to blow their noses for seven years without stopping. Spiffy's sartorial innovations were legend, and he was the first man ever to wear gloves on his head. Because of extra-sensitive skin, Spiffy's underwear had to be made of the finest Nova Scotia salmon, carefully sliced by one particular tailor. His libertine attitudes involved him in several notorious scandals, and he eventually sued the government over the right to wear earmuffs while fondling a dwarf. In the end Spiffy died a broken man in Chichester, his total wardrobe reduced to kneepads and a sombrero.

8   Looking "spiffy," then, is quite a compliment, and one who does is liable to be dressed "to beat the band," a turn-of-the-century expression that originated from the custom of attacking with clubs any symphony orchestra whose conductor smiled during Berlioz. "Beating the band" soon became a popular evening out, and people dressed up in their finest clothes, carrying with them sticks and rocks. The practice was finally abandoned, during a performance of the *Symphonie fantastique* in New York when the entire string section suddenly stopped playing and exchanged gunfire with the first ten rows. Police ended the melee but not before a relative of J. P. Morgan's was wounded in

the soft palate. After that, for a while at least, nobody dressed "to beat the band."

9   If you think some of the above derivations questionable, you might throw up your hands and say, "Fiddlesticks." This marvelous expression originated in Austria many years ago. Whenever a man in the banking profession announced his marriage to a circus pinhead, it was the custom for friends to present him with a bellows and a three-year supply of wax fruit. Legend has it that when Leo Rothschild made known his betrothal, a box of cello bows was delivered to him by mistake. When it was opened and found not to contain the traditional gift, he exclaimed, "What are these? Where are my bellows and fruit? Eh? All I rate is fiddlesticks!" The term "fiddlesticks" became a joke overnight in the taverns amongst the lower classes, who hated Leo Rothschild for never removing the comb from his hair after combing it. Eventually "fiddlesticks" meant any foolishness.

10   Well, I hope you've enjoyed some of these slang origins and that they stimulate you to investigate some of your own. And in case you were wondering about the term used to open this study, "the cat's pajamas," it goes back to an old burlesque routine of Chase and Rowe's, the two nutsy German professors. Dressed in oversized tails, Bill Rowe stole some poor victim's pajamas. Dave Chase, who got great mileage out of his "hard of hearing" specialty, would ask him:

> Chase: Ach. Herr Professor. Vot is dot bulge under your pocket?
> Rowe: Dot? Dot's de chap's pajamas.
> Chase: The cat's pajamas? Ut mein Gott?

11   Audiences were convulsed by this sort of repartee and only a premature death of the team by strangulation kept them from stardom.

Post-reading Questions

Content

1. In the first paragraph, Allen explains the purpose of his essay. What is that purpose? Why would Allen provide a guide to more interesting slang origins if he is not interested in them?

2. How did the expression "to eat humble pie" develop? What was its original meaning and how did it change? Does Allen's explanation seem reasonable?

3. What two sayings derived from marital customs does Allen define? What do his explanations suggest about the relationship between the sexes through the ages?

Strategies and Structures

1. How does beginning and concluding his essay discussing "She's the cat's pajamas" provide a framing device for this essay?
2. What pattern does Allen follow in each paragraph? Why?
3. What techniques does Allen use to make his essay humorous? Do you find the use of humor disturbing or distracting? Why or why not? What is the purpose of the humor in this essay? Whom is he making fun of?

Language and Vocabulary

1. Vocabulary: *frenzy, culinary, winch, decadent, hemorrhaged, wiener, ointment, treacle, libertine, brothel, burlesque.* Using five related words from this list, write a sentence for each, based on a common theme. Once you have written your five sentences, combine them into a unified paragraph. Use additional sentences to provide coherence where necessary.
2. What linking devices does Allen use to lead the reader through the essay?

Group Activities

1. Make a list of five slang terms that you use every day. Look up their origins and dictionary definitions. (Such books as *Hog on Ice* or *Who Put the Butter in Butterfly?* may be helpful.) Write down the real definitions and make up your own definitions. Present each set of definitions to the class without telling the students which are the true meanings and let the class vote on which are the real definitions.
2. Make a glossary of slang terms you hear others using but feel uncomfortable using yourself.

Writing Activities

1. After doing some preliminary research, write your own definition essay explaining the slang words or phrases used by a particular group; for example, sports slang, business jargon, or cultural expressions.

2. Write a humorous essay explaining the origins of some of your own *original* slang expressions. Certain humorous devices that you may find helpful are exaggeration, absurdity, sarcasm, and irony. (You may want to consult the Glossary for definitions of these devices.)

Martha L. Henning

Of Prigs and Pigs: Revolution in the Name of Manners

Martha L. Henning holds a Ph.D. in Rhetoric and Composition. Her
book, Beyond Understanding: Appeals to the Imagination, Passions,
and Will in Mid-Nineteenth-Century American Women's Fiction,
urges readers to read more "holistically" with a change of mind that
includes the multiple faculties available to nineteenth-century
readers. She teaches writing and literature at Portland (Oregon)
Community College and really does snowboard in skirts.

Pre-reading Questions

1. Jot down a brief description of the word "manners." What does the word imply?
2. Make a list wherein you categorize types of manners (e.g., table manners, good sportsmanship, and so on). Are good manners important to you? Why or why not?

1   I iron pillowcases. So did my grandmother. And I iron napkins and handkerchiefs and the more wrinkly of the cotton and linen dishtowels. My family has enjoyed the manners of ironed kitchen linens long before my environmentally conscious twins declared disposable napkins and towels an unnecessary expenditure of wood fiber and long before those twins were in and out of their non-disposable cloth—washable and line-dried—diapers. Perhaps I learned such manners of living with durable cloth fibers from that bastion of manners, my mother. From her, I also learned never to let a television into the house. "After all," she used to say, "through such a device, some person might

appear in our living room to whom we had not been properly introduced": prophetic. My mother firmly fashioned my dress without a bit of acquiescence to fads or fashion. Living by a school teacher's wages, we maintained propriety: white gloves and hat to visit "the city," sensible saddle shoes and wool pleated skirts for school. I learned my lessons well. To this day I rarely cross-dress—as is the fashion—into pants. Oddly, this penchant for a woman to wear women's clothing often elicits second takes and comments as not many of my sex enjoy hiking, snowboarding, etc. in skirts. Perhaps it is in observance of such habits and appearances that a colleague has asked me to write of manners.

2   To learn more about writing, we can do well by turning to our elders. For health and other reasons, the ancient Greeks liked to pace around while engrossed in reflection, consideration, and speculation; Plato teaches us to explore various elements of a subject to know it better; Virginia Woolf would have me walk through the grounds of our colleges to ponder social foundations and implications. So following the leads of my predecessors, my attempt to explore ideas of manners unfolds as an excursion, beginning in the office of the college president, moving to the classroom, and coming around to a look inside the textbooks—such as this one—that students are required to buy. The walk ends up in a quagmire: evidently, several institutionalized components of our country's educational system currently discourage a culture of manners.

3   First stop, the president's office. Looking into ties between the leaders of higher education and an enmeshed business/political front, Columbia's Hofstradter Fellow, David Greenberg, laments:

> As universities have become more like other businesses, their presidencies have attracted administrators and fundraisers more than scholars and visionaries. . . . The politicians can work the statehouse for cash or friendly laws while the CEOs bring a devotion to the bottom line. . . . This mandate to pull in the money has changed the type of person who becomes a president. . . . Only 57 percent of presidents hold a Ph.D. . . . "One has to be a beggar, a flatterer, a sycophant, a court jester," echoes Botstein. . . .

In the president's office we find that our educational administrators have evolved from scholarly visionaries—who once shaped our country's cultural ideals and ideas of what it means to be educationally enriched—to become business functionaries. Working in a world of cut-throat economics, these C.E.O.s for the university often forget their roles as cultural indicators.

They often forget their predecessors' unspoken charter to engender a world that includes waiting one's turn and considering others before self-interest—that is, they sometimes forget their roles as cultural indicators of manners.

4 Next stop, the classroom. As the reins of education have passed into the hands of business leaders and their political partners, correspondingly, classroom processes and goals have become what is called "outcomes-based" education. Whatever their educational aspirations, students entering the college classroom find themselves in the grip of "college to career" curricula. The theater of the classroom has dramatically changed scenes; by the decree of administrators who readily bend to the powers of accreditation teams, a backdrop of education has given way to a backdrop of instruction. A little Latin lesson helps to differentiate "education" from "instruction." The idea "to educate" comes from "e-ducere," meaning to draw or to bring out. Here we have the image of the student as agent, drawing something out of materials. Or, we have the image of the student evolving out of a former self into a new sense of being—like a snake or butterfly, not so much shedding its former self, but emerging into a new season as a renewed creature. In another arena, the Latin root for the idea "to instruct" comes from "struere," meaning to strew around, to scatter, to build. As *con*-struct means to put things together, *in*-struct means to put things into something—usually a student. Hence we get Charles Dickens's metaphor of the student as a "little pitcher": instructors pour things into the student and the student pours those things back. Brazilian educator Paulo Freire calls this sort of activity, the "banking" concept: "an act of depositing, in which the students are the depositories and the teacher is the depositor." Whereas the educator would have the student grow into an enriched self, the instructor would have the student as vessel or "receptacle" receive information in commodity form and so demonstrate predictable "outcomes." Classroom buzzwords have evolved, accordingly, from a focus on the student or "student-centered" to a focus on what *comes out* of the student/pitcher or "outcomes-based." Students can think about manners and a mannerly world; objects cannot.

5 For our third stop we turn to the textbooks that we would have nourish and teach our culture's next generation. Not surprisingly, we find that over the decades, the production of college texts has generally mirrored the evolution we have seen as early college presidents have turned from their roles as visionaries and cultural indicators to more current roles as bureaucrats.

Also unsurprisingly, the evolution of college texts has generally mirrored the evolution we have seen as classrooms have changed from scenes of open-ended intellectual exploration and inspiration to scenes of predictable, pragmatic utilitarianism. Before the industrial revolution, early American colleges used texts written by acknowledged scholars. First-year required writing classes, for example, typically used texts of collected lectures by such Scottish neo-classicist rhetoricians as George Campbell, Hugh Blair, and/or Richard Whately. Churchmen and rhetoric professors as they were, Campbell, Blair, and Whately compiled their texts not to sell, but to promote contemplation, to promote a sense of writing as an art form, and to promote a harmonious world as based on the search for truth. Current textbook editors—important figures because they control the choices and formulation of textbooks that will reach our culture's next generation—speak openly of their evolution. As recently as 1994 a prominent editor for a prominent American textbook publishing company characterized himself as a "man of letters" who prided himself on getting the best of textbooks to print. With that editor's retirement, his replacement now straightforwardly characterizes the role of textbook editor as that of a "broker." With the publisher now characterized as "broker," the textbook author must now characterize him- or herself as the means of production. Correspondingly, the text itself has become nothing but a commodity.

6   And further correspondingly, those people whose job it is to introduce the choices of texts to professors are changing identities as well. Until recently, publishers' representatives have usually had backgrounds and graduate degrees relative to the subjects of the texts they offer. For example, a publisher's representative offering a choice of text books to an English professor usually held a Master's Degree in writing or literature. The professor and the publisher's liaison could discuss cultural issues relative to the curricular field, teaching and texts. Increasingly, however, the newly hired publishers' "reps" hold degrees not in any particular curricula field—nor even in education. Rather, this human connection between textbook publishers and professors rounds out the picture of the textbook as commodity with the boast of degrees in marketing.

7   The walk from administration building to classroom to publishing house reveals a fundamental identity and paradigm shift. Each of these three players in our educational endeavors has moved (or has been moved) from visionary to the functionary. As scholar, student, and person of letters, the visionary

usually combined expertise with experience and intellectual energy to envision a progressively bettering world. More often than not, that pursuit of a better world usually included exploring such issues as the nature of what it means to be noble or to behave in a noble manner. That is, the pursuit of a better world usually included attention to "manners" of behavior.

8   And so we come full circle. We deny ourselves manners because we admit into our living rooms, our colleges, and our lives a complex of business liaisons, outcomes, and commodities that we value much more than bettering the world. Perhaps the public is beginning to feel this lack of ideals and yearns to return to a world of ironed napkins and home-made pies. After all, one of the current era's hottest stocks on the commodities market has been Martha Stewart's marketing of the goods of graceful living. But, importantly, the goods of decorum are not the same as manners. "Manners" cannot be bought and sold as commodities. "Manners" refers to activity, what we do, and attitudes that generate behavior. Martha Stewart may sell the napkins and pie plates, but she leaves the consumer to iron those napkins and make the pies.

9   The irony, the frustration, the Catch-22 here lies (as Virginia Woolf would have us learn) in basic economic contradictions. With increasing numbers of parents feeling the need to work, we hand over our children to day-care personnel who guide our growing youngsters as they pursue children's activities. Gone are the days of children participating in adult activities, baking and fixing and building and studying alongside their parents. At the same time, rarely do instructive adults teach virtues of humility. As our children grow, they spend an average of forty hours per week (outside school) plugged into some media form, more often than not isolating themselves from social contact, sitting passively in front of televisions in their own bedrooms. We ask our teenagers to have manners, but we have trained them from birth to live in and perpetuate not a world of grace and waiting one's turn; rather, we have taught them to live in and perpetuate that world envisioned by Hobbes, Machiavelli, and social Darwinists—where human behavior "naturally" turns to individualism, private self-interest, egotism, and greed; where rules and police and prisons effectively control "naturally" corrupt human nature; where the meaning of life lies more in the struggle for existence than in celebration of human and cultural possibility.

10   In the words of the teen-age murderer and suicide, Dylan Klebold, "What is society? Just stupid human beings living off

each other." Indeed, our individualism has deepened even beyond the imagination of Hobbes, Machiavelli, and Darwin. We now exist taking care of ourselves, "because no one else will" without accountability for our actions. We insure ourselves for libel. In the world of Internet sites and e-mail we can flame and insult others while we rest safely in anonymity. Within the anonymity of mobile steel shells, drivers can yell and even shoot before darting off to hide in a camouflage of traffic. Back at the office, in the blind reviews of middle management, we can anonymously and safely unload our pained egos, disregarding the manuscript, employee, or job applicant at hand. And given a world view based in self-interest, we welcome such occasions where and when we can with anonymity diminish others and so elevate ourselves.

11   Manners, perhaps, have to do with basic cultural foundations—with how we envision what human existence together on this planet is all about. Right now, our educational systems seem to view themselves as founded in a hostile world. University administrators who spend their energies writing grants and making economically-based liaisons with business interests have little energy and mind left to ponder human existence and cultural potential. Students entering the college classroom filled with a sense of self-interest wish and expect to encounter nothing outside of what hat will efficiently and with practicality further that self-interest. Certainly, to ponder, to imagine, to contemplate, or to change their minds gets them nowhere in their goals to move from point A to point B. And the various cultural elements that should nourish us—from our college classrooms and textbooks to the articles that fill our homes—reinforce an American sense of self based more on the objects of life—the commodities—and less on living, by doing, with manners.

Post-reading Questions

Content

1. What, according to Henning, is the major reason modern society discourages a culture of manners?

2. Why might an outcome-based approach to education downplay the importance of good manners and behavior?

3. What is the difference between something that is more intellectually stimulating and something that is more utilitarian (useful)?

4. Which of the three "stops" that Henning mentions

during her essay impressed you the most and why?

5. To what extent is Henning correct in her assessment of basic "economic contradictions" in our society that pull parent and child apart, leaving the latter with little resources for exposure to and acquisition of simple types of common courtesy?

Strategies and Structures

1. Explain the difference between a *prig* and a *pig*. Why might the contrast between the two be ideal before the subtitle, "Revolution in the Name of Manners"?

2. Henning uses a variety of sentence patterns throughout her essay; cite a few of them, and explain why a writer would not want to rely on a single sentence pattern for conveying information in an essay.

3. At one point in the essay, Henning applies the rhetorical strategy of definition to explain and advance her argument. What two words does she mention, and how is knowledge of their Latin roots relevant to her analysis?

4. Who are Hobbes, Machiavelli, and social Darwinists? How does Henning strategically use parallel structure to organize information about them directly following her list of names? Assess how her allusions provide cultural contexts for understanding Klebold's quote and the disturbing ramifications of his antisocial behavior. To what extent might Klebold's attitude toward other human beings reflect the values of a world based on "self-interest"?

5. In what way does Henning employ transitions and linking devices to connect the parts of her essay? How is her composition structured like a journey? What purpose does this serve?

Language and Vocabulary

1. Vocabulary: *prig, expenditure, propriety, pleated, elicits, excursion, institutionalize, components, enmeshed, functionaries, correspondingly, aspirations, accreditation, differentiate, pragmatic, utilitarianism, prominent, paradigm, endeavors, liaisons, commodities, contradictions, practitioners, perpetuate, egotism, libel.* Using at least ten of the above words (or forms

of the words), write a descriptive paragraph about a person (or people) who displays bad manners.

2. How would you describe Henning's style of writing, accessible or elevated? Explain your opinion, citing specific words and phrases from the essay that illustrate how and why you arrived at your conclusion. (There are no wrong answers here.)

Group Activities

1. Divide the class into groups, go back through Henning's essay, and jot down all unfamiliar names that she mentioned. Next, go to the library or go online, and research all the authors on your list. Return to class and share minibiographies about the people you have researched. In hindsight, how were the names Henning mentioned an appeal to authority? How might citing authorities in your own writing strengthen the stance you have taken?

2. After getting into groups, write collaborative paragraphs describing people with a) good manners, and b) bad manners. Use public figures or fictional characters on television, at the movies, or in books to vividly illustrate your claims with concrete examples.

Writing Activities

1. Write an essay in which you identify and explain the apparent decline in manners, respect toward others, and so on. You also might suggest a plan of action that will instill citizens with values necessary to cultivate and sustain a "society of manners."

2. Brainstorm the word "manners." How, for instance, are manners taught, reinforced, and/or destroyed? Next, reflect on how human values, behavior, and conduct directly relate to what society has come to regard as "manners." Finally, state something that you want to argue or explain as your thesis; develop it using a combination of rhetorical strategies (e.g., sentences indicating cause-and-effect relationships, points using comparison and contrast, and so on).

Jeanne Wakatsuki Houston

and

James D. Houston

Arrival at Manzanar

*Born in Inglewood, California, Jeanne Wakatsuki Houston has spent
most of her life on the Pacific coast. During World War II, her family
was moved to the Japanese-American internment camp in Manzanar,
California, for four years. Ms. Wakatsuki Houston was only seven
years old at the time, and the memories of her years there are
recorded in* Farewell to Manzanar *(1973), now in its thirtieth
Bantam printing, which she co-wrote with her husband James D.
Houston, a well-known novelist. Then in 1988, they collaborated
again in* One Can Think about Life after the Fish Is in the Canoe:
Beyond Manzanar. *The Houstons also worked on film projects
together such as* Barrio *(1978) and* The Melting Pot *(1980).
Ms. Wakatsuki Houston's essays, articles, and reviews have appeared
in numerous magazines and periodicals such as* Mother Jones,
California Living, West Magazine, New England Review, The
Reader's Digest *(Japanese edition),* Dialogue *(international edition),
and* The Los Angeles Times, *as well as several anthologies. Other
works include* Don't Cry, It's Only Thunder, *co-authored with Paul
Hensler (1984),* Beyond Manzanar: Views of Asian American
Womanhood *(1985), and* Fire Horse Woman *(1998). Among the many
awards and accolades Ms. Wakatsuki Houston has received is the
prestigious Wonder Women Award (1984), an award honoring women
over forty who have made outstanding achievements in the pursuit of
positive social change.*

Pre-reading Questions

1. Answer the following questions in your journal. What do
you know of the Japanese-American internment in the
United States during World War II? Who was confined in
these camps? Why were Japanese Americans confined?
What were the results of such internment? What were the
conditions of these camps?

2. How would you react if your family and you were suddenly asked to move to an internment camp and to give
up your possessions, property, and professions? As you
write, think of all your possible actions and the advantages and disadvantages of each one.

---

1   In December of 1941 Papa's disappearance didn't bother me
nearly so much as the world I soon found myself in.

2   He had been a jack-of-all-trades. When I was born he was
farming near Inglewood. Later, when he started fishing, we
moved to Ocean Park, near Santa Monica, and until they
picked him up, that's where we lived, in a big frame house with
a brick fireplace, a block back from the beach. We were the only
Japanese family in the neighborhood. Papa liked it that way.
He didn't want to be labeled or grouped by anyone. But with
him gone and no way of knowing what to expect, my mother
moved all of us down to Terminal Island. Woody already lived
there, and one of my older sisters had married a Terminal Island boy. Mama's first concern now was to keep the family together; and once the war began, she felt safer there than
isolated racially in Ocean Park. But for me, at age seven, the
island was a country as foreign as India or Arabia would have
been. It was the first time I had lived among other Japanese,
or gone to school with them, and I was terrified all the time.

3   This was partly Papa's fault. One of his threats to keep us
younger kids in line was "I'm going to sell you to the China-
man." When I had entered kindergarten two years earlier, I
was the only Oriental in the class. They sat me next to a Caucasian girl who happened to have very slanted eyes. I looked
at her and began to scream, certain Papa had sold me out at
last. My fear of her ran so deep I could not speak of it, even to
Mama, couldn't explain why I was screaming. For two weeks
I had nightmares about this girl, until the teachers finally
moved me to the other side of the room. And it was still with
me, this fear of Oriental faces, when we moved to Terminal
Island.

4   In those days it was a company town, a ghetto owned and controlled by the canneries. The men went after fish, and whenever the boats came back—day or night—the women would be called to process the catch while it was fresh. One in the afternoon or four in the morning, it made no difference. My mother had to go to work right after we moved there. I can still hear the whistle—two toots for French's, three for Van Camp's—and she and Chizu would be out of bed in the middle of the night, heading for the cannery.

5   The house we lived in was nothing more than a shack, a barracks with single plank walls and rough wooden floors, like the cheapest kind of migrant workers' housing. The people around us were hardworking, boisterous, a little proud of their nickname, *yo-go-re,* which meant literally *uncouth one,* or roughneck, or dead-end kid. They not only spoke Japanese exclusively, they spoke a dialect peculiar to Kyushu, where their families had come from in Japan, a rough, fisherman's language, full of oaths and insults. Instead of saying *ba-ka-ta-re,* a common insult meaning *stupid,* Terminal Islanders would say *ba-ka-ya-ro,* a coarser and exclusively masculine use of the word, which implies gross stupidity. They would swagger and pick on outsiders and persecute anyone who didn't speak as they did. That was what made my own time there so hateful. I had never spoken anything but English, and the other kids in the second grade despised me for it. They were tough and mean, like ghetto kids anywhere. Each day after school I dreaded their ambush. My brother Kiyo, three years older, would wait for me at the door, where we would decide whether to run straight home together, or split up, or try a new and unexpected route.

6   None of these kids ever actually attacked. It was the threat that frightened us, their fearful looks, and the noises they would make, like miniature Samurai, in a language we couldn't understand.

7   At the time it seemed we had been living under this reign of fear for years. In fact, we lived there about two months. Late in February the navy decided to clear Terminal Island completely. Even though most of us were American-born, it was dangerous having that many Orientals so close to the Long Beach Naval Station, on the opposite end of the island. We had known something like this was coming. But, like Papa's arrest, not much could be done ahead of time. There were four of us kids still young enough to be living with Mama, plus Granny, her mother, sixty-five then, speaking no English, and nearly

blind. Mama didn't know where else she could get work, and we had nowhere else to move *to*. On February 25 the choice was made for us. We were given forty-eight hours to clear out.

8   The secondhand dealers had been prowling around for weeks, like wolves, offering humiliating prices for goods and furniture they knew many of us would have to sell sooner or later. Mama had left all but her most valuable possessions in Ocean Park, simply because she had nowhere to put them. She had brought along her pottery, her silver, heirlooms like the kimonos Granny had brought from Japan, tea sets, lacquered tables, and one fine old set of china, blue and white porcelain, almost translucent. On the day we were leaving, Woody's car was so crammed with boxes and luggage and kids we had just run out of room. Mama had to sell this china.

9   One of the dealers offered her fifteen dollars for it. She said it was a full setting for twelve and worth at least two hundred. He said fifteen was his top price. Mama started to quiver. Her eyes blazed up at him. She had been packing all night and trying to calm down Granny, who didn't understand why we were moving again and what all the rush was about. Mama's nerves were shot, and now navy jeeps were patrolling the streets. She didn't say another word. She just glared at this man, all the rage and frustration channeled at him through her eyes.

10   He watched her for a moment and said he was sure he couldn't pay more than seventeen fifty for that china. She reached into the red velvet case, took out a dinner plate and hurled it at the floor right in front of his feet.

11   The man leaped back shouting, "Hey! Hey, don't do that! Those are valuable dishes!"

12   Mama took out another dinner plate and hurled it at the floor, then another and another, never moving, never opening her mouth, just quivering and glaring at the retreating dealer, with tears streaming down her cheeks. He finally turned and scuttled out the door, heading for the next house. When he was gone she stood there smashing cups and bowls and platters until the whole set lay in scattered blue and white fragments across the wooden floor.

13   The American Friends Service helped us find a small house in Boyle Heights, another minority ghetto, in downtown Los Angeles, now inhabited briefly by a few hundred Terminal Island refugees. Executive Order 9066 had been signed by President Roosevelt, giving the War Department authority to define military areas in the western states and to exclude from them anyone who might threaten the war effort. There was a

lot of talk about internment, or moving inland, or something like that in store for all Japanese Americans. I remember my brothers sitting around the table talking very intently about what we were going to do, how we would keep the family together. They had seen how quickly Papa was removed, and they knew now that he would not be back for quite a while. Just before leaving Terminal Island Mama had received her first letter, from Bismarck, North Dakota. He had been imprisoned at Fort Lincoln, in an all-male camp for enemy aliens.

14 Papa had been the patriarch. He had always decided everything in the family. With him gone, my brothers, like councilors in the absence of a chief, worried about what should be done. The ironic thing is, there wasn't much left to decide. These were mainly days of quiet, desperate waiting for what seemed at the time to be inevitable. There is a phrase the Japanese use in such situations, when something difficult must be endured. You would hear the older heads, the Issei, telling others very quietly, *"Shikata ga nai"* (It cannot be helped). *"Shikata ga nai"* (It must be done).

15 Mama and Woody went to work packing celery for a Japanese produce dealer. Kiyo and my sister May and I enrolled in the local school, and what sticks in my memory from those few weeks is the teacher—not her looks, her remoteness. In Ocean Park my teacher had been a kind, grandmotherly woman who used to sail with us in Papa's boat from time to time and who wept the day we had to leave. In Boyle Heights the teacher felt cold and distant. I was confused by all the moving and was having trouble with the classwork, but she would never help me out. She would have nothing to do with me.

16 This was the first time I had felt outright hostility from a Caucasian. Looking back, it is easy enough to explain. Public attitudes toward the Japanese in California were shifting rapidly. In the first few months of the Pacific war, America was on the run. Tolerance had turned to distrust and irrational fear. The hundred-year-old tradition of anti-Orientalism on the west coast soon resurfaced, more vicious than ever. Its result became clear about a month later, when we were told to make our third and final move.

17 The name Manzanar meant nothing to us when we left Boyle Heights. We didn't know where it was or what it was. We went because the government ordered us to. And, in the case of my older brothers and sisters, we went with a certain amount of relief. They had all heard stories of Japanese homes being attacked, of beatings in the streets of California towns. They were

as frightened of the Caucasians as Caucasians were of us. Moving, under what appeared to be government protection, to an area less directly threatened by the war seemed not such a bad idea at all. For some it actually sounded like a fine adventure.

18   Our pickup point was a Buddhist church in Los Angeles. It was very early, and misty, when we got there with our luggage. Mama had bought heavy coats for all of us. She grew up in eastern Washington and knew that anywhere inland in early April would be cold. I was proud of my new coat, and I remember sitting on a duffel bag trying to be friendly with the Greyhound driver. I smiled at him. He didn't smile back. He was befriending no one. Someone tied a numbered tag to my collar and to the duffel bag (each family was given a number, and that became our official designation until the camps were closed), someone else passed out box lunches for the trip, and we climbed aboard.

19   I had never been outside Los Angeles County, never traveled more than ten miles from the coast, had never even ridden on a bus. I was full of excitement, the way any kid would be, and wanted to look out the window. But for the first few hours the shades were drawn. Around me other people played cards, read magazines, dozed, waiting. I settled back, waiting too, and finally fell asleep. The bus felt very secure to me. Almost half its passengers were immediate relatives. Mama and my older brothers had succeeded in keeping most of us together, on the same bus, headed for the same camp. I didn't realize until much later what a job that was. The strategy had been, first, to have everyone living in the same district when the evacuation began, and then to get all of us included under the same family number, even though names had been changed by marriage. Many families weren't as lucky as ours and suffered months of anguish while trying to arrange transfers from one camp to another.

20   We rode all day. By the time we reached our destination, the shades were up. It was late afternoon. The first thing I saw was a yellow swirl across a blurred, reddish setting sun. The bus was being pelted by what sounded like splattering rain. It wasn't rain. This was my first look at something I would soon know very well, a billowing flurry of dust and sand churned up by the wind through Owens Valley.

21   We drove past a barbed-wire fence, through a gate, and into an open space where trunks and sacks and packages had been dumped from the baggage trucks that drove out ahead of us. I could see a few tents set up, the first rows of black barracks,

and beyond them, blurred by sand, rows of barracks that seemed to spread for miles across this plain. People were sitting on cartons or milling around, with their backs to the wind, waiting to see which friends or relatives might be on this bus. As we approached, they turned or stood up, and some moved toward us expectantly. But inside the bus no one stirred. No one waved or spoke. They just stared out the windows, ominously silent. I didn't understand this. Hadn't we finally arrived, our whole family intact? I opened a window, leaned out, and yelled happily. "Hey! This whole bus is full of Wakatsukis!"

22   Outside, the greeters smiled. Inside there was an explosion of laughter, hysterical, tension-breaking laughter that left my brothers choking and whacking each other across the shoulders.

23   We had pulled up just in time for dinner. The mess halls weren't completed yet. An outdoor chow line snaked around a half-finished building that broke a good part of the wind. They issued us army mess kits, the round metal kind that fold over, and plopped in scoops of canned Vienna sausage, canned string beans, steamed rice that had been cooked too long, and on top of the rice a serving of canned apricots. The Caucasian servers were thinking that the fruit poured over rice would make a good dessert. Among the Japanese, of course, rice is never eaten with sweet foods, only with salty or savory foods. Few of us could eat such a mixture. But at this point no one dared protest. It would have been impolite. I was horrified when I saw the apricot syrup seeping through my little mound of rice. I opened my mouth to complain. My mother jabbed me in the back to keep quiet. We moved on through the line and joined the others squatting in the lee of half-raised walls, dabbing courteously at what was, for almost everyone there, an inedible concoction.

24   After dinner we were taken to Block 16, a cluster of fifteen barracks that had just been finished a day or so earlier—although finished was hardly the word for it. The shacks were built of one thickness of pine planking covered with tarpaper. They sat on concrete footings, with about two feet of open space between the floorboards and the ground. Gaps showed between the planks, and as the weeks passed and the green wood dried out, the gaps widened. Knotholes gaped in the uncovered floor.

25   Each barracks was divided into six units, sixteen by twenty feet, about the size of a living room, with one bare bulb hanging from the ceiling and an oil stove for heat. We were assigned two of these for the twelve people in our family group; and our official family "number" was enlarged by three digits—6 plus

the number of this barracks. We were issued steel army cots, two brown army blankets each, and some mattress covers, which my brothers stuffed with straw.

26   The first task was to divide up what space we had for sleeping. Bill and Woody contributed a blanket each and partitioned off the first room: one side for Bill and Tomi, one side for Woody and Chizu and their baby girl. Woody also got the stove, for heating formulas.

27   The people who had it hardest during the first few months were young couples like these, many of whom had married just before the evacuation began, in order not to be separated and sent to different camps. Our two rooms were crowded, but at least it was all in the family. My oldest sister and her husband were shoved into one of those sixteen-by-twenty-foot compartments with six people they had never seen before—two other couples, one recently married like themselves, the other with two teenage boys. Partitioning off a room like that wasn't easy. It was bitter cold when we arrived, and the wind did not abate. All they had to use for room dividers were those army blankets, two of which were barely enough to keep one person warm. They argued over whose blanket should be sacrificed and later argued about noise at night—the parents wanted their boys asleep by 9:00 P.M.—and they continued arguing over matters like that for six months, until my sister and her husband left to harvest sugar beets in Idaho. It was grueling work up there, and wages were pitiful, but when the call came through camp for workers to alleviate the wartime labor shortage, it sounded better than their life at Manzanar. They knew they'd have, if nothing else, a room, perhaps a cabin of their own.

28   That first night in Block 16, the rest of us squeezed into the second room—Granny, Lillian, age fourteen, Ray, thirteen, May, eleven, Kiyo, ten, Mama, and me. I didn't mind this at all at the time. Being youngest meant I got to sleep with Mama. And before we went to bed I had a great time jumping up and down on the mattress. The boys had stuffed so much straw into hers, we had to flatten it some so we wouldn't slide off. I slept with her every night after that until Papa came back.

Post-reading Questions

Content

    1. Why does the mother move her family to Terminal Island? What are some of the results of the move?

    2. What does the description of the town suggest about

the people and their condition? What specific details give you these impressions?

3. What did the navy decide to do to Terminal Island? How did second-hand dealers take advantage of the situation? Why did the narrator's mother react as she did, smashing her dishes and getting angry?

4. How did the narrator feel about moving to Manzanar? What are some of her initial feelings and reactions upon arriving at the camp? What details and specifics create the first impression of Manzanar?

5. What is the impression you have after reading the description of the camp and its activities? What problems would these Japanese Americans encounter?

Strategies and Structures

1. Wakatsuki Houston's narration explains many causes and effects. What is the cause of her fear of other Asian children? What is the effect of being isolated from other Asians? How does she explain this cause and effect?

2. How does Wakatsuki Houston show the effects of being unable to speak the language of the community? What specifics make this passage so vivid and detailed?

3. What is the purpose of the episode about the second-hand dealer and the china set? Why is narration an effective means of achieving this purpose?

4. How does Wakatsuki Houston organize her material in order to make this essay easy to follow? What transitional devices and/or linking words does she use to make this organization apparent to the reader?

Language and Vocabulary

1. Often place names are used in narratives to suggest the journey a narrator or character takes; however, if we are unfamiliar with the region, these place names may confuse us. An excellent strategy for getting a sense of place is to consult a map and to try and follow the narrative journey. Wakatsuki Houston uses the following place names in her narrative: *Inglewood, Ocean Park, Santa Monica, Terminal Island, Long Beach,*

Manzanar, Boyle Heights, Los Angeles, Owens Valley.
Get a map of California and follow Wakatsuki
Houston's journey using the above vocabulary
words. Consult the essay as needed.

2. Wakatsuki Houston uses several Japanese words in
   Paragraph 5. How does she explain the meaning of
   these words? Do you find this strategy effective?
   How might you be able to use such a strategy in
   your own essays?

Group Activities

1. Many people have faced hardships because of the
   fear caused by the ignorance of another culture.
   Wakatsuki Houston explains the hardships encountered by Japanese Americans because of the U.S.
   government's ignorance of Japanese-American culture. As a group, brainstorm and discuss other instances in which whole groups of people faced
   problems and hardships because of a lack of understanding. What groups have faced problems?
   What problems have they faced? Why? Whose ignorance has caused these hardships? How have
   the persecuted people tried to deal with these
   problems?

2. Wakatsuki Houston explains how she felt about the
   camp as a child; however, she includes enough details about the reality of the camp to clearly show
   that it was not a pleasant place. First, freewrite
   about an experience which you either enjoyed or
   found unpleasant as a child but now feel different
   about. Then share your freewriting with the rest of
   the group. As you listen to others, note why we
   change our feelings about an event.

Writing Activities

1. Write about an event in which you faced prejudice
   and/or hardship because of someone's lack of understanding about you or your culture. What were the
   causes of your problems and the person's lack of understanding? What were the effects of the person's
   misunderstanding?

2. Write an essay discussing the initial impression a person(s) had made upon you and how your first impression was subject to change once you got to know that person(s). Make sure you give plenty of examples to illustrate the validity of what you say.

Additional Topics and Issues for Expository Essays

1. Compose and develop an original thesis that says something specific about visual pollution. In doing so, you may want to answer such questions as "What is visual pollution?" "Where is one likely to encounter visual pollution?" and "What can or should be done about it?"

2. Write an expository essay wherein you explain a solution to the overpopulation problem without eliminating any of the people already alive.

3. Analyze the parking problem at your college. What is the cause of it? How does it affect your daily routine, particularly the time you get up and how much study time you have? Make sure you show your reader what goes on by offering him or her a glimpse into your life.

4. Explain how economics influences and often dictates our political and social relationships with countries around the world by comparing and contrasting an economic boom to a recession. If you draw information from outside sources, make sure that you acknowledge them correctly.

5. Explain why it is important to wear all the latest fashions in order to attract a love interest. Begin with a brief discussion of the process of keeping up with the fads. How much money do you have to spend? With whom is it important to be seen? Why? Are there any long-range effects of being a slave to fashion? You will want to conclude your essay with a thoughtful analysis of your topic.

6. Write an essay wherein you demonstrate how stockpiling or spreading nuclear weapons throughout the world is a deterrent or an invitation to war.

7. After attracting your reader's interest by using a clever anecdote in your thesis, write an essay exposing why and in what ways pets fulfill an emotional void in many people's daily lives.

8. There has been much written about the effects of television on today's generation. Write an original, insightful essay wherein you explain (1) why you think people spend so many hours in front of their television sets and (2) the effect of watching too much television.

9. Is beauty really only in the eye of the beholder? Write an essay explaining why you think Americans, or a town in the United States, illustrates its preference for ugliness over beauty. Some obvious topics to examine here would be architecture, clothes (patterns, styles), landscaping, and so on. Make sure your reasoning is clear and your examples are representative of your topic. You will want to mention any exceptions to your thesis early in your essay.

10. Write an essay contrasting wanton luxuries versus human necessities. To fully develop your essay, employ additional methods of development, such as illustration and example, division and classification, and description.

11

Argumentation: The Logical Appeal

Argumentative essays should be based on sound logic. The most elemental forms of reasoning stem from induction and deduction. When preparing to write an argumentative paper, imagine you are a detective, perhaps Sherlock Holmes, the famous fictional sleuth renowned for the powers of observation that aided his deductive reasoning. Through this deductive reasoning, he was able to solve the most baffling cases. In a similar manner, by carefully observing all aspects of an argument, you may successfully draw conclusions from them, conclusions that are reasonable, logical, and verifiable.

Inductive Logic

Induction moves from the particular to the general. To use induction, you take several representative examples of a person, place, or thing and make a general observation about it. What general observation, for instance, could you make about these three facts?

- Sixty-four people lost their lives due to California's earthquake last fall.
- Forty-eight people died during the Mississippi flash flood in Louisiana last month.
- Hurricane Hugo claimed thirty-nine lives in South Carolina.

No doubt you noticed that each fact had two things in common with the others: multiple human deaths and a natural disaster.

What can we conclude by considering the three facts? *Natural disasters can be dangerous.*

The greater the number of representative examples (facts) you can offer your reader, the better. Why? Inductive arguments require a *leap in logic,* a leap from specific points to one believable general point, and the more examples you can offer, the smaller the inductive leap. When you check your argumentative essays for weak points, you frequently are searching for places where the connection between your specific points and generalizations requires your reader to place more "faith" in your word than in concrete evidence. Whenever this occurs, your inductive leap—getting from your specific points to a general, logical conclusion—is too broad and thereby unconvincing. Furthermore, since one exception to a claim like "all men like to play golf on weekends" would disprove your point, you often will want to qualify what you say using words like *most, usually,* and *often.*

Deduction

The opposite of induction, deduction, moves from general points—evidence—to a specific conclusion. A valid deductive conclusion, however, depends on the truth of its evidence (this evidence can be either of major or minor importance). The following logical statement illustrates this point. If I say *All show dogs have pedigrees* (major evidence) and that *My dog Grendel has a pedigree* (minor evidence), I could deduce that *Grendel is a show dog.* What is wrong with my reasoning? We all know that *not* every dog with a pedigree appears in dog shows; therefore, it cannot be concluded that every dog with a pedigree is automatically a show dog. Evidence that is not true can lead to untrue conclusions. To ensure that your deduction is logical and valid, qualify your major evidence with a word like *many—Many pedigree dogs are show dogs.* Deductive reasoning, therefore, should be seen as an aid in leading the reader to the conclusion you want him or her to reach. Mark Charles Fissel uses deduction in just such a way in "Online Learning and Student Success" to arrive at the conclusion many segments of American society can—or in the future, will—benefit from distance learning courses as an alternate method of instruction. However, students must voice their genuine "preferences and needs," rather than allowing cybermarketers to lead the way, and *"ultimately, it is the individual teacher who must take responsibility for the curriculum and how it is taught."*

Types of Argumentation

Are there different types of argumentation? Yes. At times, one will argue for an entire essay that something like censorship is or is not constitutional. Here, an author argues to establish what he or she believes is a convincing fact, a fact worthy of a reader's attention. A good example of an argument of fact would be found in "Peyote, Wine and the First Amendment." Douglas Laycock argues that governmental bodies in the United States—local or federal—should not regulate religious rituals and ceremonies of minor religions, particularly those of Native Americans who use peyote as part of a *"substantial tradition,"* and that their use of peyote is limited to a *"structured worship service."* In arguing his case, Laycock points out that the First Amendment guarantees "the free exercise of religion."

Grace Sumabat Mateo presents another argument of fact, in which she asserts, *"The beguiling presence of anime within North American culture cannot be ignored. We are bombarded by anime merchandise in clothing, electronic, and toy stores."* Throughout her essay, Mateo demonstrates the validity of her argument referring to multiple examples of both anime and western cartoons. Walt Disney and other animators will continue to thrive; hovever, the *"anime revolution, without a doubt, is here to stay."*

Barbara Ehrenreich's "In Defense of Splitting Up," an essay challenging the antidivorce movement's claim that children suffer more from a divorce than they do being raised in a *"bad marriage,"* represents yet another argument of fact. The essay further argues that the emotional status of children has less to do with being raised by two parents than growing up in poverty.

At times, however, writing a factual argument is only the starting point of an essay. In such an essay, a problem or issue will be identified and defined in the first few paragraphs. Then, an author will propose a logical course of action, convincing the reader of the merit of his or her solution. Arguments containing a *call to action* demand that an author impress his or her readers that a situation exists which needs to be addressed and changed. If your neighbor told you that your best friend was a terrorist and should be turned over to the police or the Federal Bureau of Investigation, what are the chances of your doing so? Without specific evidence, you would be unlikely to embark upon any plan of action. Reacting to hearsay and unsubstantiated reason makes an act impulsive, not rational or ethical. In short, provide your reader with sufficient reason to "act."

Still another form of argumentation is the argument of refutation. In such an essay, an author strives to disprove an opposing viewpoint on a topic. To do so, writers attack generalizations and faulty logic used by their counterparts. In "Soul Food," for instance, Imamu Amiri Baraka refutes (argues) that those who claim African Americans lack a distinct cuisine do not know what they are talking about. To tear apart his opposition's argument, he shows through illustration and example that foods like *grits, fried porgie,* and *black-eyed peas* are definite African-American contributions to our country's varied cultural cuisines.

Clearly Stated Thesis

Though the type of argument may be determined by your objective for writing the essay, all types of argumentation usually have one thing in common: *a strong, clearly stated thesis.* As in most compositions, a specific thesis statement will help you keep your essay focused when developing the composition, avoiding digressions and superfluous facts. Such a thesis will unquestionably lead your reader to your opinion and help frame the supporting points of the argument. An uncertain thesis is bound to result in reader as well as writer confusion.

Avoiding Fallacies

A fallacy is an incorrect or falsely reasoned fact. We could devote an entire course in logic to discussing them, but for our purposes, we'll only mention a few fallacies by name—the ones most likely to occur and weaken an argument.

1. *Ad Hominem* ("To the person"): This reasoning twists the focus of an argument by attacking the person who made it rather than arguing the issue at hand. In other words, a person guilty of *ad hominem* might spend time attempting to persuade readers that an opponent is disreputable rather than refute an argument that animals have rights.

2. *Stereotyping:* Since stereotyping inaccurately presents people, places, and things (e.g., all Californians have suntans, only Yuppies drive BMW cars, or anyone who lives in

Florida is retired), using stereotypes to support an argument will weaken rather than strengthen it.

3. *Faulty Sampling:* When you support an argument with specific examples, you must make certain that your examples are truly representative of your topic. Suppose that you argue that Americans no longer like house pets and say that recently 90 percent of the Americans surveyed said they don't own or plan to own a pet. If, however, you surveyed only ten people (nine of whom disliked animals), your examples can only be inaccurate. This points to one of the major problems in using statistics: You can make them say whatever you want.

4. *Sweeping Generalizations:* To avoid sweeping generalizations, make use of qualifying words and phrases such as *usually, often, most, some, several,* and avoid the use of absolute phrases like, *"Everybody* enjoys swimming." One person who dislikes or fears swimming makes your entire statement untrue!

5. *False Dilemma (Either / Or Fallacy):* The false dilemma fallacy oversimplifies issues by assuming that there are only two alternatives in an argument. Thus, instead of exploring possibilities, readers are forced to choose between two extremes when other choices may exist. A sentence such as "Christopher must either become a medical doctor or join the United States Marine Corps for life," for instance, inaccurately measures the number of career opportunities open to him.

6. *Post Hoc / Ergo Propter Hoc:* The Latin phrase literally translates as: "It happened after this; therefore, it happened because of this." However, just because one event follows another does not produce a logical, valid cause/effect relationship. There is no true causal relationship expressed in a sentence like: "Every time I wash my truck it rains." Washing the truck did not cause rainfall to occur. Similarly, a sentence like "Rose Anna gives Wayne a ride home after work every day; therefore, she likes to drive" is equally absurd. Rose Anna does not enjoy driving a car merely because she drops Wayne off at his house after work. Such reasoning will result in *faulty cause / effect analysis.*

Tips on Writing Argumentative Essays

1. Prewrite to determine what you wish to say about your topic. As mentioned earlier, a very clear thesis is essential,

for if you have a fuzzy, unclear thesis, your reader won't know precisely what you are arguing for or against. A seemingly uncertain writer is not too trustworthy or convincing.

2. Don't apologize for your viewpoint; justify it! This is particularly important to remember when you take an unpopular stance on a topic or issue. After all, popular opinion does not depend on ethical or logical reasoning.

3. Make sure you can defend what you claim. Have a firm basis for what you are contending. Do not assume your reader will agree with your social, political, or religious viewpoints. Avoid "leap-of-faith" arguments.

4. Present all sides of your topic/issue; otherwise, your paper is not an argument. If your opponent makes or has a good point, don't ignore it. Place it early in your essay. By acknowledging that no issue is black or white, you will seem ethical and reasonable.

5. Present your material in emphatic order (move from your weakest to your strongest argument). Otherwise, your supporting argument may seem anticlimatic or weak by comparison. Step by step, lead your reader to the conclusion.

6. Use authoritative evidence for technical information whenever you can to make what you claim believable.

7. In arguments of action, show how and why your plan of action is the most logical one to adopt. By taking time to explain who or what will benefit from your proposal, you will not only appear a logical person but also an ethical person.

8. Check your work for faulty logic and generalizations; do so in all stages of the writing process to avoid building an entire argument on a faulty premise, one that you will only have to rethink and rewrite in order to make rational sense.

Barbara Ehrenreich

In Defense of Splitting Up

An award winning reporter and essayist, Barbara Ehrenreich has written articles for a very broad range of publications, including The Atlantic Monthly, Esquire, The Nation, *the* New York Times Magazine, *the* New Republic, Vogue, Wall Street Journal, *the* Washington Post Magazine, *and* Time *where she currently serves as the concluding essayist of the magazine. Among Ehrenreich's many books are* The Hearts of Men *(1983),* Fear of Falling *(1989),* The Worst Years of Our Lives *(1990),* The Snarling Citizen *(1995),* Blood Rites: Origins and History of the Passions of War *(1998),* Nickel and Dimey: on (Not) Getting by in America *(2002), and* Our Media, Not Theirs: The Democratic Struggle Against Corporate America *(2003). As the* Boston Globe *mentioned in its review of* The Worst Years of Our Lives, *"Ehrenreich's scorn withers, her humor stings and her radical light shines on." In the following essay, originally published in the April 8, 1996 edition of* Time *magazine, Ehrenreich attacks the antidivorce movement's claim that their concern for the health and well-being of children justifies an argument to restrict divorces in the United States.*

Pre-reading Questions

1. How do you feel about the concept of marriage and divorce? Should married couples who have children face stricter or more lenient divorce laws? Defend your point of view.

2. What mental or physical harm might come to the children of an unhappy marriage? Would a divorce between parents who no longer care for each other contribute to a child's healthy growth and development or encourage delinquent behavior?

1   No one seems much concerned about children when the subject is welfare or Medicaid cuts, but mention divorce, and tears flow for their tender psyches. Legislators in half a dozen states are planning to restrict divorce on the grounds that it may cause teen suicide, an inability to "form lasting attachments" and possibly also the piercing of nipples and noses.

2   But if divorce itself hasn't reduced America's youth to emotional cripples, then the efforts to restrict it undoubtedly will. First, there's the effect all this antidivorce rhetoric is bound to have on the children of people already divorced—and we're not talking about some offbeat minority. At least 37% of American children live with divorced parents, and these children already face enough tricky interpersonal situations without having to cope with the public perception that they're damaged goods.

3   Fortunately for the future of the republic, the alleged psyche-scarring effects of divorce have been grossly exaggerated. The most frequently cited study, by California therapist Judith Wallerstein, found that 41% of the children of divorced couples are "doing poorly, worried, underachieving, deprecating and often angry" years after their parents' divorce. But this study has been faulted for including only 60 couples, two-thirds of whom were deemed to lack "adequate psychological functioning" even before they split, and all of whom were self-selected seekers of family therapy. Furthermore, there was no control group of, say, miserable couples who stayed together.

4   As for some of the wilder claims, such as "teen suicide has tripled as divorces have tripled": well, roller-blading has probably tripled in the same time period too, and that's hardly a reason to ban in-line skates.

5   In fact, the current antidivorce rhetoric slanders millions of perfectly wonderful, high-functioning young people, my own children and most of their friends included. Studies that attempt to distinguish between the effects of divorce and those of the income decline so often experienced by divorced mothers have found no lasting psychological damage attributable to divorce per se. Check out a typical college dorm, and you'll find people enthusiastically achieving and forming attachments until late into the night. Ask about family, and you'll hear about Mom and Dad . . . and Stepmom and Stepdad.

6   The real problems for kids will begin when the antidivorce movement starts getting its way. For one thing, the more militant among its members want to "re-stigmatize" divorce with

the cultural equivalent of a scarlet *D*. Sadly though, divorce is already stigmatized in ways that are harmful to children. Studies show that teachers consistently interpret children's behavior more negatively when they are told that the children are from "broken" homes—and, as we know, teachers' expectations have an effect on children's performance. If the idea is to help the children of divorce, then the goal should be to *de*-stigmatize divorce among all who interact with them—teachers, neighbors, playmates.

7   Then there are the likely effects on children of the proposed restrictions themselves. Antidivorce legislators want to repeal no-fault divorce laws and return to the system in which one parent has to prove the other guilty of adultery, addiction or worse. True, the divorce rate rose after the introduction of no-fault divorce in the late '60s and '70s. But the divorce rate was already rising at a healthy clip *before* that, so there's no guarantee that the repeal of no-fault laws will reduce the divorce rate now. In fact, one certain effect will be to generate more divorces of the rancorous, potentially child-harming variety. If you think "Mommy and Daddy aren't getting along" sounds a little too blithe, would you rather "Daddy (or Mommy) has been sleeping around"?

8   Not that divorce is an enviable experience for any of the parties involved. But just as there are bad marriages, there are, as sociologist Constance Ahrons argues, "good divorces," in which both parents maintain their financial and emotional responsibility for the kids. Maybe the reformers should concentrate on improving the *quality* of divorces—by, for example, requiring prenuptial agreements specifying how the children will be cared for in the event of a split.

9   The antidivorce movement's interest in the emotional status of children would be more convincing if it were linked to some concern for their physical survival. The most destructive feature of divorce, many experts argue, is the poverty that typically ensues when the children are left with a low-earning mother, and the way out of this would be to toughen child-support collection and strengthen the safety net of supportive services for low-income families—including childcare, Medicaid and welfare.

10   Too difficult? Too costly? Too ideologically distasteful compared with denouncing divorce and, by implication, the divorced and their children? Perhaps. But sometimes grownups have to do difficult and costly things, whether they feel like doing them or not. For the sake of the children, that is.

Post-reading Questions

Content

1. According to Ehrenreich, what percentage of American children live with a divorced parent?
2. What do some members of the antidivorce movement argue are the lasting scars of divorce on children? Specifically, how are children affected emotionally and physically?
3. When will the real problems for children begin according to the author?
4. What seems to be the real motivation behind restricting divorces and repealing "no-fault divorce laws"?
5. Do you agree with Ehrenreich's argument that the "antidivorce movement's interest in the emotional status of children would be a lot more convincing if it were linked to some concern for their physical survival"? Why or why not?

Strategies and Structures

1. How does Ehrenreich organize her argument?
2. Explain the significance of Ehrenreich's essay's title, "In Defense of Splitting Up."
3. How does Ehrenreich weaken the antidivorce movement's argument that the amount of divorces in the United States will be reduced as a result of repealing "no-fault divorce laws" and returning to a "system in which one parent has to prove the other guilty of adultery, addiction or worse"?
4. Sociologist Constance Ahrons states that just as there are bad marriages, there can be "good divorces." Explain her reasoning. How does the reference to Ahrons, an authority, add weight to Ehrenreich's argument?

Language and Vocabulary

1. Vocabulary: *rhetoric, alleged, slanders, attributable, militant, stigmatize, equivalent, deprecating, blithe, inevitable, sociologist, prenuptial.* After locating the dictionary definitions for the words on the vocabulary list, go back through the list and write a form of at least four of the words whose meaning changes with the addition of a prefix (e.g., *pre-, un-, anti-, de, re-*) or a suffix (e.g., *-ist, -able, -logy*).
2. Go through the essay. Identify and explain words and phrases that appeal to you ethically, emotion-

ally, and logically. Were there times in Ehrenreich's essay where she impressed you as particularly reasonable and trustworthy? Does she ever seem to count on emotionally charged words to *move* her readers? Explain.

Group Activities

1. Get into groups and analyze your personal responses to Ehrenreich's concluding paragraph. Would supporting services for single parent families really be "too costly" in our society? If so, what do antidivorce legislators seem most concerned with? Carefully reason a group response to this question and draft it into a collaborative paragraph or so.

2. Does the movement to "re-stigmatize divorce" and repeal "no-fault divorce laws" seem like a conservative or a liberal proposition—if either? Collaboratively brainstorm this question and then begin to consider the family backgrounds of representative political leaders to help you arrive at a conclusion or to avoid making sweeping generalizations. You might either debate your group's point of view on the antidivorce movement, or else present it in a class forum. The emphasis of this project should be based on inductive and deductive reasoning.

Writing Activities

1. Write an essay titled "In Defense of Staying Single," modeling your paper after Ehrenreich's essay. Be sure you do not rely on news statistics alone to argue your position. Instead, assemble and use plenty of representative samplings of married and single couples in the United States to support what you claim.

2. Write an essay in which you argue that restricting divorces in the United States will strengthen the family unit—regardless of a couple's feelings for each other—or that restrictions will accentuate the harm done to children in dysfunctional family relationships. Use plenty of representative examples drawn from readings, personal experience and observations to validate your claims.

Paula Gunn Allen

Who Is Your Mother? Red Roots of White Feminism

Paula Gunn Allen, a well-known Laguna (Sioux) and Lebanese poet, novelist, and essayist, has written many works touching on themes relevant to the Native-American experience. Her prose works include The Woman Who Owned the Shadows *(1983),* The Sacred Hoop: Recovering the Feminine in American Indian Traditions *(1986)—the source of the following essay,* Spider Woman's Granddaughters: Traditional Tales and Contemporary Writings by Native American Women *(1989),* Grandmothers of the Light: A Medicine Woman's Source Book *(1992),* As Long as the Rivers Flow: The Stories of Nine Native Americans *(1996), and* Off the Reservation: Reflections on Boundry-Busting, Border-Crossing Loose Canyons *(2002). Allen's considerable poetic works frequently echo themes derived from her Native-American roots, and they range from* The Blind Lion *(1974),* Coyote's Daylight Trip *(1981), and* Starchild *(1981), to* Wyrds *(1987),* Skin and Bones *(1988),* The Voice of the Turtle *(1994), and* Life Is a Disease: Selected Poems 1964–1994 *(1996).*

Pre-reading Questions

1. Most Americans have immigrant origins. An old American saying is "we've all come from somewhere else." What are your family origins? What traditions and customs—holidays, foods, beliefs—does your family still observe?

2. What are some traditions of the Native-American people? Which of these traditions can you speculate have been lost? Which of their lost traditions could enrich American society today?

1   At Laguna Pueblo in New Mexico, "Who is your mother?" is an important question. At Laguna, one of several of the ancient Keres gynecocratic societies of the region, your mother's identity is the key to your own identity. Among the Keres, every individual has a place within the universe—human and nonhuman—and that place is defined by clan membership. In turn, clan membership is dependent on matrilineal descent. Of course, your mother is not only that woman whose womb formed and released you—the term refers in every individual case to an entire generation of women whose psychic, and consequently physical, "shape" made the psychic existence of the following generation possible. But naming your own mother (or her equivalent) enables people to place you precisely within the universal web of your life, in each of its dimensions: cultural, spiritual, personal, and historical.

2   Among the Keres, "context" and "matrix" are equivalent terms, and both refer to approximately the same thing as knowing your derivation and place. Failure to know your mother, that is, your position and its attendant traditions, history, and place in the scheme of things, is failure to remember your significance, your reality, your right relationship to earth and society. It is the same as being lost—isolated, abandoned, self-estranged, and alienated from your own life. This importance of tradition in the life of every member of the community is not confined to Keres Indians; all American Indian Nations place great value on traditionalism.

3   The Native American sense of the importance of continuity with one's cultural origins runs counter to contemporary American ideas: in many instances, the immigrants to America have been eager to cast off cultural ties, often seeing their antecedents as backward, restrictive, even shameful. Rejection of tradition constitutes one of the major features of American life, an attitude that reaches far back into American colonial history and that now is validated by virtually every cultural institution in the country. Feminist practice, at least in the cultural artifacts the community values most, follows this cultural trend as well.

4   The American idea that the best and the brightest should willingly reject and repudiate their origins leads to an allied idea—that history, like everything in the past, is of little value and should be forgotten as quickly as possible. This all too often causes us to reinvent the wheel continually. We find ourselves discovering our collective pasts over and over, having to retake ground already covered by women in the preceding

decades and centuries. The Native American view, which highly values maintenance of traditional customs, values, and perspectives, might result in slower societal change and in quite a bit less social upheaval but it has the advantage of providing a solid sense of identity and lowered levels of psychological and interpersonal conflict.

5   Contemporary Indian communities value individual members who are deeply connected to the traditional ways of their people, even after centuries of concerted and brutal effort on the part of the American government, the churches, and the corporate system to break the connections between individuals and their tribal world. In fact, in the view of the traditionals, rejection of one's culture—one's traditions, language, people—is the result of colonial oppression and is hardly to be applauded. They believe that the roots of oppression are to be found in the loss of tradition and memory because that loss is always accompanied by a loss of a positive sense of self. In short, Indians think it is important to remember, while Americans believe it is important to forget.

6   The traditional Indians' view can have a significant impact if it is expanded to mean that the sources of social, political, and philosophical thought in the Americas not only should be recognized and honored by Native Americans but should be embraced by American society. If American society judiciously modeled the traditions of the various Native Nations, the place of women in society would become central, the distribution of goods and power would be egalitarian, the elderly would be respected, honored, and protected as a primary social and cultural resource, the ideals of physical beauty would be considerably enlarged (to include "fat," strong-featured women, gray-haired, and wrinkled individuals, and others who in contemporary American culture are viewed as "ugly"). Additionally, the destruction of the biota, the life sphere, and the natural resources of the planet would be curtailed, and the spiritual nature of human and nonhuman life would become a primary organizing principle of human society. And if the traditional tribal systems that are emulated included pacifist ones, war would cease to be a major method of human problem solving.

Post-reading Questions

Content

1. In the Laguna tribe, how does one establish his or her identity? What benefits does this form of identity have?

2. Name the disadvantages of not knowing your mother. What is important to the Native-American way of life?
3. Have contemporary Americans held onto their cultural origins? What forces does Allen suggest have promoted this cultural alienation?
4. What would be the results if contemporary American culture adopted traditional views of Native Americans? Why would American culture change? How would it change?
5. What are the contrasting values of contemporary American and Native-American culture? What results from the contemporary American way of life? What are the results of Native-American cultural values?

Strategies and Structures

1. How does Allen start her essay? Why does she begin her essay this way?
2. Where does Allen present her thesis? How does it help the reader to focus on the controlling idea of her essay?
3. How does Allen use comparison and contrast to support her argument not to reject our traditions? And how does she use this strategy to develop her argument that we should adopt Native-American values?
4. In the final paragraph, Allen suggests the benefits of adopting Native-American values. Why does she present all of the benefits in one paragraph? What is the result of structuring the essay this way?

Language and Vocabulary

1. Vocabulary: *matrilineal, psychic, context, matrix, self-estranged, alienated, antecedents, interpersonal.* Most of these words may cause the reader to lose track of what Allen is trying to say. Look up the definitions of the words and rewrite the sentences in which they appear using simple language. Does this in any way change the effect? How? Why?
2. Allen repeats key terms throughout the essay. What are they? How do they help unify the essay and keep it focused?

Group Activities

1. Form multicultural groups and compare your different beliefs. How have the different cultures retained or rejected their traditions? Who is the traditional head of the household in the different cultures? What are the different relationships between humanity and nature? What are the different religious beliefs? What are the different political beliefs and institutions present in the history of each culture? You may want to create a chart in which you list the different cultural beliefs under different headings such as religion, politics, or assimilation.

2. As a group, do a short research project in which you compare three different world cultures and their traditions. What are their political histories? Who have been their leaders? What are their different religious beliefs, and how have they developed over time? What have been their different beliefs about the relationship between humanity and nature? What are the different scientific discoveries that have shaped their cultures?

Writing Activities

1. Do some research on your cultural origins. You may want to interview relatives, do research in the library, and/or watch some films on your culture in the audiovisual center. After researching, write a paper in which you argue for the inclusion of one of your culture's traditions into mainstream, contemporary American culture.

2. Write a paper in which you argue for or against assimilation or the "melting-pot" theory. Explain the different benefits and disadvantages of assimilation. Explain why immigrants should or should not abandon their cultural traditions in favor of contemporary American culture.

Imamu Amiri Baraka

Soul Food

An essayist, poet, novelist, and playwright, Imamu Amiri Baraka is
well known for his plays such as The Dutchman, The Slave, The
Toilet *(1964) and* Four Black Revolutionary Plays *(1969). Other works*
include Preface to a Twenty Volume Suicide Note *(1961),* The System
of Dante's Hell *(1965),* Black Magic: Poetry 1961–1967 *(1967),*
Selected Poetry of Imamu Amiri Baraka/LeRoi Jones *(1979),* Reggae
or Not *(1982),* The Music: Reflections on Jazz *(1982),* Wise Why's Y's:
The Griots Tale *(1997), and* The Fiction of LeRoi Jones/Amiri Baraka
(1999). Baraka rejected traditional poetic forms and also the
dominant white culture. He denounced his Christian name, LeRoi
Jones, and adopted his Muslim name, Imamu Amiri Baraka which he
later shortened to Amiri Baraka. Baraka was one of the founders of
the Black Arts Movement in the 1960s, and his work—especially the
early poems—reflects a Black Nationalist's stance.

Pre-reading Questions

1. What does the essay's title suggest to the reader? Have
   you any idea what soul food is? What?

2. What do you think about when you hear the term *soul*
   linked with *food* or *music*? Have you any idea where the
   meaning you associate with such terms originated?
   Briefly write about your own "word history" for *soul* in
   your thesis notebook, writing log, or class journal.

1   Recently, a young Negro novelist writing in *Esquire* about
the beauties of America mentioned that one of the things
wrong with Negroes was that, unlike the Chinese, blacks have
neither a language of their own nor a characteristic cuisine.

And this to me is the deepest stroke, the unkindest cut of oppression, especially as it has distorted black Americans. America, where the suppliant, far from rebelling or even disagreeing with the forces that have caused him to suffer, readily backs them up and finally tries to become an honorary oppressor himself.

2   No language? No characteristic food? Oh, man, come on.

3   Maws are things ofays seldom get to peck, nor are you likely ever to hear about Charlie eating a chitterling. Sweet potato pies, a good friend of mine asked recently, "Do they taste anything like pumpkin?" Negative. They taste more like memory, if you're not uptown.

4   All those different kinds of greens (now quick frozen for anyone) once were all Sam got to eat. (Plus the potlikker, into which one slipped some throwed away meat.) Collards and turnips and kale and mustards were not fit for anybody but the woogies. So they found a way to make them taste like something somebody would want to freeze and sell to a Negro going to Harvard as exotic European spinach.

5   The watermelon, friend, was imported from Africa (by whom?) where it had been growing many centuries before it was necessary for some people to deny that they had ever tasted one.

6   Did you ever hear of a black-eyed pea? (Whitey used it for forage, but some folks couldn't.) And all those weird parts of the hog? (After the pig was stripped of its choicest parts, the feet, snout, tail, intestines, stomach, etc., were all left for the "members," who treated them mercilessly.) Is it mere myth that shades are death on chickens? (Deep fat frying, the Dutch found out in 17th century New Amsterdam, was an African specialty: and if you can get hold of a fried chicken leg, or a fried porgie, you can find out what happened to that tradition.)

7   I had to go to Rutgers before I found people who thought grits were meant to be eaten with milk and sugar, instead of gravy and pork sausage . . . and that's one of the reasons I left.

8   Away from home, you must make the trip uptown to get really straight as far as a good grease is concerned. People kill chickens all over the world, but chasing them though the dark on somebody else's property would probably insure, once they went in the big bag, that you'd find some really beautiful way to eat them. I mean, after all the risk involved. The fruit of that tradition unfolds everywhere above 100th Street. There are probably more restaurants in Harlem whose staple is fried chicken, or chicken in the basket, than any other place in the

world. Ditto, barbecued ribs—also straight out of the South
with the West Indians, *i.e.,* Africans from farther south in the
West, having developed the best sauce for roasting whole oxen
and hogs, spicy and extremely hot.

9 Hoppin' John (black-eyed peas and rice), hushpuppies
(crusty cornmeal bread cooked in fish grease and best with
fried fish, especially fried salt fish, which ought to soak
overnight unless you're over fifty and can take all that salt),
hoecake (pan bread), buttermilk biscuits and pancakes, fat-
back, *i.e.,* streak'alean-streak'afat, dumplings, neck bones,
knuckles (both good for seasoning limas or string beans), okra
(another African importation, other name gumbo), pork
chops—some more staples of the Harlem cuisine. Most of the
food came North when the people did.

10 There are hundreds of tiny restaurants, food shops, rib
joints, shrimp shacks, chicken shacks, "rotisseries" throughout
Harlem that serve "soul food"—say, a breakfast of grits, eggs
and sausage, pancakes and Alaga syrup—and even tiny booths
where it's at least possible to get a good piece of barbecue, hot
enough to make you whistle, or a chicken wing on a piece of
greasy bread. You can *always* find a fish sandwich: a fish sandwich is something you walk with, or "Two of those small sweet
potato pies to go." The Muslim temple serves bean pies which
are really separate. It is never necessary to go to some big expensive place to get a good filling grease. You *can* go to the Red
Rooster, or Wells, or Joch's, and get a good meal, but Jenny-
lin's, a little place on 135th near Lenox, is more filling, or some
place like the A&A food shop in a basement up in the 140's, and
you can really get away. I guess a square is somebody who's in
Harlem and eats at Nedicks.

Post-reading Questions

Content

1. What argument of fact does Baraka seek to establish in this essay? Does the author accomplish his
   purpose? Why or why not?

2. What methods does the author use to illustrate that
   African Americans, indeed, have a cuisine of their
   own?

3. What is the author attempting to express by his
   constant reference to "uptown"? Is this a reference
   meaningful only to African Americans? Provide several examples to illustrate your reasoning.

4. Baraka concludes his essay by saying, "I guess a square is somebody who's in Harlem and eats at Nedicks." (Nedicks is a typical American fast-food restaurant that does not serve soul food.) Why is it appropriate that he end his essay in such a manner? How does his comment reinforce his argument about African Americans?

Strategies and Structures

1. Why does the author first use African-American terms for food and later define these food terms? Does this suggest a two-part argument? In what way?
2. What is the value of slang in this composition? Do slang terms serve a strategic purpose in Baraka's argument? Explain.
3. How well does the subject of food work as a unifying device in Baraka's essay? Cite some specific examples that support your claim.

Language and Vocabulary

1. Vocabulary: *chitterling, potlikker, collards, fried porgie, grits.* How many of these words can you find in a pocket dictionary? If you are unable to find all of the words, try using an unabridged dictionary. Next, try to locate recipes for some of the above. Choose one recipe that particularly appeals to you and either cook it yourself or go to a *soul food* restaurant and order it. Then write an essay persuading your reader to try the food.
2. Does the use of slang change your conception of *soul food* to the more exotic? How? Why?

Group Activities

1. Get into diverse groups and discuss foods that are typical in each represented culture. Argue for their uniqueness. Are there any slang terms that have developed for the foods your group considers? If so, are they in common use in America today? What would be lost without the slang terms?
2. Visit a restaurant—other than fast-food restaurants like McDonalds—that serves a cuisine other than your own. Order a food you never have tasted

and also sample those foods ordered by members of your group. Then write an essay in which you defend your own food or promote the new food that you have tried.

Writing Activities

1. Compose an essay based on a cultural issue (food, clothing, habits), arguing for your topic's uniqueness to your culture. Carefully consider any opposing arguments, addressing them as necessary, in order to be convincing.
2. Write an essay arguing how and why America needs to become a multilingual society (one that speaks several languages) in order to preserve cultural differences and enrich society as a whole.

Grace Sumabat Mateo

The Anima of Anime

A renaissance woman, Grace Sumabat Mateo works in the field of In-formation Technology, yet her perception and skill in the areas of crit-ical thinking, literature, and social sciences give a broad view of life and sensitivity to all aspects of human needs and conveniences. A poet and essayist, her works have been published in everything from Projections: Brief Readings on American Culture *to* Leaf by Leaf. *Although Mateo cultivates a wide variety of interests, her children, Geoffrey and David, play a major part of her life and strongly influ-ence her concerns about the world in which they live. In the following essay, Mateo blends comparison and contrast development techniques to advance her argument about anime in western society.*

Pre-reading Questions

1. Cluster the words "cartoon" and "anime." What images and qualities do the words bring to mind? How do both words reflect culture values? Explain.

2. In your lifetime, what criticism have your heard directed at cartoons? When, where, how? Why might the very car-toons some people criticize oftentimes earn praise from other sources?

"The blue sky is infinitely high, crystal clear. . . that's what the world should be. . . a world of infinite possibilities, laid before us, crystal clear"

—*Kintasu* (Samurai X)

1   The beguiling presence of anime within North American culture cannot be ignored. We are bombarded by anime mer-chandise in clothing, electronic, and toy stores. The *Pokemon*

craze that swept the nation is but one example of how anime has surpassed the influence of mainstream American cartoon characters such as Batman and Superman. One anime series in particular, *Dragonball Z*, is one of the longest-running animated series worldwide. Hundreds of fan clubs exist in Asia, Europe, and North America. It holds a coveted place in the hearts of grade-school children and young adults alike. Very few shows can manage such widespread appeal to a broad age range. The anime revolution, without a doubt, is here to stay.

2   People use the term anime, in its most basic definition, to refer to Japanese animation. However, the phenomenon of anime has extended far beyond this limited description. Anime encompasses not only the animated video and film industry, but that of the manga (comic book) and video game industries (Izawa) as well. Anime has also transcended the national boundaries of Japan to include other countries such as Korea because the distinctive cartoon style of anime is more defining than its country of origin. If anything, Japan quickly is losing its exclusive ownership of this style of art. North American illustrators would do well to examine the underlying factors that have caused anime to be more appealing than their domestic creations.

3   Anime art is vibrant, colorful, and dynamic. Its highly stylized form is easily recognizable. Female characters such as Sailor Moon have extremely large eyes, almost non-existent noses, and petite mouths. Their figures are invariably slim and curvaceous. Similarly, male superhero characters like Goku of *Dragonball Z* often have disproportionately muscular physiques that are impossible to attain. In anime, both male and female viewers are subjected to unrealistic physical standards. Facial expressions are exaggerated to a comical extent—subtlety is not a virtue of anime art.

4   These consistent characteristics of anime serve a dual purpose. First, the features emphasized by anime style are those that address universal standards of sex appeal—the females accentuate their youth and fertility while the males display power through status or genetic superiority. Ergo, consciously or not, viewers inexplicably find anime figures to be aesthetically pleasing. Secondly, it is very difficult to determine the ethnic origin of anime characters. Whereas *Batman* and *Superman* are undoubtedly Caucasian, anime characters display a blend of Asian and European traits. Since both genders often sport unusual hair colors and styles, such as blue bouffants or golden Mohawks, the lines of ethnicity become even further blurred. In

Dragonball Z, the fighters begin as dark-eyed and dark-haired figures, but become blue-eyed and blond as their power levels jump to a higher level (a Japanese yearning for westernization?). This ethnic ambiguity lends itself beautifully to allowing a wider range of viewers to identify with the characters.

5   Although the majority of anime stories take place in outer space or in some other time era, they still have the tendency to portray characters in a more true to life perspective. Naturally, Japanese social customs and culture are somewhat reflected in the shows, but they add an appealing sense of reality and domesticity. It is not unusual to see a hero being told to do homework, eat a meal, or go to the bathroom. In one amusing scene in a *Dragonball Z* movie, two of its flying child-heroes, Goten and Trunks, decide to play a game of writing their names in the sky while they relieve themselves. Imagine Batman and/or Superman engaging in such an activity! North American-made animated shows are often plagued with the handicaps of censors and political correctness. They are sanitized to the point of blandness.

6   The anime storylines found in anime shows also tend to be more complex than in North American made animation. Typically, western animators rely on conventional, black and white plots and characters. Superman and his arch-nemesis, Lex Luthor, for instance, are representative of the black and white nature of western cartoons. Superman, the archetypal *ultimate* boy scout, clearly contrasts with Lex Luthor, the supreme manifestation of greed and evil. While viewers expect and even relish the conflict between good and bad, they know full well that, in the end, good will prevail—no surprises.

7   Similarly, Disney films are characterized by their handsome/ beautiful protagonists, cute animal sidekicks, and sinister-looking villains. Without even knowing the storyline, one could tell who the "bad guy" is within multiseconds of a Disney movie! Only in one of its more recent releases, *Lilo and Stitch,* has Disney departed from this predictable formula. In this movie, Stitch, the main character, is actually a genetically engineered alien creature designed to be indestructible but destructive of everything in its way. Stitch's evolution into a socially acceptable citizen of earth and his relationship with Lilo signify Disney's recognition that this new generation of cartoon viewers demands more depth and complexity, even in animated storylines.

8   Anime stories, in contrast to traditional western storylines, are known for their intricacy. Characters have multidimen-

sional aspects to their nature, and rather than being black or white, individuals often find themselves in the gray area. Two of the most popular characters of *Dragonball Z* are Vegeta and Piccolo. Both originated as villains but subsequently found themselves fighting alongside the main hero, Goku. Throughout the show, however, it is clear that their combative and contradictory personalities continue to afflict them as a team, bringing forth extremely entertaining interactions. Anime assumes a certain level of maturity and sophistication from its viewers. Major protagonists are often seriously wounded or even killed during battle, making the plots far less predictable than their North American counterparts. For example, we all know that the Joker will never succeed in killing Batman; by contrast, in *Dragonball Z*, the villain Majin Boo killed many of the shows protagonists. Although the heroes did have a method of returning from the grave (through dragonball wishes), the intrigue of "when" and "how" still compels viewers and draws them further into the plot. In anime, there is no guarantee of a happy ending or immediate gratification.

9   Those new to anime often are concerned by the violence and sexual content of a significant portion of anime movies. However, there is a cultural difference between east and west that must be understood. In America, almost anything cartoon is relegated to the children's section. Due to Disney's popular formula for American-animated movies, people in this country tend to view all animated films as being family fare. The assumption of sanitized subject matter should not apply for foreign films. In Asia, anime is a genuine form of entertainment for adults. The biggest domestic movie hit of all time in Japan is *Monoke-hime* (Princess Monoke), a non-juvenile animated film by Miyazaki Hayao (Kenji). Anime has overtaken live-action film production in Japan, largely due to the latter's inherent budget and creative limitations (Kenji). Anime offers a relatively inexpensive alternative that can often surpass the visual and intellectual appeal of live-action films. Just as people scrutinize live-action movies for their viewing appropriateness, they should also maintain the same vigilance for anime films.

10   Paradoxically, the world of anime is one that offers a sense of reality coupled with a liberating door to fantasy. Characters perform mundane chores, experience doubt and angst, and have troubled relationships as we do, yet they can also travel to other worlds, interact with aliens, and perform superhuman feats of strength and agility. As with our lives, it is difficult to predict how an anime story will end. The appeal of anime and its growing

popularity in mainstream America marks an intellectual and emotional growth in popular consciousness. Perhaps we are ready for a new level of entertainment and creativity; perhaps we no longer need the guarantee of a happy ending.

> "Always with the end comes hope and rebirth."
> —*Sailor Saturn* (Sailor Moon)

Post-reading Questions

Content

1. Where does Mateo place the thesis of her essay? Why?
2. List some of anime's dominant characteristics.
3. Where do the majority of "anime" stories occur?
4. Explain the significant cultural differences in the way people in the east and west perceive the function of cartoons.
5. Why does Mateo claim that anime storylines tend to be more complex than in American animation? To what extent do you agree with her assessment and why?

Strategies and Structures

1. Why do you imagine Mateo chose to preface her thesis paragraph and follow her concluding paragraph with a quotation by an anime character? What do they add to the essay?
2. Following her thesis paragraph, Mateo spends time defining anime before returning to argue her thesis. How does this affect the persuasive merit of her argument?
3. Mateo notes that anime contains several consistent characteristics that serve a dual purpose. Briefly mention some of the consistent characteristics listed in your response to Content Question 2 and then explain their dual purpose in context.
4. Anime stories, despite their fantastical elements, often depict an appealing sense of domesticity, according to Mateo. How does she justify this comment? In your opinion, would the same statement apply to Western cartoons? Why or why not?
5. In what way does Mateo's concluding paragraph pull together the parts of her essay and refocus her argument?

Language and Vocabulary

1. Vocabulary: *anima, beguiling, coveted, phenomenon, transcended, curvaceous, ergo, domesticity, blandness, arch-nemesis, manifestation, multiseconds, evolution, multidimensional, relegated, inherent, mundane, paradoxically, angst.* After checking the definitions for vocabulary words, consider how Mateo uses the majority of them to express a quality or modify other words. Then, select at least seven such words, go to a thesaurus, and locate an antonym (word with opposite meaning) and synonym (word with similar meaning) for each.

2. Make a list of some specific instances in this essay where Mateo's language indicates or suggests her attitude towards her subject. Then, do the same thing to a recent composition you have written.

3. Return to the word "anima" in Mateo's essay title and then locate a general dictionary definition of the word, as well as Carl Jung's definition of anima. Which definition do you think Mateo was alluding to, if not both? Explain.

Group Activities

1. Mateo blends the rhetorical strategies of illustration and example, definition, comparison and contrast to argue "the anime revolution, without a doubt, is here to stay." Gather in groups, pair off, and have each sub-group go back though the essay, identifying instances where she uses specific rhetorical modes of development to develop it. Next, reassemble in your groups and share your insights and record them on a single sheet. Finally, as a class, compare and contrast group findings.

2. In a computer-assisted classroom, pair off and explore the world of cartoons online. Have one person jot down your impressions of such popular cartoons in western society as *The Simpsons, The Flintstones, Daffy Duck, Bugs Bunny, Spiderman, Batman, Justice League, South Park*, and so on. Also consider Disney and other animated movies such as *Shrek* and *Toy Story*. What are the defining characteristics of the cartoons you looked up (e.g., color, style, and so on) on the Internet? Make a copy of your findings for each group member to refer to in a writing activity.

Writing Activities

1. Construct an essay where you compare and contrast characters in an anime cartoon and a western cartoon or movie to argue a specific point.
2. After brainstorming the topics of sex and/or violence in twenty-first century cartoons, write an essay arguing that anime, western cartoons, or both tend to promote violence and exploit sex in North and South America or vice versa. Use sound reasoning, plenty of representative examples, and analysis to prove your argument.

Douglas Laycock

Peyote, Wine and the First Amendment

Essayist Douglas Laycock presently serves as the Alice McKean Young Regents Chair in Law at the University of Texas, Austin. His works include Modern American Remedies *(1985) and* The Death of the Irreparable Injury Rule *(1991). Douglas's essay first appeared in* The Christian Century *on October 4, 1989.*

Pre-reading Questions

1. Make a list of freedoms and practices you feel are guaranteed by the First Amendment. If you are uncertain what the First Amendment is, get a copy of the U.S. Constitution and look it up. Where does freedom of religion fit into our inalienable rights?

2. To your knowledge, is the continuance or growth of non-Christian religions, rituals, and ceremonies (excluding Satanism and death cults) discouraged in America? How many non-Christian religious shows have you seen on television?

3. What is your attitude toward the use of drugs (wine and other alcoholic beverages are drugs) in religious ceremonies? Does it matter that these drugs have been in use for centuries?

---

1   This fall the U.S. Supreme Court will consider arguments in a case that goes to the very heart of the constitutional guarantee of free exercise of religion. The court will decide whether the state can prohibit a religious ritual, and if so, what kinds of dangers justify such an extraordinary prohibition. This litigation involves not a practice of a mainstream faith but the peyote ritual of the Native American Church.

2   Peyote, or mescal, is a small cactus that grows in the southwest U.S. and in northern Mexico. It produces buds or tubers, called buttons, that have hallucinogenic properties. Peyote is an illegal drug, but the federal government and twenty-three states permit its use in at least some religious ceremonies. Federal drug authorities issue licenses to grow and sell peyote to religious users. But the case before the court comes from Oregon, which has no such exemption.

3   If the Supreme Court focuses too narrowly on drugs in this case and misses the larger issue of religious ritual, it could create a devastating precedent for religious liberty. For the Native American use of peyote has substantial parallels to Christian and Jewish uses of wine. If the peyote ritual is allowed only by legislative grace and not by constitutional right, the right to participate in communion, the Passover Seder and sabbath rituals may rest on no firmer footing.

4   The Oregon case is an odd vehicle for addressing such an issue. It is not a criminal prosecution; questions about criminal prohibitions are involved only because the court reached out for them. Alfred Smith and Galen Black were drug- and alcohol-abuse counselors at a nonprofit agency. When their supervisor learned that they had consumed peyote at a religious service, he discharged them for violating the agency's absolute rule against drug or alcohol use. The supervisor later testified that "we would have taken the same action had the claimant consumed wine at a Catholic ceremony." But he offered no evidence that anyone had actually been discharged for drinking communion wine, and he did not claim to have inquired about which of the churches his employees attended used wine and which only grape juice.

5   Smith and Black first complained that their employer had discriminated against them based on their religion. Without admitting the charge, the employer changed its absolute rule against religious use of drugs, and it paid Smith and Black some of their lost pay. They agreed not to insist on being reinstated to their jobs.

6   Smith and Black also filed claims for unemployment compensation. A long line of Supreme Court cases holds that states must pay unemployment compensation to employees who lose their jobs because of their religious beliefs. Employees who refuse to work on their sabbath have been the principal beneficiaries of this rule (in another case a worker lost his job in a brass mill because he refused to help manufacture tank

turrets). The Oregon courts followed these cases and awarded unemployment compensation to Smith and Black.

7 The U.S. Supreme Court vacated the judgment, deciding that if Oregon could send Smith and Black to prison for chewing peyote, it could surely refuse to pay them unemployment compensation. Therefore, the court reasoned, the constitutional status of Oregon's criminal prohibition of peyote was logically prior to the unemployment-compensation issue. It sent the case back to the state courts to ask whether Oregon would recognize a religious exception to its criminal laws against possession or consumption of peyote.

8 Oregon's Supreme Court, which had already concluded that this question was irrelevant, dutifully answered that in its judgment criminal prosecution of Smith and Black would violate the federal Constitution. Their consumption of peyote was a constitutionally protected exercise of religion; therefore, Oregon could not send them to prison or refuse to pay them unemployment compensation.

9 The U.S. Supreme Court has agreed to hear the case again. Presumably it intends to decide whether Smith and Black could be sent to prison, even though no one has shown the slightest interest in sending them there. If it has second thoughts about this exercise in judicial activism, it may retreat to the narrower issue and decide only whether Smith and Black are entitled to keep their unemployment compensation.

10 The opinions of the Oregon courts provide few details about exactly what Smith and Black did with peyote. Opinions in other cases provide more information about the peyote ritual, based on the testimony of witnesses and of anthropologists who have studied it. The peyote ritual is no modern innovation designed to evade the drug laws. Native Americans have practiced it at least since 1560, when it was first described in Spanish records. Today the ritual is practiced in substantially similar form from northern Mexico to Saskatchewan. Believers come from many Native American tribes, although it is not the major religion of any tribe. The faith has absorbed some Christian teachings as well, but peyote remains at the heart of its theology and practice.

11 To the believer, peyote is a sacramental substance, an object of worship and a source of divine protection. Peyote is the focus of the worship service, much as the consecrated bread and wine are the focus of mass and communion. The cases speak of prayers being directed to peyote; I suspect that the believer

thinks of himself as praying to the holy spirit who is present in the peyote.

12   The believer may wear peyote on his person for protection; soldiers have worn a large peyote button in a beaded pouch suspended from their necks. While there is no parallel in Christian theology, there is ample parallel in Christian folk-belief—a consecrated communion wafer worn around the neck has been thought to be the best defense against Dracula, and crosses and medals are put to similar use against modern dangers.

13   Finally, and most important for the question before the court, participants in the ritual believe that peyote intoxication enables them to experience God directly. Peyote is consumed for this purpose only at a "meeting," convened and controlled by a leader. It is a sacrilege to use peyote for a non-religious purpose. A meeting is a solemn and somewhat infrequent occasion. Participants wear their finest clothing. They pray, sing and perform ceremonies with drums, fans, eagle bones and other symbolic instruments.

14   The central event is the consumption of peyote in quantities sufficient to produce intoxication. At the appointed time, the leader distributes up to four buttons to each adult participant. There is an opportunity for participants to take additional buttons at a later point in the ceremony. The buttons are extremely bitter, and difficult to chew and swallow. Some groups use a tea brewed from the buttons, but chewing the buttons appears to be the norm.

15   The meeting lasts from sundown Saturday to sunrise Sunday. In the morning, the leader serves breakfast. By then all effects of the peyote have worn off, and the participants leave in a sober state. Smith and Black were fired for participating in a service that, apparently, went according to this generic description.

16   The First Amendment guarantees the free exercise of religion and forbids the governmental establishment of religion. One of the amendment's central purposes is to ensure that religious belief and practice be as free as possible from government regulation. There are limits to this freedom when serious and immediate harm is threatened; hardly anyone believes in a constitutional right to practice human sacrifice. But the Supreme Court has repeatedly said that government can limit religious liberty only for compelling reasons that cannot be served in any other way.

17   Another central function of the First Amendment is to ensure that small, unfamiliar, and unpopular religions get equal

treatment with larger, well-known, and politically influential religions. In those compelling cases in which religious liberty must be restricted, the restrictions must be applied neutrally.

18   This principle of neutrality requires us to compare the peyote ritual to the rituals of mainstream faiths. Peyote is not the only mind-altering drug used in a religious ritual. Many Christians drink wine at communion. For Jews, a prayer over wine is part of the sabbath service, sabbath meals, all religious holidays and special religious events such as weddings and circumcisions.

19   Wine was once illegal in the U.S., just as peyote is now. But the National Prohibition Act, passed after ratification of the 18th Amendment, exempted wine "for sacramental purposes, or like religious rites." State prohibition laws, some of which survived into the 1960s, either had similar exemptions or at least were not enforced against religious users. (Contemporary local prohibition laws rarely require exemptions; they generally restrict the sale of alcohol, but permit private consumption of alcohol purchased elsewhere.)

20   Why is it that the religious use of wine was exempt everywhere during Prohibition, but the religious use of peyote is exempt in only half the states today? If Oregon may constitutionally punish the religious use of peyote, may it not also punish the religious use of wine? Could Oregon ban communion wine and require that all Christians use grape juice instead? The Supreme Court does not have to answer these questions formally; no case about wine is before it. But it should think hard about these questions, to make sure it is not suppressing a small and unfamiliar religion on the basis of principles it would not apply to a mainstream faith.

21   Oregon may respond that peyote is simply more dangerous than wine. I do not know whether that is true; I am sure that wine is more widely abused. But the court will assume that the legislature had good reason for its ban. It should inquire into dangerousness only in the narrow context of religious use. The judicial question is this: if the Constitution protects the religious use of wine when legislatures believe that wine is so dangerous it has to be banned, does the Constitution also protect religious use of peyote at a time when legislatures believe peyote must be banned? If sacramental uses of wine are protected and sacramental uses of peyote are not, it must be because of some compelling difference between the drugs or the rituals.

22   Each of the Christian and Jewish uses of wine is similar to the peyote ritual in some ways, and quite different in others. Communion resembles the peyote ritual in the liturgical and

theological centrality of the wine in the worship service. For many Christians, there are further similarities in the reverence and even adoration for the consecrated wine and the belief that the deity is present in the wine.

23   However, no one gets intoxicated on communion wine. Well, hardly anyone. In traditions that believe in the real presence of Christ, the priest or pastor may get tipsy from drinking the consecrated wine that is left over at the end of the service, since the blood of Christ cannot just be poured down the drain. This consequence could perhaps be avoided by recruiting enough helpers, but in some denominations only clergy and designated assistants are permitted to help.

24   Not even the matter of intoxication distinguishes Purim, the celebration of the Jews' deliverance from a genocidal plot during the Babylonian captivity. Some Jewish traditions teach a duty to celebrate Purim to the point of drunkenness. Jews drink four cups of wine at the Passover Seder, which commemorates the Exodus from Egypt. Prayer over a single cup of wine is part of the sabbath service and of sabbath meals.

25   But one important difference is that an essential part of the peyote ritual is to experience God through the mind-altering effects of the drug; that is not part of the communion service in any Christian tradition, and it is not part of any Jewish celebrations or rituals. Purim, the most intoxicating Jewish celebration, is only a minor festival. Because Purim is far less central theologically, a decision that Oregon could ban the peyote ritual would clearly imply that it could ban the use of intoxicating amounts of wine to celebrate Purim.

26   In an important sense it is a greater violation of religious liberty to ban a ritual that is at the theological heart of a faith than to ban a peripheral celebration. But either act limits religious liberty. We should be uncomfortable with governmental bans on minor religious festivals, or with judges deciding which festivals are important enough to deserve full constitutional protection and which are not. A court that starts down that path might eventually convince itself that wine is not central to the sabbath or to the celebration of Passover, or that the use of wine is not central to communion. The government could acquire a de facto power to review theology and liturgy.

27   If the court considers communion or the Passover Seder or the sabbath, its instinct will be to regard these as constitutionally protected. If it considers only peyotism, its instinct may be to consider it a weird and dangerous practice. Comparing familiar and presumptively protected faiths to an unfamiliar one

is a way of guarding against unrecognized bias. But this cautionary device will not work if the court jumps at any possible distinction to rationalize its prejudices in favor of the familiar.

28   Thus, the ultimate question is whether Oregon's reasons for prohibiting the peyote ritual are compelling, and, if the peyote ritual is to be distinguished from Christian and Jewish rituals, whether the distinctions are compelling. The only plausible distinction is that Christian and Jewish uses are generally less intoxicating—but there are important exceptions even to that.

29   The distinction is further blurred by the mystical tradition in every major world religion, including Christianity and Judaism. The mystics often seek to experience God through altered states of consciousness, generally induced by trance or meditation instead of drugs. So neither the use of mind-altering drugs nor the achievement of altered consciousness distinguishes peyotism from mainstream faiths. It is only the combination of these two things that arguably distinguishes peyotism.

30   The most one can say without exceptions is that only in peyotism is drug-induced altered consciousness part of the central religious event. That difference is compelling only if peyote intoxication under the controlled conditions of a meeting poses a serious danger to the participants or others. To say only that Oregon disapproves of peyote intoxication is merely to restate Oregon's disapproval of this mode of worship. Oregon's disapproval does not provide a compelling reason to forbid a religious ritual. . . .

31   It may be that as a practical matter religious use of mind-altering drugs will be limited to groups that can point to some substantial tradition and that limit the use of drugs to structured worship service. Perhaps the practical difficulties of enforcing the drug laws will prevent any broader protection of religious liberty. But both familiar and unfamiliar groups can show a substantial tradition and a structured worship service. At least Christians, Jews and peyote worshipers fall into this category. Peyote worship should be constitutionally protected, and Smith and Black should be allowed to keep their unemployment compensation.

Post-reading Questions

Content

1. What is Laycock's concern in this essay? Why does he claim that "peyote worship should be constitutionally protected"?

2. Did Smith and Black's supervisor treat them fairly when he discharged them for using peyote in a religious ceremony? Explain.

3. In what way is the Christian and Jewish use of wine similar to and different from the Native-American use of peyote in religious rituals?

4. Why is it ironic that alcohol, a drug introduced by Western society into Native-American culture, was "exempt" from Prohibition when used for religious purposes, but the use of peyote, a Native-American drug used by American Indians in religious rituals for centuries, is allowed only in "half the states today"?

5. How does the reader know that Laycock is not advocating peyote use for the sake of a *high?*

Strategies and Structures

1. How does Laycock use the First Amendment to strengthen his argument in this essay?

2. This essay begins and concludes with references to U.S. governing bodies and laws. Why is the separation of church and state an essential part of his argument?

3. How does Laycock demonstrate that peyote is a "sacramental substance, an object of worship and a source of divine protection"? What makes his argument logical?

4. Why does Laycock point out how Smith and Black are discriminated against by their employer, the Oregon courts, and the Supreme Court? Why does the employer make them agree not to ask for job reinstatement? Why does the Supreme Court decide to make no judgment? What does Laycock want us to conclude from all these points? Does his strategy work? Why or why not?

5. Why does Laycock want us to feel uncomfortable with the government and judges deciding which religions and religious rituals are important, and which are not? What is his purpose for pointing out what these bans can lead to?

6. After reading this article, what deductions can you make about the legal attitude and treatment of minor religions by the U.S. courts and the government in general? What do you feel is more important to

American society: the religious practices of many, the religious practices of a few, or both?

Language and Vocabulary

1. Vocabulary: *hallucinogenic, litigation, denomination, sacrilege, sacramental, consecrated.* Define the above words, then choose one and write an extended definition incorporating your own views and/or observations on the subject.

2. Three of these words—*sacrilege, sacramental,* and *consecrated*—have the same root—*sacr, secr*— which comes from Latin and means *holy* or *sacred.* Words with this root deal with religion or ritual. For a journal entry, find at least five more words with the same root and compose two or three paragraphs in which you discuss something that is sacred or holy to you, using each of your chosen words at least two times.

Group Activities

1. Does our Constitution guarantee the rights of all or just a few? Are some religions better than others? Divide the class into two groups, one assuming the role of a mainstream religion and the other a minority religion, and debate the issue. Following the debate, each student should write a summary of the opposing group's argument, noting its strengths and weaknesses.

2. When and where does censorship infringe on individual rights? Get in small groups and discuss how prohibiting traditions and rituals is censorship. (You first will have to have a clear idea of what censorship involves.) What examples of censorship in America today does your group agree with? Why? Now discuss what this censorship might lead to in the future. Finally, write a collaborative essay in which you argue for or against censorship of an ideal, a practice, or a privilege.

Writing Activities

1. Compose an essay arguing that all drug use in religious ceremonies or rituals should be outlawed,

including the use of alcohol. Anticipate your reader's reaction to your proposal and defend your thesis with clear reasoning and concrete examples.

2. Write an essay arguing that our freedom of worship in America is in jeopardy if the U.S. government does not stop tampering with the mystical religious traditions and the legality of rituals in practice today.

Mark Charles Fissel

Online Learning
and Student Success

*Mark Charles Fissel is a Fellow of the Royal Historical Society. He
received his Ph.D. from the University of California at Berkeley and
has published* English Warfare 1511–1642, The Bishops' Wars:
Charles I's Campaigns Against Scotland 1638–1640, *and articles on
educational technologies. A former dean of Harris Manchester College
(Oxford) and a Fulbright Senior Lecturer at Bogazici University
(Istanbul), Fissel specializes in faculty development. His essay
provides a counterpoint to his previous contribution to* Visions, *an
encomium to distance learning, based on the decade he taught via
interactive television (1988–1997).*

Pre-reading Questions

1. What images does the word *online* bring to mind?
2. Have you ever thought of taking an online course? Have
   you or any of your friends taken an online college course?
   Why?

1   Americans are being told that computerized instruction,
drawing from the resources of the World Wide Web, will empower the individual learner much as a decade ago televised
instruction linked learning communities.

2   Allegedly "knowledge" is expanding, doubling every eighteen months, so that there is more "knowledge" outside of the
academy than within its hallowed precincts. Simultaneously,
we are becoming "student-centered" educators. Elementary
and secondary school students employ multimedia technology

in their at least partially "virtual" classrooms. We are, justifiably, concerned with inculcating critical thinking skills in learners, and not so much with memorization (or what we might call "data retrieval"). Never before have we focused so steadily upon the learner, and provided students with such an array of educational tools. And this optimal environment for study defies space and time. Asynchronous learning and the Internet provide the student with unprecedented opportunities to learn outside the traditional classroom. This halcyon era of public and self-directed Enlightenment surely has produced better students. Legislators, taxpayers, students, and teachers understandably have a right to expect such results. The educational technologists have predicted and promised a brave new world. What are the results?

3   Mean SAT/SAT I scores for college-bound high school seniors have declined since 1972, implying that the age of computers did not accelerate student learning ("Table 1: Mean SAT Scores of Entering College Class, 1967–97"). It may be that learning has become more challenging. Computer technology moves large amounts of data very quickly. The development of critical thinking skills and reflective learning require time and patience, two commodities in rather short supply in the digital culture (Leibowitz A67). While some students have achieved notable success with the new technology, others struggle. When we consider allegations of grade inflation, try to explain the flourishing of home schooling, and the flight to private schools, one must conclude that "computer age" education is still beset with problems.

4   In the meanwhile, many traditional universities have declared their withdrawal from the "remediation business." In other words, students who do not meet some of the academic standards of a given institution find it increasingly difficult to convince universities to admit them with the understanding that they will take non-credit "remedial" classes to make up their deficiencies. Obsessed with quantifiable and measurable "student success," and dependent upon product-minded political institutions for funding, fewer universities feel willing to "take a chance" on a promising but underqualified applicant.

5   Where, then, will these students go, who have been turned away from the gates of the traditional university? Worldwide Web entrepreneurs already offer round-the-clock tutoring (Carr A45). Virtual universities are quick to advertise their own merits as an alternative to the residential or commuter college. Private institutions, such as the University of Phoenix, market "digital degrees," much as a corporation would offer products and

service. State-funded virtual institutions, for example the Florida Gulf Coast University, have appeared, offering online students the prestige of being part of a university system electronically.

6   Digital learning in the virtual university is supposed to "make that liberal arts ideal even broader." Not only will the online students have greater flexibility as to *when* they learn, they will also have more courses (and instructors) to choose from. William Draves, president of the Learning Resources Network, claims digital learning will "be more personalized because you as an individual learner will get more feedback on what you know and how you're proceeding and you'll have your curriculum tailored toward your learning needs" (Chaudry). Even though "online" learning may involve "megaclasses" of 1,000 or more students, taking multiple choice exams, Draves predicts a better education for students that will be more affordable, as automation and high enrollments push down the cost of tuition ("A Distance-Learning Forecast Calls for Megaclasses" A47). "Universities have to be businesses in the Information Age. They have to be cost effective. They have to bring their prices down," insists Draves.

7   But at what cost? Historian David Noble points out that "distance education has always been not so much technology driven as profit driven." While it is indisputable that the Internet has made accessible a greater volume of information, the promotion of virtual universities entails the automation of higher education. Unlike Draves, Noble believes that Web-based instruction necessarily imposes uniformity on curricula, while taking intellectual property from teachers and giving it to institutions. A college education ceases to be an experience and becomes increasingly a commodity in a highly capitalized world. Noble's assertions are buttressed by the evidence of alliances between corporate entrepreneurs and university administrations. UCLA brokered a deal with Onlinelearning.net, Berkeley with AOL, the University of Colorado with Real Education, and numerous university systems with WebCT. Now labor union–busting mogul Rupert Murdoch, through his News International conglomerate, is forging an alliance among multinational corporations and universities in order to establish a global distance education venture ("5 Corporations Reportedly Bid to Join Universities in Distance Learning" A55). Where Draves applauds colleges' assimilation of capitalist techniques and mentality, Noble sees in it the degradation of students to identityless cogs in a vast machine and the destruction of academic freedom. In an age where information is both wealth and power, the commercialization of colleges and

the standardization of a corporately owned curriculum, is a real and present danger (Noble).

8 The justification for the privatization and monopolization of higher education is that online technology helps students learn better. However, the jury is still out on that argument (Merisotis and Phipps 13–17). At a university in Texas, an acclaimed graduate course taught exclusively online garnered complaints by students who protested that they had come to that campus for a classroom experience. The administration felt compelled to offer a "traditional" section of the course, through another instructor.

9 Virtual universities (like home schooling) will flourish under certain conditions. Highly motivated and self-directed students will doubtless bloom in the virtual university. Isolated learners, too, will reap benefits from the ether. But in this bewildering world of exponentially increasing knowledge and techno-solitude, many citizen-students will opt for the safe havens of traditional colleges and universities. Education, in all millennia, has been a social activity. Building upon the centuries-old traditions of classroom instruction, professors (with student input), can make wise choice of the technologies available to complement, supplement, and expand their learning environment. In the words of the executive director of the American Association for History and Computing, "The most effective use of technology is being made in small classes that also provide face-to-face interaction" (Trinkle A60).

10 What does "online" learning mean to teachers? Academicians are in danger of selling their curricula to the highest bidder, usually a corporate custodian with no pedagogical and ethical commitment to educating society. What about students? Student organizations, especially those with a national membership, should initiate surveys to determine student preferences and needs. We hear a lot from the cyber-marketers, such as WebCT's splashy full-page advertisements in the *Chronicle of Higher Education*. But we've not provided a forum for the average student to express how technology might help that student succeed. And, ultimately, it is the individual teacher who must take responsibility for the curriculum and how it is taught.

Works Cited

"A Distance-Learning Forecast Calls for Megaclasses." *Chronicle of Higher Education.* 10 Dec. 1999: A47. *Chronicle of Higher Education Online.* Online. 11 Dec. 1999.

Carr, Sarah. "Another Web Company Eyes Academe, This One Offering Tutoring Assistance." *Chronicle of Higher Education*. 3 Dec. 1999: A45. *Chronicle of Higher Education Online*. Online. 5 Dec. 1999.

Chaudry, Lakshuni. "Cyber-School's Never Out." An Interview with William Draves. *Wired Digital Inc.* For William Draves' network, see *http://www.lern.org*. He has published *Teaching Online* (Learning Resources Network, 1999).

"5 Corporations Reportedly Bid to Join Universities in Distance Education." *Chronicle of Higher Education*. 3 Dec. 1999: A55. *Chronicle of Higher Education Online*. Online. 5 Dec. 1999.

Leibowitz, Wendy. "Technology Transforms Writing and the Techniques of Writing." *The Chronicle of Higher Education*. 26 Nov. 1999: A67. *Chronicle of Higher Education Online*. Online. 1 Dec. 1999.

Merisotis, J.P. and R.A. Phipps. "What's the Difference? Outcomes of Distance vs. Traditional Classroom-Based Learning." *Change* 1.3 (May–June 1999): 13–17. Based on a report by the Institute for Higher Education Policy.

Noble, David. *Digital Diploma Mills*. New York: Knopf, 2000. Noble's quotations were drawn from a four part online version of the same work. N. pag. His book, *The Religion of Technology* (Penguin, 1999) is highly recommended to students.

"Table 1: Mean SAT Scores of Entering College Class, 1967–97." *College Board Online*. *http://www.collegeboard.org/index_this/sat/cbsenior/yr1999/NAT/72-99.html*.

Trinkle, Dennis. "Distance Education: A Means to an End, No More, No Less." *Chronicle of Higher Education*. 6 Aug. 1999: A60. *Chronicle of Higher Education Online*. Online. 1 Dec. 1999.

Post-reading Questions

Content

1. What is Fissel's thesis? For what does he argue?
2. Who will benefit from online learning the most?
3. Does online learning take away from or add to the learning experience? How?
4. Which occupations have the most to gain from online learning? Why?

5. Where will the students needing basic skills instruction turn once four-year colleges turn their backs on remedial education? What is remediation, anyway? Could an emphasis on online education create another area of remediation?

Strategies and Structures

1. How does Fissel ethically appeal to his readers? That is, how does he structure his essay and what materials does he present in order to make him trustworthy?
2. In what way does Fissel's diction (word choice) reflect the struggle between virtual learning and the education received in the classroom?
3. How does the use of comparison and contrast help the author to argue his thesis? What conclusion does he reach?
4. How does Fissel actively engage readers to contemplate what it would be like to treat education as a business? Does it make sense that one can buy and sell knowledge? Can an education be packaged as a consumer item? Why or why not?
5. In what way does Fissel strategically use outside sources in his essay? What does the use of outside sources suggest about him? Do you find his use of outside, authoritative sources effective and convincing? Why or why not?

Language and Vocabulary

1. Vocabulary: *virtual, inculcating, asynchronous, halcyon, allegations, quantifiable, entrepreneurs, curriculum, commodity, buttressed, conglomerate, privatization, monopolization, techno-solitude, exponentially, millennia, pedagogical, cyber-marketers, forum.* How many of the preceding words deal with online learning? Can you find all of those words in the dictionary? If you can't, what do you suppose the electronic industry has done to our modern vocabulary and why? Go to your college computer science or engineering department or talk with one of the students majoring in these subjects to discover how these industries have added to our vocabulary.
2. Fissel's vocabulary contains many words of more than one syllable. Many of these begin with prefixes

(one or more letters attached to a word which change its meaning). Identify five such words and show what the meaning of the root word is and also list how the prefixes have changed that meaning. Find five other words that begin with each of the prefixes and define them.

Group Activities

1. Before gathering as a group, individually locate the distance education or an online courses Web site at your college—or any other college, for that matter. Then, take the "distance education self-assessment test." How did you do on the test? Bring the results of your experience back to your group and compare and contrast how different members were diagnosed. How helpful did your group members find the self-assessment test in determining if online instruction would or would not be ideally suited to their individual learning styles? Jot down any additional questions your group believes would benefit students who are unsure of digitized learning is for them.

2. Visit your campus Distance Learning Center for online courses and television instruction, and interview the director or a staff member. What services do they offer? Which segment of the student population uses these services the most? According to your campus's Distance Learning Center, how might such services promote student success in college courses? What is your opinion on the matter? Gather together again as a class and have each group share findings from interviews. Finally, use your conclusions as the basis for a student-directed technology forum, a forum that addresses the possible merits and disadvantages of online instruction for the average student.

Writing Activities

1. Write an essay wherein you argue or refute the fact that online college courses offer students a viable alternative to traditional methods of classroom instruction. Consider the five "W" journalistic

questions—who, what, when, where, why—while prewriting on this topic. Then, after drafting your argumentative essay, return to them and question your statements of fact, locating and correcting fallacies in logical reasoning.

2. There are many debates about educational practices besides the current focus on traditional instructional methods and distance education delivery systems: collaborative/interactive activities versus lecture/discussion, heterogeneous versus homogeneous classrooms, home versus public education, and large versus small classrooms—to name a few. Research one of these debates (1) on the Internet, (2) in your library by reading newspapers, magazines, and books, (3) by interviewing your instructors and college administrators, and (4) by soliciting the opinions of your fellow students. Then write an essay in which you argue for one instructional method over another. To what extent might most future instructional methods integrate some aspect of technology or multimedia into them?

Additional Topics and Issues for Argumentative Essays

1. Write an essay arguing that experience is—or is not—the best teacher. Make sure you provide several representative examples to convince your reader.

2. Argue for one of the following two positions: Money is a basic necessity to happiness, or money creates a feeling of happiness but not true contentment. What observations or experiences lead you to your conclusion?

3. In an argumentative essay, disprove the popular idea that video games deteriorate reading abilities. In fact, you might want to show that video games enhance reading abilities.

4. Select a popular television show and argue that it does or does not reflect the values of the average American. For example, do the characters in *Everybody Loves Raymond, Moesha, Dharma and Greg, 7th Heaven,* or *The Simpsons* resemble the sorts of people who are your neighbors?

5. To what extent could your eating habits indicate something about your personality? One variation of this topic

might be to argue that being a vegetarian is healthier than being a meat-eater or vice versa.

6. Sexually violent crimes are on the rise. Many lawmakers feel that to reduce such violations we must extend the death penalty to include rapists, child molesters, and those guilty of incest. Take a position on this issue and support it.

7. Some people claim that technology has made Americans lazy. For example, we use calculators to figure out math problems and spell checkers rather than learning to use a dictionary. Argue either in favor of or against the use of this technology and indicate where the line must be drawn between practicality and convenience.

8. Dr. Jack Kevorkian received notoriety for his assistance with numerous suicides. Euthanasia, or mercy killing, usually of the terminally ill or clinically brain-dead (those kept alive by machines), has been a debated issue for the past three decades. In this overcrowded world is it either logical or moral to keep these people alive at a great expense and burden to society? Or should every life be considered sacred and valuable?

9. Select a current issue of social concern such as a national health plan for all United States citizens. Look carefully at the pros and cons of each side of the topic or issue you choose, eliminating information or supporting arguments which are the result of fallacies in reasoning. Finally, take a position and construct an argumentative essay around it. To establish yourself as an ethical, trustworthy source, make sure you present both sides of the issue. (Ignorance of refutation will undermine your argument.)

10. On July 19, 1993, President Clinton presented a "don't ask, don't tell" compromise to gays and lesbians serving in the armed forces. Neither those who favored nor those who opposed homosexuals in the military were satisfied. In a well-reasoned essay, argue why gays and lesbians should or should not be allowed to serve unconditionally in the military, free from discrimination due to an alternate lifestyle. (You may want to research how countries like Canada and Australia have successfully dealt with this issue.) Since this is an argumentative essay embracing logic, reason, and critical thinking, you should eliminate material that is emotionally charged or not verifiable. Your objective here is to convince your reader of your position by virtue of deductive and inductive reasoning, facts, and statistics.

12

Persuasion: The Emotional Appeal

Like formal argumentative essays, persuasive essays attempt to convince readers of a point or issue. However, while authors tend to stick solely to logic and facts (induction and deduction in particular) in formal argumentative essays, they often appeal to a reader's emotions—which frequently are not logical—in persuasive essays. Some common emotional responses would be indignation, joy, fear, love, hatred, compassion, greed, lust, disgust, and jealousy. Understandably, to "play down" the emotions (pathos) behind an argument, most persuasive essays make overt appeals to logic (logos) and ethics (ethos).

How much do our personal values and prejudices toward different words, issues, or situations influence our judgment? Quite a bit! In the past few years, the word *democracy* has stirred people's emotions, often uniting them in a cause, for they associate democracy with positive issues and inalienable rights, especially equality. Note how often leaders will preface their remarks with something like, "In the spirit of democracy," suggesting a group consensus rather than an individual opinion. Now, take the same phrase and picture a recent U.S. president saying, "In the spirit of communism, I offer you the following resolution. . . ." In America, where communism has been a "dirty" word for decades, the president's resolution—no matter how logical, fair, and humanitarian—would probably not have received any serious consideration because of the negativity associated with communism. Authors make use of words that elicit emotions in persuasive essays to assist their arguments; authors count on emotional responses to influence readers where logic alone may not impress, motivate, or convince them.

We target different emotional responses for different situations. Bruce Henderson emotionally appeals to his readers' imagination (fueled by an endless supply of science-fiction movies wherein computers or robots end up dominating the human race) as he discusses his trip to the LARCS (Ladera Ranch Community Services) housing tract in his essay "Recent Developments." While the fully digitalized, "smart" houses initially may sound exciting, even futuristic, the combination of *ethos, pathos,* and *logos* in his essay enables him to lead readers to the conclusion that *"greed and need must be balanced against preservation of the environment for all to enjoy, and against a standard of living which, despite the rosy and cozy promises of the Ladera Ranch brochure, may be inevitably developed into decline."* Though light-hearted in tone, Phyllis McGinley's "Women Are Better Drivers" engages her readers by addressing *stereotypes* and *sexism*. After making early concessions about things men "can do" or "have done" better than women (e.g., create atomic bombs), she states two things in which women excel: having babies and driving automobiles. The first claim is undeniable; men couldn't carry a child to term if they wanted to because they are not biologically equipped for it! McGinley's second claim may run into more opposition, so the majority of her examples are geared to persuade the reader that women are better drivers than men because they are more reasonable, more cautious, more practical—especially when it comes to taking advice and jotting down directions—and generally, more skilled (a result of their extensive practice). Michael Dorris controls an emotionally charged issue, fetal alcohol syndrome, by drawing on logical appeals to his reader. He offers facts, statistics, and references to authorities to make his essay tangible and approachable. *Ethos* is ever present in this essay; Dorris makes an appeal to our better instincts—the humanitarian in all of us. Beneath all of this, of course, is an appeal to the reader's emotions: *outrage* and *indignation* over society's lack of concern about the need for prenatal services and facilities to address the needs of pregnant alcoholics and drug users. He is counting on such righteous indignation—emotion—to move people to act; thus far, logic and ethics alone have obviously not been enough. In "Never Too Old" we see yet another example of an emotional appeal—an appeal to fear and apprehension. Tammerlin Drummond shatters illusions about senior citizens as she points out that they are the fastest-growing HIV-infected population in the United States, and that the AIDS virus is not usually contacted through blood transfusions.

Organizing Persuasive Compositions

Persuasive essays are organized like any argument. Initially, you will want to focus in on the topic or issue of discussion, state your thesis, define terms, and present your argument in emphatic order. For instance, in the essay titled "Drugs," Gore Vidal clearly states his argument on how to stop most American drug addiction in his first paragraph: "Simply make all drugs available and sell them at cost." He then goes on to clarify and define some of the key issues, like *freedom of choice,* and in making parallels with an emotionally charged historical event (Prohibition and its failures), Vidal argues his thesis. Though chances are Vidal has not made us all *believers* of his thesis, he has at least made us consider the merit of his argument by the end of the essay, possibly giving us reason to evaluate and reevaluate our own positions on the issue.

Dealing with emotions can be very tricky. While appealing to a person's feelings may be the most direct way you have of convincing someone of your point of view, uncontrolled emotional appeals can also make you seem like an excitable author, one who is led by the passion of the moment. Just bear in mind that it is difficult for a reader to maintain a high level of emotional intensity in a composition, so you need to keep focused on your argument and limit your emotional appeal only to those responses that further your ultimate objective. For instance, don't be sentimental if you are hoping to enrage your reader.

Tips on Writing Persuasive Essays

1. Target your audience. That is, become acquainted with the values of those you address and use your knowledge of their likes, dislikes, fears, and prejudices when selecting words. Your objective here is to get your reader involved emotionally as well as intellectually in your topic.

2. Determine your reason(s) for bringing your reader around to your point of view. Do you want to convince him or her

that a problem exists? Do you want your reader to support a plan of action you have devised? Or do you want to disprove something another person has said?

3. When you develop the body of your essay, stay focused. Check your thesis occasionally to keep the controlling idea of your composition fresh in your mind. Make sure the facts and details in your body paragraphs have not wandered from your argument.

4. Integrate verifiable facts with information that is geared more to emotional responses than logical reasoning. Doing so will balance your composition, thus not appearing to be based on illogical conclusions from emotional reactions to your topic.

5. Maintain an ethical standpoint; enable your reader to "trust" your material.

Gore Vidal

Drugs

Born in 1925, Gore Vidal has been a controversial essayist, novelist, and social critic for the past four decades. He has successfully written all major forms of literature and is well known for novels like City and the Pillar *(1948),* Julian *(1964),* Myra Breckenridge *(1968),* 1876 *(1976),* Burr *(1981), and* Lincoln *(1984). Among his other works are* At Home: Essays 1982–1988 *(1988),* Empire *(1988),* Hollywood: A Novel of America in the 1920's *(1990),* Live from Golgotha *(1992),* The Gospel According to Gore Vidal *(1993),* United States Essays, 1951–1991 *(1993),* Palimpsest *(1995), and* The Smithsonian Institution *(1998),* Sexually Speaking: Collected Sex Writings *(1999),* The Golden Age *(2000),* The Last Empire: Essays 1992–2000 *(2001), and* Perpetual War for Perpetual Peace. *The following article, "Drugs," was written in 1970, and yet its content seems as relevant today as when he originally wrote it. People still look for solutions which would curb the tide of drug abuse in the United States against great odds. The recent discovery of CIA (Central Intelligence Agency) involvement in drug trafficking to inner cities to finance covert operations (e.g., the Iran/Contra affair) might suggest the government's lack of commitment to a sincere "war on drugs."*

Pre-reading Questions

1. Examine your present attitude toward drugs. When you hear the word *drugs*, what is the first thing that pops into your mind?

2. What is the current attitude toward drug use in American society? When and where is drug use socially acceptable?

1   It is possible to stop most drug addiction in the United States within a very short time. Simply make all drugs available and sell them at cost. Label each drug with a precise description of what effect—good and bad—the drug will have on the taker. This will require heroic honesty. Don't say that marijuana is addictive or dangerous when it is neither, as millions of people know—unlike "speed," which kills most unpleasantly, or heroin, which is addictive and difficult to kick.

2   For the record, I have tried—once—almost every drug and liked none, disproving the popular Fu Manchu theory that a single sniff of opium will enslave the mind. Nevertheless, many drugs are bad for certain people to take and they should be told why in a sensible way.

3   Along with exhortation and warning, it might be good for our citizens to recall (or learn for the first time) that the United States was the creation of men who believed that each man has the right to do what he wants with his own life as long as he does not interfere with his neighbor's pursuit of happiness (that his neighbor's idea of happiness is persecuting others does confuse matters a bit).

4   This is a startling notion to the current generation of Americans. They reflect a system of public education which has made the Bill of Rights, literally, unacceptable to a majority of high school graduates (see the annual Purdue reports) who now form the "silent majority"—a phrase which that underestimated wit Richard Nixon took from Homer, who used it to describe the dead.

5   Now one can hear the warning rumble begin: if everyone is allowed to take drugs everyone will and the GNP will decrease, the Commies will stop us from making everyone free, and we shall end up a race of Zombies, passively murmuring "groovy" to one another. Alarming thought. Yet it seems most unlikely that any reasonably sane person will become a drug addict if he knows in advance what addiction is going to be like.

6   Is everyone reasonably sane? No. Some people will always become drug addicts just as some people will always become alcoholics, and it is just too bad. Every man, however, has the power (and should have the legal right) to kill himself if he chooses. But since most men don't, they won't be mainliners either. Nevertheless, forbidding people things they like or think they might enjoy only makes them want those things all the more. This psychological insight is, for some mysterious reason, perennially denied our governors.

7   It is a lucky thing for the American moralist that our country has always existed in a kind of time-vacuum: we have no public memory of anything that happened before last Tuesday. No one in Washington today recalls what happened during the years alcohol was forbidden to the people by a Congress that thought it had a divine mission to stamp out Demon Rum— launching, in the process, the greatest crime wave in the country's history, causing thousands of deaths from bad alcohol, and creating a general (and persisting) contempt among the citizenry for the laws of the United States.

8   The same thing is happening today. But the government has learned nothing from past attempts at prohibition, not to mention repression.

9   Last year when the supply of Mexican marijuana was slightly curtailed by the Feds, the pushers got the kids hooked on heroin and deaths increased dramatically, particularly in New York. Whose fault? Evil men like the Mafiosi? Permissive Dr. Spock? Wild-eyed Dr. Leary? No.

10   The Government of the United States was responsible for those deaths. The bureaucratic machine has a vested interest in playing cops and robbers. Both the Bureau of Narcotics and the Mafia want strong laws against the sale and use of drugs because if drugs are sold at cost there would be no money in it for anyone.

11   If there was no money in it for the Mafia, there would be no friendly playground pushers, and addicts would not commit crimes to pay for the next fix. Finally, if there was no money in it, the Bureau of Narcotics would wither away, something they are not about to do without a struggle.

12   Will anything sensible be done? Of course not. The American people are as devoted to the idea of sin and its punishment as they are to making money—and fighting drugs is nearly as big a business as pushing them. Since the combination of sin and money is irresistible (particularly to the professional politician), the situation will only grow worse.

Post-reading Questions

Content

   1. Vidal states that it is possible to "stop most drug addiction in the United States within a very short time." What is the basis of his argument? Do you find it convincing or weak? Support your position.

2. What parallel do you see between Congress's mission to "stamp out the Demon Rum" earlier in this century and its present mission to punish drug users?

3. How persuasive is Vidal's claim that the American moralist "has always existed in a kind of time-vacuum"?

4. Some readers of this essay have taken offense at Vidal's use of masculine nouns and pronouns in paragraphs 3 and 6. What is your opinion of this? Do his references imply that only men will become drug users? How? Why or why not?

Strategies and Structures

1. Vidal balances logic and emotion in this essay to accomplish his objective. Where are some examples of sound reasoning (logic)? How does the author appeal to his reader's emotional prejudices toward drug use and drug users?

2. How well does Vidal address your concerns regarding drug use in American society? Does he seem to consider both sides of the issue carefully? How? What does he omit in his argument?

3. What is the effect of Vidal's final paragraph? How does it relate to his thesis? Why does he conclude a "reasonable" solution to America's drug problem is unrealistic?

4. How does Vidal establish himself as an authority on drug use? How would his argument be less persuasive if he had omitted his background on the issue?

Language and Vocabulary

1. How is Vidal's thesis echoed by simple word choice?

2. What words in this essay did you respond to emotionally? Were such words used to support his position on drugs or present the opposing point of view?

3. Check a *Who's Who in America* at your library for background information on Dr. Spock and Dr. Leary. What were they famous for doing? Why do you imagine Vidal refers to them?

Group Activities

1. Have each member of your group collect articles relating to drug use from different newspapers, magazines,

and journals for a week. When you meet again with your group, compare your findings. Were most of the articles you collected extremely biased? How? Were minorities unfairly associated with drug use?

2. Collect articles on alcohol abuse, alcohol consumption, and alcohol-related deaths in America for one week. Based on your findings, develop sound ethical reasons for readvocating Prohibition and present your material in a group forum.

Writing Activities

1. Write an essay refuting Vidal's conclusion that a reasonable solution to drug addiction will never be reached because "[t]he American people are as devoted to the idea of sin and its punishment as they are to making money—and fighting drugs is nearly as big a business as pushing them." Appeal to your reader on a logical and emotional level.

2. Develop an argument which persuades your reader that legalizing drugs and drug paraphernalia would decrease crime as well as disease. Consider both sides of the issue and address opposing points of view.

Phyllis McGinley

Women Are Better Drivers

Phyllis McGinley was a prolific essayist and poet. Her works include
One More Manhattan *(1937),* Times Three *(1961), and numerous
other books of poetry and several essay collections:* The Providence of
the Heart *(1959),* Sixpence in Her Shoe *(1964), and* Saint-Watching
(1969). McGinley first published the following article in The
American Weekly *in 1959. Of particular interest here is the way
McGinley approaches her topic by appealing to her reader logically,
ethically, and emotionally.*

Pre-reading Questions

1. Do you (or someone you know) tend to romanticize your
   automobile, bicycle, or motorcycle and treat it as something more than it is? Have you named your car? Do you
   use it to show off? (Respond to these questions in your
   journal.)

2. What do you think makes any set of standards meaningful and worth aspiring to? In what way does your *value
   system* help to determine your *standards?* Can one effectively argue that one set of values is better than another?
   Justify your response.

1   That men are wonderful is a proposition I will defend to the
death. Honest, brave, talented, strong and handsome, they are
my favorite gender. Consider the things men can do better
than women—mend the plumbing, cook, invent atom bombs,
design the Empire waistline and run the four-minute mile.
They can throw a ball overhand. They can grow a beard. In
fact, I can think of only two accomplishments at which women
excel. Having babies is one.

2   The other is driving an automobile.

3   Don't misunderstand me. Some of my best friends are male drivers. And they seldom go to sleep at the wheel or drive 90 on a 45-mile-an-hour road or commit any other of the sins of which statistics accuse them. But insurance companies have been busy as bees proving that I don't get around among the right people.

4   New York State—where I live—has even made it expensive to have sons. Car insurance costs much more if there are men in the family under 25 driving than if there are only women. Obviously the females of the species make the best chauffeurs.

5   They ought to. They get the most practice. Aside from truck and taxi drivers, it is women who really handle the cars of the nation. For five days of the week they are in command—slipping cleverly through traffic on their thousand errands, parking neatly in front of the chain stores, ferrying their husbands to and from commuting trains, driving the young to schools and dentists and dancing classes and Scout meetings. It is only on Saturdays and Sundays that men get their innings, not to speak of their outings, and it is over weekends when most of the catastrophes occur.

6   Not that men are responsible for *all* the accidents. Some are caused by women—by the little blonde on the sidewalk at whom the driver feels impelled to whistle. Or by the pretty girl sitting in the front seat for whom he wants to show off his skill, his eagle eye, and the way he can pull ahead of the fellow in the red sports car.

7   But it isn't caution and practice alone which make the difference between the sexes. It's chiefly an attitude of mind. Women—in my opinion—are the practical people. To them a car is a means of transportation, a gadget more useful, perhaps, than a dish washer or a can opener, but no more romantic. It is something in which we carry the sheets to the laundry, pick up Johnnie at kindergarten and lug home those rose bushes.

8   Men, the dear, sentimental creatures, feel otherwise. Automobiles are more than property. They are their shining chariots, the objects of their affections. A man loves his car the way the Lone Ranger loves his horse, and he feels for its honor on the road. No one must out-weave or out-race him. No one must get off to a better jack-rabbit start. And no one, but no one, must tell him anything while he's driving. My own husband, ordinarily the most good-tempered of men, becomes a tyrant behind the wheel. "Shouldn't we bear south here?" I inquire

meekly on our Saturday trips to the country. Or, "Honey, there's a gray convertible trying to pass."

9 "Who's driving?" he snarls like Simon Legree, veering stubbornly north or avoiding, by a hair, being run into.

10 Women drivers, on the other hand, *take* advice. They are used to taking it, having had it pressed on them all their lives by their mothers, teachers, beaus, husbands, and eventually their children. And when they don't know their routes exactly, they inquire at service stations, from passers by, from traffic officers. But men hate to ask and, when they are forced to do so, seldom listen.

11 Have you ever overheard a woman taking down directions on the phone? "Yes," she says affably. "I understand. I drive up that pretty road to the Danbury turn-off. Then I bear left at the little antique shoppe that used to be a barn—yellow with blue shutters. Then right at a meadow with two beech trees in it, and a couple of black cows. Up a little lane, just a tiny way beyond a cornfield, and that's your place. Yes. With a Tiffany-glass carriage lamp in front. Fine. I won't have any trouble." Nor does she.

12 A man has too much pride to take such precautions. "O.K." he says impatiently. "Two point seven miles off the Post Road. A left, a rotary, another left. Six point three to—oh, never mind. I'll look it up on the map."

13 When they don't insist on traveling by car, men travel by chart. I've nothing against road maps, really, except the way they clutter up the glove compartment where I like to keep tissues and sun glasses. But men have a furtive passion for them.

14 When my husband and I are planning a trip, he doesn't rush out like me to buy luggage and a new wardrobe. He shops for maps. For days ahead of time he studies them dotingly; then I am forced to study them en route. Many a bitter journey have I taken past the finest scenery in America with my eyes glued to a collection of black and red squiggles on a road map, instead of on the forest and canyons we had come all the way across the country to behold.

15 "Look!" I cry to him as we rush up some burning autumn lane. "Aren't the trees glorious!" "What does the map say?" he mutters. "I've marked a covered bridge about a quarter of a mile along here. That's where we turn." If we should ever approach the Pearly Gates together, I know exactly how the conversation will run. "See all the pretty stars," I'll be murmuring happily. "And, oh, do look over there! Isn't that the City of Gold?"

16   "Never mind your golden cities," he'll warn me sternly, as he nearly collides with a meteor. "Just keep your eye on the map."

Post-reading Questions

Content

1. Where is the controlling idea for the essay located?
2. What are some of the things McGinley concedes that men can do better than women? Are the items on her list all really compliments? Explain.
3. From the author's point of view, what are the major reasons for women being better drivers than men?
4. According to McGinley, in what ways are cars more than simply "property" to men?
5. Who was Simon Legree? How does reference to him firmly characterize the author's portrait of male drivers?
6. From whom have women had advice *"pressed on them all their lives"*? How does the author claim men usually respond to advice? Do you agree or disagree with her? Why or why not?

Strategies and Structures

1. How does the author's account of a typical trip by automobile illustrate differences in the male/female *mind-set?*
2. In what way does McGinley address "values" in order to argue her thesis? Do you find her argument persuasive?
3. What is the tone of McGinley's essay? How does it assist her in arguing her thesis? Why?
4. How does including dialogue in this essay add to its appeal?
5. The author concludes her essay with a comment on what it would be like to drive through the *"Pearly Gates"* with her husband. How do these comments thoroughly illustrate the difference in *attitudes* or *mind-sets* between men and women?

Language and Vocabulary

1. Vocabulary: *chauffeurs, routes, Tiffany-glass, furtive, dotingly.* After you locate definitions for all of the above words, return to *furtive* (an adjective) and *dotingly* (an adverb) and write a total of four origi-

nal sentences using each word as an adjective and an adverb. (You can locate the adverbial form of *furtive* and the adjective form of *dotingly* in your dictionary.)

2. What is the author referring to when she mentions the *"Pearly Gates"* and notices the *"City of Gold"*? How does an understanding of her allusion enrich a reader's sense of the final two paragraphs?

Group Activities

1. For an entire week, have each member of your group jot down daily observations of (1) how women tend to take advice as opposed to men, and (2) how women take down directions to get somewhere in contrast to men. At the end of a week, get together in your group and share your findings. Then prepare a brief class presentation wherein you refute or add support to McGinley's arguments.

2. Cruise around town, a shopping mall, or your campus with members in your group and note the particular driving habits of men and women. Based on what you witness, what generalizations can your group make about each gender? What stereotypes could you form? Are all stereotypes formed this way? Come to class with your group's stereotypes and conclusions about male and female drivers; be prepared to share your information with the rest of the class.

Writing Activities

1. Construct an essay persuading your readers of the superiority of women or men at performing some activity (e.g., cooking, parenting, or sports). Imitate the author's style by inserting humor into your writing.

2. Write an essay wherein you try to persuade your reader that men and women have fundamentally different conversational styles which bear a direct relationship to their behavior. Use plenty of representative examples drawn from personal experience, readings, and observations to support your argument.

Michael Dorris

Fetal Alcohol Syndrome

Arriving at Dartmouth in 1972, Michael Dorris joined and later directed the Native-American studies program there. Shortly after, he left to devote his time to writing. Dorris has many scholarly publications to his credit, including Native Americans: Five Hundred Years After *(1977) and* A Guide to Research on North American Indians *(1983). He also wrote* A Yellow Raft in Blue Water *(1987),* Rooms in the House of Stone *(1993),* Guests *(1994),* Morning Girl *(1994),* Paper Trail: Essays *(1995), and* Cloud Chamber: A Novel *(1997). He cowrote* The Crown of Columbus *(1992) with his wife, author/poet Louise Erdrich. Sadly, Dorris took his own life on April 11, 1997. Chronically depressed for years, Dorris had become overwhelmed with anxiety over the ending of his fifteen-year marriage to Erdrich and over allegations of sexual abuse. In his suicide note, he apologized for the "inconvenience" he caused and further stated: "I was desperate. I love my family and my friends and will be peaceful at last." Prior to his marriage to Erdrich in 1981, Dorris, a single parent, adopted three children. One of them, Adam, was a victim of fetal alcohol syndrome (FAS). The following essay was written as an epilogue for* The Broken Cord *(1989), a nonfiction book which chronicled his six-year scholarly study of FAS and his life with Adam.*

Pre-reading Questions

1. Freewrite with a focus on the topic of *alcohol*. What do you associate with drinking?

2. Have you ever read anything about fetal alcohol syndrome? Should the U.S. provide treatment centers for pregnant women who are alcoholics? Why or why not?

1   Since the publication of this book [*The Broken Cord*] in August 1989, several new scientific discoveries have corroborated the dangers of prenatal alcohol use. The *New England Journal of Medicine* (8/17/89) reported that drinking during breast-feeding may cause "slight but significant" damage to an infant's motor development. Year-old children of women who had one or more drinks a day scored lower on psychomotor tests than children whose mothers had less than one drink per day.

2   On January 11, 1990, the same journal published an even more startling finding—that women as a gender process alcohol differently from men. Dr. Charles S. Lieber and his colleagues in the United States and Italy announced, according to Gina Kolata's front-page *New York Times* report: "Women become drunk more quickly than men because their stomachs are less able to neutralize alcohol. . . . The finding is even more pronounced among alcoholic women, because the stomach apparently stops digesting alcohol at all." With less of the enzyme that breaks down alcohol, a proportionately greater part of what women drink enters the bloodstream as pure ethanol—30 percent more than for men of similar weight who drink the same amount. But men and women usually aren't the same weight, and therefore one drink for an average woman is roughly equivalent to two or more drinks for a man.

3   Laboratory researchers at Washington University in St. Louis, Missouri, had potentially disturbing news for alcoholic fathers as well. In January 1990 Dr. Theodore J. Cicero, a pharmacologist, described the results of an experiment in which "alcoholic" male rats were bred with healthy females. While their male offspring (the focus of the first study; female offspring will also be tested) had normal body weight at birth, they did not perform as well as their counterparts on memory tests in mazes. The study suggests that alcohol may damage the rat's sperm, thus passing on genetic defects in the same way as do other toxic substances.

4   Meanwhile, the number of drug-impaired babies continues to rise and preliminary research suggests that the long-term effects of illegal drugs, such as crack cocaine, on learning behavior are similar to those of ethanol. According to one recent survey, upwards of 11 percent of all infants born in the United States in 1988 tested positive for cocaine or alcohol the first time their blood was drawn. A New York City Health Department official estimated that births to drug-abusing mothers had increased there by about *3,000 percent* in the past ten years.

5   Why? Some causes are obvious. Only one residential treatment program (Odyssey House) for pregnant women exists in New York, where the State Assembly Committee on Alcoholism and Drug Abuse estimates that "twelve thousand babies will be born addicted in New York City in 1989, and the number of children in foster care has doubled in two years from twenty-seven thousand in 1987 to more than fifty thousand today, mainly because of parental drug abuse." Sixteen percent of all American women who give birth have had inadequate prenatal care—increasing to 33 percent for unmarried or teenage mothers, 30 percent for Hispanic mothers, and 27 percent for black women.

6   The effects of this neglect are by no means restricted to impoverished urban areas. *The Cardova* [Alaska] *Times* reported on August 3, 1989, that "Alaska has the highest estimated incidence of FAS babies in the nation, and certain portions of the state record the highest FAS rate among any population in the world."

7   Although the legislatures of Arizona, Illinois, Minnesota, Oregon, Pennsylvania, New Hampshire, and Florida have recently created study committees or passed laws aimed at addressing the needs both of pregnant alcohol and drug abusers *and* of their unborn babies, much more effort and funding are needed if an unprecedented national health crisis is to be averted. A drug-impaired baby is destined for, at best, an adult life of sorrow and deprivation, and at worst, for a fate governed by crime, victimization, and premature death. But fetal alcohol syndrome is preventable—it need not happen ever again. The future of society, in this instance more than in most, is in our hands. We can't claim ignorance any longer.

Post-reading Questions

Content
1. What is the focus of this essay?
2. What are the effects of prenatal alcohol abuse on the children of men and women who drink?
3. Where is there a residential treatment program for women who are alcoholics?
4. What state has the highest percentage of fetal alcohol syndrome?
5. In addition to alcoholism, what other drugs tend to impair babies at birth? What reasons does Dorris provide for the increase in such births?

Strategies and Structures

1. What effect does the use of statistics in this essay have on the reader?
2. How does Dorris's appeal to authority assist him in establishing himself as ethical, logical, and trustworthy as an author? In what way is his essay emotionally charged?
3. In what way does the author's use of transitions and linking devices provide a sense of chronology and coherence in this essay?
4. How does Dorris's early argument of fact lead to his call for immediate action in the concluding paragraph?
5. How might society itself be responsible for the perpetuation of fetal alcohol syndrome?

Language and Vocabulary

1. Vocabulary: *corroborated, prenatal, motor development, psychomotor, neutralize, enzyme, ethanol, pharmacologist, toxic, unprecedented, deprivation, victimization, fetal alcohol syndrome.* After establishing the definitions of these words, use several of the words in a paragraph, written from the point of view of the baby suffering with fetal alcohol syndrome, persuading people not to use alcohol and/or drugs.
2. In what way is Dorris's word usage scientific or matter-of-fact? Does he use any figurative language to discuss FAS? Explain what reasons he may have had for his choice of words.

Group Activities

1. Research the issue of fetal alcohol syndrome by looking in popular magazines or medical journals for a class forum. Take advantage of the resources on your campus; interview drug-awareness counselors or health service individuals. What you may want to do is to have each group focus on one social, economic, or ethnic group. This way every group will have something unique to contribute at the forum. Ultimately, determine ways that you, as members of the community, can assist in the elimination of fetal alcohol syndrome.

2. To determine the effects of drinking in a different arena, contact the police academy on your campus or the police department in your community and, as a group, quiz them in order to obtain the sort of facts and statistics that Dorris uses to substantiate his claims in the essay. Keep the information that your group uncovers for Writing Activity 1.

Writing Activities

1. Using several facts and statistics drawn from Group Activity 2, back up the emotionally charged issue of what would be a just punishment for those who commit manslaughter while driving under the influence. Your persuasive essay should initially contain an argument of fact, and throughout your essay you should urge your reader that the punishment you prescribe is logical, fair, and just. (In other words, don't rely on "an eye for an eye, a tooth for a tooth" reasoning.)

2. Write an essay in which you illustrate the seriousness of a social issue and convince your readers that action must be taken immediately to address the situation. Attempt to engage the readers' emotions and stir them into action using statistics and specific examples.

Tammerlin Drummond

Never Too Old
Sexually Active Seniors Are One of the Fastest-Growing HIV-Infected Populations in the U.S.

Tammerlin Drummond, whose articles are frequently featured in Time *magazine, writes on issues of immediate social concern. In the following essay, for instance, Drummond examines the little-known fact that as we move into the new millennium, senior citizens constitute the fastest-growing segment of HIV-infected patients in the United States.*

Pre-reading Questions

1. What do you consider "sexually active"? Which age group do you think is the most promiscuous and why?
2. Make a list of qualities and activities you associate with "senior citizens." Upon what did you base your insights? Television? Movies? Parents, grandparents, aunts, uncles?

1 Sue Saunders, a Fort Lauderdale, Fla., grandmother, had the symptoms: rapid weight loss, rashes, fever. But when she went to her local health clinic, a nurse asked incredulously, "What's an old woman like you doing getting an HIV test?"

2 Saunders' positive result came as a shock to the nurse, but it shouldn't have. Seniors are one of the fastest-growing HIV-infected populations in the U.S. Sunny south Florida, a magnet for retirees, has the largest concentration of people 50 or older with HIV. Seniors account for 14% of AIDS cases in Dade, Broward and Palm Beach counties, compared with 10% nationally. "You've got people contracting it later in life," says Drace Langford, a member of the Florida HIV/AIDS and Aging Task Force. But there are also seniors who have been living

with HIV for years, thanks to the effectiveness of the new AIDS "cocktails."

3   Before blood screening became mandatory, most older people got HIV from transfusions. But since such transmissions have been all but eliminated, medical workers are being forced to confront the fact that seniors are getting infected primarily during sex. Promiscuity is common in senior centers, where the ratio of women to men averages 7 to 1. Since fear of pregnancy is no longer a concern, many seniors don't use condoms. And Viagra has added more fuel to an already volatile mix. Physically fit single men, dubbed "condominium Casanovas," often flit from one woman to the next, sometimes passing along AIDS. Widowers often hire prostitutes. The manager of a Miami apartment complex once asked former Miami Beach geriatric counselor Vincent Delgado to speak to an 82-year-old woman who brought young men to her apartment for sex whenever she got her Social Security checks. "She said she was going to die anyway," Delgado said, "and to leave her alone and let her enjoy life."

4   Public health officials blithely assumed that seniors weren't at risk because, of course, they didn't have sex. But the increasing numbers are challenging that assumption. The American Association of Retired Persons has produced an AIDS-prevention video called *It Could Happen to Me*, which is distributed to senior citizens nationwide. Meanwhile, public health officials are handing out condoms at senior complexes, offering free HIV tests and training a cadre of the elderly as counselors to help educate their peers about the dangers of unsafe sex.

5   Even so, this demographic group is often difficult to reach. Many elderly people are reluctant to discuss their intimate life with strangers. "A lot of people were taught that you don't air your dirty laundry," says John Gargotta, supervisor for the Senior HIV Intervention Project, an AIDS advocacy group. Most troubling, though, is that doctors often fail to consider HIV as a possible illness among their senior patients. As a result, the elderly are often misdiagnosed. Also, AIDS symptoms like dementia and weight loss can mimic the ravages of old age. "So there is a higher prevalence of people being diagnosed in the month of death," says Dr. Karl Goodkin, an associate professor at the University of Miami School of Medicine. Goodkin, who is conducting a national study on the rate of cognitive impairment in HIV-infected elderly, says the virus proceeds to full-blown AIDS twice as fast in seniors, making early detection all the more crucial.

6   Early intervention saved Sue Saunders. Her HIV was diagnosed eight years ago, but she is alive today, thanks in part to

protease inhibitors. Meanwhile, she has made it her mission to warn others about the dangers of high-risk sex in the golden years. 'I'd just like to save one life," she says.

Post-reading Questions

Content

1. Why was Saunders' HIV positive result a shock to the nurse and to most other people?
2. Before blood-screening became mandatory, how did most seniors become HIV positive?
3. What is an AIDS "cocktail?" (You may need to research the answer to this question in your library or online.)
4. The author contends that "widowers often hire prostitutes" as a partial explanation for how seniors get AIDS. Is she convincing? How might further representative examples strengthen her argument?
5. Why are senior citizens often the most difficult group to reach when teaching about "the dangers about unsafe sex"?

Strategies and Structure

1. How does Drummond use statistics to support her discussion points? Do her statistics seem convincing? Why or why not?
2. Subtitles are frequently used to enable readers to predict what will happen in an essay. How well does Drummond's subtitle fulfill this function and why? What would you have predicted about the essay without the subtitle?
3. How does Drummond develop her essay? That is, in what way does she unify her information and establish a clear sense of direction from the beginning to the end of her essay?
4. Explain how the shock value of the author's material establishes a powerful call to action that practicing safe sex has no age barrier?
5. Describe the tone of the essay. What does it add to Drummond's informative exposition?

Language and Vocabulary

1. Vocabulary: *HIV, incredulously, effectiveness, transfusion, transmission, promiscuity, Viagra, volatile, condominium, Casanova, blithely, cadre, advocacy,*

dementia, mimic, prevalence, cognitive, impairment, protease inhibitors. Make a two-part list in which you place all the words above that have to do with medicine in column one and the others in column two. How does the author's diction (word choice) reinforce the seriousness of her topic?

2. Take another look at the list you made in question one. Note how many words tend to be argumentative in nature. Write something about how the author's words could be even more persuasive in convincing seniors to be more aware and thus more careful about the dangers of indiscriminate sex.

Group Activities

1. Assemble in small groups and make a list of five-to-ten questions each member will use to interview seniors in their community. Ask them what they think of this essay. (You probably will have to paraphrase it for them.) When you get back together, share your responses and establish some statistics of your own.
2. Carefully go back through Drummond's essay noting the strengths and weaknesses of her argument. Next divide the class into two parts. The first group will research information on the Internet to back up the author's claim. The second group will seek facts and statistics to disprove what she says. Finally, have each group debate the reality and consequences of sexually active seniors.

Writing Activities

1. Compare and contrast the emotional and physical needs of senior citizens as presented in Barrett's essay "Old Before Her Time" in Chapter 3 and Drummond's essay "Never Too Old."
2. How did this essay contradict your impressions of senior citizens, and how do you feel about them now? Compose an essay relating your feelings about this topic. In what way does innocence affect our perceptions differently than experience?

Bruce Henderson

Recent Developments

Bruce Henderson is a Professor of English at Fullerton College in Southern California. Educated at Oberlin College, the University of Washington (Seattle), and State University of New York at Albany, he has published poetry and academic and journalistic articles for countless magazines, anthologies, and newspapers such as the Orange County Weekly *and* Wishbone *zine. Henderson currently serves as editor of* inside english, *the professional journal of the English council of California Community Colleges. During ten years of residence in Southern California, he has become a local activist for preserving the environment through the Sierra Club and other organizations, and he continues critical research on future large-scale planned developments.*

Pre-reading Questions

1. What is a "smart" house or "smart" car? What advantages do each promise, and what might be the frequently unmentioned disadvantages?

2. What would be your ideal home and why? Bearing your immediate impressions in mind, freewrite with focus, explaining your feelings about the need for, or indifference to, privacy in your ideal home.

1   The housing tract in which I currently reside could almost be described as socialist. Not because of politics, but because in some ways it defies the American Dream of the single-family home with white picket fence and private swimming pool in the back yard, which the homeowner mows, edges and occasionally rototills. Instead, no one homeowner owns the land—technically, we all do. Each little house sits near its share of greenbelt, open

central lawn with communal swimming pool, playground area or open field. My development was built in the early 1970s, in the bygone era of "low-density." We pay a modest association fee to hire a crew of professional gardeners to do the mowing, edging, tree-trimming, rototilling and so forth.

2   A brand-new housing tract is now under construction about ten miles away, called Ladera, which my fiancée and I toured recently. It is being heavily promoted to young families who seek the relatively wide open spaces of South Orange County in which to raise their kids (two-thirds of the people of Orange County live in North Orange County, and L.A. County is even more densely populated). The site itself used to be pristine rolling hills about 15 miles from the Pacific Ocean. The Los Angeles *Times* has featured Ladera in front page stories and a special local real estate section, making one wonder whether the newspaper made investments in the project. To our surprise we even saw the new development appear in an ad on the screen of a local movie theater.

3   These home models tout the latest technical innovation: hookup to the Internet. Ladera is thus advertised as a forward-looking "online community" where neighbors will be able to communicate with one another at the click of a mouse. In fact, according to their brochure, as the homes are built in the usual phased construction, the available units do not just become available, they "come online."

4   Signs, flags and banners herald our approach to the model homes located off a brand-new parkway apparently built expressly to provide access to this instant city of what will eventually be over 8,000 houses. We park on a leveled dirt parking area alongside mostly sport utility vehicles and late-model cars. The development broadcasts its trademarked marketing theme: "Roots. And Wings," in brochures and on specially labeled bottles of spring water given away as promotional tools at a stand next to a makeshift bus stop at which prospective buyers can board a jitney to view home sites. An unintended irony of this theme, of course, is that building the project necessitates destruction of natural animal and plant habitat— the real roots and wings which have been displaced.

5   As you approach the model homes you notice that the "yard" or lot in which it is set consists of a narrow pathway hugging the house walls which barely affords room for an outdoor bench, a birdhouse and a path to the trash cans. This arrangement, of course, is designed to maximize the number of homes which can be squeezed onto the overall parcel of land upon

which Ladera is being built; in short, this is clearly a high-density development.

6   Inside, the houses maximize large windows and high atrium/entryways. My first thought is that, given how closely the homes will be packed together, buyers will need to install a lot of curtains to maintain privacy. We also note that the walls do not afford much unwindowed space for bookcases, but enough for, say, a TV stand or a wine rack. Upstairs, the bedrooms have been decorated with photos from the 1950s, and 40s swing music plays from hidden speakers. At first we are puzzled by this retro decor, until we realize that the intent is to subliminally conjure for the target customers, baby boomers with kids, the atmosphere of their original childhood homes.

7   We also find, upstairs, the specially built closet to house the computer Internet hookups and equipment. Reading further in the Ladera brochure, this Ladera Life network will enable residents to "publish community news" and "link residents to one another, local businesses, community, social and recreational activities and to the World Wide Web." All this sounds exciting and forward-looking until we read about how the hookup will beam in messages from a "select number of businesses dedicated to providing goods and services to Ladera Ranch." The fine print on the brochure, so small that many would need a magnifying glass to decipher the words, announces that homeowners will pay for the hookup "whether or not they choose to use the highspeed data service, and whether or not they obtain any benefit . . . from such services . . . monthly equipment fees, franchise fees and/or applicable sales tax additional."

8   How many homeowners will resist using the data service, especially since they must pay for it regardless? So the arrangement becomes clear: Ladera Life will in effect function as a vehicle for piping in advertisements and offers from area businesses concerning virtually every aspect of living, whether business, social or recreational. Big Brother may not be watching you, but he will be exhorting you, via the compulsory Internet hookup, to buy vacation packages, to shop at particular markets, and to buy a membership at the local gym. Furthermore, a community organization with the acronym LARCS (Ladera Ranch Community Services) will "host a spectrum of innovative community-based activities." The fine print warns that "Membership is automatic" and will be funded by "community enhancement fees on residential sales and resales, nondeductible contributions, user fees, corporate alliances and

partnerships. . . ." Translation: an activity organization which you will pay for, whether you want to participate or not, will orchestrate community-oriented activities which, ominously, involve corporate alliances.

9 We realize we are out of camera film and take a break in our touring to drive to the nearest store to buy more. As we enter the market we are struck by the upscale fare. This is no 7-Eleven; the store features a long deli case full of prepared delicacies, plus a plethora of fully stocked wine racks with announcements of tasting events. Adjacent businesses seem even less practical than the market: nail parlors, beauty salons, florists. Neighborhood stores usually cater to the budgets and tastes of those living in the neighborhood, so it becomes evident who the intended buyers of Ladera Ranch homes will be, which is also a strong indication of the selling prices of these new homes. The most expensive models will sell for over $1,000,000.

10 However, the more modest homes (the brochure pledges that some will be priced at "less than $200,000") seem to be represented by the models we return to, which are priced at about $265,000. We notice an outside balcony on one that reminds me of an experience I had in Disneyland. While you could actually enter the ground-floor building, the second story was severely foreshortened, so that while it appeared that people could sit on the balcony as in a classic western town, in fact the "balcony" was only about two feet wide and the "staircase" which appeared to lead up to it could not really be used. So it was with the "balcony" on the Ladera model home; the railings appeared to be carved ornamental wood, but were really flat boards cleverly shaped by machine to resemble custom work. I would not be too confident in stepping out of the second-story bedroom onto this "balcony" and leaning on its flimsy railing, nor was this "balcony" actually open to the touring public.

11 As we finally drove out of the development, we were startled to notice a dead coyote lying on the shoulder of the parkway directly opposite the Ladera entrance road. Massive grading is underway by armies of bulldozers droning through the hills, and of course trees, shrubbery and other cover and food for wildlife are the first features to be cleared. Antonio Parkway will soon be a busy thoroughfare with cars whizzing by at all hours of the day and night, sometimes inevitably killing animals who formerly ranged freely on the land and don't know any better but to try to cross the road.

12 One might argue that people need houses to live in, and new developments such as Ladera easily win the approval of

most city councils and chambers of commerce based on the lure of new tax revenues and more bodies to shop at local stores. But what are the real long-range costs? With over 8,000 new homes, Ladera alone will dump upwards of 16,000 cars on local roads, typically for several trips each per day. Then there is the question of infrastructure. Who is going to build all the new elementary schools, the additions to or expansion of the local high schools to accommodate all those new kids? Who will build the libraries and fire stations? Who will pay for adding additional lanes to existing roads to accommodate all that extra traffic?

13   One answer, of course, is local taxpayers, who never had any real vote about whether they wanted more development in the first place. An item mentioned on the Ladera Web site, though not in the brochures they hand out, concerns Mello-Roos, cleverly characterized as an advantage to the new homebuyers in that they can move more quickly (than local government might) to get community facilities up and running. What Mello-Roos really does is pass the expenses of infrastructure on to the homebuyers themselves in the form of a mandatory surcharge on their mortgage payments, rather than developers taking any responsibility for the considerable expenses involved.

14   In fact, many of the builders and subcontractors who put up these tracts are not even based in California, but in states such as Texas or Arizona. They come in, slap up the houses, and go home; they do not plan to live there themselves, nor be around for whatever the consequences may be. In some notorious cases, developers building on hillsides in Orange County ignored long-standing geology reports indicating underground streams, so that with the first winter rains homes slid down the hill, or else foundations cracked as the homes "settled." Another obvious problem with building on any hills, of course, is that California is earthquake country. But building on hills means views, which serve as an excuse to overprice the home, so the temptation proves too much for many builders. Other new home buyers suffer the consequences of plain old shoddy construction. In San Juan Capistrano some homes were built so poorly that just about everything that could go wrong with them did. While it is possible to sue the builders, this can prove difficult since the web of independent subcontractors all point fingers at each other, or else are impossible to even track down, and in any case the home buyers' money is tied up for years in litigation, while they may have to resort to renting temporary shelter after being forced to leave an unsafe house.

15   The pressure for new developments in turn leads to pressure for new roads, not just to handle future volumes of traffic, but more importantly to provide highway access for future commuters. In fact Orange County has recently seen the construction of a network of new toll roads, privately funded through bonds and private investors, and therefore beyond the reach of many existing regulatory rules. One unfortunate result is that a new toll road is being planned to bisect an existing state park in South Orange County, where people pitch tents or park RVs to camp near the ocean. Along the route of another toll road already built through the Laguna Hills, the names of eleven new "cities" (huge future housing developments) have already been copyrighted. In a county with little effective public transportation, such a long-range increase in residential density flirts with disaster, but only for residents, not the out-of-state-developers.

16   In nearby California counties development is actively discouraged by limiting access to water rights, as in San Luis Obispo and Monterey counties. Merely buying a parcel on which to build does not allow you to build immediately, but only when your site comes up in its due turn on the local water list, which in some instances could take as long as ten years. Many prospective builders/buyers instead opt to buy an existing home rather than wait for the right to build new ones. In the city of Santa Barbara there is a statute forbidding construction of any new walls. An owner may get a permit to add a second story, for example, but not to build out with a new addition, and certainly not to build additional homes.

17   Such tactics might seem undemocratic, but what about those people who in fact moved there first and have been part of the local community for years? The very reasons they might have moved there in the first place could be threatened by massive new construction, which can also affect the value of their existing homes, and could even result in a new toll road running through their backyard.

18   And finally, there are environmental issues, including runoff and erosion, pollution of the ocean, destruction of native plants and wildlife, the filling in of natural wetlands and other significant potential problems. One has to wonder just how many people the Western environment can sustain, given real limits to sources of fresh water. Already several states are fighting over access to Colorado river water. and fantastic schemes have been proposed for bringing more fresh water to the area. Indeed, the story of Los Angeles has historically been

the story of finding water to slake the thirst of an ever-expanding population, from the draining of the Owens Valley to the defeated proposal to build a multibillion dollar Peripheral Canal to drain San Francisco Bay. Greed and need must be balanced against preservation of the environment for all to enjoy, and against a standard of living which, despite the rosy and cozy promises of the Ladera Ranch brochure, may be inevitably developed into decline.

Post-reading Questions

Content

1. What seems to be some of the major difference in the *low-density* housing developments of the 1970s and the *high-density* housing developments of the late 1990s and early twenty-first century?

2. Who will end up paying for all the community services, roads, and so on for new *high-density* homes? Would this arrangement be fair? Why or why not?

3. Explain what Henderson meant by "Big Brother may not be watching you, but he will be exhorting you, via the compulsory Internet hookup . . . " (paragraph 8).

4. Henderson asserts "many of the builders or subcontractors who put up these tracts are not even based in California, but in Texas or Arizona." What have they and other developers frequently ignored, and what were the consequences?

5. Ultimately, what effect will more and more housing tracts have on the environment, national parks, and area resources (water, gas, electricity)? What specific examples does Henderson provide to illustrate his points?

Strategies and Structures

1. In what way does Henderson's use of first person narrative figuratively lead readers through the housing developments to which he refers?

2. Why does Henderson spend his introductory paragraph discussing the housing tract that he lives in as "almost socialist"? How does this prepare readers for his analysis of the Ladera housing tract? If Henderson's own *low-density* housing is "almost socialist," how would you characterize the Ladera tract?

3. What sort of linking words and phrases—transitional words—does Henderson use in his essay? How do they assist in indicating time and space order?

4. How does Henderson's use of irony in this essay help to highlight issues he finds outrageous with respect to recent developments in his neighborhood? Also, how is humor expressed though ironic points to alert readers to the downside of smart housing tracts—readers who might have otherwise have been defensive about his criticism?

5. In his concluding paragraph, what "call to action" does Henderson make to his readers? How do the contents of his essay lead logically and ethically to his conclusion?

Language and Vocabulary

1. Vocabulary: *socialist, pristine, tout, innovation, brochures, prospective, irony, necessitates, habitat, displaced, maximize, high-density, atrium, retro, subliminally, conjure, exhorting, compulsory, spectrum, enhancement, residential, alliances, plethora, adjacent, balcony, thoroughfare, whizzing, inevitably, commerce, infrastructure, accommodate, mortgage, subcontractors, shoddy, litigation, regulatory, copyrighted, opt, statute, sustain.* After checking the definitions for each of the above vocabulary words, make three lists and label one "Descriptive Words," another "Technological Terms," and still another "Legal Language." Next, based on your knowledge of each word's dictionary and suggested meanings, place them on the appropriate list and attempt to use at least three of the words in your next essay.

2. Which words, phrases, and passages in this essay do you find particularly ironic (see Glossary) and why?

Group Activities

1. In groups of two or so, go visit an "open house" for a housing tract or a mobile home park or a "grand opening" at a shopping mall, restaurant, and so on. Gather as much literature or verbal information about the place as possible, and then draft a brief description of the place. Finally, critique how accu-

rately the *open house* or *grand opening* portrayed itself in advertising materials.

2. Gather together in groups of four or five people and discuss the references and examples Henderson uses to illustrate his points and draw his conclusions. To what extent does your group agree with Henderson's analysis of housing tracts? Please justify your answers.

Writing Activities

1. Write an essay wherein you reflect upon, describe, and/or critique some sort of recent development where you live. You need not restrict yourself to houses, shopping malls, or business buildings. New freeways, roads, dams, airports, water treatment plants, subways, and so on would be equally vivid examples of the good and bad side of any development.

2. Does development bring greater benefits in terms of taxes, housing opportunities, and convenience, than it does problems in terms of environmental degeneration and disruption of communities? Take a position on this issue, and then write an argumentative essay, persuading readers of your position. Support and analyze all claims with examples drawn from personal experience, observations, and readings.

A North Chinese/Vietnamese Elder As Told To James M. Freeman

I Want to Live Without Trouble

James M. Freeman, professor of anthropology, has focused his teaching, research, and community service on India and Indochinese refugees. His most significant publications are Untouchables: An Indian Life History *(1979) and* Hearts of Sorrow: Vietnamese-American Lives *(1989), which won a 1990 American Book Award and the Outstanding Book Award of the Association for Asian-American Studies. In the following excerpt from* Hearts of Sorrow: Vietnamese-American Lives, *the speaker, identified as a "North Chinese / Vietnamese Elder," lived under communist rule for more than twenty years before, unwillingly, he immigrated to America. This, in part, may explain his rather critical attitude toward American society and Vietnamese refugees in particular.*

Pre-reading Questions

1. How do you feel about America? Would you die for it? Why or why not?
2. Is it more important to be an individual or a part of a group in American society? Why?
3. What do you believe makes living in America desirable? How can a person be considerate toward others if he or she is preoccupied with making money?

1   During the time of French rule, those of us who were Chinese were set apart from others. People were afraid that when

the Chinese gained wealth, they'd send it back to China. As a Chinese, I was considered a foreigner, and I carried Chinese papers. Because of this, when I was in high school, I was exempt from entrance exams and could enter the high school.

2   When the Communists took over, our position at first was good because China was considered close friends with North Vietnam. They praised China, and so the Chinese participated in all activities from 1954 to around 1960 or 1962. As a minority group, the Chinese had privileges reserved for them, such as entrance into the university without high grades.

3   The treatment of the Chinese depended on how friendly Vietnam and China were at any moment. When war broke out between China and Vietnam, we were asked to leave. I was expelled because I allowed a relative to stay in my house illegally, that is, I failed to report to the proper authorities that someone had come to live in my house. For this, my neighbors distrusted me. Actually, I was not expelled by any official document. Rather, they used my relative's visit as a pretext to put pressure on me, with veiled and indirect threats. The Administrative Committee of the Ward invited me to meet with them. The Public Security Agent explained, "For your protection against the Chinese aggression, we have to bring you to another place in the countryside." When I came back home, the Public Security Agent came to my house and asked, "Do you have any relatives in Hong Kong? You should leave."

4   After that, I understood that I could no longer stay on in Hanoi. I said, "I am poor; I have no relatives in Hong Kong."

5   The Public Security Agent said, "See if you can sell anything, even the door, but not the house, to give you the money to go."

6   The house was very big; that's why they didn't want to let us sell it. We were very bewildered. We were now old. I had no career except my government job. How could we survive? I didn't actually want to go, but so many of our relatives had left already, and that gave me a very good impetus, urged me to go.

7   I had lived all my life around Hanoi; I had never been to other provinces, never to South Vietnam. Many of my friends and relatives never thought I would go; they were quite surprised when I left for Hong Kong. My wife's sister, resident in America for six months, sponsored us, and three months later, we arrived in the United States.

8   When I lived in North Vietnam, even though I was not hungry, the food was meager. Even though I had money, I couldn't buy much food. My entire monthly salary was not enough to

cover our food needs. For a North Vietnamese arriving in America, it is really paradise; we can buy food so easily, so cheaply! I live on public assistance. President Reagan wants to cut our aid. I don't think his cuts will affect us much, and I accept them because of his big efforts to resist the Communists. That's on the physical life, the material life.

9   I have talked with many Vietnamese, and they say that even though they have a good material life, their sentimental life is not good, not relaxed, not at ease. Those Vietnamese who are less than 30 years of age will be integrated into American society. Those people who are 30 to 50 years old and those over 50 still miss their old society; they cannot fully integrate. If 50 years later the two cultures can be integrated, then the people will feel more at home. Once people live here, they must have an American soul. When people think of becoming a United States citizen, they think of the benefits, the jobs, the travel abroad. They never think, for example, of patriotism, of attachment or devotion to their adopted country. But if they think only of benefits, what will they do if there is aggression against the United States? Will they stand and fight for their country, or will they run away?

10   If you don't have a good foundation, no ideals, no attachment, then you won't die for your country. The majority of Vietnamese are like that now. They are not devoted to America. I think that America should create those kinds of people who will fight for their country. That should be the criterion for education in America.

11   The bad thing about America is that there is too much freedom. Americans think only about the maximization of profit, what they can do that will benefit themselves. There is too much individualism and freedom of one group at the expense of others, with little concern for the common good. Every community thinks of itself too much, not of the country, so people can sell secrets to the Russians just for money, for profit.

12   Some U.S. Congressmen proposed measures to lessen accidents on the highways, but other Congressmen and lobbyists opposed this because it affects capitalists. If a proposal for the good of everybody affects their profits, companies lobby or buy off the Congressmen.

13   Because of the division between legislative, judicial, and executive branches, the president is always affected. Every time he wants to make a decision he is controlled and hindered; he has to consult with the legislative branch and he cannot make quick and good decisions. The presidential term is only four

years. How can all of the projects or plans be carried out in such a short time? Leaders can have a long-range view on many matters, maybe 20 years, but their term is too short to carry it out.

14 Because of too much freedom, Americans are so *careless* about so many things. When they go out on the streets, they do not wear shirts, or dresses, some use the flag for shorts and for trousers. But the flag is symbolic of the country.

15 Many people who stretch their legs on the bus don't leave room for other people. Some women put handbags on the seats and don't let others sit down. I use the bus often; I see such disregard for people.

16 On American Independence Day, not many houses hang out flags. People are individualistic, and even neighbors do not know one another's names. One night, an old American man was robbed near my house; his wallet was taken, but no one seemed to care. Passersby watched as the man was dragged into the bushes and robbed. They did nothing.

17 Another point of too much freedom: Americans do not have many children, and the trend to remain single is on the rise. In my view, a superpower should have as many people as possible to be strong. Compare the populations of other superpowers; many are populous; many countries are really scared about the population of China.

18 If the Constitution could be changed and not too much freedom were allowed, I think America would be better off. For example, freedom of the press is excessive. If they would try to help and say something good about the government instead of criticizing it, they could not be exploited by the Russians, who use these negatives in their propaganda.

19 In the American educational system, both technology and human relations and values should be given equal emphasis. Family values, such as relationships between grandparents, parents, and children, should be introduced into the educational system. Too much emphasis is put on technology to the neglect of humans, so that when people grow up, they only think of money and profits at the expense of everything else. That's all they know.

20 I have tried to be humble. I've been here only a short time, but the things I've told you are really big. People think too much about themselves. They are too selfish, too individualistic.

21 There's much that's good in America. In their deeds, Americans are energetic and great; they do great things. When I came here to live, I found in my contacts with Americans that

they were honest. If a teacher doesn't know something, he doesn't pretend; instead, he says he doesn't know. When I was in high school, I took a philosophy class in which the teacher made a mistake. He stated the wrong century in which Auguste Comte was born. A student discovered that. The teacher, in trying to cover this up, said, "There are two Auguste Comtes." What I like about Americans is that they admit they don't know.

22   Vietnamese refugees in the United States are very much anti-Communist. They try to identify those who show some sympathy with Communism. It is not accidental that in the last two years (1982–1984) two people (elsewhere in America) have been murdered, for they openly praised the Communist regime. When a respected professor wrote an article in which he referred to Ho Chi Minh as "Uncle Ho," people got very angry: "He's not our uncle; he destroyed the country."

23   Once I met some South Vietnamese military officers who said, "I hate Americans. Because of American policy we lost and have to suffer here."

24   I replied, "You should not complain about this because America should put the interests of its own 200 million people first, above those of South Vietnam's 20 million. All Vietnamese suffered, not just you." They became quite angry at my remarks. Because I come from the North, people believe I sympathize with the Communists. This makes it difficult to live, and now I'm very cautious. I'm old now; I don't want to have trouble, just to live in peace. My family heredity is that people do not live long. I don't want to do anything to affect my life. I just want to live a few more years.

Post-reading Questions

Content

1. Throughout this essay, the author expresses a fear of strangers. What are some of the more effective examples of this? How does this fear or distrust of strangers serve the purpose of his essay?

2. How does the author's discussion of Americans as careless, inconsiderate people relate to his theme of a society with too much freedom?

3. What parallels does the North Chinese/Vietnamese Elder draw between the perils of the Vietnamese society he grew up in and those faced in the United States? Do you think his earlier experiences in

Vietnam influenced his later critical view of America? Why?

4. According to the author, what dangers to American society are brought about by too much individualism?

Strategies and Structures

1. Why does the author begin his essay by recounting his experiences as a Chinese minority in Vietnam? What foundation does this lay for the rest of the essay?

2. Why does the author conclude his essay on a positive note? What purpose does this serve? What impressions are you left with in regard to the author?

3. The author constantly reminds us that he is an ethnic minority, no matter where he has lived. How has this fact influenced the way he observes the world around him? In what way does this repetition provide a "cohesive" (linking) device for the essay as a whole?

4. To what extent does the author support the arguments he presents to the reader? Why, in some instances, does his method of writing evoke an emotional response from you? Cite specific examples that particularly inflamed you.

Language and Vocabulary

1. Vocabulary: *aggression, capitalism, communism, criterion, individualistic.* Write down your personal definitions for each of these words. Then, on a separate piece of paper titled "Dictionary Definitions," write down the literal (dictionary) definitions of the words. (*Note:* Some of these words are concepts and require a lengthy explanation; to do justice to this assignment, avoid attempting shortcuts.) Compare the differences between what you associate with the words and what their real definitions are. Finally, after considering the literal and your personal definitions, write a short persuasive essay in which you develop a thesis and argue an issue about one of the words (e.g., aggression is healthy, capitalism is bad).

2. Choose six words from the essay that evoke an emotional response in you and write a paragraph in which you use those words to refute the argument that there is too much freedom in America.

Group Activities

1. Assemble the class into two groups: one advocating complete freedom and the other advocating totalitarianism, and prepare for a two-round debate. For round 1, appeal primarily to your audience's emotions (pathos). Then, during round 2, rationally argue and defend your group's point of view. Follow up the class debate with an evaluation of the most effective methods of persuasion.

2. Write a collaborative, persuasive essay on one of the themes in this essay (e.g., Americans lack devotion to their country) wherein your group attempts to achieve an ideal balance among logic, ethics, and emotions.

Writing Activities

1. Do you believe that an individual's obsession with money has driven him or her to ignore his or her brothers and sisters? Is less personal concern about freedom and money the only way for people to care about fellow human beings? Write a persuasive essay based on your point of view.

2. Is blind allegiance to one's country the only way to demonstrate loyalty or patriotism, or in this highly technical age, is the "one world" concept more important? Integrating fact with emotion, write a persuasive argument based on this issue.

Additional Topics and Issues for Writing Persuasive Essays

1. Write an essay in which you persuade the school to give you a scholarship. You will want to consider why you are a worthy beneficiary and how your scholarship will further your education.

2. Devise an original thesis about the current position of men, women, children, and/or elderly people in American society. Then write a persuasive essay calling for a change in the way they are presently treated.

3. Write an essay in which you persuade your audience that general education courses are useless. How do you expect

college to prepare you for your major? In what way do general education courses assist you in achieving your goals? Avoid arguments like "I could get my college degree a lot sooner if I did not have to have a general education."

4. Write an essay persuading your classmates and families to discontinue the use of plastics and/or Styrofoam (petroleum-based products).

5. Persuade your audience in a well-developed essay that all international boundaries should be dissolved and that we should all become citizens of one world with one governing body, a government that includes the best of all existing political ideologies.

6. Write an essay defending a society that respects an individual's right to an alternate lifestyle.

7. Write a persuasive essay calling for drastic yet fitting punishment for those who sexually, psychologically, and physically abuse others.

8. Compose an essay wherein you defend two or three vices you have. Attempt to convince your reader that what society commonly views as a vice (e.g., smoking, drinking, gambling) is—in your case at least—a virtue.

9. Summarize the differences between two opposing points of view (e.g., we should or should not allow people who have tested positive for the AIDS virus to immigrate to America), and then argue for one of the positions.

10. Pick a word such as *prejudice* and write a persuasive essay convincing your reader that the popular definition of the word is misleading and that your definition is more appropriate or useful. Support your claims with a clear definition of terms and examples drawn from authoritative references and personal observations.

Glossary of Literary and Rhetorical Terms

Acronym   A word formed from the first letter or letters of subsequent parts of a compound term. For instance, International Business Machines becomes IBM, the Equal Rights Amendment becomes the ERA, the Central Intelligence Agency becomes the CIA, and the Bureau of Indian Affairs becomes the BIA.

Active Verbs   Verbs that show rather than just tell your reader what you are talking about. For instance, write *David practices law* instead of *David is a lawyer.* (See **Voice.**)

Adjectives   Words that can indicate the quality of a noun or its equivalent (e.g., the *slippery* pavement, the *rocky* soil, the *blue* sky). Typically, adjectives answer questions like "which kind?" and "which one?"

Adverbs   Words that modify verbs, adjectives, other adverbs, and complete sentences:

Verbs:	Ngan drove *swiftly.*
Adjectives:	The cat was *extremely* frisky.
Adverbs:	Deborah spoke *very* slowly.
Sentences:	*Desperately,* Kevin pleaded his case to the jury.

Alliteration   The repetition of the same letters or sounds at the beginning of two or more words that are next or close to each other (e.g., My mother makes mashed potatoes on Mondays).

Allusion   A term used when making reference to a famous literary, historical, or social figure or event. For instance, a reference to Watergate refers to (alludes to) political corruption, or more recently, "To Wag the Dog" alludes to a calculated political diversion.

Analogy   An extended comparison where an unfamiliar topic is explained by noting its similarity to something familiar.

Analysis   To closely inspect and come to a conclusion on something by separating the topic or issue into parts in order to better understand the whole.

Anecdote   A short story that illustrates a point.

Antonym   A word that has an opposite meaning to another word (e.g., *Happy* is the antonym of *sad,* and *young* is the antonym of *old*).

Argumentation   One of the four major forms of essay writing, the others being narration, exposition, and description. In an argument, you prove your point by establishing the truth about a topic or issue. In doing so, revealing the fallacies of another's argument may prove invaluable. For a detailed discussion of argumentation, see Chapter 11.

Audience   Those you address when you write (e.g., friends, professors, public servants). You must consider whether your audience knows nothing or a lot about your topic.

Brainstorming   Individually or collectively solving a problem by considering and/or rejecting ideas. A writer brainstorms to generate ideas on a topic and then focuses on a specific controlling idea which will lead to a topic sentence or a thesis statement.

Cause and Effect   See Chapter 9.

Classification   See Chapter 8.

Cliché   A trite or worn-out expression that either becomes a stereotype or meaningless in its original context. Example: *I'm as hungry as a horse! It's raining cats and dogs!* (How often have you pictured a hungry horse eating or dogs and cats falling from the sky when someone makes either of those remarks?)

Clustering   A type of brainstorming where all the ideas one has about a topic or an issue are written down, circled, and related. Clustering words creates a visual picture of the relationships between ideas which are associated with a topic. For further discussion on this method of "prewriting," see Chapter 1.

Coherence A term used to refer to the clear, logical relationship between words, phrases, clauses, and paragraphs. In writing, we use traditional devices and linking words to achieve coherence.

Colloquial Expressions Informal expressions, somewhere between slang and formal language. Colloquialisms are acceptable in speech but not formal writing.

Comparison and Contrast See Chapter 7.

Concrete/Abstract Concrete words may stand by themselves and be understood because they are perceived through the five senses: touch, taste, sight, smell, and sound. For instance, we can touch, see, and hear a small child; thus the word *child* is concrete. However, the child's *anger* would be abstract since it is perceived only through its relationship with another word. Abstract words define ideas, concepts, and attitudes (love, hate, ethical, indifference, honesty, pride) and tend to be subjective in their interpretation.

Concrete Nouns See **Concrete/Abstract**

Connotation The meanings or implications associated with a particular word beyond its literal definition. For instance, while a hospital denotes an institution which provides medical care for people, the word also suggests (connotes) fear, pain, misery, and possibly death. (See **Denotation.**)

Context Words that occur before and after a specified word or words and determine its/their meaning.

Controlling Idea The main idea expressed in a paragraph or an essay.

Deduction A form of reasoning which moves from general points to a specific conclusion. See Chapter 11 for a detailed discussion of deductive logic. (See **Induction.**)

Definition See Chapter 5.

Denotation The literal or dictionary definition of a word. (See **Connotation.**)

Description See Chapter 3.

Diction An author's word choice. Diction also deals with word usage (e.g., concrete/abstract expressions, denotation/ connotation, colloquialisms).

Division See Chapter 8.

Essay Map An essay map is using three or more ideas which are attached to your thesis statement, providing you with the controlling ideas for your body paragraphs. In essence, an essay map tells you where to go by providing a specific direction.

Ethos The ethical (what is right or wrong) appeal in an essay.

Euphemism The substitution of a mild expression for a harsh one. For example, it is common practice in today's business world to state that one is *terminated* or *laid off* instead of *fired.*

Evidence Facts and examples which prove what you claim.

Exposition A form of writing where the author's main purpose is to explain or expose a topic or an issue.

Fallacy Faulty logic. (See Chapter 11.)

Figures of Speech Terms which are used to add variety to your essay where points are discussed *figuratively* instead of literally. Some of the common forms of figures of speech include the use of metaphor, simile, hyperbole, and personification (listed elsewhere in this Glossary).

Freewriting Spontaneous writing in which one does not stop to edit material, the objective being merely to generate ideas for one unified paragraph or essay. (See Peter Elbow's essay "Freewriting" in Chapter 1.)

Generalization A statement made without a foundation in fact or supporting evidence.

Hyperbole   A figure of speech wherein one greatly exaggerates to emphasize a point. Example: *Tom went through hell to get a yellow rose for his mother.*

Idiom   The use of words unique to a particular group or language.

Illustration and Example   See Chapter 4.

Imagery   Concrete expressions which appeal to the senses, often employing the use of figurative speech to produce mental pictures.

Induction   A form of reasoning which takes several specific points and leads to a generalization about them. See the introduction to Chapter 11 for a more detailed discussion of inductive logic. (See **Deduction.**)

Introduction   In a short essay, the introduction acquaints the reader with the theme or topic which will be explored in depth within the body. Traditionally, one's thesis statement appears in the latter part of an introductory paragraph and provides a focus or direction for developing the remainder of the paper.

Irony   Irony is a figure of speech wherein the author states his or her intention in words that carry an opposite meaning. Irony can also be situational.

Jargon   Like slang, jargon consists of words or phrases particular to a specific profession or social group. Computer operators, for instance, use terms such as *interfacing* or *networking.* The problem is that many people do not know the definitions of these words, and if you use them in an essay, it will be necessary to define them.

Lexicon   A list of words or a wordbook such as a dictionary.

Linking Words   Basically, linking words are connectors that refer to transitions and subordinating, coordinating, and adverbial conjunctions.

Logos   An appeal to logical order which comes from the ancient Greeks as the source of world order.

Metaphor   A comparison without the use of *like* or *as.* For instance, a simile would state: *My professor is like a prison warden.* A metaphor would simply state: *My professor is a prison warden.*

Mood   The mood is the emotional tone of a work (e.g., gloomy, optimistic, pessimistic, cheerful).

Myth   Tales and stories about supernatural heroes, heroines, gods, goddesses, and monsters, which originated before written language and were passed on to succeeding generations through the oral tradition of storytelling. The purpose of many primitive myths—and modern myths—is to interpret natural phenomena such as creation and the seasons.

Narration   One of the major forms of writing. Narration is used to relate what happened at an event or a number of events. In essence, a narrative tells a story. (See Chapter 2 for further discussion on narration.)

Paradox   A situation or statement which, although it is contradictory to what reason dictates, is nevertheless true. Example: *The starving people at the edge of town were the happiest people I have ever met.*

Parallelism   Constructing word groups into consistent and balanced patterns using the same grammatical forms. For example, nouns should be combined with similar nouns (*Doctors, lawyers,* and *accountants* were in the room), adjectives with like adjectives (The gardener planted *yellow, white,* and *red* roses), verbs with similar verbs (*We studied, ate,* and then *slept* for ten hours).

Paraphrase   To put someone else's ideas or written material into your own words.

Parody   A device whereby an author employs humor to make fun of a particular situation or another piece of literature.

Pathos   An appeal to the emotions of readers that arouses pity, sympathy, sorrow, and so on.

Persona   A character or voice used as the speaker of an essay or short story. The attitudes of the persona frequently differ from those of the author.

Personification   A form of figurative speech, personification is the treatment of animals or inanimate objects as if they were human. Example: *The rose breathed a sigh of relief as the morning sun touched her, bringing warmth and life to her cold petals.*

Persuasion   Like argumentation, persuasion is a form of writing where an author attempts to convince his/her reader of something. In contrast to argumentation, however, persuasion includes words that elicit an *emotional* rather than a rational, logical response from a reader to achieve the writer's ultimate objective. That is, the author appeals to one's emotions (pathos) and ethics (ethos) in addition to logic (logos). (See Chapter 12.)

Point of View   The perspective from which an essay or story is written. In formal writing, point of view is expressed in first person, wherein the author uses the pronoun "I," and third person, which is a more subjective form of writing, wherein the writer uses "he," "she," or "it" as the narrator. Point of view may also refer to an author's attitude toward his or her subject matter.

Prefix   Something added to the beginning of a word to change its meaning or give it a new meaning (e.g., un + wanted = unwanted; re + united = reunited).

Prewriting   A spontaneous listing of thoughts to aid in the composition of your essay or paragraph. Prewriting techniques include clustering, free-writing, listing, and mapping.

Purpose   The objective or reason for writing.

Rhetoric   The study of the elements, such as structure or style, used in writing or speaking.

Rhetorical Question   A question which the author offers the reader, with the intention of promoting thought. Often, an author will answer his or her own question within the body of an essay.

Root Word   A base word to which prefixes and suffixes are added.

Sarcasm   Heavy-handed verbal irony where a person expresses dislike or disapproval in a caustic, demeaning, jeering manner. Sarcasm is intended to ridicule and hurt by taunting an individual in a snide manner.

Satire   A form of writing which pokes fun at social conventions or attacks the follies of the human race, with the hope of getting the reader to reconsider the issue and thus improve the human condition.

Science Fiction   A form of writing in which imagination is the differentiating characteristic of the writer, as well as the reader. It came into being with the new world of invention and technology and is reputed to have begun with Jules Verne. It deals with topics that are not part of our times but usually are set in the future and/or on distant planets.

Simile   A comparison with the use of *like* or *as*. Examples: *Andrea's hands were as cold as frost. Chris's pants look like shreds of tissue paper.*

Slang   While slang is often colorful and descriptive, such language is considered vulgar and/or informal and never should be employed in a formal essay.

Strategy   The method for approaching, analyzing, and writing about a topic.

Stereotype   Giving qualities to a particular person, race of people, or situation which are overly generalized and are not a fair representation of the person, place, or thing to which they refer.

Style   How a writer expresses what he or she wants to say. Important factors in style are word use, sentence structure, and voice.

Suffix   A syllable(s) added to the end of a word or root word to give the word a new meaning, a different grammatical function, or form a new word (e.g., wise + est = superlative form of the adjective *wise*).

Summary   Condensing your own or someone else's work into a shorter composition. Summaries are useful for a writer to get a good sense of a larger work, but they are only a starting point for analysis.

Support   Facts, details, and examples which illustrate the validity of your points.

Syllogism   A three-part form of reasoning consisting of a major premise, a minor premise, and a conclusion. See the introduction to Chapter 11 for examples.

Symbol   Something which stands for or represents something other than itself (e.g., a flag, just a piece of cloth, can represent a country and thus is a symbol for it).

Synonym   Synonyms are words with similar meanings (e.g., skinny/ thin, desire/want). Synonyms should be used with care because no two words mean precisely the same thing. (See **Connotation**.)

Syntax   Syntax refers to the arrangement of words in a sentence.

Theme   Subject or topic on which a person writes or speaks. (*Note:* A theme may also refer to a short essay.)

Thesis   The main or controlling idea that a writer seeks to prove in his or her essay.

Tone   The expressing of a writer's mood or attitude toward his or her subject through the use of carefully chosen words.

Topic Sentence   Much like a thesis, a topic sentence is the controlling idea of a paragraph and is usually stated at the beginning of a paragraph. The sentences that follow must support the topic to provide unity for the paragraph.

Transitions   Transitions are words or word groups that aid the writer in moving from one point to the next. Some common transitions include *before, after, thus, therefore, however, moreover, nevertheless.*

Uncountable Noun   Words which cannot be plural since they are considered as a group, i.e., furniture, homework, rice, spaghetti, and so on.

Understatement   Intentionally downplaying an important point or a serious situation. Consider the following sentence: *After losing her car, house, and every cent she had to her name, Colleen was a bit annoyed.* To say Colleen was *a bit annoyed* understates the true gravity of the situation. (See **Irony**.)

Unity   To provide unity in a composition, the writer must stick to the controlling idea he or she has established without digressing from that major discussion point.

Voice   There are two voices—active and passive. In the active voice, the subject *does* the acting (e.g., the hunter *shot* the wolf), and in the passive voice the subject *receives* the action of the verb (e.g., the wolf *was shot by* the hunter).

Photo Credits

Literary Credits

Chapter 9

"Growing Up With Two Moms" by Megan McGuire, from *Newsweek,* November 4, 1996. Copyright © 1996. Newsweek, Inc. All rights reserved. Reprinted by permission.

"The Naked Face" by Karen Ray. Copyright © 1985 by Karen Ray.

"Guilt" by Phillip Persky. Copyright © 1999 by Phillip Persky.

"Labor and Capital: The Coming of Catastrophe" by Carlos Bulosan, from *If You Want to Know What We Are: A Carlos Bulosan Reader.* Copyright © 1983 by Aurelio Bulosan. Reprinted by permission of West End Press and Aurelio Bulosan.

"Eating With Immigrants" by Rose Anna Higashi. Permission granted by the author.

Chapter 10

"Sharing Tradition" by Frank La Pena, from News From Native California, Vol. 4, No. 1. Copyright © 1989. Reprinted by permission.

"Curanderismo: A Healing Art" by Cynthia Lopez, from *Intercambios Magazine,* Winter 1990 Vol. 5, No. 1. Reprinted by permission of Intercambios.

"How I Started Writing Poetry" by Reginald Lockett, from *California Childhood* by Reginald Lockett. Copyright © 1988. Reprinted with permission by Creative Arts Books Company, Berkley.

"Slang Origins" by Woody Allen, from *Without Feathers* by Woody Allen. Copyright © 1972, 1973, 1974, 1975 by Woody Allen. Reprinted by permission of Random House, Inc.

"Of Prigs and Pigs: Revolution in the Name of Manners" by Martha L. Henning. Copyright © 1999 by Martha L. Henning.

"Arrival at Manzanar" by Jeanne Wakatsuki Houston and James D. Houston from *Farewell to Manzanar* by Jeanne Wakatsuki Houston and James D. Houston. Copyright © 1973 by James D. Houston. Reprinted by permission of Houghton Mifflin, Co.

Chapter 11

"In Defense of Splitting Up" by Barbara Ehrenreich, from *Time,* April 6, 1996. Copyright © 1996 Time Inc. Reprinted by permission.

"Who Is Your Mother? Red Roots of White Feminism" by Paula Gunn Allen from *The Sacred Hoop* by Paula Gunn Allen. Copyright © 1986 by Paula Gunn Allen. Reprinted by permission of Beacon Press.

"Soul Food" by Imamu Amiri Baraka, from *Home: Social Essays* by Imamu Amiri Baraka. Copyright © 1986 by LeRoi Jones. Reprinted by permission of William Morrow & Company, Inc.

"The Anima of Anime" by Grace Sumabat Mateo. Permission granted by the author.

"Peyote, Wine and the First Amendment" by Douglas Laycock. Copyright © 1989 Christian Century Foundation. Reprinted by permission from the October 4, 1989, issue of *The Christian Century.*

"Online Learning and Student Success" by Mark Charles Fissel. Copyright © 1999 by Mark Charles Fissel.

Chapter 12

"Drugs" by Gore Vidal, from *Homage to Daniel Shays: Collected Essays 1952–1972* by Gore Vidal. Copyright © 1970 by Gore Vidal. Reprinted by permission of Random House, Inc.

"Women Are Better Drivers" by Phyllis McGinley. Copyright © 1959 by Hearst Publications Corporation. Reprinted with special permission of King Features Syndicate.

"Fetal Alcohol Syndrome" by Michael Dorris from *The Broken Cord* by Michael Dorris. Copyright © 1989 by Michael Dorris. Reprinted by permission of HarperCollins.

"Never Too Old" by Tammerlin Drummond. Copyright © 1999 Time, Inc. Reprinted by permission.

"Recent Developments" by Bruce Henderson. Copyright 1999 © by Bruce Henderson.

North Chinese/Vietnamese Elder: "I Want to Live Without Trouble," as told to James M. Freeman. Reprinted from *Hearts of Sorrow: Vietnamese-American Lives* by James M. Freeman with the permission of the publishers, Stanford University Press. Copyright © by the Board of Trustees of Leland Stanford Junior University

Index